Building Better Students

Building Better Students

Preparation for the Workforce

EDITED BY

JEREMY BURRUS

KRISTA D. MATTERN

BOBBY D. NAEMI

RICHARD D. ROBERTS

OXFORD
UNIVERSITY PRESS

Oxford University Press is a department of the University of Oxford. It furthers
the University's objective of excellence in research, scholarship, and education
by publishing worldwide. Oxford is a registered trade mark of Oxford University
Press in the UK and certain other countries.

Published in the United States of America by Oxford University Press
198 Madison Avenue, New York, NY 10016, United States of America.

CIP data is on file at the Library of Congress
ISBN 978–0–19–937322–2

9 8 7 6 5 4 3 2 1

Printed by Sheridan Books, Inc., United States of America

CONTENTS

> We cannot always build the future for our youth, but we can build our youth for the future.
>
> —FRANKLIN D. ROOSEVELT (1940)

I am proud of my son, who graduated from Roosevelt University this year, and I have been predisposed to think of quotations from Eleanor and Franklin Roosevelt. This FDR quote seems particularly apt as I offer a few reflections about this important and scholarly edited volume, *Building Better Students: Preparation for the Workforce*. We live in a dramatically and rapidly changing, diverse world. Thus, as the contributors to this volume express, it is important to *rethink* what we teach our students and how we teach them to optimize their preparation to succeed in work and life.

The *2016 PDK Poll of the Public's Attitudes Toward the Public Schools* asked, "What do you think should be the main goal of public school education: to prepare students academically, to prepare them for work, or to prepare them to be good citizens?" The 1,221 American adults who were interviewed were split over their priorities: 45% said that preparing students academically is the main goal, whereas 25% said the main purpose is to prepare students for work and 26% endorsed good citizenship (Langer Research Associates, 2016). If "all of the above" were an option, I imagine that most Americans and the volume editors would vote for all three. Also noteworthy is the fact that when it comes to selecting strategies for improving public schools, many more Americans support offering more technical or skill-based classes (68%) than more honors or advanced academic classes (21%).

Jeremy Burrus, Krista Mattern, Bobby Naemi, and Richard Roberts (Chapter 1) introduce this book with three challenging questions: Is the world of work changing? If so, what types of education and skills are needed for workers to succeed in this new context? Finally, is it necessary to change our educational systems to "build better students" who have the skills it takes? They answer that technological innovation is changing the ways in which we live and work. Changes in the ways we work are leading to a changing job market that requires a high level of education and a particular set of intrapersonal and interpersonal skills. Many of the new entrants into the workforce lack foundational social and emotional skills needed to succeed. Burrus and colleagues propose two general solutions to prepare students for workplace readiness and success: improving college retention rates and fostering students' intrapersonal and interpersonal skills.

The editors structured this volume in an enjoyable and engaging way. They recruited world-class scholars to contribute three or four research- and theory-based chapters to three groundbreaking sections: "Rethinking How We Define and Measure Workforce Readiness," "Rethinking How We Prepare Students for the Workforce," and "Bridging the Gap Between College and Workforce Readiness." Then they enlisted other thought leaders who wrote integrative commentaries with constructive critiques about each chapter in their section. The editors conclude with an outstanding synthesis of themes raised by contributors and propose a broad taxonomy and working definition of workforce readiness.

It was pleasing to read the final chapter (Chapter 15), which offers the unifying framework we yearn for when reading individual chapters in an edited book. Naemi and colleagues refer to Patrick Kyllonen's (Chapter 5) "Tower of Babel" concept, in which he posits that a lack of alignment in terminology and frameworks inhibits progress in a field and then asks how to get the disciplines of educational psychology, organizational psychology, education, business, and public policy to communicate more effectively with each other. Rather than complaining (as most others have before them) that a unifying model for stakeholder in government, business, and schools cannot be achieved, Naemi et al. take a giant step forward by proposing the following heuristic framework that includes four higher-order sets of skills: (a) *intrapersonal skills*, such as maintaining motivation and stress management; (b) *interpersonal skills*, including multicultural appreciation, cross-cultural competence, and working with others; (c) *cross-cutting cognitive skills*—which are useful across multiple domains—such as creativity, critical thinking, problem solving, and judgment; and (d) *cognitive skills*, such as general mental ability, subject-specific knowledge, and job-specific knowledge.

This framework builds from and coordinates with two increasingly influential employability frameworks described by Hope Clark (Chapter 11) in her informative chapter on "Linking Education and Employment: A Foundational Competency Framework for Career Success." The Employability Skills Framework is an online resource available on the website of the US Department of Education (2016). It describes employability skills as general skills that are required for success in the labor market at all levels of employment, and it is based on a crosswalk and integration of existing employability frameworks and standards. The skills fall into three broad categories: effective relationships (including intrapersonal and interpersonal skills), workplace skills, and applied knowledge. Similarly, the common employability skills model promoted in business by the National Network of Business and Industry Associations (2014) highlights four areas: personal skills, people skills, applied knowledge, and workplace skills. It seems, at last, like there is momentum for a unifying framework to enhance communication and progress.

Of all the holistic frameworks to advance educating students to be college, career, community, and life ready, Naemi et al's model is the one that could be most useful in improving future educational research, practice, and policy. In certain respects, it aligns with the social and emotional learning (SEL) framework that my colleagues and I at the Collaborative for Academic, Social, and Emotional Learning (CASEL) have advanced for more than two decades (Weissberg, Durlak, Domitrovich, & Gullotta, 2015). SEL involves the processes through which children and adults acquire and effectively apply the knowledge, skills, attitudes, and abilities necessary to understand and manage emotions, set and achieve positive goals, feel and show empathy for others, establish and maintain positive relationships, and make responsible decisions. CASEL has identified five interrelated sets of cognitive, affective, and behavioral competencies: Self-awareness and self-management are intrapersonal competencies; social awareness and relationship skills are interpersonal competencies; and responsible decision-making about personal and social situations involves personal, social, and cognitive skills. There is compelling evidence that these skills can be taught and that the ability to coordinate these competencies when dealing with daily situations and challenges provides a foundation for more positive attitudes and social behaviors, fewer conduct problems, less emotional distress, and improved grades and test scores (Durlak, Weissberg, Dymnicki, Taylor, & Schellinger, 2011). Despite positive theory and research accomplishments that point to the importance of addressing students' social and emotional development, the Naemi model challenges the field of SEL to more thoughtfully embrace cognitive and cross-cutting cognitive skills as part of a comprehensive, systemic educational model. The five CASEL competence clusters all have social–cognitive and cognitive–affective components—which is why we do not refer to them as noncognitive skills. However, the roles that skills such as creativity, critical thinking, and general knowledge play should have greater salience in future SEL theory building, research, and program design.

Murano and Roberts's (Chapter 14) advocacy for evidence-based SEL programming at the primary, secondary, and tertiary education levels as an important approach to foster both college and workforce readiness is to be applauded. The field of SEL has focused primarily on promoting students' positive social behavior, academic performance, health, and citizenship. A gap in the recent 37-chapter *Handbook on Social and Emotional Learning: Research and Practice* was that it did not include a contribution on SEL and preparation for the workplace (Durlak, Domitrovich, Weissberg, & Gullotta, 2015). The powerful case that the current contributors make to connect the promotion of social-emotional competence to success in work will ensure that this glaring omission will not happen again. If fact, I anticipate that the next decade of SEL research, practice, and policy will focus on fostering improved approaches to career and technical education as one of its highest priorities, if not its highest. This will involve the creation of well-designed preschool through college programs that are developmentally sound with standards for what students should know and be able to do and effective assessment systems that support the efforts of educators and employers to build better students and workers.

Of course, there are many other positive features to commend in this book. For now, I conclude with a few final expressions of intellectual appreciation. The chapter on conscientiousness by Brent Roberts and Patrick Hill (Chapter 9) is enormously informative and important. Although there is compelling research linking conscientiousness to school and workplace success, there have not been sufficient descriptions of how conscientiousness develops across childhood and into adulthood or what the necessary ingredients are to enhance conscientiousness in today's children and youth. Roberts and Hill elaborate on developmental, personal, relational, and environmental considerations that will help to link research on conscientiousness—which is often misconstrued as a fixed trait that applies only to adults—to school-based SEL programming that fosters students' self-awareness, self-management, and responsible decision-making skills. The chapters on cross-cultural competence (Jennifer Klafehn, Chapter 4) and preparing students for workplace diversity (Jamie Lester, David Kravitz, and Carrie Klein, Chapter 6) will also be mind-expanding for readers. As 21st century educational settings and workplaces become increasingly diverse, there is a growing need for multiculturally and globally competent students and workers who interact effectively with people from different backgrounds and cultures. These authors argue convincingly that we should make research-based efforts to enhance emotion perception, perspective taking, relationship skills, and, more broadly, cross-cultural learning a priority for student learning. In closing, I express my admiration and gratitude to the editors and chapter authors for their academically rigorous and boundary-spanning contributions. I wholeheartedly and excitedly believe that they have achieved the hope the editors express in the final chapter (Chapter 15): This important volume will inform and improve the quality of future theory and research to prepare students for fulfilling and meaningful work, and it will foster future collaborations to promote effective policies and practice in educational and work settings.

Roger P. Weissberg
University of Illinois at Chicago

REFERENCES

Durlak, J. A., Domitrovich, C. E., Weissberg, R. P., & Gullotta, T. P. (Eds.). (2015). *Handbook of social and emotional learning: Research and practice.* New York, NY: Guilford.

Durlak, J. A., Weissberg, R. P., Dymnicki, A. B., Taylor, R. D., & Schellinger, K. B. (2011). The impact of enhancing students' social and emotional learning: A meta-analysis of school-based universal interventions. *Child Development, 82,* 405–432.

Langer Research Associates. (2016, September). Why school? Americans speak out on education goals, standards, priorities, and funding—The 48th annual PDK Poll of the Public's Attitudes Toward the Public Schools. *Phi Delta Kappan, 98,* N1.

National Network of Business and Industry Associations. (2014, July 22). *Common employability skills—A foundation for success in the workplace: The skills all employees need no matter where they work.* Retrieved from http://businessroundtable.org/sites/default/files/Common%20Employability_asingle_fm.pdf

Roosevelt, F. D. (1940, September 20). Address at University of Pennsylvania. Online by G. Peters & J. T. Woolley, *The American Presidency Project.* Retrieved from http://www.presidency.ucsb.edu/ws/?pid=15860

Weissberg, R. P., Durlak, J. A., Domitrovich, C. E., & Gullotta, T. P. (2015). Social and emotional learning: Past, present, and future. In J. A. Durlak, C. E. Domitrovich, R. P. Weissberg, & T. P. Gullotta (Eds.), *Handbook of social and emotional learning: Research and practice* (pp. 3–19). New York, NY: Guilford.

US Department of Education. (2016). *Employability Skills Framework.* Retrieved from http://cte.ed.gov/employabilityskills

Why do we educate our youth? Universal education is the norm in our current society, but the very nature of norms means that we rarely question them; after all, they are "normal." Thus, the question, "What is the purpose of education?" is rarely asked. When artificial intelligence one day invents a time machine, we can go back in time and ask our forefathers and foremothers what they thought about this question. Answers are likely to range from "instructing youth in religious doctrine, to preparing them to live in a democracy, to assimilating immigrants into mainstream society, to preparing workers for the industrialized 20th century workplace" (Sloan, 2012, p. 1). It will probably come as no surprise that our current society seems to favor the "preparing the workforce" purpose of education. A 2012 Gallup poll found that 96% of Americans thought that education beyond high school is either somewhat or very important for getting a good job (Gallup, 2013). These Americans seem to be correct. It is projected that by the year 2018, most new jobs created in the United States will require some kind of college degree (Carnevale, Smith, & Strohl, 2010; US Bureau of Labor Statistics, 2013). Plainly, there is a recognition of the importance of adequately preparing our students for the 21st century workforce.

People tend to be very good at saying the right things. Acting on the right thing, or changing policy to enact the right thing, is more difficult. Thus, the fact that we are failing to produce enough college graduates to fill the positions that require a college education might be predicted by simply taking human nature, and the nature of human politics, into account. At least in recent history, we have seemed to be unable or unwilling to enact policy changes that may serve to increase the number of college graduates. Action requires changing norms (or the status quo), and changing norms gets people out of their proverbial "comfort zones." Accordingly, a shortfall of approximately 3 million college-educated workers is projected by 2018 (Carnevale et al., 2010). Thus, we have the ubiquitous "skills gap." The term "skills gap" has been introduced to describe the difference between the skills a society or organization needs in its workforce and the skills the workforce possesses. One aspect of the skills gap is an education gap. It might be disheartening to some, however, that it very well might be the case that simply increasing the number of college-educated workers still might not close the skills gap. There is much evidence for this (Mattern et al., 2014). For example, although there were 7.9 million unemployed in the United States in December 2015, there were also 5.6 million job openings in the country (Gillespie, 2016), suggesting a shortage of sufficiently skilled workers. Furthermore, large-scale surveys of US employers have found that entry-level college-educated employees are underprepared for their jobs (Casner-Lotto & Barrington, 2006; Hart Research Associates, 2010). It is important to note that this issue is not isolated to the United States. There is evidence that employers in Europe are also experiencing similar problems (Cedefop, 2015).

In recognition of this, we (the editors of this book) applied for and were awarded a grant from the American Education Research Association to host a conference to bring together some of the world's leading researchers to discuss these issues. Included were leading thinkers in the fields of industrial/organizational psychology, education, and economics. We also received support from Educational Testing Service and The College Board, and we thank all three organizations for their generosity. We decided to call our conference "Building Better Students: Preparation for Life After High School." The conference title was a nod to a book edited by Wayne Camara and Ernest Kimmel called *Choosing Students: Higher Education Admissions Tools for the 21st Century* (Camara & Kimmel, 2005)—the implication being that because a lot of good thinking has been done on how to select students for college, it was now time for more thinking on how to *prepare* them for college (and the workforce). We held our conference in Washington, DC, on December 8–10, 2010. Conference information, including presentation slides and videos, can be found at http://www.ets.org/c/15481/index.html.

It seemed logical that the next step would be to publish a book based on the conference proceedings. There is a well-known phenomenon discovered in the field of social psychology called the *planning fallacy*, whereby people tend to underestimate the time it takes to complete complex tasks (Buehler, Griffin, & Ross, 1994). We unofficially estimate that 90% of people who have attempted to publish an edited book have experienced the planning fallacy, and we are no exception. The process of securing a publisher, authors understandably dropping out of the book because of busy schedules, recruiting new authors, and the writing and editing process has taken several years, and now, finally, here we are. Along the way, the theme of the book shifted to focus on workforce readiness only, and the final title reflects this shift in focus: *Building Better Students: Preparation for the Workforce*. We think that the end product was worth the wait.

Burrus, Mattern, Naemi, and Roberts (the editors) begin the book (Chapter 1) by making an argument for why we do indeed need to build a better workforce. In this chapter, they provide one theory for how the skills gap came to be (the flourishing of technology has changed the job market and skills required to succeed in the new job market) and what it will take to close this skills gap (more education and a greater focus on training noncognitive skills). The rest of the book is divided into three sections, although there is certainly overlap in content across each.

The first section is titled "Rethinking How We Define and Measure Workforce Readiness." Sackett and Walmsley (Chapter 2) open this section by "setting the stage" for workplace readiness and personnel selection. In their very informative chapter, they (a) discuss definitions of workforce readiness, (b) present themes of common procedures for personnel selection, (c) summarize efforts to build taxonomies of workplace readiness, and (d) present some recent research they have conducted to identify personality attributes that are important for workplace readiness. In Chapter 3, Whorton, Casillas, Oswald, and Shaw present skills they have identified as especially crucial for the 21st century workforce. They state that three major factors—interpersonal, technological, and international (e.g., globalization) forces—are influencing the relative importance of workplace skills. They argue that these three factors are causing the following skills to become more important: customer service, teamwork, safety, creativity, critical thinking, metacognition, cross-cultural knowledge and competence, and ethics and integrity. Next, Klafehn (Chapter 4) focuses on a specific skill identified by Whorton et al. that she (and we) believe is a critical 21st century skill: cross-cultural competence (3C). She defines 3C as an "individual's ability to successfully navigate cross-cultural contexts" and provides a discussion of how four essential 3C skills can be developed using Piaget's theory of cognitive development as an organizing framework. These four 3C skills are cultural self-awareness, metacognition, emotion regulation, and perspective taking. In Chapter 5, Kyllonen provides a commentary and synthesis of these three chapters.

Section 2 is titled "Rethinking How We Prepare Students for the Workforce." In the first chapter of this section, Lester, Kravitz, and Klein (Chapter 6) discuss an issue related to 3C that we believe will become increasingly important over the coming years—workplace diversity—and how to prepare workers for it. In this chapter, Lester et al. discuss the presence of diversity on college campuses and how having a diverse workforce can be beneficial, and they make recommendations for how to prepare the workforce for diversity. Chernyshenko, Chan, Hoon-Ho, Uy, and Loo (Chapter 7) next discuss the importance of entrepreneurial skills in the 21st century and the development of a survey to measure aspirations for entrepreneurial, professional, and leadership careers. As careers become more "boundaryless" in the 21st century, workers become freer to determine the trajectory of their careers rather than remaining in a single occupation their entire lives. Thus, Chernyshenko and colleagues developed an important scale measuring intention, motivation, and self-efficacy toward such a lifestyle. Importantly, this scale can be used in providing developmental feedback to college students. Relatedly, but on a broader scale, Su and Nye in Chapter 8 focus on something we believe to be understudied—the influence of vocational interests and person–environment fit on job performance, career success, and academic achievement. In their chapter, they discuss recent evidence for the relationship of interests to the three outcomes and two mechanisms through which interests predict these outcomes. That is, interests serve both as a source of motivation and as a way of capturing the fit between a person and his or her environment. In doing so, they make a compelling argument for the assessment of interests and their use in career guidance. In Chapter 9, Roberts and Hill present a model for improving conscientiousness, which they refer to as the "sourdough" model of conscientiousness because the process for developing conscientiousness parallels the process of baking a loaf of sourdough bread. This is an especially important model because conscientiousness has been shown to be an important determinant of both school (Poropat, 2009) and work success (Barrick, Mount, & Judge, 2001). Roberts and Hill state that the "ingredients" of conscientiousness include a sense of effortful control, the ability to plan for long-term goals, regulatory systems that allow for the adoption of long-term goals, and, finally, a motivational desire to commit to others. They then outline a series of steps intended to increase each of these "ingredients." Finally, Clark, Double, and MacCann conclude this section (Chapter 10) with a reflection on these four chapters.

The third and final section of the book is titled "Bridging the Gap Between College and Workforce Readiness." In the first chapter of this section, Clark (Chapter 11) presents an overview of frameworks for organizing foundational academic and workplace competencies. Foundational competencies were based primarily on job-analysis methods. She concludes by providing recommendations for building a common language between educators and employers for describing foundational competencies. In Chapter 12, Schmitt discusses the development and validation of a set of noncognitive constructs that added to the prediction of grade point average (GPA) and other important outcomes in a sample of college students. These measures included a series of situational judgment tests, biodata measures, and other types of measures. He argues that such measures should be considered for use in college selection both because they predict outcomes besides GPA very well and because they effectively measure constructs that are valued by employers. Next, Golubovich, Su, and Robbins (Chapter 13) highlight the need to bridge education and work by ensuring that people complete education with the skills they need to enter the workforce. In doing so, these authors introduce an international framework for summarizing the skill requirements for middle skills jobs from both a US and an international perspective. They conducted extensive analyses of both the Occupational Information Network (O*NET) and the International Standard Classification of Occupations (ISCO) databases in developing their comprehensive framework. Of key importance, they also present a research agenda for validating an assessment of these key skills. In Chapter 14, Murano and Roberts provide a commentary and summary of these three chapters.

We thoroughly enjoyed each of these chapters and the process of editing this book. Along the way, we identified several themes that run through the book, which we discuss at length in a final chapter (Chapter 15). To give the reader a sense of the major issues we uncovered in advance, the following are a few that we identified:

- Noncognitive skills/personality are becoming increasingly important for the 21st century workforce, both in the United States and internationally.
- Noncognitive skills/personality can be developed.
- The proliferation of technology and globalization have had a powerful impact on the nature of work. This leads to a greater need for skills such as cross-cultural competence, entrepreneurship, and dealing with diversity.
- We should pay attention to what really interests students and try to develop these interests.
- The skills that it takes to succeed in higher education and the workforce are likely similar, and there is a need for better communication between these entities.

These are clearly points to think about while we attempt to "build better students."

In conclusion, we are very proud of this work that has been years in the making and believe it makes a substantial contribution to our thinking on workforce readiness. Specifically, the goal of this book was to formulate principles for providing a scientific model of workforce readiness. To achieve this goal, the book includes a series of views on theoretical and practical issues on workforce readiness. Theoretical issues addressed include defining workforce readiness and identifying the knowledge, skills, and abilities (KSAs; both cognitive and noncognitive) necessary to be considered workforce ready. Practical issues include how to validly and reliably measure these dimensions; how to incorporate these KSAs into the current kindergarten through grade 12 and postsecondary curriculum to reduce, if not eliminate, the "skills gap"; and discussion of potential interventions that can be implemented to best educate students for the work demands of the 21st century. To this end, we think we have been successful. More globally, our hope is that this book will in turn inform future theory, research, and practical applications.

REFERENCES

Barrick, M. R., Mount, M. K., & Judge, T. A. (2001). Personality and performance at the beginning of the new millennium: What do we know and where do we go next? *International Journal of Selection and Assessment, 9*, 9–30.

Buehler, R., Griffin, D., & Ross, M. (1994). Exploring the "planning fallacy": Why people underestimate their task completion times. *Journal of Personality and Social Psychology, 67*, 366–381.

Camara, W., & Kimmel, E. W. (Eds.). (2005). *Choosing students: Higher education admissions tools for the 21st century.* Mahwah, NJ: Erlbaum.

Carnevale, A. P., Smith, N., & Strohl, J. (2010). *Help wanted: Projections of job and education requirements through 2018.* Indianapolis, IN: Lumina Foundation.

Casner-Lotto, J., & Barrington, L. (2006). *Are they really ready to work? Employers' perspectives on the basic knowledge and applied skills of new entrants to the 21st US workforce.* New York, NY: The Conference Board, Corporate Voices for Working Families, Partnership for 21st Century Skills, and Society for Human Resource Management.

Cedefop. (2015). *Matching skills and jobs in Europe: Insights from Cedefop's European Skills and Jobs Survey.* Retrieved from http://www.cedefop.europa.eu/en/publications-and-resources/publications/8088

Gallup. (2013). *America's call for higher education redesign: The 2012 Lumina Foundation study of the American public's opinion on higher education.* Retrieved from https://www.luminafoundation.org/files/resources/americas-call-for-higher-education-redesign.pdf

Gillespie, P. (2016). *America has near record 5.6 million job openings.* Retrieved from http://money.cnn.com/2016/02/09/news/economy/america-5-6-million-record-job-openings/

Hart Research Associates. (2010). *Raising the bar: Employers' views on college learning in the wake of the economic downturn.* Washington, DC: Author.

Mattern, K. D., Burrus, J., Camara, W. J., O'Connor, R., Hanson, M. A., Gambrell, J., Casillas, A., & Bobek, B. (2014). *Broadening the definition of college and career readiness: A holistic approach.* Iowa City: IA: ACT.

Poropat, A. E. (2009). A meta-analysis of the five-factor model of personality and academic performance. *Psychological Bulletin, 135,* 322–338.

Sloan, W. M. (2012). What is the purpose of education? *Education Update, 54.* Retrieved from http://www.ascd.org/publications/newsletters/education-update/jul12/vol54/num07/What-Is-the-Purpose-of-Education%C2%A2.aspx

US Bureau of Labor Statistics. (2013, December). Overview of projections to 2022. *Monthly Labor Review.*

ACKNOWLEDGMENTS

It is customary to include acknowledgments at the beginning of a book, and despite our innovative spirits, we see no reason as to why we should buck this trend in a book dedicated to creating better students and, ultimately, citizens. We thank a number of organizations for helping fund both the proceedings of the "Building Better Students: Preparation for Life After High School" conference and the writing of this book, with its slightly narrower focus on building students for the emerging workforce. These powerhouse organizations, along with various support structures they provided, included the American Educational Research Association (AERA), Educational Testing Service (ETS), The College Board, ACT, and Professional Examination Service. In addition, we would be remiss not to thank Pete Swerdzewski for his help conceptualizing and planning the initial conference from which the current volume promulgated, as well as Mary Lucas, Jennifer Minsky, Ben Orchard, Zhitong Yang, Teresa Jackson, and Matthew Ventura for their help during the conference. We also thank Professor Roger Weissberg, a recognized authority in the assessment and teaching of academic, social, and emotional learning who graciously agreed to write the Foreword to this edited volume.

During the writing of our respective chapters and the editing of this book, ETS, The College Board, ACT, and Professional Examination Service provided the facilities necessary to undertake and complete this work. We also extend our gratitude to senior management of these respective institutions, most notably Marten Roorda (CEO) at ACT, Wayne Camara (Senior Vice President) at ACT and (former Vice President) at The College Board, Ida Lawrence (Senior Vice President) at ETS, and Robert Block (CEO) and Simmy Ziv-el (Vice President) at Professional Examination Service.

Edited volumes can be very difficult to produce, as anyone who has set out on this onerous task will testify. We are indebted to Dana Marie Murano for her work pulling together the important pre-production pieces, including formatting all the chapters and compiling tables. Special thanks to the production team at Oxford University Press for making the final stretch of this process tolerable. Abby Gross and Courtney McCarroll were fantastic at pushing, encouraging, and cajoling us along the way and answering our countless questions with no complaints whatsoever.

No arduous undertaking can reach completion without continuous support, steadfast encouragement, and difficult sacrifice from all involved. First and foremost, we thank our wonderful children—Andrew and Joshua Burrus and Matthew Dean Roberts and Caspian Sondre Aicher-Roberts—who have variously lost us for stretches of time as we dealt with logistical issues and wrote our own pieces. We are blessed to have you in our lives and hope and trust that as you move along your professional paths, our work on this volume and beyond, directly or indirectly, will be of help to you. We love you dearly.

To the following friends, family, students, and/or colleagues, many thanks to you for your advice, for listening to us as we vented our frustrations, and for just plain being there: Meghan Brenneman, Bennett Burrus, Larry Burrus, Mary Margaret Kerns, Mabel Letheby, Ana Lipnevich, Mary Lucas, Carolyn MacCann, Jonathan Martin, Karla Mattern-Jones, Farin Mirvahabi, Gabriel Olaru, Kevin Petway, Richard Powell, Lynne Ream, Rebecca Rhodes, Rob Schneider, Ralf Schulze, Emily Shaw, Selina Weiss, Oliver Wilhelm, Franklin Zaromb, and Fritz Mattern (who we know is proudly smiling from heaven).

Finally, an edited book would be nothing without its contributions from the acclaimed scholars who we asked to give of their time, expertise, and knowledge to prepare chapters on topics that we believed needed special attention. We are indebted to each and every one of you for the various chapters appearing in this volume. We appreciate your critical contributions and your willingness to cope with a challenging task and to respond to our suggestions with grace, dignity, and efficiency. Because of your joint efforts, we believe the volume is coherent, hugely informative, and possibly even influential.

We hope this book will give readers a deeper understanding and appreciation of the current state of the art in assessment and intervention in workforce readiness. Please enjoy this volume, and do not hesitate to drop us a line should the book raise some questions.

Jeremy Burrus
Krista D. Mattern
Bobby D. Naemi
Richard D. Roberts

CONTRIBUTORS

Alex Casillas
ACT, Inc.
Iowa City, IA

Kim-Yin Chan
Division of Strategy, Management,
    and Organization
College of Business
Nanyang Technical University
Singapore

Olexander S. Chernyshenko
Division of Strategy, Management,
    and Organization
College of Business
Nanyang Technical University
Singapore

Hope Clark
ACT, Inc.
Iowa City, IA

Indako E. Clarke
School of Psychology
University of Sydney
Sydney, Australia

Kit S. Double
School of Psychology
University of Sydney
Sydney, Australia

Juliya Golubovich
Center for Academic and
    Workforce Readiness and
    Success
Educational Testing Service
Princeton, NJ

Patrick L. Hill
Department of Psychology
Carleton University
Ottawa, Ontario, Canada

Ringo Ho Moon-Ho
Division of Psychology
School of Humanities and Social
    Sciences
Nanyang Technical University
Singapore

Jennifer Klafehn
Center for Academic and
    Workforce Readiness and
    Success
Educational Testing Service
Princeton, NJ

Carrie N. Klein
Department of Higher Education
George Mason University
Fairfax, VA

David A. Kravitz
School of Business
George Mason University
Fairfax, VA

Patrick C. Kyllonen
Center for Academic and Workforce
    Readiness and Success
Educational Testing Service
Princeton, NJ

Jaime Lester
Department of Higher Education
George Mason University
Fairfax, VA

Carolyn MacCann
School of Psychology
University of Sydney
Sydney, Australia

Dana M. Murano
Department of Educational
    Psychology
The Graduate Center, City University
    of New York
New York, NY

Christopher D. Nye
Department of Psychology
Michigan State University
East Lansing, MI

Frederick L. Oswald
Department of Psychology
Rice University
Houston, TX

Steven B. Robbins
WorkFORCE Innovation
Educational Testing Service
Princeton, NJ

Brent W. Roberts
Department of Psychology
University of Illinois
Champaign, IL

Paul R. Sackett
Department of Psychology
University of Minnesota
Minneapolis, MN

Neal Schmitt
Department of Psychology
Michigan State University
East Lansing, MI

Amy Shaw
Department of Psychology
Rice University
Houston, TX

Rong Su
Department of Psychological
    Sciences
Purdue University
West Lafayette, IN

Marilyn Uy
Division of Strategy, Management,
    and Organization
College of Business
Nanyang Technical University
Singapore

Philip T. Walmsley
Office of Human Resources
    Management
Personnel Research and Assessment
    Division
US Customs and Border Protection
Washington, DC

Roger P. Weissberg
Department of Psychology
University of Illinois at Chicago
Chicago, IL

Ryan Whorton
Educational Testing Service
Princeton, NJ

Emma Yoke Loo Sam
Nanyang Technical University
Singapore

Building Better Students

Do We Really Need to Build Better Students?

JEREMY BURRUS, KRISTA D. MATTERN, BOBBY D. NAEMI,
AND RICHARD D. ROBERTS ■

> Change will not come if we wait for some other person or some other time. We are the ones we've been waiting for. We are the change that we seek.
>
> —Barack Obama (2008)

Many have argued that the way we work, what we work to achieve, and how we go about unifying these two endeavors is rapidly changing.[1] It is a story frequently told by the contemporary press and a recurring theme throughout the length and breadth of this book. If the requirements to succeed in the world of work are changing, then the world of workers may also need to change, perhaps precipitously, to meet these demands. If this statement is true, then it begs at least three questions: Is the world of work truly changing? If so, what kind of education and skills are required for workers to succeed in this new world? Finally, do workers currently have the education and skills necessary to succeed, or is there a need to alter our education systems in order to "build better students"?

In essence, as both the editors of this book and authors of its first chapter, we wanted an opening argument that provided a broad, evidence-related rationale for why we see a need to build better students. Furthermore, in the spirit of the quote from Barack Obama, 44th President of the United States, we viewed ourselves as not only commentators but also agents of change in a domain that will continue to impact generations to come. As a first step in this pursuit, we discuss the three questions raised in the opening paragraph. Next, we provide evidence that the world of work is indeed changing and, by extension, that this new world of work demands that its workers be more educated and possess a different mix of skills than those that were previously required. In a final section, we argue that the current workforce falls short in these areas. This then lays out the terrain for the remaining chapters of the book, which seek to redress this unfortunate, but entirely tractable (or so we believe), state of affairs.

THE EVOLVING NATURE OF WORK

One important mechanism that contributed to the change in the nature of the workplace is the rapid growth of technology that occurred in the latter half of the 20th century and that continues to this day. In this chapter, we focus on technological innovation, although certainly many other interrelated factors have also influenced the world of work, such as globalization, political and macroeconomic factors, and cultural shifts in attitudes toward work. Figure 1.1 provides a heuristic model that attempts to illustrate one path through which technological innovation has led to changes in the types of skills needed for a productive 21st century workforce. The arrows in Figure 1.1 represent the passage of time, with each factor on the left preceding, and partially causing, the factors that follow to the right. As Figure 1.1 illustrates, we posit that technological innovation has led to changes in many of the activities conducted at work. For instance, the development of the Internet has led to the Internet being used at work in countless impactful ways, whether for communication, research, or general work activities. This change in work activities has helped spur changes in the structure of the world's job market, with growth observed in some occupations and decline in others. Some jobs, for example, have become nearly obsolete (e.g., switchboard operators and travel agents) because of changes in the way that work is accomplished, whereas others (e.g., information security analysts and data scientists) are growing at an increasingly faster rate (Deming, 2015; US Bureau of Labor Statistics, 2015). Finally, this change in the world's job market requires a change in both workers' educational attainment and the skills required to fill new job openings (Carnevale, Smith, & Strohl, 2010). For instance, regarding the examples mentioned previously, usually a high school education is required for switchboard operators and travel agents, whereas a bachelor's degree is required for information security analysts, and some level of graduate training is required of data scientists. The model is explicated in the paragraphs that follow.

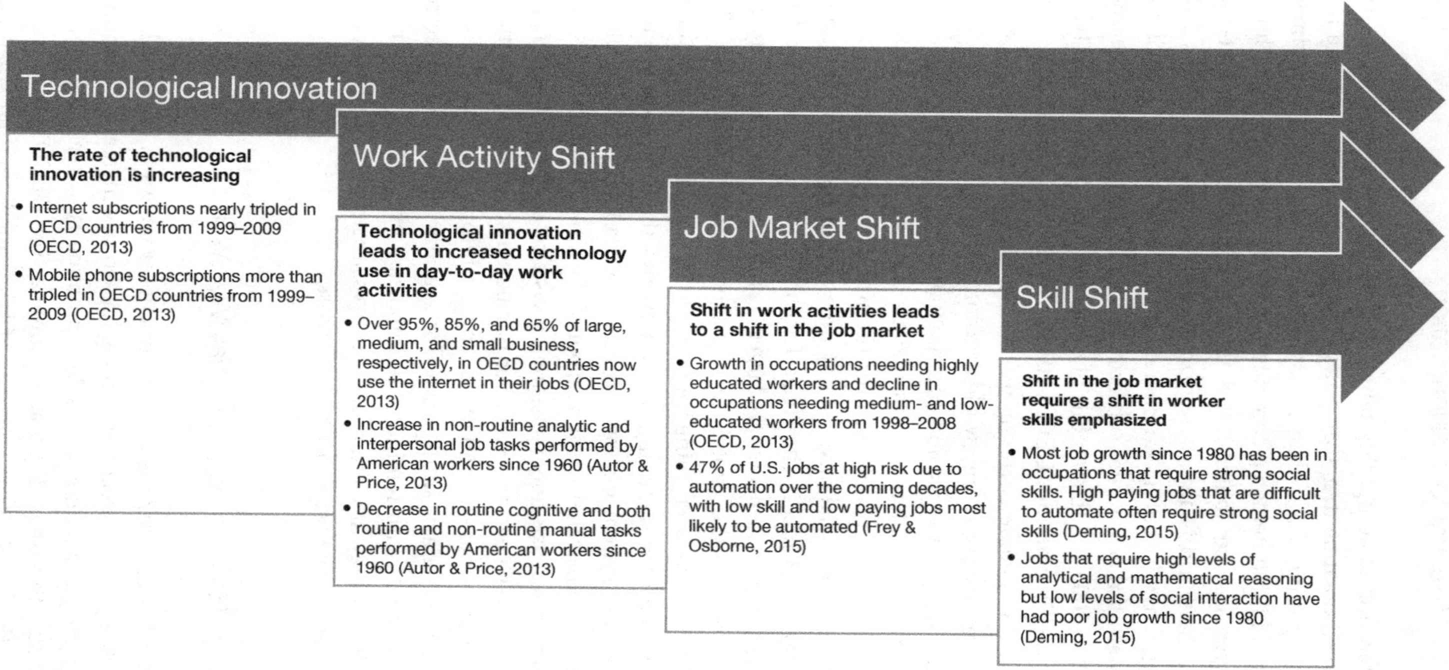

Technological Innovation

The rate of technological innovation is increasing

• Internet subscriptions nearly tripled in OECD countries from 1999–2009 (OECD, 2013)
• Mobile phone subscriptions more than tripled in OECD countries from 1999–2009 (OECD, 2013)

Work Activity Shift

Technological innovation leads to increased technology use in day-to-day work activities

• Over 95%, 85%, and 65% of large, medium, and small business, respectively, in OECD countries now use the internet in their jobs (OECD, 2013)
• Increase in non-routine analytic and interpersonal job tasks performed by American workers since 1960 (Autor & Price, 2013)
• Decrease in routine cognitive and both routine and non-routine manual tasks performed by American workers since 1960 (Autor & Price, 2013)

Job Market Shift

Shift in work activities leads to a shift in the job market

• Growth in occupations needing highly educated workers and decline in occupations needing medium- and low-educated workers from 1998–2008 (OECD, 2013)
• 47% of U.S. jobs at high risk due to automation over the coming decades, with low skill and low paying jobs most likely to be automated (Frey & Osborne, 2015)

Skill Shift

Shift in the job market requires a shift in worker skills emphasized

• Most job growth since 1980 has been in occupations that require strong social skills. High paying jobs that are difficult to automate often require strong social skills (Deming, 2015)
• Jobs that require high levels of analytical and mathematical reasoning but low levels of social interaction have had poor job growth since 1980 (Deming, 2015)

Figure 1.1 The influence of technological innovation on worker education and skill requirements.

Flourishing of Technological Innovation

The proliferation of computing power and its influence on our everyday lives has been well documented. Computers that were once the size of a room had far less computing power than today's handheld devices. It is estimated that more than 2 billion personal computers were in use by 2015 (see http://www.worldometers.info/computers) and that the number of Internet-connected devices in the world is anywhere from 8 to 10 billion (Soderbery, 2013). The Organization for Economic Co-operation and Development (OECD) released a report stating that Internet subscriptions in OECD countries nearly tripled from 1999 to 2009 and that mobile phone subscriptions more than tripled during that same time period (OECD, 2013). Worldwide, it is estimated that more than 3.2 billion people currently use the Internet, an increase of 806% since 2000 (see http://www.internetworldstats.com/stats.htm).

This technological explosion has dramatically changed the way much of the world lives and interacts with one another. Today, we can communicate instantaneously with people all over the world through e-mail, instant messaging, Skype, and social media at any time, day or night. Information spreads quickly over social media sites (e.g., Facebook), so much so that it has even been suggested that such sites are largely responsible for transformative social movements, such as the "Arab Spring" that occurred in 2010 (Rosen, 2011). We can purchase nearly everything we need without leaving home and often have it delivered the very same day. Many activities that historically relied on the human memory system are now accomplished via the aid of technology. We no longer need to remember street names and the most direct route between point A and point B because global positioning systems optimally navigate routes for us. We no longer need to remember our parents' or friends' phone numbers because smartphones store all of our contact information. We no longer need to remember birthdays, anniversaries, or appointments because electronic calendars provide us with reminders of important events. In summary, the ways in which technology has influenced our lives are myriad. Naturally, technology has also changed the ways in which we work.

Technology Has Changed the Way We Work

Technology has changed the way we work in several ways. The speed of computing, data analysis, and decision-making has greatly increased. Communication happens nearly instantaneously. Telecommuting is increasingly more common as we are able to work collaboratively online. The OECD (2013) has estimated that more than 95%, 85%, and 65% of large, medium, and small businesses, respectively, in OECD countries currently use the Internet in their operations. One key driver of change is automation because computing and robots are now able to take the place of humans in completing several types of tasks. It is estimated that the supply of industrial robots will be 186,000 in Asia, 55,000 in Europe, and 40,000 in the Americas by the end of 2017 (International Federation of Robotics, 2014, as cited in Frey & Osborne, 2015). This supply is expected to grow as robots become cheaper and more technologically sophisticated. Frey and Osborne provide examples of the types of activities robots are now able to do: "[R]obots are beginning to be used for a diverse range of professional service tasks, with sales continuing to grow for milking robots, robotic fencers, mobile barn cleaning robots, underwater robots and medical robots for assisted surgery" (p. 34). In turn, Autor and Price (2013) found that the share of routine cognitive and routine manual work tasks has fallen sharply since 1960. In general, routine tasks are tasks that follow relatively well-defined procedures, whereas nonroutine tasks refer to types of tasks that cannot be automated. Whereas computers can be programmed to complete routine tasks, they cannot be programmed to complete nonroutine tasks. By contrast, the share of nonroutine analytic and nonroutine interpersonal tasks has been on the rise since 1960. Nonroutine analytic tasks require skills such as problem solving, critical thinking, and creativity, whereas nonroutine interpersonal tasks require skills such as persuasion, empathy, and teamwork. Thus, it is no surprise that these changes in work activities coincide with an increase in the use of technology at work.

THE EVOLVING JOB MARKET

The Shift in the Way We Work Has Contributed to a Shift in the Job Market

One would expect that the job market should change in response to technological change, as occupations that are routine, and thus can be conducted by computers and robots, are eliminated and nonroutine jobs grow. Evidence suggests that this is the case. For example, the OECD (2013) has reported that the number of occupations requiring highly educated workers grew from 1998 to 2008. Frey and Osborne (2015) have estimated that 47% of US jobs are at risk due to automation in the coming years, with the jobs most at risk being the ones that are low paying and most likely to be automated (a point that, at the time of writing, should be of some concern for the espoused policies of the 45th President of the United States, Donald Trump). Consistent with these findings, an investigation of the top 30 fastest growing occupations indicates that the majority require at least some postsecondary education (US Bureau of

Labor Statistics, 2015), with 87% classified as zone 3^2 or higher (O*NET, 2016). Table 1.1 provides a complete list of the top 30 occupations expected to show the largest growth (as percentage change) during the next decade.[3]

Not only has the job market changed structurally in response to technological innovation but also there have been structural changes *within* jobs as a response to technological innovation. Although we are unaware of any research that has explicitly examined the issue, we predict that many job descriptions have changed throughout the years as a function of improving technology. Take the role of a psychology professor as an example. The job of a psychology professor consists, essentially, of research, teaching, and service (e.g., committee work). At least two of these three job responsibilities—research and teaching—have been greatly impacted by technology. Research is impacted in many ways, including the following:

- Studies can be conducted in less than 1 hour because of the availability of crowd-sourced participant pools.
- Statistical analyses can be conducted much more quickly with the use of software.
- Papers can be written very quickly due to modern word processing software, and they can be reviewed and published even quicker with the advent of open-source digital publishing platforms.
- Dissemination of one's research is greatly enhanced through Internet sources.

The impact of technology on professors' job responsibilities has several potential implications. For example, professors might be expected to publish more often given the relative ease of conducting research now compared with several decades ago. Likewise, teaching is impacted by technology in a number of ways. Each of these might also have important implications. For example:

- Lectures are conducted via PowerPoint rather than on a chalkboard.
- Students can communicate with professors at any time through e-mail and even social media.
- Computer simulations of events close to real life are possible; one can see the workings of the brain, for example, in far more elaborate detail than was ever possible by reading a text.
- Students can access learning materials over the Internet—often for free.

It would not be difficult to generate examples of how technology has significantly influenced the roles and responsibilities in other occupational fields (e.g., medicine, astrophysics, and engineering).

Table 1.1 TOP 30 PROJECTED FASTEST GROWING OCCUPATIONS FROM 2014 TO 2024 AND CORRESPONDING JOB ZONE

Occupation	Percentage Change (2014 to 2024)[a]	Job Zone[b,c]
Wind turbine service technicians	108.0	3
Occupational therapy assistants	42.7	3
Physical therapist assistants	40.6	3
Physical therapist aides	39.0	3
Home health aides	38.1	2
Commercial divers	36.9	3
Nurse practitioners	35.2	5
Physical therapists	34.0	5
Statisticians	33.8	5
Ambulance drivers and attendants, except emergency medical technicians	33.0	2
Occupational therapy aides	30.6	3
Physician assistants	30.4	5
Operations research analysts	30.2	5
Personal financial advisors	29.6	4
Cartographers and photogrammetrists	29.3	4
Genetic counselors	28.8	5
Interpreters and translators	28.7	4
Audiologists	28.6	5
Hearing aid specialists	27.2	3
Optometrists	27.0	5
Forensic science technicians	26.6	4
Web developers	26.6	3
Occupational therapists	26.5	5
Diagnostic medical sonographers	26.4	3
Personal care aides	25.9	2
Phlebotomists	24.9	3
Ophthalmic medical technicians	24.7	3
Nurse midwives	24.6	5
Solar photovoltaic installers	24.3	2
Emergency medical technicians and paramedics	24.2	3
Total, all occupations	*6.5*	*All*

[a]Data from US Bureau of Labor Statistics (2015).

[b]Data from O*NET (2016).

[c]Zone 1: Some of these occupations may require a high school diploma or GED certificate. Zone 2: These occupations usually require a high school diploma. Zone 3: Most occupations in this zone require training in vocational schools, related on-the-job experience, or an associate's degree. Zone 4: Most of these occupations require a 4-year bachelor's degree, but some do not. Zone 5: Most of these occupations require graduate school.

In summary, it is apparent that technology has not only changed the structure of the job market but also changed the structure of jobs themselves. Most pointedly, technology has allowed for more efficient work production processes/higher levels of productivity, as well as led to the need for increased facility with a variety of tools and forms of communication compared to the past.

The Shift in the Job Market Has Contributed to a Shift in the Skills Required of Workers

The job market's increasing emphasis on nonroutine and nonautomated occupations necessitates workers with the requisite education and skills to fill these jobs. In particular, these jobs seem to require a more highly educated workforce. One analysis found that, in 1973, approximately 66% of all jobs in the United States required a high school diploma or higher (Carnevale et al., 2010). By 2007, the percentage had increased dramatically, with 89% of jobs requiring a high school diploma or higher and 51% requiring some type of training after high school. It is projected that by 2020, 35% of jobs will require at least a bachelor's degree and 30% of jobs will require some college or an associate's degree (Carnevale, Smith, & Strohl, 2013). Another analysis found that occupations requiring a master's degree are projected to have high growth through 2022, whereas those that require a high school diploma or less are projected to have little growth (US Bureau of Labor Statistics, 2013).

Second, many of these jobs require strong *noncognitive* skills—"noncognitive" in the sense that they are typically not highly correlated with cognitive ability (Kyllonen, Lipnevich, Burrus, & Roberts, 2014). Noncognitive skills have also been referred to as personal skills, personal qualities, character traits, and psychosocial skills. Among these noncognitive skills, social skills seem to be especially important to the changing world of work. For instance, Deming (2015) found that most US job growth since 1980 could be attributed to an increase in difficult-to-automate jobs requiring strong social skills. Furthermore, he found that jobs requiring high levels of analytical and mathematical reasoning, but low levels of social skills, experienced poor growth since 1980. Survey research of US employers also suggests that noncognitive skills, as well as more broad cross-cutting capabilities, are greatly valued in today's workforce. A 2006 survey of US employers found that skills such as communication, work ethic, teamwork, and critical thinking were often considered more important than traditional academic skills (Casner-Lotto & Barrington, 2006). A 2010 survey found that US employers thought that colleges should put more emphasis on teaching and developing students' communication, critical thinking, complex problem solving, ethical decision-making, teamwork, and creative skills (Hart

Research Associates, 2010). Furthermore, a study developed a parsimonious framework of the most important skills needed for college-educated workers based on O*NET data (Burrus, Jackson, Nuo, & Steinberg, 2013). Specifically, a principal component analysis of the importance ratings of knowledge, skills, abilities, and work styles of the 536 occupations in O*NET that require at least some college education informed the development of the framework. The final framework included five skills, of which three were noncognitive in nature: teamwork, communication skills, and achievement/innovation. The other two skills were problem solving (which may also have some noncognitive components) and fluid intelligence. Note that the need for noncognitive skills is not merely an American issue but, rather, of great consequence throughout the world. For example, policy issues regarding noncognitive skills are increasingly being recognized as important in large-scale testing programs such as the Programme for International Student Assessment (Naemi et al., 2013).

The evidence seems clear that today's students will have to be more educated and possess a different set of skills than students in previous generations in order to succeed in the 21st century workplace. These demands appear to have arisen, at least in part, because technological innovations have changed the way in which work is accomplished, which, by extension, has influenced the very makeup of the labor market. A major thesis of the current book is that there is a need to "build better students," however, a discussion of whether today's students are meeting or falling short of these requirements is first necessary. This is discussed in the next section (for a review of these issues, see Mattern et al., 2014).

IS THERE A NEED TO "BUILD BETTER STUDENTS"?

Education Shortfall

How well is the United States doing to meet the education demands of an evolving job market, which requires a more educated workforce? Evidence suggests not very well. It has been projected that the US economy will need 5 million more workers with an associate's degree or higher by 2020 than will be available (Carnevale et al., 2013). Furthermore, the United States seems to be falling behind other countries in producing college graduates. In 2008, the United States had the third highest percentage of individuals obtaining an associate's degree, behind only China and Japan (Carnevale & Rose, 2010). The picture looks bleaker when analyses are limited to 25- to 34-year-olds. Among this group, the United States ranks 10th, with just 42% of this age group obtaining a college degree. If the current trend holds, it is possible that the United States will have to recruit much of its workforce from other countries to keep up with demand. Indeed, this already seems to be happening because half of all US workers in science, technology, engineering, and mathematics (STEM) occupations with graduate degrees come from foreign countries (Information Technology Industry Council, 2012). Undoubtedly, the educational outlook does not paint an optimistic picture for the future of the US economy. Less clearly articulated is how other countries compare on these metrics, but it is likely the situation is not something about which only citizens from the United States should be concerned.

Skill Shortfall

There is evidence that even if the United States were producing enough college graduates, many would still be unprepared for work. A 2006 survey of more than 400 employers found that 11% of 2-year and 9% of 4-year college graduates who were new entrants into the workforce were rated as "deficient" in their overall preparation (Casner-Lotto & Barrington, 2006). By contrast, 10% and 24% were rated as "excellent" in their overall preparation, respectively. The most common deficiencies were written communication, self-direction, and creativity for 2-year college graduates and written communication and leadership for 4-year college graduates. In another survey, 60% of employers stated that 2-year colleges and universities needed improvement in preparing students for the workforce, and 68% said that 4-year colleges and universities needed to improve their students (Hart Research Associates, 2010). Yet another survey found that only 42% of employers agreed that colleges and universities were doing a good job of "ensuring that college graduates possess the full set of skills and knowledge that they will need for success" compared to 74% of students who believed their skills and knowledge to be adequate (Hart Research Associates, 2015). This discrepancy suggests that students lack awareness of the skills and knowledge they need to be successful in today's workforce.

In line with this argument, a summary of employer and student perceptions on college graduates' preparation of specific skills is displayed in Table 1.2. Percentages reflect the number of people who believe that recent college graduates are "well prepared." There are at least two important points to note. First, many of these skills are noncognitive in nature. Second, the discrepancy between student and employer perceptions persists for each skill. Specifically, across all skills, more than half (54%) of students think recent college graduates are well prepared compared to less than one-fourth (24%) of employees. Note that the skill shortfall—both cognitive and noncognitive in nature—is not simply restricted to students in the United States; it is a global problem (Cedefop, 2015). In summary, much existing survey research evidence

Table 1.2 PERCENTAGE OF EMPLOYERS AND STUDENTS WHO BELIEVE THAT RECENT
COLLEGE GRADUATES ARE "WELL PREPARED" IN EACH SKILL

Skill	Employers (%)	Students (%)
Working in teams	37	64
Staying current on technologies	37	46
Ethical judgment and decision making	30	62
Locating, organizing, and evaluating information	29	64
Oral communication	28	62
Working with numbers/statistics	28	55
Written communication	27	65
Critical/analytical thinking	26	66
Being innovative/creative	25	57
Analyzing/solving complex problems	24	59
Applying knowledge/skills to the real world	23	59
Awareness/experience of diverse cultures in the United States	21	48
Staying current on technologies on developments in science	21	44
Working with people from different backgrounds	18	55
Staying current on global developments	18	43
Proficient in other languages	16	34
Awareness/experience of diverse cultures outside the United States	15	42

SOURCE: Data from Hart Research Associates (2015).

suggests that employers perceive a lack of skill in many of their recent hires, despite the hires having earned a college degree.

SUMMARY: LOOKING FORWARD TO CHANGE

The purpose of this chapter was to examine whether there is a need to "build better students" and to set the stage for the rest of the book. In this chapter, we provided evidence that better prepared students are indeed needed if they are to succeed in the new world of work. Our reasoning can be summarized by the following six points:

1. Technological innovation is proliferating and has changed the way we live.
2. Technological innovation has also changed the way we work.

3. Changes in the way we work have led to structural changes in the job market, with some occupations growing and others shrinking in number. Technological innovation has also led to structural changes within jobs themselves.
4. These growing occupations tend to require a high level of education and a particular set of skills. Many of these skills are noncognitive in nature.
5. At the current rate, we are not producing enough highly educated students to fill these occupations.
6. Many of the new entrants into the workforce do not possess the requisite skills (which are increasingly noncognitive in nature) needed to succeed, even if they are highly educated.

Thus, the need to build better students is apparent. The chapters in this book offer several suggestions for ways to bolster student readiness and success. Next, two general suggestions that follow from the previous sections of this chapter are offered.

Improve College Retention Rates

Many students enter college academically unprepared and thus find it difficult to graduate with a degree. For example, in 2007–2008, approximately one-fifth of first-year undergraduate students had to take a remedial course (US Department of Education, 2013). Furthermore, a large-scale survey found that only 26% of college instructors thought the students they taught arrived at college "well" or "very well" prepared (ACT, 2013). In addition, 31% of the ACT-tested high school graduating class of 2015 met none of the four college readiness benchmarks in English, reading, mathematics, and science (ACT, 2015). These benchmarks correspond to the ACT scores associated with a 50% chance of obtaining a B or higher or an approximately 75% chance of obtaining a C or higher in corresponding college courses. Given these statistics, it is probably not surprising that only 6 of 10 college students earn a degree within 6 years (US Department of Education, 2016).

Of course, one way to improve college retention would be to increase the amount that students learn in high school, which presumably would lead to better grades in first-year college courses. This is important because it is well known that students who perform poorly in the first year are most likely to drop out of college (Pascarella & Terenzini, 2005). Moreover, grades are predictive of college completion over several demographic characteristics (Adelman, 1999). Another less obvious way to improve retention would be to foster the development of student noncognitive skills. Research has shown that factors such as having academic goals, high achievement motivation, and high academic discipline are related to retention in college (Allen, Robbins, Casillas, & Oh, 2008; Robbins et al., 2004). Furthermore, emotional stability, conscientiousness, agreeableness, and extraversion all predict retention via their relationship with adjustment to college (Credé & Niehorster, 2012). This discussion of noncognitive skills leads us to our second point.

Emphasize the Development of Noncognitive Skills

In addition to college retention, noncognitive skills predict a host of academic, work, and life outcomes. For example, noncognitive skills have been shown to predict positive outcomes such as the following:

- Academic performance (Poropat, 2009)
- Job performance (Barrick, Mount, & Judge, 2001)
- Job satisfaction (Judge, Heller, & Mount, 2002)
- Happiness (Diener & Lucas, 1999)
- Health (Bogg & Roberts, 2004) and longevity (Roberts, Kuncel, Shiner, Caspi, & Goldberg, 2007)
- Marital satisfaction (Watson, Hubbard, & Wiese, 2000)
- Peer relationships (Jensen-Campbell et al., 2002)
- Volunteerism (Penner, 2002)

They have also been shown to predict negative outcomes, including the following:

- Academic discipline rates and truancy (MacCann, Duckworth, & Roberts, 2009)
- Behavioral problems (Ge & Conger, 1999)

It is important to note that noncognitive skills predict academic and work outcomes many years into the future. For instance, one study found that 6-year-olds who scored higher on measures of behavioral problems were more likely to drop out of high school than 6-year-olds who did not demonstrate such problems (Moon, 2012). Another study found that children's level of conscientiousness predicted their occupational status, wages, and job satisfaction 60 years later (when controlling for cognitive ability; Judge, Higgins, Thoresen, & Barrick, 1999). Furthermore, 10th-grade students' work ethic ratings predicted their educational attainment and earnings 10 years later (controlling for cognitive ability; Lleras, 2008). These findings suggest that it may be important to focus on and foster children's noncognitive skills at early ages. Consistent with this assertion, recent work has shown that school programs that teach noncognitive skills through *social and emotional learning* (SEL) programs have a benefit-to-cost ratio of $11 to $1 for society, both in the United States and elsewhere (Belfield et al., 2015). That is, the monetary benefits of implementing an SEL program far outweigh the costs in terms of reducing the prevalence of substance abuse, delinquency, and mental health issues and increasing social competence. Given that the data clearly point to a positive return on investment, a component of educational reform should focus on investing both local, national, and global resources into inculcating, scaling, and evaluating these programs.

CONCLUSION

The evidence provided in this chapter, as well as that provided in the chapters that follow, makes a strong case that we as a society need to find a way to "build better students." We provided two potential solutions to this problem: increasing college retention and fostering noncognitive skills. Many of the chapters in this book further develop these, and other, options in greater detail. In the process, we are beholden to the insightful quotation with which this chapter began and mention it again, for the reader also can play a pivotal role: "Change will not come if we wait for some other person or some other time. We are the ones we've been waiting for. We are the change that we seek" (Obama, 2008). This book represents more than words on pages; it is a call to action. We argue that, as a society, we must come together to support the better preparation of our youth and, in turn, ensure a strong, effective workforce for generations to come.

NOTES

1. All statements expressed in this article are the authors' and do not reflect the official opinions or policies of the any of the authors' host affiliations.
2. O*NET (Occupational Information Network) classifies jobs into one of five zones based on the typical education level required. Refer to Table 1.1 for the job zone definitions.
3. O*NET refers to the Occupational Information Network, an extensive job analysis of more than 900 jobs. Jobs are classified into one of five zones based on the typical education level required. Refer to Table 1.1 for the job zone definitions.

REFERENCES

ACT. (2013). *ACT National Curriculum Survey 2012: Policy implications on preparing for higher standards.* Iowa City, IA: Author.

ACT. (2015). *The condition of college & career readiness 2015.* Iowa City, IA: Author.

Adelman, C. (1999). *Answers in the toolbox: Academic intensity, attendance patterns, and bachelor's degree attainment* (Document PLLI 1999-8021). Washington, DC: US Department of Education.

Allen, J., Robbins, S. B., Casillas, A., & Oh, I. S. (2008). Third-year college retention and transfer: Effects of academic performance, motivation, and social connectedness. *Research in Higher Education, 49,* 647–664.

Autor, D. H., & Price, B. (2013). The Changing Task Composition of the US. Labor Market: An Update of Autor, Levy, and Murnane (2003). Retrieved from http://economics.mit.edu/files/11661

Barrick, M. R., Mount, M. K., & Judge, T. A. (2001). Personality and performance at the beginning of the new millennium: What do we know and where do we go next? *International Journal of Selection and Assessment, 9,* 9–30.

Belfield, C., Bowden, B., Klapp, A., Levin, H., Shand, R., & Zander, S. (2015). *The economic value of social and emotional learning.* New York, NY: Center for Benefit–Cost Studies in Education.

Bogg, T., & Roberts, B. W. (2004). Conscientiousness and health behaviors: A meta-analysis. *Psychological Bulletin, 130,* 887–919.

Burrus, J., Jackson, T., Nuo, X., & Steinberg, J. (2013). *Identifying the most important 21st century workforce competencies: An analysis of the Occupational Information Network (O*NET)* (Research Report ETS RR-13-21). Princeton, NJ: Educational Testing Service.

Carnevale, A. P., & Rose, S. J. (2010). *The undereducated American.* Washington, DC: Georgetown University, Center on Education and the Workforce.

Carnevale, A. P., Smith, N., & Strohl, J. (2010). *Help wanted: Projections of job and education requirements through 2018.* Indianapolis, IN: Lumina Foundation.

Carnevale, A. P., Smith, N., & Strohl, J. (2013). *Recovery: Job growth and education requirements through 2020.* Washington, DC: Georgetown Public Policy Institute.

Casner-Lotto, J., & Barrington, L. (2006). *Are they really ready to work? Employers' perspectives on the basic knowledge and applied skills of new entrants to the 21st US workforce.* New York, NY: The Conference Board, Corporate Voices for Working Families, Partnership for 21st Century Skills, and Society for Human Resource Management.

Cedefop. (2015). *Matching skills and jobs in Europe: Insights from Cedefop's European skills and jobs survey.* Retrieved from http://www.cedefop.europa.eu/en/publications-and-resources/publications/8088

Credé, M., & Niehorster, S. (2012). Adjustment to college as measured by the Student Adaptation to College questionnaire: A quantitative review of its structure and relationships with correlates and consequences. *Educational Psychology Review, 24,* 133–165.

Deming, D. J. (2015). *The growing importance of social skills in the labor market* (No. w21473). Cambridge, MA: National Bureau of Economic Research.

Diener, E., & Lucas, R. E. (1999). Personality and subjective well-being. In D. Kahneman, E. Diener, & N. Schwarz (Eds.), *Well-being: The foundations of hedonic psychology* (pp. 213–229). New York, NY: Russell Sage Foundation.

Frey, C. B., & Osborne, M. (2015). *Technology at work: The future of innovation and employment*. Retrieved from http://www.oxfordmartin.ox.ac.uk/downloads/reports/Citi_GPS_Technology_Work.pdf

Ge, X., & Conger, R. D. (1999). Adjustment problems and emerging personality characteristics from early to late adolescents. *American Journal of Community Psychology, 27*, 429–459.

Hart Research Associates. (2010). *Raising the bar: Employers' views on college learning in the wake of the economic downturn*. Washington, DC: Author.

Hart Research Associates. (2015). *Falling short? College learning and career success*. Washington, DC: Author.

Information Technology Industry Council, the Partnership for a New American Economy, and the US Chamber of Commerce. (2012). *Help wanted: The role of foreign workers in the innovation economy*. Washington, DC: Author.

International Federation of Robotics. (2014). *World Robotics 2014: Executive summary*. Retrieved from http://www.diag.uniroma1.it/~deluca/rob1_en/2014_World Robotics_ExecSummary.pdf.

Jensen-Campbell, L. A., Adams, R., Perry, D. G., Workman, K. A., Furdella, J. Q., & Egan, S. K. (2002). Agreeableness, extraversion, and peer relationships in early adolescents: Winning friends and deflecting aggression. *Journal of Research in Personality, 36*, 224–251.

Judge, T. A., Heller, D., & Mount, M. K. (2002). Five-factor model of personality and job satisfaction: A meta-analysis. *Journal of Applied Psychology, 87*, 530–541.

Judge, T. A., Higgins, C. A., Thoresen, C. J., & Barrick, M. R. (1999). The big five personality traits, general mental ability, and career success across the life span. *Personnel Psychology, 53*, 621–652.

Kyllonen, P. C., Lipnevich, A. A., Burrus, J., & Roberts, R. D. (2014). *Personality, motivation, and college readiness: A prospectus for assessment and development* (ETS RR-14-06). Princeton, NJ: Educational Testing Service.

Lleras, C. (2008). Do skills and behaviors in high school matter? The contribution of noncognitive factors in explaining differences in educational attainment and earnings. *Social Science Research, 37*, 888–902.

MacCann, C., Duckworth, A., & Roberts, R. D. (2009). Identifying the major facets of conscientiousness in high school students and their relationships with valued educational outcomes. *Learning and Individual Differences, 19*, 451–458.

Mattern, K. D., Burrus, J., Camara, W. J., O'Connor, R., Gambrell, J., Hanson, M. A., . . . Bobek, B. (2014). *Broadening the definition of college and career readiness: A holistic approach*. Iowa City, IA: ACT.

Moon, S. H. (2012). *Decomposing racial skill gaps in the US*. Unpublished manuscript, University of Chicago, Department of Economics.

Naemi, B., Gonzalez, E., Bertling, J., Betancourt, A., Burrus, J., Kyllonen, P. C., . . . Roberts, R. D. (2013). Large-scale group score assessments: Past, present, and future. In D. H. Saklofske, C. B. Reynolds, & V. L. Schwean (Eds.), *Oxford handbook of child psychological assessment* (pp. 129–149). Cambridge, England: Oxford University Press.

Obama, B. (2008). Barack Obama's Feb. 5 speech. *New York Times*. Retrieved from http://www.nytimes.com/2008/02/05/us/politics/05text-obama.html

O*NET. (2016). *Browse bright outlook occupations*. Retrieved from https://www.oneton-line.org/find/bright?b=1&g=Go#foot1

Organisation for Economic Co-operation and Development. (2013). *OECD skills out-look 2013: First results from the Survey of Adult Skills*. Retrieved from https:/www.oecd.org/skills/piaac/Skills%20volume%201%20(eng)--full%20v12--eBook%20 (04%2011%202013).pdf

Pascarella, E. T., & Terenzini, P. T. (2005). *How college affects students: A third decade of research* (Vol. 2). San Francisco, CA: Jossey-Bass.

Penner, L. A. (2002). Dispositional and organizational influences on sustained volun-teerism: An interactionist perspective. *Journal of Social Issues, 58*, 447–467.

Poropat, A. E. (2009). A meta-analysis of the five factor model of personality and aca-demic performance. *Psychological Bulletin, 135*, 322–338.

Robbins, S. B., Lauver, K., Le, H., Davis, D., Langley, R., & Carlstrom, A. (2004). Do psychosocial and study skill factors predict college outcomes? A meta-analysis. *Psychological Bulletin, 130*, 261–288.

Roberts, B. W., Kuncel, N. R., Shiner, R., Caspi, A., & Goldberg, L. R. (2007). The power of personality: The comparative validity of personality traits, socioeconomic status, and cognitive ability for predicting important life outcomes. *Perspectives on Psychological Science, 2*, 313–345.

Rosen, R. J. (2011). *So, was Facebook responsible for the Arab Spring after all?* Retrieved from http://www.theatlantic.com/technology/archive/2011/09/so-was-facebook-responsible-for-the-arab-spring-after-all/244314

Soderbery, R. (2013). *How many things are currently connected to the "Internet of things" (IoT)?* Retrieved from http://www.forbes.com/sites/quora/2013/01/07/how-many-things-are-currently-connected-to-the-internet-of-things-iot

US Bureau of Labor Statistics. (2013, December). Overview of projections to 2022. *Monthly Labor Review*.

US Bureau of Labor Statistics. (2015). *Fastest growing occupations*. Retrieved from https://www.bls.gov/emp/ep_table_103.htm

US Department of Education, National Center for Education Statistics. (2013). *First year undergraduate remedial coursetaking: 1999–2000, 2003–2004, 2007–2008* (NCES 2013- 013). Washington, DC: National Center for Education Statistics.

US Department of Education, National Center for Education Statistics. (2016). *The con-dition of education 2016* (NCES 2016- 144). Washington, DC: National Center for Education Statistics.

Watson, D., Hubbard, B., & Wiese, D. (2000). General traits of personality and affec-tivity as predictors of satisfaction in intimate relationships: Evidence from self- and partner-ratings. *Journal of Personality, 68*, 413–419.

Rethinking How We Define and Measure Workforce Readiness

Workplace Readiness and Personnel Selection

Setting the Stage

PAUL R. SACKETT AND PHILIP T. WALMSLEY ∎

In this overview chapter, we discuss four principal topics. First, we offer a brief conceptual overview of the various ways in which the concept of "workplace readiness" is currently used. Second, we offer an overview of central themes in the area of personnel selection, with an eye toward putting workplace readiness efforts in perspective. Third, we summarize a current substantive model of workforce readiness, providing links to prospects for measurement in a personnel selection environment. Finally, we summarize some of our recent research on personality attributes valued at work as a vehicle for discussing some important issues in assessing workplace readiness.

There are three main options for students upon completion of high school: higher education, the civilian workforce, and the military. Under the rubrics of "workforce readiness" and "college and career readiness," questions regularly arise as to the degree to which students are prepared for these postsecondary endeavors (Casner-Lotto & Barrington, 2006). One set of questions focuses on issues of academic achievement that are clearly central to the mission of secondary education: Are students acquiring the subject-specific content knowledge and more general learning and problem-solving skills needed in higher education, civilian, and military workplace environments? A second set of questions focuses on attributes beyond the knowledge/skill/ability domains, referred to variously as "personality characteristics," "noncognitive attributes," "soft skills," "social and emotional competencies," or "21st century skills," among other labels (National Research Council, 2011). These questions address whether students are entering the workforce with the capability to apply these "soft skills" successfully. The labels listed previously are used in reference to a wide array of attributes, such as dependability, resilience, and cooperation. Attention to these attributes derives from a number of disciplines. Personality at work is a widely studied topic in industrial and organizational psychology (Christiansen & Tett, 2013). Noncognitive attributes are rapidly growing topics of study in labor economics (Cobb-Clark & Tan, 2011; Heckman, Stixrud, & Urzua, 2006). In the field of education, classroom interventions aimed at "social and emotional skills" are the topic of a meta-analysis by Durlak, Weissberg, Dymnicki, Taylor, and Schellinger (2011).

"Workforce readiness" has emerged as a commonly used term with widely differing meanings. The term is commonly paired with the somewhat parallel concept of "college readiness," which addresses the issue of whether youth completing high school are prepared to succeed in college. Given that common postsecondary pathways include entering the civilian workforce, entering the military, and pursuing some form of further education, there is interest in examining commonalities in what is needed for success in each of these domains. "Career readiness" is sometimes used as an alternate term for workplace readiness, commonly when paired with college readiness, permitting the euphonious pairing of "college and career readiness" (Stone & Lewis, 2012; US Department of Education, 2010).

OVERVIEW OF THE CONCEPT OF WORKPLACE READINESS

To set the stage, consider a small sampling of definitions of workforce readiness found in the literature. First, ACT (2013) offers the following as a definition: "A 'work ready' individual possesses the foundational skills needed to be minimally qualified for a specific occupation as determined through a job analysis or occupational profile" (p. 3). "Foundational skills" are defined as fundamental portable skills that can be applied across a wide variety of occupations and that serve as the basis for subsequent advanced skill development. ACT operationalizes eight foundational skills: applied mathematics, reading for information, locating information, applied technology, writing, teamwork, observation, and business writing. Note that these include both "traditional" cognitive skills (e.g., mathematics and reading) and skills commonly falling under the rubric of "soft skills" or "noncognitive skills" (e.g., teamwork).

Second, Conley (2010) focuses on the commonalities between college and career readiness and defines these as

> the level of preparation a student needs in order to enroll and succeed—without remediation—in a credit-bearing course at a postsecondary institution that offers a baccalaureate degree or transfer to a baccalaureate program, or in a high quality certificate program that enables students to enter a career pathway with potential future advancement. (p. 1)

He differentiates between "career ready," which focuses on preparation for a career pathway, and "work ready," which focuses on basic expectations regarding workplace behavior and demeanor. He identifies four domains within the broad notions of college and career readiness: cognitive strategies (e.g., problem formulation and communication), content knowledge (e.g., technical knowledge and skills), learning skills (e.g., goal setting, persistence, and time management), and transition skills (e.g., understanding workplace norms and expectations). Although elements of these four domains are broadly applicable, Conley acknowledges that different occupations and work settings have different requirements, and thus the set of skills that any given individual needs to be work ready in the occupation to which he or she aspires will vary.

Third, a joint project between The Conference Board, the Partnership for 21st Century Skills, Corporate Voices for Working Families, and the Society for Human Resource Management (Casner-Lotto & Barrington, 2006) titled "Are They Really Ready to Work?" surveyed employers to obtain perceptions of the importance of 20 basic knowledge domains (e.g., speaking, reading, writing, and mathematics) and applied skills (e.g., professionalism/work ethic and teamwork/collaboration) for new workplace entrants with three levels of education attainment (high school, 2-year college graduates, and 4-year college graduates). These perceptions of importance were paired with judgments of the degree to which these new workplace entrants were prepared (on a scale from deficient to adequate to excellent) in each of these 20 domains, in addition to a judgment of overall preparedness for work. They did not offer a formal definition of workplace readiness, but it is implicit in the operationalization previously presented: Workforce-ready individuals are at least adequate in attributes rated as important in the workplace.

The resulting aggregate perceptions reflect the percentage of employers using each response category (e.g., 43% of employers rated new high school graduates as deficient in their overall preparedness for the workplace). Unfortunately, the report at times makes a subtle, but important, shift and wrongly interprets these aggregate perceptions as the percentage of new entrants who fall into each category (cf. p. 31). That 24% of employers rated 4-year college graduates as "excellent" in their preparation does not permit an inference that 24% of college graduates fall into the "excellent" category. This is highlighted here because the aggregate percentage of new entrants meeting a particular readiness standard is a statistic that is commonly of interest. One could obtain a direct judgment of this statistic or could roll up data from systems that directly assess the readiness of each individual.

This brief overview of a sampling of approaches to workplace readiness can be parsed to identify a set of features on which the approaches differ. First, they differ in the set of attributes that are considered. For example, the ACT model contains 8 attributes, whereas The Conference Board model contains 20. All three of the approaches to workplace readiness include both "traditional" cognitive attributes (e.g., reading and math) and noncognitive "soft skill" attributes (e.g., teamwork). Note that the inclusion of attributes from the cognitive and noncognitive domains is not universal. The College Board, for example, offers benchmarks for college and career readiness based solely on the reading, math, and writing subtests of the SAT (The College Board, n.d.). It does acknowledge the importance of other attributes; the focus solely on SAT scores is a function of their widespread use and ready availability for use in computing a readiness index rather than reflecting a belief that noncognitive attributes are not relevant to readiness.

Second, they differ in whether their perspective on readiness is general versus occupation specific. For example, The Conference Board perspective is general because it examines perceptions of whether new workforce entrants with a given level of educational attainment (e.g., high school diploma) are ready for success in the workplace as a whole. In contrast, the ACT model and Conley model define readiness in terms of meeting the demands of a specific occupation. A given individual would be deemed ready for some occupations and not for others.

Third, they differ in whether their focus is at the individual level or the aggregate level. The ACT model, for example, can be applied at the individual level: A given student can be evaluated as to whether he or she meets the entry threshold on the attributes relevant to a particular occupation. Approaches that evaluate readiness at the individual level also have the potential for aggregation: If a random or representative sample of students is evaluated, results can be pooled to permit statement about the percentage of students who meet a readiness standard for a given occupation. In contrast, The Conference Board approach operates at an aggregate level because employers report the importance of each attribute and their evaluation of whether new workplace entrants as a whole are deficient, adequate, or excellent. This is certainly useful information, shedding light on which attributes generate, for example, the highest percentage of "deficient" ratings. However, the approach is not designed to evaluate readiness at the individual student level.

Fourth, they differ in whether or not they specify the level of each attribute that is needed to be classified as workplace ready. This is related to the individual versus aggregate distinction drawn previously. In order to classify an individual student as workplace ready, either on a single attribute or across a profile of attributes, it is necessary to determine the level of the attribute needed for readiness. For example, the ACT model uses a job-analytic procedure to determine the needed level of each attribute for a particular occupation on a 5-point scale, and it assesses student standing on each attribute on a comparable 5-point scale. In contrast, approaches operating at the aggregate level do not necessarily need to specify the needed level of the attribute, as in the case of The Conference Board approach.

Fifth, they differ in whether they define readiness in terms of preparation to succeed on the job (e.g., the ACT and The Conference Board approaches) or in terms of preparation to succeed in a career-relevant training program (the Conley approach). Conceptually, a broader array of attributes may be relevant to job success than to training success.

In summary, approaches to workplace readiness vary on a variety of dimensions (Table 2.1). Absent a consensual definition, there is the potential for confusion because different approaches can yield very different results as to

Table 2.1 DIMENSIONS FOR COMPARING APPROACHES FOR DEFINING WORKPLACE READINESS

No.	Dimension	Description/Examples
1	Attributes considered	There is a wide range in terms of number of attributes considered, from 2 or 3 to more than 20. Some approaches include attributes from both cognitive and noncognitive domains; other approaches focus on a single domain.
2	General versus occupation-specific	Some approaches consider success in the workplace as a whole; others focus on specific occupations.
3	Individual versus aggregate-level focus	Some approaches can be used to evaluate an individual's readiness; others provide information only in aggregate.
4	Specification of the level of attribute required	Some approaches use methods to identify the level of an attribute required at entry to work; others identify an attribute as relevant without specifying the needed level of the attribute.
5	Entry to job versus entry to career training	Some approaches focus on readiness as entry to the job; others focus on entry to job training.

whether a given individual would meet a standard for being labeled "workplace ready," as well as yielding differing results as to the aggregate level of preparedness of a particular youth cohort.

OVERVIEW OF PERSONNEL SELECTION

We offer some observations about personnel selection in organizations because workplace readiness programs are necessarily linked to selection systems in organizations. Note that there are at least two potentially complementary, but potentially divergent, ways to think about a successful workplace readiness program. One is that a workforce-ready individual is prepared to meet selection standards for workplace entry; the other is that the individual has the skills to perform effectively once hired. Ideally, these two would be perfectly complementary: Organizations would select for precisely those attributes that contribute the most to subsequent effective job performance. However, it is possible that employers are incorrect in their beliefs as to the attributes most important for job performance. In fact, there is a body of literature that documents considerable discrepancies between findings in the scientific literature and the beliefs of human resource managers. For example, Rynes, Colbert, and Brown (2002) presented a list of 35 true–false statements regarding research findings to a large sample of human resource managers. Only 18% disagreed with the false statement that conscientiousness was a better predictor of job performance than intelligence. Sixteen percent disagreed with the false statement that values are a better predictor of performance than intelligence. Thirty-two percent disagreed with the false statement that integrity tests were not useful predictors because they were easy to fake. Note that this is not per se evidence that inappropriate decisions are made in determining which attributes to include in employee selection systems. Such decisions may include input from a variety of individuals, and incorrect beliefs on the part of some may be countered by correct information from others. Nonetheless, these findings do at the least suggest the value in separately examining scientific evidence about what attributes are valued by organizational decision makers as well as data about which attributes predict work outcomes.

There is a very large body of scientific knowledge about personnel selection techniques, and personnel selection is one of the most studied topics within the field of industrial and organizational psychology. We offer here a very high-level overview of organizational selection practices because we believe this will be useful in understanding how workforce readiness efforts can link to these practices.

Theme 1: There Is High Variance in Selection Procedures Used in Employment Settings

Perhaps the most basic observation to be made is that organizational selection practices are extremely varied. This is in strong contrast to selection in the higher education context, in which variations are relatively modest, at least in the United States. Students expect that factors to be considered will be high school academic performance, performance on one of two dominant admissions tests (SAT and ACT, except at schools presenting themselves as test optional), an application form, letters of recommendation, and a personal essay. A select set of schools conduct interviews. In contrast, an individual presenting him- or herself as a candidate for a given job and a given employer faces a far more varied array of potential hurdles. Tests may be used, but rather than the well-known admissions tests, with which students have ample advance opportunity to familiarize themselves, there are hundreds and perhaps thousands of different tests commercially marketed to organizations for use for selection. In addition, a great many tests are developed in-house by individual organizations and thus are unique to those organizations. These tests can measure a wide variety of attributes, including knowledge, skill, ability, judgment, personality, interests, and values. A wide variety of measures other than traditional tests may be used, including methods for obtaining background information (from simple application blanks to lengthy and formally scored biographical data forms and accomplishment records and to reference, credit, and criminal background checks), interviews (which may range from informal unstructured interviews to highly structured interviews with prespecified questions and formal scoring systems), and simulations (ranging from online or paper-based in-baskets to immersive day-in-the-life assessment centers).

With some frequency, surveys of employers are conducted regarding the use of selection practices. For example, the Society for Human Resource Management (2005) surveyed 282 human resource professionals and reported the percentage of employers making use of each method listed in its survey. Among the results are that 40% report using skills testing, 26% use aptitude testing, 34% use personality testing, 11% use work simulations, and 7% use assessment centers. Note that the focus is on whether the organization makes use of a method, and a "yes" response means that the method is used for at least some screening decisions. A "yes" to aptitude testing may mean that such tests are broadly used across jobs within the organization or that they are used selectively for only a single job. Thus, the finding that 26% of organizations use aptitude testing does not permit an individual to infer "If I apply for a job, I have a 26% chance of being asked to complete an aptitude test."

Another issue related to these survey findings is a key distinction between *constructs* and *methods* (Arthur & Villado, 2008; Hunter & Hunter, 1984). Constructs refer to the attributes being measured; methods refer to the type of measurement device used to measure the construct. A given construct could be measured using multiple methods. For example, conscientiousness could be assessed by a standardized personality test, an interviewer could attempt to draw inferences about conscientiousness through a series of questions about past work experiences, or a situational judgment test could be designed to present candidates with a series of scenarios and a set of possible responses that reflect differing degrees of conscientiousness. Conversely, a given method, such as an interview or a situational judgment test, could be designed to measure any of a wide variety of constructs. One interview may be in effect an orally administered job knowledge test, whereas another interview focuses exclusively on interpersonal skills. Thus, data on the percentage of employers who use interviews or situational judgment tests do not make clear which constructs the employer is attempting to measure. More nuanced research might survey users of situational judgment tests to ascertain the frequency with which that method is used to assess various constructs (e.g., job knowledge, teamwork, or integrity).

Yet another issue related to surveys of employer usage of selection methods is that some measures yield scores on a variety of constructs. For example, many personality measures produce scores on a wide array of attributes. Knowing that an employer is making use of a particular personality measure tells us little about what attributes the employer is seeking. Although the test may produce scores on, for example, 10 attributes, a given employer may attend to scores on only 5 of these. In addition, the 5 attended to by one employer may be different from the 5 attended to by another.

In summary, employers use a wide array of selection measures; nominally similar measures (e.g., interviews) may be used to assess widely varying attributes; and even when the same measure is used by multiple employers, the employers may attend to differing subsets of the measured attributes.

Theme 2: There Is High Variance in How Employee Selection Procedures Are Used

At first glance, designing a selection system may seem straightforward: Just decide which selection measures to use and then use them. However, there are a number of decisions to be made in designing a selection system, such that two employers deciding to use the same set of selection procedures (e.g., a cognitive ability test, a conscientiousness measure, and an interview) can use them in very different ways. De Corte, Sackett, and Lievens (2011) outline the set of decisions to be made in designing a selection system.

The first is the decision as to which predictors to use, which De Corte et al. (2011) label the *predictor subset decision* problem. This decision is based on a wide variety of factors, which may include organizational priorities (e.g., which is more highly valued—technical competence or interpersonal skills?), and various constraints, such as the speed by which selection decisions need to be made and limit on the cost of the selection process.

The second decision, which De Corte et al. (2011) refer to as the *selection rule decision*, involves choosing between a compensatory and a noncompensatory selection scheme (or a combination of both). In a compensatory scheme, lower scores on one predictor may be compensated for by higher scores on others, whereas the decision to maintain a given minimum cut-off level for at least one of the predictors leads to a noncompensatory scheme. For example, assume that a verbal ability test and a mathematical ability test are used. If scores on the two are added together, the approach is compensatory: One gets the same total score of 100 with 50 on each test or with 25 on one and 75 on the other. Alternately, a minimum on each may be specified; for example, a score of 50 on each test is needed. The choice between a compensatory and noncompensatory system is at times a matter of organizational preference; at other times, there are stronger grounds for a noncompensatory system. For example, there may be threshold levels of given skills that are viewed as so critical for safe and effective job performance that a score below that threshold cannot be compensated for by other skills.

A third decision issue is the choice between single- and multiple-stage designs—the *selection staging decision*. In a single-stage system, all the predictors are administered prior to any screening decisions, whereas in multistage systems the predictors are administered in several stages, with only those that pass the previous stage(s) moving on to subsequent stages. When opting for a multistage approach, the *sequencing of the predictors* over the stages constitutes a fourth decision in the design process. For example, given a choice to use an ability test, a conscientiousness measure, and an interview, one might use the two tests first because they are less expensive and then interview a subset of candidates who perform above some standard on the tests. With the use of the ability test and the conscientiousness measure, if they are used in a compensatory manner, a fifth decision is the *weighting of the predictors*. A simple approach is to weight the tests equally, but differing weights are possible (e.g., double-weighting ability). Weights may be empirically determined (e.g., regression weights), job-analytically based (e.g., predictors are weighted by the number of job tasks for which the attribute in question is rated as important), or judgmentally weighted based on organizational values or rules. Note that predictor weighting is an important decision in noncompensatory procedures when information from multiple hurdles is used in determining final scores for ranking or grouping candidates. If scores from multiple predictors (e.g., the ability test, conscientiousness measure, and interview), some of which were used to reduce the applicant pool (ability and conscientiousness), are combined into a final score, care must be taken to ensure the effective weights of each predictor match the intended weights.

Sixth, and finally, but only in case of multistage selection systems, *retention decisions* must be made, specifying at each intermediate stage the proportion of initial applicants who will be retained for further scrutiny in the next stage. For example, if a composite of ability and conscientiousness is used at an initial stage to determine who moves on to a subsequent interview, the proportion of candidates moving to the next stage may be very large (e.g., 90%) or very small (e.g., 10%). When the proportion moving to the next stage is large, the selection procedure may be viewed as a "screen-out" approach, in which the tests are used only to exclude those with very low scores. When the proportion moving on to the next stage is small, the selection procedure may be viewed as a "screen-in" approach, in which only those with high test scores move on for further consideration.

All of these decisions highlight the fact that simply knowing that a given attribute (e.g., conscientiousness) is part of an employer's selection system tells us little about *how* that attribute is used. It may be part of a compensatory system such that a low score may be overcome by a high score on other attributes. It may be used in a noncompensatory manner as an initial screen with a very low cut-off score. It may be used in a noncompensatory manner with a high cut-off score. In short, broad questions such as "What level of conscientiousness qualifies an individual as workplace ready?" do not lend themselves to a ready answer. A particular level of conscientiousness may meet one employer's standard but not meet another's.

One additional summary point is that even with formal decisions made for each aspect of selection system development outlined by De Corte et al. (2011), there still may be variation across organizations in how final selection decisions are made. Organizations may differ in the rules and procedures used to make final hiring decisions. In some cases, test scores may be algorithmically combined and applicants hired on a top-down basis, leaving little discretion for a single decision maker. In other cases, applicants may be placed in bands or categories in which they are viewed as indistinguishable (or equally qualified) on the basis of test scores. In yet other cases, information from multiple predictors may be holistically reviewed and combined through individual judgment or group consensus meetings before making decisions. Hiring decision makers may be given substantial latitude in these situations. Although evidence shows that mechanical data combination procedures tend to yield superior decision accuracy for workplace performance relative to clinical or holistic data combination (Kuncel, Klieger, Connelly, & Ones, 2013), the use of any particular strategy is a matter of organizational strategy or policy.

Theme 3: Organizations Differ in the Aspects of Performance They Value

Although it is a truism that organizations want to hire individuals who will be high performers, it is critical to recognize that performance is a multifaceted construct. A widely accepted principle within the field of personnel selection is that to develop a selection system, one must begin by specifying the criterion of interest. Using a simple example, if told "We want a selection system for supermarket cashiers," the response is to question the organization further: Do you want cashiers who are fast in scanning groceries, friendly in dealing with customers, or reliable in their attendance? Some firms may emphasize speed and efficiency; others may emphasize friendliness. Some may want a balance between each of these. This has implications for the subsequent selection system: The individual attributes that predict who will be quick in scanning groceries are likely to be very different from those that predict warm and friendly customer interactions.

Importantly, the choice to, for example, focus on predicting speed and efficiency versus friendly customer interaction is a matter of organizational values. It is not appropriate for the selection researcher to assert that the organization should value one outcome versus the other. The researcher can inform the organization about the degree to which a given outcome is predictable, but the choice of the outcome(s) of interest is ultimately a matter of organizational strategy. This also has implications for workplace readiness because it highlights the fact that even nominally similar jobs (e.g., supermarket cashier) may require differing attributes depending on the organization in question.

Theme 4: The Validity of Selection Procedures Varies by the Criterion of Interest

A commonly asked question is "How well does selection procedure X [e.g., cognitive ability tests and personality tests] predict job performance?" There is an enormous literature on the criterion-related validity of selection procedures, with an overall summary of this literature offered by Schmidt and Hunter (1998). Table 2.2 outlines Schmidt and Hunter's summary of the mean validity

Table 2.2 CRITERION-RELATED VALIDITY AND PREVALENCE OF USE ESTIMATES
FOR PERSONNEL SELECTION METHODS

Predictor	Meta-Analytic Validity Estimate[a]	Approximate Prevalence in the United States[b]
General mental ability	.51	2.09
Work sample	.54	1.40
Integrity	.41	1.09
Conscientiousness	.31	1.62
Structured interviews	.51	3.27[*]
Unstructured interviews	.38	4.78[†]
Job knowledge tests	.48	—
Job tryout procedure	.44	2.02
Peer ratings	.49	—
T&E[c] behavioral consistency	.45	—
Reference checks	.26	4.02
Job experience (years)	.18	—
Biodata	.35	1.21
Assessment centers	.37	—
T&E[c] point method	.11	4.12[‡]
Years of education	.10	4.47
Interests	.10	1.15
Graphology	.02	1.09
Age	−.01	—

[a]Adapted from Schmidt and Hunter (1998).

[b]Adapted from Ryan et al. (1999). The response scale values from Ryan et al. are as follows: 1, never; 2, rarely (1–20%); 3, occasionally (21–50%); 4, often (51–80%); and 5, almost always or always (81–100%). Several values in the "Approximate Prevalence" column required judgment calls to match with predictors tabled by Schmidt and Hunter (1998); these are listed as follows:

[*]This value is taken from Ryan et al.'s value for "group/panel" interviews;

[†]this value is taken from Ryan et al.'s value for "one-on-one" interviews. These pairings for "group/panel" and "one-on-one" interviews were used because the use of multiple interviewers tends to be associated with a greater degree of structure than a one-on-one interview in practice (Campion, Palmer, & Campion, 1997), although group interviews may still be unstructured or one-on-one interviews conducted in an otherwise structured manner. We calculated the validity–prevalence correlation with these structured–unstructured pairings swapped. The $r = -.13$ became $r = -.07$; indicating the same pattern of results.

[‡]This value is taken from Ryan et al.'s (1999) value for "application forms"; note the match with the T&E point method assumes that applications are scored by crediting amount of training and experience.

[c]T&E, training and experience.

of each of a large number of selection procedures. We offer a number of comments on the table. First, it presents grand averages across studies and settings and thus does not present information as to the degree to which validity varies from setting to setting. Second, the performance measures used may vary from study to study, and they may not be directly comparable from predictor to predictor. For example, cognitive ability tests top the list in the Schmidt and Hunter table. However, upon closer examination, the outcome measures used in the studies reflect almost exclusively the criterion of task performance. In the case of our prior example of supermarket cashiers, this would be speed and accuracy in processing groceries. Gonzalez-Mulé, Mount, and Oh (2014) examined how well cognitive ability tests predict other important criteria, such as citizenship behavior (helping others and supporting the organization) and the avoidance of counterproductive work behavior. The overall message is that although cognitive ability tests are excellent predictors of task performance, they are much less effective predictors of citizenship and the avoidance of counterproductivity. This returns us to Theme 3: We need to know what aspects of performance are particularly valued by the organization in order to offer advice as to which predictors are most effective. The supermarket chain that values speed and accuracy in processing groceries should focus on different predictors of that facet of performance than would a chain that values customer service orientation most highly. Furthermore, once the predictor choice is made, the sequence in which predictors are administered and the manner in which they are scored, combined, and weighted take us back to Theme 2.

A second way to illustrate this point is to examine the relationship between employers' use of each predictor and the predictor's expected validity. In addition to the validity estimates provided by Schmidt and Hunter (1998), Table 2.2 presents the results of a survey examining the prevalence of use of various selection methods (Ryan, McFarland, Baron, & Page, 1999). Ryan et al. surveyed 52 US employers, each with more than 1,000 employees. Correlations between prevalence of predictor use and validity coefficient result in a slight negative relationship ($r = -.13$).[1] This could be indicative of at least two conditions. First, it may show that employers tend not to use selection methods with the highest relative validity coefficients. If task performance is the valued criterion, this presents a potential issue of increasing employers' awareness of which predictors are most likely to achieve their goals. Alternatively, it could reflect that across employers, differing aspects of performance were viewed as most important, with predictors chosen based on those value judgments. This could mean that attention to validity across multiple aspects of performance is needed before concluding that employers routinely use selection procedures suboptimal for meeting their goals.

Theme 5: The Opportunity to Be Selective Is a Scarce Resource

Continuing with the supermarket cashier example, a common reaction upon confronting the issue of whether to use selection tools to predict speed and accuracy, customer service, or dependability in attendance is to assert that one wants to predict all of these. The list of attributes on which one might wish to screen can quickly become quite long. However, the key constraint is the size of the applicant pool relative to the number of openings. Imagine that there are 100 applicants and 50 openings. One could screen on the single attribute one values most highly, and thus all selected employees would score in the top of the score distribution. However, if one wants to screen on two attributes (assume for simplicity here that the two are uncorrelated with each other), one can only set cut-off scores at the 25th percentile on each. With five attributes, one can only set cut-off scores at the 10th percentile on each. Thus, much depends on the size of the available applicant pool relative to the number of openings. Change the previous example to 1,000 applicants for 50 openings, and one can set much higher cut scores. However, the fundamental message is always the same: With any given ratio of applicants to openings, one can set a more stringent standard on a smaller set of attributes or a less stringent standard on a larger set of attributes. Thus, careful consideration of the performance outcomes that are most valuable to an organization is required, such that a thoughtful decision as to how to "spend" one's opportunity to be selective is made.

Theme 6: Selection Is But One Approach to Achieving High Performance

Screening for valued attributes is but one strategy for achieving high employee performance. Others are possible. For example, rather than hiring individuals with specific knowledge and skills, one could attempt to impart the knowledge and skill to new hires via training. Rather than trying to control employee theft by screening out applicants on the basis of personality attributes proven to be predictive of theft, one could put into place various control systems, such as security cameras, limiting what employees can bring into or out of the workplace, or close supervision. To encourage higher levels of productivity, performance incentives can be put into place. The point is not to argue against selection: Identifying individuals with attributes conducive to desired workplace behavior is indeed valuable. However, there are times when the opportunity to be selective is very limited. There are also times when a strategic decision is made to focus one's selectivity on one set of attributes and to manage other aspects of performance via other systems such as those mentioned elsewhere in this chapter.

A CURRENT SUBSTANTIVE WORKING TAXONOMY OF WORKFORCE READINESS

Previously in this chapter, we identified several dimensions on which workforce readiness models can be compared. Against the backdrop of measurement procedures in personnel selection, we now address the substance of the descriptors used to discuss workforce readiness. The goal is to offer a reasonable, if broad, working taxonomy within which various models of workforce readiness can be classified.

At the outset, we noted that a variety of labels have been used for these attributes, such as "personality characteristics," "noncognitive attributes," "soft skills," "social and emotional competencies," or "21st century skills." In some cases, differences in labels may be semantic only; the vague nature of the labels allows open interpretation and interchangeability. In other cases, the labels may not be interchangeable upon inspection: For instance, "noncognitive attributes" imply a domain characterized by exclusion of "cognitive attributes," which usually include reasoning and analytic abilities or complex problem-solving skills (DeYoung, 2011). That these cognitive attributes are often included in discussions of "21st century skills" implies that all the labels are not interchangeable. This is a difficult problem to solve but one that needs to be recognized as an obstacle for taxonomic work and cumulative research. The issue is similar to efforts among psychologists to discretely define what is meant by "competencies" relative to "knowledge" (collections of discrete facts, rules, or information about a domain), "skills" (proficiency in completing tasks or applying knowledge), "abilities" (relatively enduring general capacities), and "other characteristics" (e.g., personality, interests, and motivational tendencies) (Campion et al., 2011; Morgeson & Dierdorff, 2011).

Kyllonen (2012) summarized lists of personal attributes included in models of workforce readiness. He presented a taxonomy drawn from work from contributors to multiple workshops held by the National Academy of Sciences (NAS) and National Research Council (NRC, 2011), the Partnership for 21st Century Skills (Casner-Lotto & Barrington, 2006), the Assessing and Teaching of 21st Century Skills organization (ATC21S; Binkley et al., 2012), and academic researchers (Oswald, Schmitt, Kim, Ramsay, & Gillespie, 2004;

Shultz & Zedeck, 2011), among others. Because Kyllonen describes the constituent studies in detail, we present the summary taxonomy including the following three domains emerging from his review, with exemplar attribute descriptors:

1. Cognitive skills: critical thinking, problem solving, creativity
2. Interpersonal skills: communication skills, social skills, teamwork, cultural sensitivity, dealing with adversity
3. Intrapersonal skills: self-management, self-regulation, time management, self-development (lifelong learning), adaptability, executive functioning, conscientiousness

We make several observations about this working taxonomy. First, the research on which it is built involves multiple methods. Several large-scale surveys of employers were conducted asking about current practices in organizations and the importance of various attributes for employment. Examples include a survey of 400 employers by The Conference Board (Casner-Lotto & Barrington, 2006) and a survey of 2,000 employers by the McKinsey Global Institute (Manyika et al., 2011). One interesting element of the McKinsey survey is a focus on qualifications including attributes from the three descriptor areas offered in the previous taxonomy: Historically, "qualifications" were often taken to mean knowledge-based requirements indicated by applicants' education or experience. The inclusion of elements across the taxonomy may reflect a broadening focus. A second method involved assembly of expert panels for the purposes of identifying descriptors (Binkley et al., 2012). In some cases, judgmental categorization procedures were used to derive final lists of categories (Oswald et al., 2004). These panels appeared to focus more on literature reviews than on employer trends, but in instances such as the series of workshops held by the NRC (2011), expert panelists considered a variety of research-based and employer-based information. A third method involved differing focus on attributes judged as currently needed for success versus attributes judged as important for future work role requirements. These forecasting studies bear similarity to strategic forms of job analysis (Schneider & Konz, 1989). The key point is that the variety of methods triangulate on the common set of attribute descriptors included in the working taxonomy presented previously.

A second observation is that the taxonomy descriptors fall into "can do" and "will do" domains (Cortina & Luchman, 2012). "Can do" attributes relate to those applied when one's capability to perform maximally on a measurement instrument or task is the key question—such as with many measures of cognitive skills. "Will do" attributes are those applied in typical performance, usually when measurement is intended to provide insight into one's tendency to behave in certain ways over time—such as with the interpersonal or intra-personal skill examples shown in the working taxonomy. The distinction between the two domains offers implications for variability in prospects for developing proficiency on a given attribute: In general, "will do" attributes are often regarded as more changeable than "can do" attributes. In addition, the inclusion of the two domains corresponds with generally accepted models of the determinants of work performance in industrial and organizational psy-chology (Campbell, McCloy, Oppler, & Sager, 1993), such that future research may explore placement of workplace readiness models into robust theories of work performance.

A third observation is that the identified attributes extend beyond the knowl-edge and skill domains historically emphasized in educational environments but are consistent with the types of "competencies" that employers often seek. This represents the source of potential gaps in students' proficiency on these attributes when emerging from the education environment relative to employ-ers' expectations. Although the sizes of these gaps require future research, they are the major source of dialogue and debate about what attributes should be targeted for development in education and training if successful placement into the workplace is a primary goal.

Our fourth and final observation returns us to the table of personnel selec-tion tools presented in the discussion of personnel selection (see Table 2.2): The methods used for establishing the importance of the workplace readiness attri-butes in the taxonomy (surveys and expert panels) differ from the methods used to assess an individual's standing on the attributes. Industrial and orga-nizational psychology and educational measurement researchers have exam-ined the utility of various measurement approaches for making valid inferences about examinees on the basis of the scores they produce (see Table 2.2). Many methods for assessing an individual's standing on these attributes exist, but there is rarely, if ever, a one-size-fits-all solution for which method(s) to use. If limited to one measurement method for a given workplace readiness attri-bute, in some cases, self-report testing procedures may present the best avail-able method for evaluating proficiency (e.g., ability tests, personality tests, or situational judgment inventories). In other cases, methods involving structured observer evaluation may prove most advantageous (e.g., work samples or struc-tured interviews). As noted in the discussion of personnel selection, the deci-sion about which method (or combination of methods) to use must involve consideration of several factors—no broad statement can be made about the superiority of a given procedure for all cases.

ONE EXAMINATION OF KEY ASPECTS OF WORKPLACE READINESS WITH A FOCUS ON PERSONALITY

We illustrate some research approaches to shedding light on workplace readiness, summarizing and drawing from some of our prior research (Sackett & Walmsley, 2014). Our focus was on the domains commonly labeled as soft skills or social–emotional competencies. We view constructs in these domains as trait labels (e.g., dependability and cooperativeness) or behaviors (e.g., teamwork) that can be viewed as manifestations of these traits. Within psychology, a high-level organizing framework is the five-factor model of personality (Big Five; McCrae & Costa, 1997). Barrick, Mount, and Judge (2001) offer a series of adjectives intended to describe the five factors: (a) Conscientiousness involves being dependable, achievement-striving, hardworking, persevering, and orderly; (b) agreeableness involves being cooperative, flexible, tolerant, and forgiving; (c) emotional stability involves being calm, self-confident, and resilient; (d) extraversion involves being sociable, talkative, assertive, and active; and (e) openness to experience involves being curious, broad-minded, intelligent, and cultured. Each of these can also be usefully broken down into subfacets (e.g., conscientiousness is commonly viewed as having dependability, achievement-striving, orderliness, and cautiousness facets; Dudley, Orvis, Lebiecki, & Cortina, 2006), although our focus here is the overall factor level.

To address the question, "Which personality attributes are most important in the workplace?" Sackett and Walmsley (2014) integrated three distinct research approaches. The first was to examine the research literature on the use of measures of the Big Five factors to predict work behaviors. This literature examines which attributes are useful for predicting valued job behaviors such as completing tasks well (labeled "task performance"), contributing to a positive work environment (labeled "organizational citizenship behavior"), and avoiding counterproductive behavior such as theft or withdrawal (labeled "counterproductive work behavior"). For this approach, the relative importance of the personality attributes is operationalized in terms of the size of validity coefficients relating these attributes to various facets of job performance (here, validity coefficients are correlations aggregated using meta-analysis procedures). Although very useful, a key limitation is that there is no necessary relationship between what the research literature reveals and the value that employers place on these attributes. Employers may be unaware of the research literature, or they may discount it based on their personal perspective. The second body of research operationalized importance as the value that employers place on an attribute when considering applicants for employment, operationalized by the dimensions that employers evaluate in structured interviews. The third approach operationalized importance in terms of direct ratings of attribute importance for a very large number of occupations gathered as part of a systematic job analysis system developed by the US Department of Labor known as O*NET (Occupational Information Network; Peterson, Mumford, Borman, Jeanneret, & Fleishman, 1999).

Sackett and Walmsley (2014) found clear agreement across the research strategies in that attributes related to conscientiousness and agreeableness are highly important for workforce readiness across a variety of occupations that require a variety of training and experience qualifications (i.e., differ in job complexity), with conscientiousness emerging as the single most important facet. Table 2.3 contains a summary of the results. The various lines of evidence differed as to the relative importance of extraversion and emotional stability, with emotional stability more important in our most wide-reaching data, namely the O*NET analyses. Openness to experience was the least important facet. It is most useful to see reasonable convergence between what validation research indicates as the most important attributes, the set of attributes valued by employers, and the attributes rated most highly in large-scale job-analytic work. These findings suggest that, at least in terms of interviews, employers often focus on attributes that are both rated as important for and predictive of successful performance. A second conclusion, from an alternate perspective, is that it appears that applicants would do well to develop and emphasize these characteristics in the job search process.

Note that the primary focus was on identifying attributes most widely valued in the workplace. The finding that conscientiousness is on average the most highly valued attribute certainly does not mean that that attribute is most highly valued for all occupations, or most highly valued by all individual interviewers even within an occupation within which that attribute is identified as generally most highly valued. The primary focus on the most generally valued attributes is particularly useful for designing broad interventions (e.g., addressing questions such as "Should a school system wish to invest in a program aimed at one or more 'soft skills,' which of these skills should receive top priority?"). In contrast, consider a given individual who aspires to a career in a particular occupation (e.g., a police officer or a laboratory scientist). Here, occupation-specific information would be useful, and a student might work with a guidance counselor to identify occupation-specific information (e.g., O*NET attribute ratings for that occupation). For example, a meta-analysis by Vinchur, Schippmann, Switzer, and Roth (1998) focused exclusively on the prediction of performance in sales occupations. Vinchur et al. report that conscientiousness is the top-ranked Big Five personality predictor, followed in order by extraversion (perhaps not surprising in a sales environment), openness to experience, emotional stability, and agreeableness. As another example, although not based on a meta-analytic strategy, Dunn, Mount, Barrick, and Ones (1995) examined the importance

Table 2.3 Summary of Most Important Personality Attributes in the Workplace

Personality Attribute	Research Approach for Determining Importance		
	Validity for Predicting Job Performance	Frequency of Use by Employment Interviewers	Importance Ratings in Occupational Analyses
Conscientiousness	Top-ranked predictor Overall job performance Task performance Organizational citizenship behavior Counterproductive work behavior	Most frequently assessed attributes are facets of conscientiousness Dependability Responsibility Need for achievement	Dependability is ranked among the top 3 attributes in 95% of job families. Integrity is ranked among the top 3 attributes in 68% of job families.
Agreeableness	Second-ranked predictor Organizational citizenship behavior Counterproductive work behavior Third-ranked predictor Overall Job Performance Task Performance	Second-most frequently assessed attributes are interpersonal skills related to agreeableness Working with others Teamwork Cooperation	Cooperation and concern for others are ranked among the top 3 attributes in 50% of job families.
Emotional stability	Third-ranked predictor Task performance Organizational citizenship behavior Counterproductive work behavior	Less frequently assessed attributes are facets of emotional stability Stress tolerance Self-control	Self-control and stress tolerance are ranked among the top 3 attributes in 50% of job families.
Extraversion	Second-ranked predictor Overall job performance Task performance	Third-most frequently assessed attributes are extraversion and related concepts Persuading and negotiating Leadership	Tends to be relatively lower rated Not rated in top 3 with the exception of management jobs

that managers gave to Big Five dimensions in a policy-capturing task. Although conscientiousness emerged as the most important attribute across jobs, differences were found for specific occupations (e.g., openness to experience was most important for news reporters, and extraversion was most important for insurance sales agents). Thus, decisions about workforce readiness for a specific occupation should make use of available data for that occupation, in addition to the broad results discussed here. However, given that occupational plans often change, even the student with a specific occupational aspiration would be well advised to attend to information about broadly valued attributes.

Although personality is often viewed as a stable individual difference characteristic, we differentiate between personality as underlying disposition, which may indeed be very stable, and personality as patterns of behavior, for which we review multiple lines of evidence suggesting that change is indeed possible. A variety of bodies of literature contribute to the case for the possibility for personality change. First, there is a body of literature on test–retest correlations for self-report personality measures over time. A typical range of correlation values is .40–.60 for 4- to 10-year intervals in young to middle adult samples (Nye & Roberts, 2013). Although the retest literature does not address the mechanisms behind this instability (e.g., how much change is developmental versus intervention based), the fact that these correlations are far from 1.0 indicates that there is considerable change in self-reported personality. Second, there is a literature on change in personality as a result of work-specific experiences, with the general finding that successful work experiences are associated with positive changes in social dominance, conscientiousness, and emotional stability (for a review, see Nye & Roberts, 2013). Third, Shaffer and Postlethwaite (2012) report meta-analytic findings showing that self-report personality measures that are contextualized (e.g., seeking descriptions of behavior at work versus behavior in general) are markedly more predictive of job performance than are noncontextualized measures. This permits the inference that behavior at work is different from behavior in general, which is consistent with the notion that the demands and reward contingencies of work settings influence the behavior/reputation aspects of personality. Finally, there is a large literature on interventions aimed at social and emotional competencies in kindergarten through grade 12 (K–12) education. These include attributes such as recognizing and managing emotion, establishing positive relationships, and making responsible decisions. Durlak et al. (2011) report a meta-analysis of 213 intervention studies with control groups, showing change in self-reports and externally observed behavior.

These various lines of evidence support the notion that even if underlying dispositions prove quite fixed, patterns of behavior reflecting an attribute are indeed changeable. Some people may find it dispositionally quite easy to, for example, keep track of multiple work tasks and projects, whereas others may realize that they are not dispositionally detail-oriented. Nonetheless, if persuaded that workplace success requires organization and order, they may learn to make use of day planners, checklists, and various other aids in order to behave in counterdispositional but effective ways in the workplace. Thus, we do not view fixed dispositions as an impediment to making use of findings that particular attributes are important at work as the basis for interventions.

We believe these findings are important for various constituencies. First, individuals interested in evaluating their readiness for various workplace settings may find the results as to the most broadly valued attributes useful for self-assessment and for self-directed or counselor-directed change efforts. Knowledge of what is valued and rewarded is a key driver of change. Individuals with as-yet undeveloped career plans may find it most useful to focus on our overall findings, whereas individuals with a more specific focus may find it most useful to focus on occupation-specific O*NET data. Second, K–12 interventions aimed at improving workplace readiness may make use of these findings to choose the target attributes for interventions. Absent resources for individually tailored interventions, a focus on attributes identified as most broadly valued would appear to have the most promise. Third, we have observed universities offering personal and professional development courses to augment traditional academic instruction. These may include formal assessment, via mechanisms such as self-report personality measures and peer evaluations. A pairing of information about current standing on attributes of interest with information about what organizations value and reward may be a most useful developmental experience. Fourth, our findings may be useful for organizations working with jobseekers to aid in making them more attractive to employers. Research on the most effective approaches for behavior change on the particular attributes valued in the workplace would be most welcome.

CONCLUSION

In this chapter, we identified several dimensions on which models of workplace readiness can be described and compared. We also summarized a broad taxonomy that may prove useful for integrating the varied approaches for defining attributes related to workplace readiness. With those models and dimensions in mind, we offered a set of themes characterizing major considerations in designing and implementing personnel selection procedures used to make hiring decisions. Personnel selection is an applied science with a long history of defining and measuring applicants' standing on individual difference attributes, related to job requirements, that are legitimately testable at the time of selection. These themes illustrate factors in need of consideration if one were to implement a model of workplace readiness in a personnel selection program. The themes also illustrate the variety of practices associated with personnel selection in organizations. Finally, the procedures and findings of work by Sackett and Walmsley (2014) were presented as an illustration of strategies for addressing complex questions associated with workplace readiness. Once these foundations are in place, other questions can be explored, such as "How well prepared are students for demands of the workplace in terms of these workplace readiness attributes?" and "Can and should secondary education invest resources in developing these attributes in students?"

NOTE

1. We thank Jeffrey M. Cucina for discussion related to this analysis.

REFERENCES

ACT. (2013). *Work readiness standards and benchmarks: The key to differentiating America's workforce and regaining global competitiveness.* Iowa, City, IA: Author.

Arthur, W., & Villado, A. J. (2008). The importance of distinguishing between constructs and methods when comparing predictors in personnel selection research and practice. *Journal of Applied Psychology, 93*(2), 435–442.

Barrick, M. R., Mount, M. K., & Judge, T. A. (2001). Personality and performance at the beginning of the new millennium: What do we know and where do we go next? *International Journal of Selection and Assessment, 9*, 9–30.

Binkley, M., Erstad, O., Herman, J., Raizen, S., Ripley, M., Miller-Ricci, M., & Rumble, M. (2012). Defining twenty-first century skills. In P. Griffin, B. McGaw, & E. Care (Eds.), *Assessment and teaching of 21st century skills* (pp. 17–66). New York, NY: Springer.

Campbell, J. P., McCloy, R. A., Oppler, S. H., & Sager, C. E. (1993). A theory of performance. In N. Schmitt & W. C. Borman (Eds.), *Personnel selection in organizations.* San Francisco, CA: Jossey-Bass.

Campion, M. A., Fink, A. A., Ruggeberg, B. J., Carr, L., Phillips, G. M., & Odman, R. B. (2011). Doing competencies well: Best practices in competency modeling. *Personnel Psychology, 64*(1), 225–262.

Campion, M. A., Palmer, D. K., & Campion, J. E. (1997). A review of structure in the selection interview. *Personnel Psychology, 50*, 655–702.

Casner-Lotto, J., & Barrington, L. (2006). *Are they really ready to work? Employers' perspectives on the basic knowledge and applied skills of new entrants to the 21st century US workforce.* New York, NY: The Conference Board, Corporate Voices for Working Families, Partnership for 21st Century Skills, and Society for Human Resource Management.

Christiansen, N. D., & Tett, R. P. (2013). *Handbook of personality at work*. New York, NY: Routledge.

Cobb-Clark, D. A., & Tan, M. (2011). Noncognitive skills, occupational attainment, and relative wages. *Labour Economics*, *18*(1), 1–13.

Conley, D. T. (2010). *College and career ready: Helping all students succeed beyond high school*. Hoboken, NJ: Wiley.

Cortina, J. M., & Luchman, J. N. (2012). Personnel selection and employee performance. In N. W. Schmitt & S. Highhouse (Eds.), *Handbook of psychology: Volume 12. Industrial and organizational psychology* (2nd ed., pp. 143–183). Hoboken, NJ: Wiley.

De Corte, W., Sackett, P. R., & Lievens, F. (2011). Designing pareto-optimal selection systems: Formalizing the decisions required for selection system development. *Journal of Applied Psychology*, *96*(5), 907–926.

DeYoung, C. G. (2011). Intelligence and personality. In R. J. Sternberg & S. B. Kaufman (Eds.), *The Cambridge handbook of intelligence* (pp. 711–737). Cambridge, England: Cambridge University Press.

Dudley, N. M., Orvis, K. A., Lebiecki, J. E., & Cortina, J. M. (2006). A meta-analytic investigation of conscientiousness in the prediction of job performance: Examining the intercorrelations and the incremental validity of narrow traits. *Journal of Applied Psychology*, *91*, 40–57.

Dunn, W. S., Mount, M. K., Barrick, M. R., & Ones, D. S. (1995). Relative importance of personality and general mental ability in managers' judgments of applicant qualifications. *Journal of Applied Psychology*, *80*(4), 500.

Durlak, J. A., Weissberg, R. P., Dymnicki, A. B., Taylor, R. D., & Schellinger, K. B. (2011). The impact of enhancing students' social and emotional learning: A meta-analysis of school-based universal interventions. *Child Development*, *82*(1), 405–432.

Gonzalez-Mulé, E., Mount, M. K., & Oh, I. S. (2014). A meta-analysis of the relationship between general mental ability and nontask performance. *Journal of Applied Psychology*, *99*(6), 1222–1243.

Heckman, J. J., Stixrud, J., & Urzua, S. (2006). *The effects of cognitive and noncognitive abilities on labor market outcomes and social behavior* (No. w12006). Cambridge, MA: National Bureau of Economic Research.

Hunter, J. E., & Hunter, R. F. (1984). Validity and utility of alternative predictors of job performance. *Psychological Bulletin*, *96*(1), 72–98.

Kuncel, N. R., Klieger, D. M., Connelly, B. S., & Ones, D. S. (2013). Mechanical versus clinical data combination in selection and admissions decisions: A meta-analysis. *Journal of Applied Psychology*, *98*(6), 1060–1072.

Kyllonen, P. C. (2012). *Measurement of 21st century skills within the Common Core State Standards*. Paper presented at the Invitational Research Symposium on Technology Enhanced Assessments, May 7–8, 2012.

Manyika, J., Lund, S., Auguste, B., Mendonca, L., Welsh, T., & Ramaswamy, S. (2011). *An economy that works: Job creation and America's future*. Washington, DC: McKinsey Global Institute.

McCrae, R. R., & Costa, P. T. (1997). Personality trait structure as a human universal. *American Psychologist*, *52*, 509–516.

Morgeson, F. P., & Dierdorff, E. C. (2011). Work analysis: From technique to theory. In S. Zedeck (Ed.), *APA handbook of industrial and organizational psychology* (Vol. 2, pp. 3–41). Washington, DC: American Psychological Association.

National Research Council. (2011). *Assessing 21st century skills: Summary of a workshop.* Washington, DC: National Academies Press.

Nye, C. D., & Roberts, B. W. (2013). A developmental perspective on the importance of personality for understanding workplace behavior. In N. Christiansen & R. Tett (Eds.), *Handbook of personality at work* (pp. 796–818). New York, NY: Routledge.

Oswald, F. L., Schmitt, N., Kim, B. H., Ramsay, L. J., & Gillespie, M. A. (2004). Developing a biodata measure and situational judgment inventory as predictors of college student performance. *Journal of Applied Psychology, 89*(2), 187–207.

Peterson, N. G., Mumford, M. D., Borman, W. C., Jeanneret, P. R., & Fleishman, E. A. (Eds.). (1999). *An occupational information system for the 21st century: The development of O*NET*. Washington, DC: American Psychological Association.

Ryan, A. M., McFarland, L., Baron, H., & Page, R. (1999). An international look at selection practices: Nation and culture as explanations for variability in practice. *Personnel Psychology, 52*(2), 359–391.

Rynes, S. L., Colbert, A. E., & Brown, K. G. (2002). HR professionals' beliefs about effective human resource practices: Correspondence between research and practice. *Human Resource Management, 41*(2), 149–174.

Sackett, P. R., & Walmsley, P. T. (2014). Which personality attributes are most important in the workplace? *Perspectives on Psychological Science, 9*(5), 538–551.

Schmidt, F. L., & Hunter, J. E. (1998). The validity and utility of selection methods in personnel psychology: Practical and theoretical implications of 85 years of research findings. *Psychological Bulletin, 124*(2), 262–274.

Schneider, B., & Konz, A. M. (1989). Strategic job analysis. *Human Resource Management, 28*(1), 51–63.

Shaffer, J. A., & Postlethwaite, B. E. (2012). A matter of context: A meta-analytic investigation of the relative validity of contextualized and noncontextualized personality measures. *Personnel Psychology, 65*, 445–494.

Shultz, M. M., & Zedeck, S. (2011). Predicting lawyer effectiveness: Broadening the basis for law school admission decisions. *Law & Social Inquiry, 36*(3), 620–661.

Society for Human Resource Management. (2005). SHRM weekly on-line survey, March 15, 2005. Retrieved from http://www.slideplayer.com/slide/7466076/, January 2, 2016.

Stone, J. R., & Lewis, M. V. (2012). *College and career ready in the 21st century: Making high school matter*. New York, NY: Teachers College Press.

The College Board. (n.d.). College and career readiness pathway. Retrieved from https://pathway.collegeboard.org

US Department of Education. (2010). *A blueprint for reform: The reauthorization of the Elementary and Secondary Education Act*. Retrieved from http://www2.ed.gov/policy/elsec/leg/blueprint

Vinchur, A. J., Schippmann, J. S., Switzer, F. S., & Roth, P. L. (1998). A meta-analytic review of predictors of job performance for salespeople. *Journal of Applied Psychology, 83*, 586–597.

Critical Skills for the 21st Century Workforce

RYAN WHORTON, ALEX CASILLAS,
FREDERICK L. OSWALD, AND AMY SHAW ■

Several major co-occurring economic forces have profoundly disrupted the nature of work in the 21st century from work carried out in the past. First, *technology* often serves to improve the quality and augment the aggregate productivity of the work that employees carry out across a range of jobs (e.g., global positioning systems for delivery drivers; brain scans for neurosurgeons). Notably, there is a rising reality (and fear) that technology will serve to replace many types of workers entirely (e.g., automated customer service, robots for specialized manufacturing, and unmanned aircraft and cars; Donofrio & Whitefoot, 2015). Second, *the rise of the service economy* increasingly requires employees to communicate, coordinate, and cooperate with teammates and customers more frequently and effectively than ever before—sometimes in remote or virtual environments that heavily rely on technology. Third, the growing trend toward *globalization* reflects unprecedented levels of innovation, along with increased managerial and strategic operations that address technology and teamwork across borders, cultures, and time zones. Managers and employees alike need to be adaptable across cultural and geographic locations, and they also face unique adjustment challenges when striving to achieve work–life balance in jobs that require frequent global travel and relocation. These three powerful economic forces—technology, the rise of the service economy, and globalization—contribute critically to the rise of what has been coined *21st century skills*. Although many of these skills are not new, in that they were used in the work of the past, the requirements of today's work and workforce have made certain skills more frequently needed, needed at a higher level, and otherwise indispensable.

Before we identify and review a set of critical 21st century skills, we first remind ourselves of the fundamental features of what constitutes a skill. Being fundamental, these features are important to remember, and they are unchanging, even when the types of skills needed in today's workforce are in fact changing rapidly.

WHAT IS A SKILL?

A generic definition of *skill* is "the level of proficiency on a specific task or group of tasks. The development of a given skill or proficiency on a given task is predicated in part on the possession of relevant basic abilities" (Fleishman & Quaintance, 1984, p. 163). Researchers have offered many other definitions of the term *skill* at various levels of refinement (e.g., specific skills (Fleishman & Quaintance, 1984) and general skills in the U.S. Department of Labor's content model (https://www.onetcenter.org/content.html/#cm2)), so it is useful to review considerations that are common to these definitions, such as the following:

1. *Is the skill general or specific?* A general skill, such as critical thinking or communication, can be viewed as more similar to an ability or an aptitude because it covers broad domains and therefore requires extended and extensive experience to improve upon. By contrast, a very specific skill, such as balancing a checkbook, can be viewed as something that is clearly trainable, because the content is well specified and fairly limited in scope. Clearly, general and specific skills are related; for example, people who possess a more general skill in mathematics may more easily learn new specific types of math such as calculus; and likewise, people who accumulate more specific skills in math are simultaneously developing their more general mathematical reasoning skills. Just as there is a general versus specific aspect to the definition of a skill, training interventions have been similarly pitched at more general versus more specific levels, with general-skill training being viewed as having a wider impact, but specific-skill training being viewed as more feasible and often focused on reaching practical goals. Highly complex skills are often specific to a domain,

such that the specific knowledge required to acquire the skill does not transfer to other skills; however, some aspects of that knowledge might generalize to related areas (e.g., knowledge of the structure of a computer programming language might facilitate the learning of other programming languages).

2. *Is the skill cognitive, physical, or affective in nature?* Some skills are mostly thought of as information based and cognitive in nature (e.g., STEM skills), and other skills may require physical action and are thus facilitated by physical ability (e.g., running a marathon). A third set of skills falls more heavily in the affective domain, and these skills are often referred to as "soft skills" (e.g., empathy skills and customer service skills require expression of genuine interest and concern). Of course, many skills draw from each of these three domains, perhaps in different combinations over time (e.g., over time, a skill that was originally more cognitive in nature can become more automatic and therefore more physically and affectively driven).

3. *How much is the skill dependent on the type of environment?* Environmental characteristics that can inhibit or enhance training- and performance-relevant skills include the pacing, ordering, and predictability of the task; the spacing and quality of practice; the quality of results and feedback; the influence of supervisors, coaches, role models, and peers; and the assistance of technology in skill development and performance (see Oswald, Hambrick, & Jones, 2007, Table 4.1). In addition to attaining a skill, maintaining the skill once it is attained might recruit these characteristics once again, as well as others.

4. *How much effort does the skill require?* Some skills must always be performed with a high level of cognitive, physical, or emotional effort to achieve the results that are desired, perhaps because the environment is relatively unpredictable (e.g., troubleshooting an electronic repair; improvisational comedy). Other skills might be performed with less effort because the environment facilitates a high level of performance, the environment is not very challenging, the person is prepared with scripts to be enacted, or the person has a high level of prerequisite ability and experience in the domain. A skill or its aspects can become more automatic over time as a person gains experience, meaning that attentional and cognitive demands can be reduced at the same time that psychomotor and motor functions improve (Kanfer & Ackerman, 1989; Proctor & Dutta, 1995). Some have equated skill almost purely with automaticity (Rasmussen, 1983), but we make no such association here, because skills call

upon strategies, rules, and knowledge that may be subject to change in unpredictable environments. Thus, to apply a skill successfully, a person might need to switch back and forth from automatic processing to effortful control as characteristics and demands of the person and the environment change over time (Beier & Oswald, 2012). This continuous switching itself may be a skill that develops over time.

5. *How does the level of performance reflect the level of skill?* Some skills seem to be captured by a person's level of performance in a relatively straightforward manner (e.g., typing skill might be defined as average words per minute of typing from general or technical samples of text that represent the domain of interest). For other skills, measuring levels of performance may be more difficult and error-prone, such as when the domain is multidimensional or "fuzzy" (e.g., negotiating skill), when the skill itself changes (e.g., when cultural knowledge changes and influences skill in bilingualism), or when there are many environmental factors that also influence performance beyond individual skill (e.g., teamwork and bad weather).

Despite these complexities—and perhaps because of them, sometimes—we believe that leveraging the research literature and subject matter experts (SMEs) to define a skill domain more precisely will yield multiple benefits. It increases our understanding of the value of skills in the workforce; it provides clearer implications for how skills can be developed through training and intervention; and it suggests how human capital can be best invested in skill development, to the benefit of organizations and employees alike.

21ST CENTURY SKILLS

Given the previously discussed definition and attendant considerations for a skill, there are a huge number of skills that would qualify as 21st century skills. After reviewing the research literature and related academic discussions of 21st century skills, we identified three broad forces—technology, the rise of the service economy, and globalization—that lead us to focus on nine 21st century skills; they are summarized in Table 3.1. We are limited in how extensively we can discuss each of these skills (e.g., entire books have been dedicated to each of them, individually or in combination; see Pellegrino & Hilton, 2012), but we believe that readers will derive unique value from the overview of the subset of critical 21st century skills covered here.

Table 3.1 CRITICAL 21ST CENTURY SKILLS

	Central Skill Area		
Skill	Interpersonal	Technological	International
1. Leadership	x		
2. Customer service	x		x
3. Teamwork	x		x
4. Safety	x		x
5. Creativity		x	x
6. Critical thinking		x	
7. Metacognition and self-regulation		x	
8. Cross-cultural knowledge and competence	x		x
9. Ethics and integrity	x		x

Leadership

Organizations always require leaders who plan, cultivate, and inspire the success of their employees; yet both leaders and employees in the 21st century workforce are generally less loyal to any particular organization. This is supported by data from organizational development consulting companies that indicate how the majority of the U.S. employees tend to be disengaged from their work (Aon Hewitt, 2014; Gallup, 2013). This lack of engagement is partially attributed to a lack of effective leaders or managers possessing the leadership skills that serve to motivate and engage the workforce within the span of their control. Organizational research consistently points to the need for positive leadership behavior, because it is consistently found to be associated with better subordinate learning and performance outcomes (Burke et al., 2006). Also, we know that leadership capabilities are important even in those who are not formal leaders but often find themselves leading teams, projects, and their own tasks and careers.

Employees who are not trained as leaders, and who have been exposed to ineffective leaders, will often view leadership narrowly as a transaction: If an employee works hard and effectively, the manager rewards that employee; employees who do not work hard or effectively get punished (Bass & Riggio, 2005). This approach can be effective in some circumstances, especially when tasks and rewards can be coupled tightly in terms of time and causality, but often this is not the case, and those leaders who focus on the larger picture—which includes building relationships and leading by example—may often be more effective. In fact, research has found these latter types of transformational and socialized charismatic leadership styles to be associated with increased employee adoption of organizational values (Brown & Treviño, 2009) as well as productivity (Burke et al., 2006). Trust in leaders has been framed within a mediational model, in which both leader and follower characteristics contribute to cognitive and affective leader perceptions of trust; these perceptions then drive various outcomes of performance, attitudes, and intentions that in turn contribute to future trust in the leader (Dirks & Ferrin, 2002).

New leaders seeking to develop their skills usually benefit from some form of coaching, training, or mentoring. Training leaders in transformational leadership skills appears to improve perceptions by their direct reports (Kelloway, Barling, & Helleur, 2000), as well as increase both leader and work unit effectiveness (Judge & Piccolo, 2004; Lowe, Kroeck, & Sivasubramaniam, 1996). Moving beyond training, an ongoing mentoring relationship with a more seasoned leader can assist the developing leader. The mentor can work with the developing leader over time to provide feedback, suggest resources, offer career guidance, and act as a role model. This type of relationship has been found to work best when the mentor and mentee have similar interpersonal styles, backgrounds, and common interests (Buckingham, 2012).

Customer Service

Providing customers and clients with high-quality service has been and continues to be a priority for organizations and the U.S. economy as a whole. As of 2014, 120 million workers (approximately 77% of the labor force) were employed in the service sector (U.S. Bureau of Labor Statistics, 2013c), which includes workers in professional, retail, utilities, management, education, and health services. This number is expected to increase to 130 million workers by 2022, accounting for most of the U.S. economic growth in that period (Henderson, 2013). To keep up with the need for high-quality customer service, more service workers will need to be able to communicate with customers and clients, to get results, and to be perceived as friendly and empathetic while learning about and fulfilling customer needs (Koenig et al., 2011). Models of service quality include aspects of the customer service experience that are very dependent on the skills of customer service representatives. For example, the well-established SERVQUAL model describing service quality (Parasuraman, Zeithaml, & Berry, 1985) organizes the content of service quality into five categories: tangibles (the physical appearance of people or things related to the company), reliability (delivering on service promises), responsiveness (providing customer assistance quickly), assurance (employee ability to convey trust and confidence), and empathy (individualized attention to the needs of each customer). Thus, customer service is one way that employees can successfully perform as friendly ambassadors for their organization.

At the employee level, high-quality customer service can be best achieved through two general approaches: selecting service-oriented employees, and providing employees with training and feedback on how best to serve customers. Employees who are predisposed to want to help others, and to be likeable and calm while doing so, can be specifically selected from job applicant pools using personality inventories (Hogan, Hogan, & Busch, 1984). These customer service orientation inventories tend to evaluate candidates on a combination of personality characteristics, such as Agreeableness, Conscientiousness, and Emotional Stability (Ones, Viswesvaran, & Dilchert, 2005). In addition to selecting customer service employees with desirable characteristics, the desirable customer-service behaviors that people possessing these characteristics might naturally engage in can be trained in others. These trainable behaviors include using specific language and tone, following through on promises, and acting on anticipated future customer needs (Raub & Liao, 2012). Research from a variety of service industries, including medicine (Mayer, Cates, Mastorovich, & Royalty, 1998), banking (Pattni, Soutar, & Klobas, 2007), and hospitality (Garavan, 1997), suggests that training on the basics of customer service can translate into decreased customer complaints and increased customer satisfaction and loyalty.

Given the importance of customer service for the competitiveness of organizations, training for communication and empathy skills should be a priority. In addition to such training, employees must believe that their organization values providing customers with high-quality service. This concept is referred to as *service climate*, and it is a shared perception by members of an organization that service is a core principle valued and prioritized by management; it is typically informed by whether and how the organization incentivizes employee service behaviors (Schneider, White, & Paul, 1998). Service climate depends on buy-in from organizational leadership, which results in better employee attitudes, less employee stress, greater customer satisfaction, and positive financial outcomes (Hong, Liao, Hu, & Jiang, 2013).

Teamwork

Another 21st century skill that continues to grow in importance is teamwork. Because teams can strategically draw on the diverse pool of talent and efforts from each group member, work teams are able to complete larger projects that individuals simply cannot (West, 2012). Teams can even eliminate the need for direct work group supervision, allowing organizations to be more efficient

(Salas, Stagl, & Burke, 2004). The key to teamwork, like any work function, is to ensure that team members possess the skills needed to function effectively together. With this in mind, teamwork generally results in better work performance when it consists of effective communication, coordination, and cohesiveness. Furthermore, good teamwork tends to increase the job satisfaction of team members (LePine, Piccolo, Jackson, Mathieu, & Saul, 2008).

The need to train workers on teamwork skills is widely understood. The job search website, CareerBuilder, polled a large sample of hiring managers and found that 60% of them cited team orientation as a quality they seek in applicants (CareerBuilder, 2014). Similarly, during their 2011 meetings to discuss 21st century skills, representatives of the National Research Council identified skills needed for success in the workplace, listing the ability to work productively in teams and groups as a general skill set desired by employers (Koenig et al., 2011). Higher education also recognizes the importance of training for teamwork skills, as evidenced by the listing of teamwork as a practical skill on the Association of American Colleges and Universities' (2007) list of essential learning outcomes.

Good teamwork requires workers to possess the aforementioned skills of communication, coordination, and cohesiveness, which are related to both interpersonal skills and team performance regulation skills (Rousseau, Aubé, & Savoie, 2006; Stevens & Campion, 1999). Interpersonal skills relevant for teamwork include communicating effectively with team members, motivating team members, resolving conflicts, and solving problems in a collaborative manner. This also includes the ability to influence others on a team, which can be useful for developing group consensus (Zhuang, MacCann, Wang, Liu, & Roberts, 2008) and for effective informal mentorship. Team performance regulation skills refer to the team's ability to set goals, monitor progress toward those goals, and plan and organize the activities of group members in a timely manner, so that individual efforts are properly coordinated and balanced. Effective training interventions need to consider both interpersonal and team-regulation skills because they are both required for effective teamwork. For example, the U.S. Department of Labor (2012) offers a set of exercises for helping workers understand how to participate in group decisions, support peers with complementary skills, communicate important information, and accomplish goals through group effort. Curricula focusing on these basic teamwork behaviors can better prepare people for the 21st century workplace.

Safety

A lack of workplace safety skills can be fatal for a worker and legally consequential for the organization. Hence, workplace safety skills are some of the most critical skills for many jobs in the 21st century workforce (e.g., in hospitals, on oil rigs, and at construction sites). In the United States alone, there were 4,383 workplace fatalities and nearly 2.8 million workplace injuries recorded in 2012 (U.S. Bureau of Labor Statistics, 2013a, 2013b). Although not every workplace accident is preventable, many of these tragedies are caused by workers failing to follow simple safety procedures that are already imposed by government requirements. Thus, it is important for employers and employees alike that workers possess the skills necessary to do their jobs safely and, perhaps more important, that they apply the skills they possess. The Occupational Safety and Health Administration (OSHA) has detailed policies about requirements for safety training, and these requirements are typically based on the content of the job. For example, workers who encounter chemical, radiological, or mechanical hazards as a part of their jobs are required by law to train on the proper use, maintenance, and disposal of personal protective equipment (OSHA, 2014). Individual states also require specific types of training for specific types of work, such as Ohio's requirement for public school personnel to take part in safety and violence prevention training (Ohio Department of Education, 2013).

It should also be noted that many organizations offer training beyond what is required by law, which can improve employee confidence in the work environment and in the organization as a whole. Companies often offer training on proper body mechanics for lifting objects, which is a sensible intervention given that almost half of workplace injuries can be classified as strains, sprains, or tears (U.S. Bureau of Labor Statistics, 2014). Providing safety knowledge to workers increases the likelihood that work tasks will actually be performed safely, in turn reducing the occurrence of workplace accidents and injuries. With regard to how to increase the application of workplace safety skills once safety knowledge is learned, perhaps the most important point to make is that safety compliance is heavily determined by positive organizational culture regarding safety protocols. Organization-wide culture based on solid safety training, in which employees also monitor and reward each other's safe behaviors, is ideal. Often, safety skills are underutilized due to a perceived lack of organizational culture for safe behavior at work, particularly when those perceptions are shared within one's immediate work group (Christian, Bradley, Wallace, & Burke, 2009). In other words, believing that coworkers are concerned about safe practices at work appears to be just as important as individual knowledge of safety procedures for ensuring safe work behavior. Moreover, organizations should foster a culture of reporting safety infractions to management in order to inform the timing and nature of safety training and protocol design (Reason, 2000). Workers should feel comfortable reporting "close calls" to management without fear of disciplinary action; otherwise, both safety and the safety culture can be meaningfully compromised. It is often the case that the cause of accidents can be traced to some aspect of the situation in which the accident occurred, not just to the irresponsible actions of individuals. Line employees who do the work that requires safety training are key voices in the development of effective training because they can provide rich, high-quality feedback on safety protocols (Wirth & Sigurdsson, 2008). To ensure that safety training is as effective as possible, it is critical for both culture and leadership to encourage employees to provide safety-related feedback that is based on training knowledge and best practice.

Creativity

Creativity is a critical skill contributing to organizational success, adaptation, and survival within any industry and market (Reiter-Palmon, 2011). Thus, the study of creativity in the workplace has seen a resurgence. Although laypeople may use the term creativity somewhat interchangeably with innovation, the psychological literature has defined *creativity* as the early stages of a problem-solving process (e.g., identifying the problem and generating ideas and solutions), whereas *innovation* is defined as the later-stage development and implementation of creative ideas as well as the subsequent acceptance of creative products by stakeholders in an organization (Mumford, 2001; West, 2003). In other words, creativity is required for innovation.

Regarding the type of creativity, two major types have been offered: incremental and radical. *Incremental creativity* is defined as ideas that imply modifications to existing practices, processes, or products, whereas *radical creativity* is defined as ideas that differ substantially from existing practices and alternatives and may not rely on any prior ideas or paradigms (Gilson & Madjar, 2011). In organizational contexts, both types of creativity are important for facilitating innovation.

In terms of the antecedents that contribute to creativity, a meta-analysis (Hammond, Neff, Farr, & Schwall, 2011) found several key sets of factors to be important: individual differences (Openness to Experience and intrinsic motivation), job characteristics (role expectations, creative self-efficacy, job complexity, job autonomy, and job self-efficacy), and organizational characteristics (climate for innovation, supervisor support, and leader–member exchange). These three groupings or factors suggest that it is helpful to consider them in a multilevel sense, such that job or organizational characteristics contribute to overall creativity, but how much these characteristics contribute also might depend on the individual differences listed previously. Future research might examine such cross-level interactions further in a multilevel data set. Making the aforementioned distinction between incremental and radical creativity may also be helpful in understanding creativity, as may longitudinal modeling that can examine how creative processes unfold over time.

Creativity is a joint function of (a) creative individuals, who might be creative in almost any situation, and (b) environments that can stimulate creativity in almost any individual. The meta-analysis by Hammond et al. (2011) suggests that individual differences do predict creativity; however, there also is research suggesting that at least some types of creativity are trainable. One notable example of training for creativity is the Systematic Inventive Thinking (SIT) method that was inspired by Altshuller's (1984) work on the theory of inventive problem solving (TIPS; see also Goldenberg, Mazursky, & Solomon, 1999). Altshuller and colleagues developed TIPS based on information from hundreds of thousands of inventions across many different fields, leading to the extrapolation of generalizable patterns or "templates" in the nature of inventive solutions. In short, the SIT method rests on research that shows that many creative solutions have underlying patterns and logic that can be defined and taught to others (Boyd & Goldenberg, 2013).

This work reveals how templates create useful constraints that individuals can apply to boost creative output, where users are forced to apply creativity to the resources with which they are already familiar and have close at hand. In other words, contrary to the popular notion that creativity has to come from "outside the box," according to practitioners of the SIT method, creative solutions to problems can often be found "inside the box" by applying creativity to current knowledge and expertise (Boyd & Goldenberg, 2013). This suggests that by providing individuals with training on how to use the SIT tools and similar methods, we can often train people with job experience to increase their creative output.

Another way to foster creativity is for organizations to cultivate and promote the types of work teams and organizational climates that are associated with higher creative output. With regard to teams, research suggests that two different types of motivation play a role in whether teams are more likely to generate creative ideas: *epistemic motivation* (the degree to which teams engage in systematic information processing and dissemination) and *prosocial motivation* (the degree to which team members seek collective, rather than personal, gain) (De Dreu, Nijstad, Bechtoldt, & Baas, 2011). Furthermore, research on organizational climate suggests that leader–member exchange may contribute to creativity by providing all team members with the support that can address their job-related problems and needs, which in turn can increase member self-efficacy to engage in flexible team problem solving, yielding more creative team outcomes (Liao, Liu, & Loi, 2010). As described by Iyer and Davenport (2008), Google is an organization generally recognized for its consistently creative output. The organization is well known for attracting employees who are part of the so-called creative class (i.e., researchers, engineers, architects, and design-ers), who are well educated and highly motivated. In addition to the talent it recruits, Google provides and maintains an organizational climate that sup-ports inquiry, provides autonomy, encourages broad participation, and toler-ates failures as long as something can be learned from them.

Critical Thinking

In its examination of the skills that are most prioritized by employers, the Partnership for 21st Century Skills found that critical thinking was a top-five skill for high school and both 2- and 4-year college graduates (Casner-Lotto & Barrington, 2006). The preference for applicants with high-quality criti-cal thinking skills is likely to continue to increase, particularly with regard to college-educated workers, for whom demands on cognitive ability and effec-tive problem solving are increasing. Economic projections suggest that by 2018, most jobs for college graduates will be in fields such as health care, managerial work, and the STEM fields (Carnevale, Smith, & Strohl, 2010)—fields in which desirable employees advance new knowledge, troubleshoot or prevent complex technical and interpersonal problems, and interact with a wide diversity of other professionals.

In order to discuss this topic effectively, let us consider what is meant by *critical thinking*, because it is defined in a variety of ways by scholars. Many, if not most, of these definitions are quite broad. According to Bangert-Drowns and Bankert (1990), critical thinking is "the ability and willingness to test the validity of propositions" (p. 3), a definition that incorporates both ability and motivational characteristics. Meanwhile, the Foundation for Critical Thinking (2014) defines the construct as "the art of analyzing and evaluating thinking with a view to improving it." This operationalization appears more focused on cognitive strategy but does not indicate whether or how "improved" thinking would be achieved. Other views of critical thinking break the construct down into components, including recognizing assumptions and evaluating arguments (Watson & Glaser, 2012). The authors of this chapter prefer the definition pro-vided by Halpern (1998), who defined critical thinking as "the use of cognitive skills or strategies that increase the probability of a desirable outcome" (p. 450). This definition, although brief, captures the important distinction and proba-bilistic relationship between the outcome and the cognitive skills and strate-gies that contribute to it. Often, researchers and policymakers seek to "increase critical thinking skills," where the focus is either on improving cognitive strate-gies or skills, with little attention paid to what outcomes are being affected, or on outcomes or "metrics" that are thought to be a function of critical thinking, with little attention paid to whether improvement on these outcomes will, due to improvements in critical thinking, generalize to other outcomes of personal or societal importance.

Historically, critical thinking has often been considered a generic or general skill set, something like "being smart," where one's high or low levels of critical thinking apply to any situation or content area (Ennis, 1989). However, contemporary researchers have deeply questioned this assumption. Kuncel (2011) finds little empirical evidence that critical thinking is a general or transferrable skill and attributes the often-cited improvements in critical thinking scores that follow critical thinking interventions to training effects that essentially teach to the test. He notes that learning content knowledge about a topic is a necessary requirement for critical thinking to take place, and generally, educators are better off investing in improving students' content knowledge than on some sort of general critical thinking skill. Furthermore, he suggests that cognitive strategies for approaching and interpreting information vary in important ways from subject to subject. For example, awareness of the gambler's fallacy and sampling bias is particularly useful for thinking critically about psychological research topics, but for chemistry or physics topics, other types of critical thinking are required. Similar to Kuncel, Anderman (2011) also posits that training for thinking critically should be taught within a meaningful context and should be based on repeated efforts to make domain-specific thinking strategies more efficient, routine, and comfortable through repeated practice. Moreover, he notes that educators should specifically train students to be mindful of the conditions in which their critical thinking skills might be transferrable to other content areas, because this knowledge transfer often does not occur automatically. For example, statistics instructors might encourage their students to apply the concept of the representativeness of sample data when interpreting the results of political polls, and physics instructors can note that the principle of inertia is important when considering how fast to drive and how closely to follow other cars on the road. In short, providing context, practicing basic knowledge, and carefully encouraging and evaluating (and not assuming) the transfer of knowledge to new content areas all appear to be important considerations for fostering critical thinking.

Metacognition and Self-Regulation

Today's effective learners need to be actively engaged in finding skill development opportunities and in building the skills they need for successful careers in the 21st century. Learners who are merely passive recipients of information will likely be less successful. Investigation into best learning practices has led researchers to focus on learning strategies, learner-directed behaviors, processes, and study skills that contribute to learning performance (Farrington et al., 2012) as a means to achieve learning success and ultimately career success. In general, learning strategies refer to sets of adjustments in behaviors, feelings, and thought processes that can help students and workers to be more productive and/or effective when they spend time on formal or informal learning tasks. The ability to execute and benefit from these strategies appears to be somewhat distinct from cognitive ability (Snow & Lohman, 1984), and meta-analysis has found support for positive effects of learning strategies on learning outcomes (Hattie, Biggs, & Purdie, 1996). Although there is no clear consensus regarding what psychological constructs and processes are involved in learning strategies, two generally agreed upon components are metacognition and self-regulation.

Metacognition refers to the act of thinking about one's own cognition and making a conscious decision to control it (Flavell, 1979). In the context of learning, metacognition allows learners to reflect on their learning efforts to date: what those efforts are, how successful those efforts have been in achieving the goal of understanding concepts, and how those efforts might be feasibly and usefully changed to adapt to a given learning context (Credé & Kuncel, 2008). In contrast, *self-regulation* refers to the learners' application of metacognition—either naturally or through training—to the learning process in order to achieve specific learning goals (Farrington et al., 2012). Winne and Hadwin (1998) describe a four-phase self-regulation process that involves metacognition: First, the learners must orient themselves to the task by assessing both the difficulty and their prior knowledge of the learning task. Note that this assessment need not necessarily be objective to promote engagement and learning, although self-assessment likely contains objective components. Next, learners must assess their learning goals by outlining the specific criteria of success associated with the learning task. These criteria imply a constructive learning process to reach the goals of success, especially when the criteria are more specific and proximal (e.g., "Read this chapter carefully") rather than vague or distal (e.g., "Write my dissertation") (Locke & Latham, 2002). Third, learners must apply metacognitive effort to the learning and adjust their strategy once it is decided that the present strategy is not effective (or less effective than other possible strategies). Sometimes short-term "shortcut" strategies can lead to short-term payoffs at the expense of long-term benefits; in contrast, long-term strategies can sometimes be less beneficial in the short term but more durable in the long term (Beier & Oswald, 2012). As a last step, learners may consider what the learning experience taught them about learning tasks more generally, whether in this particular domain or in analogous tasks in other domains.

Thinking about learning, and willfully directing this thinking toward a learning task, can yield diverse and cumulative benefits for learners. Receiving training in learning strategies can provide learners in a variety of situations with the skills they need to take ownership of their own learning process and maximize learning effort. Baird (1986) observed that students who were trained in metacognition, regardless of their initial interest in the topic, were more aware of their own learning practices and had more positive attitudes toward learning. Pennequin, Sorel, Nanty, and Fontaine (2010) found that a metacognition-based intervention was related to improved problem-solving ability in math, particularly for low-achieving students for whom learning may have profound long-term benefits (e.g., basic life skills and employability). Keith and Frese (2005) examined self-regulation in college students, finding that those trained to self-regulate during computer training exercises learned software more effectively than those who were trained on the software alone. Note that meta-cognition and self-regulation can even benefit those with high ability, in terms of being able to deal with emotional intrusions that are not always related to intelligence (e.g., fear of failure) and promote efficient learning. In addition to individual benefits, teams benefit from the meta-cognitive and self-regulatory strategies of their members. Dierdorff and Ellington (2012) found that the average level of self-regulation across members of a work team is positively related to team efficacy, team cooperation quality, and team decision-making. Conditions and cases in which the team benefit is greater than the sum of its parts remain largely an empirical question.

Cross-Cultural Knowledge and Competence

One area of 21st century skills in which more emphasis has been placed is in the cross-cultural competence and knowledge domain, as is evidenced in Chapter 4 of this volume. Cross-cultural competence (3C) refers to a general capability to have successful interactions with others in intercultural situations (Deardorff, 2006). Aside from cross-cultural knowledge (i.e., knowledge of the norms and practices of other cultures), most scholarly conceptualizations of 3C include metacognitive and motivational components (Ang & Van Dyne, 2008; Deardorff, 2006; Thomas, 2006). This suggests that in addition to awareness of the cultural expectations of others, people must know how those expectations are different from their own and then, to navigate those differences effectively, be willing to expend effort to be flexible, open, and empathetic in the way they communicate. In addition, some research suggests that emotional regulation is an important part of 3C because the management of stress is important for effectively adjusting to the people and environment associated with a new culture (Matsumoto & Hwang, 2013). Cross-cultural skills are both directly and indirectly related to a variety of positive outcomes for those living or working in a culture other than their own, including better job performance and more successful expatriate adjustment (Morris & Robie, 2001).

Cross-cultural competence is important for a variety of jobs, and training for this skill will need to become more prevalent in today's multinational and hyperconnected workforce. Researchers estimate that 20–40% of all expatriates sent abroad for work return home early (Black & Mendenhall, 1989; Kim & Slocum, 2008; Mendenhall, Dunbar, & Oddou, 1987), where the inability to adjust to the host country's culture has been cited as a common problem (Okpara & Kabongo, 2011; Tung, 1982). Many of these expatriates work in management and professional positions, which are projected to comprise 11% of the workforce by 2018 (Carnevale et al., 2010). Another group for whom 3C skills are of great importance is military personnel, who often receive assignments and relocations throughout the world. Although the armed forces have historically provided training on the content of the culture of interest (e.g., customs, language, and politics), it is necessary to train personnel to have mindfulness of differences in perspective in real time (Abbe & Halpin, 2009). Soldiers, officers, and other military personnel must routinely consider differences in the motivations of those in the host culture, maintaining their mission while ensuring they are able to manage their emotions and the stress associated with these complex efforts.

In addition to those who work abroad, many students and employees can greatly benefit from stronger intercultural skills in their home country. Many schools and workplaces are diverse and intercultural due to the diversity of a city, the nature of business communications in partnerships with companies abroad, or the presence of expatriates in one's organization. Regardless of the reason, many people live and work in environments in which they routinely interact with people who have different cultural expectations of interpersonal interactions. The same general principles of knowledge, self-awareness, and motivation to achieve successful interpersonal interactions are useful in cross-cultural situations as well (Herfst, van Oudenhoven, & Timmerman, 2008). Perhaps the greatest impediment to progress in this area concerns the measurement of 3C, which is often done via self-report instruments, does not incorporate specific cultural expectations, and in these two respects can be indistinguishable from personality assessment (Matsumoto & Hwang, 2013).

With the sustained practical interest in training 3C by organizations and the military, it is not surprising that the research literature has arrived at some recommendations on best practices for 3C training. Morris, Savani, Mor, and Cho (2014) have summarized this literature and have provided some recommendations. First, these authors recommend using specific types of training materials that are more innovative than what is typical for adult learners. Although books and classes are certainly helpful, web-based tools and software can offer additional engagement and realism and thus be more conductive to acquiring the foundation of structured declarative knowledge necessary for 3C. Additionally, examining an array of foreign documents online (translated using web tools if necessary) is a way of drawing primary cultural knowledge directly from the host culture, thus providing a contextual cultural learning experience. Second, these authors emphasize the need to prepare for situations in the host country in which the causes and effects of social interaction may be initially confusing. Learning to interpret situations correctly by examining critical incidents—or those situations whose nature, causes, or outcomes differ in the host and the home country—can help future expatriates prepare for their travel. For example, it is very useful to have foreknowledge of what actions or reactions may be considered offensive during conversations in the host country or how to behave when one is in the home of a host country native. This approach allows expatriates to enter situations with greater cultural awareness that helps to avoid misinterpretations and behavioral awkwardness or gaffes. Last, Morris and colleagues recommend learning to imitate customary gestures, greetings, and rituals, usually expected on a moment's notice, that will help ease expatriates into the host culture and allow them to know how to act before understanding why these actions are culturally appropriate. Given the large amount of knowledge likely needed for an expatriate to prepare for traveling to a foreign country for a work assignment, this approach is beneficial because it focuses more on the necessary behavior and less on the reasons why, which may be very nuanced and complex.

Ethics and Integrity

Adherence to ethical principles of behavior and generally knowing right from wrong are important qualities for both students and workers to possess. Nearly all jobs provide opportunities for people to lie, steal, or otherwise be unethical, and so employers seek out those individuals who possess integrity—people who are consistent in their values and actions and can be trusted with the company's time, resources, and reputation (Becker, 1998; Casner-Lotto & Barrington, 2006). Ethical thinking is relevant to a variety of job functions, including decision-making, problem solving, communication, customer service, and teamwork (Binkley et al., 2012). Moreover, meta-analytic research on assessment of integrity for employee selection has shown that ethics can usefully predict job performance, training performance, counterproductive work behavior, and job turnover (Berry, Sackett, & Wiemann, 2007; Van Iddekinge, Roth, Raymark, & Odle-Dusseau, 2012).

Although integrity and ethical behavior are important for students and employees, they are perhaps especially important for leaders, who are entrusted with vast responsibilities in managing others and managing organizational resources. Leading by ethical example can also set a culture for ethical behavior in the organization, and it can establish appropriate relationships with subordinates (Bass & Steidlmeier, 1999); conversely, a lack of ethical behavior in top leaders can have widespread destabilizing and demoralizing effects on employees. Belief in the high integrity of leaders is obviously tied to the actual integrity of leaders, and such belief has been shown to be related to valued employee outcomes, such as increased organizational commitment, job performance, and reduced intentions to quit (Dirks & Ferrin, 2002). In addition to the effect of leaders' integrity on their followers, ethical leaders guide organizational decisions to be in compliance with laws and, whenever possible, to make decisions that will cast their organization in a positive light in the eyes of the public and relevant stakeholders.

Research indicates that ethics training can lead to a positive influence on ethical behavior. Grady and colleagues (2008) studied the effects of ethics training on the behavior of nurses, finding that both foundational coursework and continuing education training in ethics translated into greater utilization of ethics committees and increased ethical decision-making when faced with an ethical dilemma. One reason to implement ethics training is to give employees the awareness and skills to monitor intensive goal setting and employee incentivization, which ordinarily can lead toward meeting any ethically-questionable behaviors with *motivated blindness*, the human tendency to ignore relevant information that is contradictory to a person's interests and goals (Bazerman & Tenbrunsel, 2011; Ordóñez, Schweitzer, Galinsky, & Bazerman, 2009). For example, tying performance evaluation and compensation to ever-increasing sales goals can encourage employees to pressure customers to buy more than they are comfortable purchasing, and incentivizing speed of product to market can result (and has resulted) in executive management ignoring serious and legitimate concerns regarding product safety. These types of actions erode trust and can have serious consequences for the welfare of others, as well as for the productivity—and even the survival—of the organization.

CONCLUSION: FURTHER UNDERSTANDING OF 21ST CENTURY SKILLS

Much more work remains to be done by researchers and practitioners to contribute to a better understanding of the nature of 21st century skills. Our perspective is that great progress can be made on this front by considering these skills in an integrated manner, such as (a) across societal, educational, and organizational contexts; (b) across cognitive and noncognitive skill domains (as shown in Table 3.1; see also Mattern & Hanson, 2015); and (c) across different research disciplines (e.g., educational psychology, vocational psychology, industrial–organizational psychology, and economics). In fact, a more integrative approach seems essential to address effectively the "skills gap," which refers to the discrepancy between the skills and skill levels that workers have and the skills and skill levels that employers seek out. As noted in a report by Educational Testing Service (2015), younger workers in the United States currently entering the workforce lack the skills they need to be competitive in today's international job market.

This chapter is our contribution to the large and important discussion regarding the changing nature of work. First, we discussed disruptive economic forces and noted that advances in technology, increased demand for customer service workers, and the expansion of industry across borders have caused employers to demand a broader and more diverse set of skills of prospective employees. Second, we examined the term *skill* and discussed the ways in which skills can differ. Skills can be broad or narrow and require intelligence, emotional control, and/or physical abilities that not all people possess. Some skills require substantial effort to be exhibited, whereas others can become automatic over time, and the measurement of the performance of skills requires careful consideration of both individual effort and the context in which the skills are performed. Third, rather than attempting to provide an exhaustive list of 21st century skills, we presented an examination of nine skills that we view to be directly related to the three aforementioned economic forces that are redefining work.

Many books, articles, and the popular press have pointed to the educational system as the main culprit for the skills gap (Association of American Colleges and Universities, 2007; Casner-Lotto, & Barrington, 2006). However, a different treatment of the "skills gap" is presented by Cappelli (2012), whose book acknowledges the gap but re-examines and redefines it as a function of revised employer expectations in those they hire and technological advances that dramatically shift workforce needs and requirements. A rapidly changing demography is also a key factor because this also contributes to a shifting distribution of skills in the workforce (Carnevale, Hanson, & Gulish, 2013; Kirsch, Braun, Yamamoto, & Sum, 2007), and even self-perceptions of skills vary by demographics and can affect the decision to persist in a particular job (McGonagle, Fisher, Barnes-Farrell, & Grosch, 2015). Also, economic models have considered the skills gap as a function of a variety of factors, including the skill levels of jobs within an organization, the composition of skilled jobs in an organization, the wages that jobs demand, the effect of technology on demand for job skills, and the unemployment rate (Albrecht & Vroman, 2002;

Autor, Levy, & Murnane, 2003). It is only through these multiple conceptual and interdisciplinary approaches that we will be able to understand, measure, and develop 21st century skills in a manner that adequately and directly serves today's incredibly diverse and dynamic demographic, economic, educational, and workforce realities.

REFERENCES

Abbe, A., & Halpin, S. M. (2009). The cultural imperative for professional military education and leader development. *Parameters, 10,* 20–31.

Albrecht, J., & Vroman, S. (2002). A matching model with endogenous skill requirements. *International Economic Review, 43,* 283–305.

Altshuller, G. S. (1984). *Creativity as an exact science: The theory of the solution of inventive problems.* Amsterdam: Gordon & Breach.

Anderman, E. M. (2011). *The teaching and learning of twenty-first century skills.* Paper presented at the National Research Council's 21st century skills workshop. Retrieved from https://atecentral.net/downloads/175/Anderman%20Final%20Submission%20After%20Conference.pdf

Ang, S., & Van Dyne, L. (2008). Conceptualization of cultural intelligence: Definition, distinctiveness, and nomological network. In S. Ang & L. Van Dyne (Eds.), *Handbook of cultural intelligence: Theory, measurement, and applications* (pp. 3–15). Armonk, NY: Sharpe.

Aon Hewitt. (2014). *2014 trends in global employee engagement.* Retrieved from http://www.aon.com/attachments/human-capital-consulting/2014-trends-in-global-employee-engagement-report.pdf

Association of American Colleges and Universities. (2007). *College learning for the new global century: A report from the National Leadership Council for Liberal Education & America's Promise.* Washington, DC: Author.

Autor, D. H., Levy, F., & Murnane, R. J. (2003). The skill content of recent technological change: An empirical exploration. *Quarterly Journal of Economics, 118,* 1279–1333.

Baird, J. R. (1986). Improving learning through enhanced metacognition: A classroom study. *European Journal of Science Education, 8*(3), 263–282.

Bangert-Drowns, R. L., & Bankert, E. (1990). *Meta-analysis of effects of explicit instruction for critical thinking.* Paper presented at the annual meeting of the American Educational Research Association, Boston, MA.

Bass, B. M., & Riggio, R. E. (2005). *Transformational leadership.* London, England: Psychology Press.

Bass, B. M., & Steidlmeier, P. (1999). Ethics, character, and authentic transformational leadership behavior. *Leadership Quarterly, 10,* 181–217.

Bazerman, M. H., & Tenbrunsel, A. E. (2011). Ethical breakdowns. *Harvard Business Review, 89,* 58–65.

Becker, T. E. (1998). Integrity in organizations: Beyond honesty and conscientiousness. *Academy of Management Review, 23,* 154–161.

Beier, M. E., & Oswald, F. L. (2012). Is cognitive ability a liability? A critique and future research agenda on skilled performance. *Journal of Experimental Psychology: Applied, 18*, 331–345.

Berry, C. M., Sackett, P. R., & Weimann, S. (2007). A review of recent developments in integrity testing research. *Personnel Psychology, 60*, 271–301.

Binkley, M., Erstad, O., Herman, J., Raizen, S., Ripley, M., Miller-Ricci, M., & Rumble, M. (2012). Defining twenty-first century skills. In P. Griffin, B. McGaw, & E. Care (Eds.), *Assessment and teaching of 21st century skills* (pp. 17–66). Dordrecht, the Netherlands: Springer.

Black, J. S., & Mendenhall, M. (1989). A practical but theory-based framework for selecting cross-cultural training methods. *Human Resource Management, 28*, 511–539.

Boyd, D., & Goldenberg, J. (2013). *Inside the box: Why the best business innovations are right in front of you.* London, England: Profile Books.

Brown, M. E., & Treviño, L. K. (2009). Leader–follower values congruence: Are socialized charismatic leaders better able to achieve it? *Journal of Applied Psychology, 94*, 478–490.

Buckingham, M. (2012). Leadership development in the age of the algorithm. *Harvard Business Review, 90*, 86–94.

Burke, C. S., Stagl, K. C., Klein, C., Goodwin, G. F., Salas, E., & Halpin, S. M. (2006). What types of leadership behaviors are functional in teams? A meta-analysis. *Leadership Quarterly, 17*, 288–307.

Cappelli, P. (2012). *Why good people can't get jobs: The skills gap and what companies can do about it.* Philadelphia, PA: Wharton Digital Press.

CareerBuilder. (2014). *Overwhelming majority of companies say soft skills are just as important as hard skills, according to a new CareerBuilder survey* [Press release]. Retrieved from http://www.careerbuilder.com/share/aboutus/pressreleasesdetail.aspx?sd=4/10/2014&id= pr817&ed=12/31/2014

Carnevale, A. P., Hanson, A. R., & Gulish, A. (2013). *Failure to launch: Structural shift and the new lost generation.* Washington, DC: Georgetown University, Center for Education and the Workforce.

Carnevale, A. P., Smith, N., & Strohl, J. (2010). *Help wanted: Projections of job and education requirements through 2018.* Indianapolis, IN: Lumina Foundation.

Casner-Lotto, J., & Barrington, L. (2006). *Are they really ready to work? Employers' perspectives on the basic knowledge and applied skills of new entrants to the 21st century US workforce.* New York, NY: The Conference Board, Corporate Voices for Working Families, Partnership for 21st Century Skills, and Society for Human Resource Management.

Christian, M. S., Bradley, J. C., Wallace, J. C., & Burke, M. J. (2009). Workplace safety: A meta-analysis of the roles of person and situation factors. *Journal of Applied Psychology, 94*, 1103–1127.

Credé, M., & Kuncel, N. R. (2008). Study habits, skills, and attitudes. *Perspectives on Psychological Science, 3*, 425–453.

De Dreu, C. K. W., Nijstad, B. A., Bechtoldt, M. N., & Baas, M. (2011). Group creativity and innovation: A motivation information processing perspective. *Psychology of Aesthetics, Creativity, and the Arts, 5*, 81–89.

Deardorff, D. K. (2006). Identification and assessment of intercultural competence as a student outcome of internalization. *Journal of Studies in International Education, 10*, 241–266.

Dierdorff, E. C., & Ellington, J. K. (2012). Members matter in team training: Multilevel and longitudinal relationships between goal orientation, self-regulation, and team outcomes. *Personnel Psychology, 65*, 661–703.

Dirks, K. T., & Ferrin, D. L. (2002). Trust in leadership: Meta-analytic findings and implications for research and practice. *Journal of Applied Psychology, 87*, 611–628.

Donofrio, N. M., & Whitefoot, K. S. (Eds.). (2015). *Making value for America: Embracing the future of manufacturing, technology, and work*. Washington, DC: National Academies Press.

Educational Testing Service. (2015). *America's skills challenge: Millennial and the Future*. Princeton, NJ: Author.

Ennis, R. H. (1989). Critical thinking and subject specificity: Clarification and needed research. *Educational Researcher, 18*, 4–10.

Farrington, C. A., Roderick, M., Allen worth, E., Nagoya, J., Keyes, T. S., Johnson, D. W., & Bee chum, N. O. (2012). *Teaching adolescents to become learners: The role of non-cognitive factors in shaping school performance—A critical literature review*. Chicago, IL: Consortium on Chicago School Research.

Flavell, J. H. (1979). Metacognition and cognitive monitoring: A new area of cognitive-developmental inquiry. *American Psychologist, 34*, 906–911.

Fleishman, E. A., & Quaintance, M. K. (1984). *Taxonomies of human performance*. Orlando, FL: Academic Press.

Foundation for Critical Thinking. (2014). *Critical thinking: Where to begin*. Retrieved from http://www.criticalthinking.org/pages/critical-thinking-where-to-begin/796

Gallup. (2013). *State of the American workplace: Employee engagement insights for U.S. business leaders*. Retrieved from http://www.gallup.com/strategicconsulting/163007/state-american-workplace.aspx

Garavan, T. N. (1997). Interpersonal skills training for quality service interactions. *Industrial and Commercial Training, 29*, 70–77.

Gilson, L. L., & Madjar, N. (2011). Radical and incremental creativity: Antecedents and processes. *Psychology of Aesthetics, Creativity, and the Arts, 5*, 21–28.

Goldenberg, J., Mazursky, D., & Solomon, S. (1999). Toward identifying the inventive templates of new products: A channeled ideation approach. *Journal of Marketing Research, 36*, 200–210.

Grady, C., Denis, M., Seen, K. L., O'Donnell, P., Taylor, A., & Ulrich, C. M. (2008). Does ethics education influence the moral action of practicing nurses and social workers? *American Journal of Bioethics, 8*, 4–11.

Halpern, D. F. (1998) Teaching critical thinking for transfer across domains. *American Psychologist, 53*, 449–455.

Hammond, M. M., Neff, N. L., Farr, J. L., & Schwall, A. R. (2011). Predictors of individual-level innovation at work: A meta-analysis. *Psychology of Aesthetics, Creativity, and the Arts, 5*, 90–105.

Hattie, J., Biggs, J., & Purdie, N. (1996). Effects of learning skills interventions on student learning: A meta-analysis. *Review of Educational Research, 66*, 99–136.

Henderson, R. (2013, December). Industry employment and output projections to 2022. *Monthly Labor Review*.

Herfst, S. L., van Oudenhoven, J. P., & Timmerman, M. E. (2008). Intercultural effectiveness training in three Western immigrant countries: A cross-cultural evaluation of critical incidents. *International Journal of Intercultural Relations, 32*, 67–80.

Hogan, J., Hogan, R., & Busch, C. M. (1984). How to measure service orientation. *Journal of Applied Psychology, 69*, 167.

Hong, Y., Liao, H., Hu, J., & Jiang, K. (2013). Missing link in the service profit chain: A meta-analytic review of the antecedents, consequences, and moderators of service climate. *Journal of Applied Psychology, 98*, 237–267.

Iyer, B., & Davenport, T. H. (2008). Reverse engineering Google's Innovation Machine. *Harvard Business Review, 86*, 58–68.

Judge, T. A., & Piccolo, R. F. (2004). Transformational and transactional leadership: A meta-analytic test of their relative validity. *Journal of Applied Psychology, 89*, 775–768.

Kanfer, R., & Ackerman, P. L. (1989). Motivation and cognitive abilities: An integrative aptitude/treatment interaction approach to skill acquisition. *Journal of Applied Psychology, 74*, 657–690.

Keith, N., & Frese, M. (2005). Self-regulation in error management training: Emotional control and metacognition as mediators of performance effects. *Journal of Applied Psychology, 90*, 677–691.

Kelloway, E. K., Barling, J., & Helleur, J. (2000). Enhancing transformational leadership: The roles of training and feedback. *Leadership & Organization Development Journal, 21*, 145–149.

Kim, K., & Slocum, J. W. (2008). Individual differences and expatriate assignment effectiveness: The case of U.S. based Korean expatriates. *Journal of World Business, 43*, 109–126.

Kirsch, I., Braun, H., Yamamoto, K., & Sum, A. (2007). *America's perfect storm: Three forces changing our nation's future*. Princeton, NJ: Educational Testing Service.

Koenig, J. A., & the Committee on the Assessment of 21st Century Skills. (2011). *Assessing 21st century skills: Summary of a workshop*. Washington, DC: National Academies Press.

Kuncel, N. R. (2011, January). *Measurement and meaning of critical thinking*. Paper presented at the National Research Council's 21st century skills workshop. Retrieved from https://atecentral.net/downloads/209/Kuncel_Measuring%20Critical%20Thinking_Paperpdf

LePine, J. A., Piccolo, R. F., Jackson, C. L., Mathieu, J. E., & Saul, J. R. (2008). A meta-analysis of teamwork processes: Tests of a multidimensional model and relationships with team effectiveness criteria. *Personnel Psychology, 61*, 273–307.

Liao, H., Liu, D., & Loi, R. (2010). Looking at both sides of the social exchange coin: A social cognitive perspective on the joint effects of relationship quality and differentiation on creativity. *Academy of Management Journal, 53*, 1090–1109.

Locke, E. A., & Latham, G. P. (2002). Building a practically useful theory of goal setting and task motivation. *American Psychologist, 57*(9), 705–717.

Lowe, K. B., Kroeck, K. G., & Sivasubramaniam, N. (1996). Effectiveness correlates of transformational and transactional leadership: A meta-analytic review of the MLQ literature. *Leadership Quarterly, 7*, 385–425.

Matsumoto, D., & Hwang, H. C. (2013). Assessing cross-cultural competence: A review of available tests. *Journal of Cross-Cultural Psychology, 44*, 849–873.

Mattern, K., & Hanson, M. A. (2015). ACT holistic framework of education and work readiness. In W. Camara, R. O'Connor, K. Mattern, & M. A. Hanson (Eds.), *Beyond academics: A holistic framework for enhancing education and workplace success* (pp. 1–9). Iowa City, IA: ACT.

Mayer, T. A., Cates, R. J., Mastorovich, M. J., & Royalty, D. L. (1998). Emergency department patient satisfaction: Customer service training improves patient satisfaction and ratings of physician and nurse skill. *Journal of Healthcare Management, 43*, 427–441.

McGonagle, A., Fisher, G. G., Barnes-Farrell, J. L., & Grosch, J. (2015). Individual and work factors related to perceived work ability and labor force outcomes. *Journal of Occupational Health Psychology, 19*, 231–242.

Mendenhall, M. E., Dunbar, E., & Oddou, G. (1987). Expatriate selection, training and career-pathing: A review and critique. *Human Resource Management, 26*, 331–345.

Morris, M. A., & Robie, C. (2001). A meta-analysis of the effects of cross-cultural training on expatriate performance and adjustment. *International Journal of Training and Development, 5*, 112–125.

Morris, M. W., Savani, K., Mor, S., & Cho, J. (2014). When in Rome: Intercultural learning and implications for training. *Research in Organizational Behavior, 34*, 189–215.

Mumford, M. D. (2001). Something old, something new: Revisiting Guildford Press's conception of creative problem solving. *Creativity Research Journal, 13*, 267–276.

Occupational Safety and Health Administration. (2014). *General requirements* (Standard 1910.132). Retrieved from https://www.osha.gov/pls/oshaweb/owadisp.show_document?p_id=9777&p_table=STANDARDS

Ohio Department of Education. (2013). *Safety and violence prevention training now required of K-12 professionals*. Retrieved from http://www.pccsd.net/ourpages/auto/2011/8/24/55780245/Safety%20and%20Violence%20Prevention%20Training%20Now%20Required.pdf

Okpara, J. O., & Kabongo, J. D. (2011). Cross-cultural training and expatriate adjustment: A study of Western expatriates in Nigeria. *Journal of World Business, 46*, 22–30.

Ones, D. S., Viswesvaran, C., & Dilchert, S. (2005). Personality at work: Raising awareness and correcting misconceptions. *Human Performance, 18*, 389–404.

Ordóñez, L. D., Schweitzer, M. E., Galinsky, A. D., & Bazerman, M. H. (2009). Goals gone wild: The systematic side effects of overprescribing goal setting. *Academy of Management Perspectives, 23*, 6–16.

Oswald, F. L., Hambrick, D. Z., & Jones, L. A. (2007). Keeping all the plates spinning: Understanding and predicting multitasking performance. In D. H. Jonassen (Ed.), *Learning to solve complex scientific problems* (pp. 77–97). Mahwah, NJ: Erlbaum.

Parasuraman, A., Zeithaml, V. A., & Berry, L. L. (1985). A conceptual model of service quality and its implications for future research. *Journal of Marketing, 49*, 41–50.

Pattni, I., Soutar, G. N., & Klobas, J. E. (2007). The impact of a short self-management training intervention in a retail-banking environment. *Human Resource Development Quarterly, 18*, 159–178.

Pellegrino, J. W., & Hilton, M. L. (Eds.). (2012). *Education for life and work: Developing transferable knowledge and skills in the 21st century*. Washington, DC: National Research Council.

Pennequin, V., Sorel, O., Nanty, I., & Fontaine, R. (2010). Metacognition and low achievement in mathematics: The effect of training in the use of metacognitive skills to solve mathematical word problems. *Thinking & Reasoning, 16,* 198–220.

Proctor, R. W., & Dutta, A. (1995). *Skill acquisition and human performance*. London, England: Sage.

Rasmussen, J. (1983). Skills, rules, and knowledge: Signals, signs, symbols, and other distinctions in human performance models. *IEEE Transactions on Systems, Man, and Cybernetics, 13,* 257–266.

Raub, S., & Liao, H. (2012). Doing the right thing without being told: Joint effects of initiative climate and general self-efficacy on employee proactive customer service performance. *Journal of Applied Psychology, 97,* 651–667.

Reason, J. (2000). Human error: Models and management. *British Medical Journal, 320,* 768–770.

Reiter-Palmon, R. (2011). Introduction to special issue: The psychology of creativity and innovation in the workplace. *Psychology of Aesthetics, Creativity, and the Arts, 5,* 1–2.

Rousseau, V., Aubé, C., & Savoie, A. (2006). Teamwork behaviors: A review and an integration of frameworks. *Small Group Research, 37,* 540–570.

Salas, E., Stagl, K. C., & Burke, C. S. (2004). 25 years of team effectiveness in organizations: Research themes and emerging needs. In C. L. Cooper & I. T. Robertson (Eds.), *International review of industrial and organizational psychology* (pp. 47–92). New York, NY: Wiley.

Schneider, B., White, S. S., & Paul, M. C. (1998). Linking service climate and customer perceptions of service quality: Tests of a causal model. *Journal of Applied Psychology, 83,* 150–163.

Snow, R. E., & Lohman, D. R. (1984). Toward a theory of cognitive aptitude for learning from instruction. *Journal of Educational Psychology, 76,* 347–376.

Stevens, M. J., & Campion, M. A. (1999). Staffing work teams: Development and validation of a selection test for teamwork settings. *Journal of Management, 25,* 207–228.

Thomas, D. C. (2006). Domain and development of cultural intelligence: The importance of mindfulness. *Group & Organization Management, 31,* 78–99.

Tung, R. L. (1982). Selection and training procedures of U.S., European and Japanese multinationals. *California Management Review, 25,* 57–71.

US Bureau of Labor Statistics. (2013a). *National census of fatal occupational injuries in 2012* (USDL 13-1699). Washington, DC: US Department of Labor.

US Bureau of Labor Statistics. (2013b). *Employer-reported workplace injuries and illnesses* (USDL 13-2119). Washington, DC: US Department of Labor.

US Bureau of Labor Statistics (2013c, December). *Employment by major industry sector, 2002, 2012, and projected 2022*. Retrieved from https://www.bls.gov/news.release/ecopro.t03.htm

US Bureau of Labor Statistics. (2014). *Occupational injuries and illnesses: A pilot study of job-transfer or work restriction cases, 2012* (USDL 14-1049). Washington, DC: US Department of Labor.

US Department of Labor. (2012). *Soft skills to pay the bills: Mastering soft skills for workplace success.* Retrieved from https://www.dol.gov/odep/topics/youth/softskills/Teamwork.pdf

Van Iddekinge, C. H., Roth, P. L., Raymark, P. H., & Odle-Dusseau, H. N. (2012). The criterion-related validity of integrity tests: An updated meta-analysis. *Journal of Applied Psychology, 97,* 499–530.

Watson, G., & Glaser, E. M. (2012). *Watson–Glaser IITM Critical Thinking Appraisal.* San Antonio, TX: Pearson.

West, M. A. (2003). Innovation implementation in work teams. In P. B. Paulus & B. A. Nijstad (Eds.), *Innovation through collaboration* (pp. 245–276). New York, NY: Oxford University Press.

West, M. A. (2012). *Effective teamwork: Practical lessons from organizational research.* New York, NY: Wiley.

Winne, P. H., & Hadwin, A. F. (1998). Studying as self-regulated learning. In D. J. Hacker, J. Dunlosky, & A. C. Graesser (Eds.), *Metacognition in educational theory and practice* (pp. 227–304). Hillsdale, NJ: Erlbaum.

Wirth, O., & Sigurdsson, S. O. (2008). When workplace safety depends on behavior change: Topics for behavioral safety research. *Journal of Safety Research, 39,* 589–598.

Zhuang, X., MacCann, C., Wang, L., Liu, L., & Roberts, R. D. (2008). Development and validity evidence supporting a teamwork and collaboration assessment for high school students. *ETS Research Report, 2008,* i–51.

Cross-Cultural Competence as a 21st Century Skill

JENNIFER KLAFEHN ■

In 1991, the US Secretary of Labor's Commission on Achieving Necessary Skills (SCANS) interviewed employers and asked them to identify the critical skills and competencies they believed were most important when considering candidates for employment (Secretary's Commission on Achieving Necessary Skills, 1991). Not surprisingly, skills related to reading, writing, and mathematics were at the top of the list, followed closely by critical thinking/problem-solving skills, as well as what the report referred to as "personal qualities," which encompassed traits such as discipline and integrity. Employers also mentioned that potential employees should be competent in a number of critical domains, particularly teamwork and technological interfacing.

Nearly a decade and a half later, a related research effort conducted by The Conference Board and the Society for Human Resource Management investigated a similar set of trends (Casner-Lotto & Barrington, 2006). Although the same basic skills and competencies that had been identified by the SCANS group remained a top priority for employers interviewed as a part of this effort, there were several new skills that emerged from these discussions as well. These new skills focused on uniquely "21st century" concerns and were projected to be most critical for employers hiring employees within the next 5–10 years.

Of all the basic skills employers said would "increase in importance" over the course of the next decade, knowledge of foreign language was the most frequently cited (63.3%). Furthermore, employers underscored the importance of future employees being able to recognize and understand the influence of culture and the role it plays in organizational contexts.

The predictions made by those employers interviewed as part of The Conference Board study could not have been more accurate, as nearly 20% of all US private-sector jobs today are accounted for by multinational corporations, including 3M, Microsoft, Coca-Cola, and Google (US Bureau of Economic Analysis, 2013). Furthermore, not only has the number of multinational employment opportunities grown significantly but also globalization, in general, has become the norm among organizations seeking to remain competitive and relevant in today's market. In response, employers are beginning to realign their hiring priorities to seek out and attract job candidates who are able to adapt to and perform effectively in environments hallmarked by cultural diversity (Hart Research Associates, 2013).

Before they ever submit a resume, however, prospective employees must first develop (or be taught how to develop) the requisite skills that will enable them to perform successfully in such environments. These skills, which include the ability to think flexibly, communicate effectively, and take the perspective of others, collectively comprise a construct known as *cross-cultural competence*. Cross-cultural competence (3C), also referred to as intercultural competence (Deardorff, 2006), intercultural sensitivity (Hammer & Bennett, 1998; Hammer, Bennett, & Wiseman, 2003), cultural intelligence (Earley & Ang, 2003; Thomas et al., 2008), or multicultural personality (van der Zee & van Oudenhoven, 2000; van Oudenhoven & van der Zee, 2002), is an individual's ability to successfully navigate cross-cultural contexts. Specifically, 3C encompasses a unique blend of knowledge, skills, abilities, and attitudes that can be universally applied across cultures to facilitate adaptation and interpersonal interactions.

Although great strides have been made to improve the operationalization of 3C, as well as better develop the means by which to assess it, the majority of research in this area remains concentrated on its role within organizational and military settings (for a review, see Gallus et al., 2014). There is certainly good reason for researchers to focus their efforts in these directions: Expatriates and deployed soldiers comprise two professional groups for whom effective cross-cultural performance is extremely critical. Given the nature of their jobs, expatriates and soldiers generally receive some form of specialized training prior to going overseas. This training can range from hour-long briefs covering basic "do's and don'ts" of the culture in question to multiday workshops designed to increase cultural awareness in general (Abbe & Gouge, 2012; Gudykunst & Hammer, 1983; see also Fowler & Mumford, 1995, 1999). Despite its apparent value to organizations, however, cross-cultural training has received mixed support in the literature concerning its effectiveness as a facilitator of cross-cultural adaptation and performance (Blake & Heslin, 1983; Kealey & Protheroe, 1996; Mendenhall et al., 2004; Puck, Kittler, & Wright, 2008). Furthermore, some individuals who travel and/or operate overseas demonstrate adaptation and performance even in the absence of formal cross-cultural training (Yamakazi & Kayes, 2004). This suggests that many of the skills enabling these individuals to effectively interact and perform in cross-cultural contexts were acquired at a stage predating their entry into the workforce.

Although it is likely that the development of 3C-relevant skills begins earlier in life as opposed to later, few researchers have explicitly investigated the development of these skills in younger (i.e., pre-professional) groups. The primary exception to this is research focusing on study abroad or international immersion programs. These studies are beneficial in that they help to illustrate the value that culturally immersive programs can offer within the context of higher education (Carlson, Burns, Useem, & Yachimowicz, 1990; Fry, Paige, Jon, Dillow, & Nam, 2009; Kitsantas, 2004; Maiworm & Teichler, 1996; Orahood, Kruze, & Pearson, 2004; Potts, 2015). Despite their documented benefits, however, study abroad programs demonstrate remarkably low participation rates, especially among minority students (Brux & Fry, 2009), due to concerns surrounding finances, familial constraints, work responsibilities, and personal safety (Salisbury, Umbach, Paulsen, & Pascarella, 2009). In fact, only 1% of all actively enrolled US college students participate in these specialized programs, the majority of whom are White females majoring in humanities or social sciences (Institute of International Education, 2014). It is therefore essential that researchers who are interested in studying cross-cultural skill development focus their attention at a level that is more widespread and inclusive in its impact—namely, the kindergarten through grade 12 (K–12) student population. By exploring how 3C and its related facets map onto the progressive development of the core skills commensurate with primary and secondary curricula, both researchers and educators can help facilitate the development of 21st century skills in today's students to better prepare them for the workforce of tomorrow.

The goal of this chapter is to investigate the extent to which 3C skills can be developed in younger, pre-professional populations and subsequently implemented into preexisting K–12 curricula. Factors that have been identified by prior research as comprising 3C (or predictive of cross-culturally competent performance) are discussed within the context of Piaget's model of cognitive development (Inhelder & Piaget, 1958; Piaget, 1952). The purpose of utilizing Piaget's model in this chapter is twofold. First, couching the discussion of cross-cultural skill development within a framework that is well known to psychologists and educators alike will help provide a theoretical foundation to those for whom the topic of 3C is relatively unfamiliar. Second, the chronological stages of Piaget's model allow for a unique presentation of cross-cultural skill development—specifically, the skills and facets identified as relevant to 3C can be separated from one another and discussed within the context of the stage at which their development is most readily facilitated. This is in contrast to other models of cognitive development, such as those of Vygotsky (1978) and Bruner (1966), which, despite their undoubted theoretical relevance, lack the necessary structure that makes a chronological presentation of cross-cultural skill development feasible. Although it should be understood that the application of Piaget's framework in this chapter and the recommendations provided herein are not intended to be prescriptive, they do serve to highlight ways in which educators may be able to incorporate activities or build upon experiences already utilized within the classroom to help cultivate critical cross-cultural skills in their students. Furthermore, addressing the development of these skills within the context of Piaget's framework may help educators identify points at which students are most likely to benefit from certain activities or experiences and prioritize their curricula accordingly.

CROSS-CULTURAL COMPETENCE: A BRIEF OVERVIEW

Before embarking on a discussion of how cross-cultural skills may be developed in the K–12 population, a brief review of the extant 3C literature, including some of its most well-known frameworks and relevant findings, is warranted.

As previously mentioned, 3C, like many other constructs (Le, Schmidt, Harter, & Lauver, 2010; Lubinski, 2004), has been referred to by researchers by a number of different names—a number that has continued to increase since initial work began on the subject more than three decades ago. Some of the earliest research pertaining to 3C focused on the development and training of cultural awareness in clinical psychologists who were faced with treating an increasingly diverse patient base (Sue, 1981; Sue et al., 1982; Wrenn, 1962). Perhaps not surprisingly, 3C research spread to the field of education with the goal of aiding teachers in overcoming the challenges of educating fully integrated, multiethnic classrooms (Banks, 1994; Little, 1993; McAllister & Irvine, 2000). An important caveat to this research, however, is that its focus was not on the development of cross-cultural skills within patients or students but, rather, the development of cross-cultural skills within the clinicians and teachers who were working with people from different cultural backgrounds. This trend of developing cross-culturally relevant skills in individuals who regularly interacted with culturally diverse groups grew to include medical practitioners

(Betancourt, 2003; Hojat et al., 2002; Purnell, 2012), first responders (Klein, Klein, Lande, Borders, & Whitacre, 2015), and lawyers (Bryant, 2001; Jacobs, 1997; Weng, 2004).

Although research in these areas was critical to ensuring the initial growth of the field, the often subjective nature of the work limited its scope of impact. It was not until the turn of the 21st century, when multicultural concerns were at the forefront of many organizational agendas, that researchers began developing frameworks and hypotheses by which to model and empirically validate their claims. This shift in focus spawned a multitude of theories that sought to address questions related to the structure, antecedents, and outcomes of 3C. Although the theories that have been developed to date are too numerous to comprehensively describe in this chapter, most can be characterized as belonging to one of two distinct groupings. The first grouping comprises theories or models that operationalize 3C as a multifaceted construct. In this sense, the "whole" of 3C is believed to be the sum of multiple, individual parts or subfacets. These subfacets are often operationalizable in their own right (e.g., openness to experience, perspective taking, metacognitive ability), but it is generally understood that they exist primarily in relation to the other subfacets that collectively make up 3C. The theory of cultural intelligence (CQ; Ang & Van Dyne, 2008; Earley & Ang, 2003) is one example of a multifaceted model. Inspired by traditional theories of intelligence, CQ is made up of four distinct but related factors: metacognitive CQ, cognitive CQ, motivational CQ, and behavioral CQ. Whereas metacognitive and cognitive CQ represent one's processing and organization of cultural knowledge, motivational and behavioral CQ represent one's willingness to engage in and adjust one's behavior during cross-cultural interactions. Previous research has shown CQ to predict numerous psychological, behavioral, and performance-related outcomes, including intercultural adjustment (Ang et al., 2007; Ward & Fischer, 2008), cooperation (Mor, Morris, & Joh, 2013), creativity, trust (Chua, Morris, & Mor, 2012), leadership performance, and multicultural team performance (Groves & Feyerherm, 2011).

The benefit of multifaceted models and theories is that they help deconstruct the contents of the 3C "black box." As a result of this work, for instance, there has been general consensus that 3C is made up of a combination of knowledge, skills, abilities, and other variables, such as personality, attitudes, and motivation (Leung, Ang, & Tan, 2014). The primary disadvantage of these models, however, is that they tend to operationalize 3C from an interindividual or between-persons perspective. In other words, multifaceted models do not explicitly account for the cognitive processes underlying 3C and its development. This can be potentially problematic, at least from a theoretical standpoint, because many of the subfacets identified in these models are actually quite malleable and readily developed through training or education (e.g., perspective taking, cultural awareness, and emotion regulation). As such, a second set of 3C models emerged that addressed these shortcomings directly. Unlike the multifaceted models, these models conceptualize 3C as a dynamic process that changes or develops in response to certain preconditions, individual differences, or contextual factors. According to these theories, 3C is less like a trait that an individual "possesses" and more like a process an individual "enacts" when navigating cross-cultural environments. One example of such process-based theories is the model developed by Thomas and colleagues (2008). Thomas' model conceptualizes 3C as a three-part system wherein one's cultural knowledge and culturally relevant skills are monitored, evaluated, and revised in response to feedback and information one receives from interpersonal interactions and the surrounding environment. This monitoring and evaluation of one's cognitive processes, referred to as cultural metacognition, is the keystone of Thomas' model in that it serves as the mechanism by which an individual's cultural knowledge and skills can be continuously updated and refined. The model's iterative design allows for endless opportunities through which individuals can improve the accuracy and efficiency of their cultural knowledge and skills, thereby increasing the likelihood of successful performance.

As previously mentioned, process models improve upon multifaceted models in that they capture the dynamic, developable nature of 3C. Often, however, process models depict the means by which 3C develops without specifying what 3C actually is. In other words, the strengths of the multifaceted models are the weaknesses of the process models (and vice versa). In an attempt to address both of these issues simultaneously, researchers from Educational Testing Service (ETS) and the US Army Research Institute (ARI) developed a comprehensive model of 3C that depicts not only the multiple components of 3C but also the means by which it develops (Brenneman, Klafehn, Burrus, Roberts, & Kochert, 2016). The ETS-ARI model is unique in that it is situated within the context of a cross-cultural interaction, such that the process of interacting with someone from a different cultural background is central to the operationalization of 3C. This process is broken into four steps, each of which progressively influences one's judgment of the situation and subsequent course of action. The first step of the process, *recognize*, reflects an individual's awareness of the situation as potentially influenced by cultural differences. Not surprisingly, self-awareness and cultural awareness are two of the skills identified as relevant to the recognize step. Once individuals have recognized that culture may influence the way an interaction unfolds, they progress to the second step in the process, *hypothesize*. The hypothesize step involves the generation of possible explanations for why an interaction has transpired and predictions about how different courses of action will influence the interaction going forward. Interpersonal skills, such as emotion recognition and perspective taking, as well as intrapersonal skills, such as metacognition, are reflected in the hypothesize step, as they help one to collect and interpret information that is necessary to generate such hypotheses and predictions. Having developed and considered a sufficient number of situationally relevant behavioral strategies, individuals must now determine which of those strategies they will enact. This third step, referred to as *decide*, is also represented in the model as a separate first step for those individuals who do not engage in the recognize and hypothesize steps prior to determining a course of action. Such automaticity in thinking can occur in cases in which the individual is familiar with the situation and the appropriate behavioral strategy is readily identifiable; this automaticity may also occur, however, in individuals who lack cross-cultural competence and are therefore less likely to consider the impact of their own and/or others' culture on the situation and its outcome. Whether premeditated or automatic, the elected strategy is enacted by individuals in the final step, *behave*. Skills related to communication, persuasion, and emotion management may be more or less applicable in this step, depending on the strategy that was ultimately selected. From here, individuals receive feedback in response to their behavior that can be positive, negative, and/or neutral in nature. This feedback, in turn, becomes a type of prior experience on which individuals can rely to inform future cross-cultural interactions.

Aside from its comprehensive coverage of the 3C domain, the ETS-ARI model highlights the components of 3C that are most amenable to training and development. The model's focus on development largely resulted from the overall purpose governing the research effort itself—that is, the Army's need to identify the components of 3C that soldiers could develop prior to, during, and following deployment overseas. Despite its military origins, however, the ETS-ARI model is universal in its conceptualization of 3C and 3C development over time. The model thus serves a dual purpose here in that it also illustrates which skills may be more readily developed in other populations, such as K–12 students.

Although not every individual will automatically engage in the four-step process when interacting cross-culturally, many of the skills contributing to or facilitating this process, including cultural awareness, metacognition, emotion perception, and perspective taking,[1] can be taught and subsequently implemented for use in future encounters. Thus, the key concern here is not identifying which components of 3C are developable but, rather, determining the best means by which to develop them. Decades of skills training research has suggested that in order to train a skill or behavior so as to reach levels of automaticity, singular, mass training events or interventions are rarely sufficient (Baddeley & Longman, 1978; Baldwin & Ford, 1988; Briggs & Naylor, 1962). Instead, training needs to be incorporated over the long term to ultimately be effective (Baddeley, 1990; Ericsson, Krampe, & Tesch-Römer, 1993), and it must be conducted in a context that is relevant to the trainee (Merrill, 2002; Noe & Colquitt, 2002). The development of cross-cultural skills is no different (Abbe & Gouge, 2012). Many cultural training programs, however, lack the continuous integration that is necessary for individuals to develop these skills adequately (Puck et al., 2008). Furthermore, suggesting to organizations or schools that they incorporate in-depth, cross-culturally focused skills training into their already full schedules or curricula is not a practical option. Instead, training should be incorporated holistically and focused according to its developmental relevance (i.e., which skills are best developed now vs. later) to maximize both its effectiveness and its efficiency. The following sections of this chapter seek to accomplish this very goal by marrying a selection of cross-culturally relevant skills with the cognitive stage(s) at which their development is most likely to be facilitated. In keeping with the suggestion that such training should be incorporated holistically, recommendations for how educators may be able to adapt their preexisting curricula to accommodate cross-cultural skills training with minimal interference are provided.

CROSS-CULTURAL COMPETENCE SKILL DEVELOPMENT ACROSS COGNITIVE STAGES

As discussed previously, this chapter's exploration of 3C skill development in K–12 populations utilizes Piaget's theory of cognitive development as its primary organizing framework. The work of Piaget was fundamental to the progression of research in developmental psychology, and it provided the field with one of the first theories of intellectual development in children and adolescents (Inhelder & Piaget, 1958; Piaget, 1952). Those who are familiar with Piaget's theory know that it conceptualizes cognitive development as a series of separate but interdependent stages. The first stage, known as the sensorimotor stage, is believed to start at birth and last until approximately 2 years of age. The sensorimotor stage represents the earliest phase of knowledge acquisition in children (facilitated largely through environmental exploration) and is hallmarked by the development of object permanence at approximately 7 months. From the sensorimotor stage, children progress to the second stage of cognitive development—the preoperational stage. The preoperational stage, which is thought to last from approximately 2 years of age until the age of 7 years, reflects a marked maturation in children's cognitive faculties, including the development of language skills and the ability to mentally represent objects, ideas, and events in memory or through imagination. Despite this growth, however, children's thinking remains highly egocentric throughout the duration of this stage, and their ability to understand problems or issues from multiple perspectives is notably absent. Rather, these higher-order cognitive processes do not begin to develop until the third stage, known as the concrete operational stage. The concrete operational stage, which is thought to occur between the ages of 7 and 11 years, is characterized by children's ability to integrate and apply logic to solving problems. At this stage, not only are children capable of making generalizations about observable phenomena but also they are able to do so with consideration of possible alternative solutions or perspectives. The caveat to the concrete operational stage, however, is that the application of logical thought is limited to concrete (i.e., subordinate) objects or stimuli. As such, children in the concrete operational stage generally struggle with solving problems that invoke hypothetical scenarios or abstract concepts. It is not until the fourth stage, the formal operational stage, that children (generally age 11 years or older) are able to think about and apply logic to abstract (i.e., superordinate) issues, such as those involving justice, faith, and ethics.

Although Piaget's multistage framework is regarded as one of the most influential theories of cognitive development to date, it does not stand without criticism (Bee & Boyd, 2010; Cohen, 1983; Lourenço & Machado, 1996; Siegel & Brainerd, 1978). Of primary concern to many critics is the fact that the theory does not stipulate why children progress from one stage to the next—just that such progression occurs and does so in a linear fashion (Brainerd, 1978; Cohen, 1983; Halford, 1989). Critics also take issue with the theory's exclusion of the influence of individual differences and social factors on cognitive development (Broughton, 1981; Ennis, 1978). Specifically, the theory fails to account for the different rates at which children are able to achieve stage-specific goals or milestones, an issue many critics suggest leads to the underestimation of children's true intellectual abilities. For instance, children who are exceptionally bright may progress through Piaget's four stages more quickly than others in their age cohort; similarly, children with learning disabilities or other cognitive impairments will likely progress at a substantially slower rate. It is also possible that some individuals may show progress or development through the four stages but only within particular domains—for example, a child may demonstrate a mastery of social skills but lack this same mastery with respect to mathematics. Piaget's theory, however, does not account for differential developmental paths, making it difficult to determine the stage (or stages) at which children should be properly classified.

Although an in-depth critique of Piaget's theory is outside the scope of this chapter, these criticisms are important to address here because they underscore the theory's intended application within the context of the present discussion—namely the use of Piaget's theory as an organizing framework is neither prescriptive nor diagnostic but, rather, serves as a means by which to illustrate the potential for cross-cultural skill development throughout various

Table 4.1 SUMMARY OF 3C SKILLS AND CORRESPONDING PIAGETIAN STAGES

3C Skill	Piagetian Stage
Self-awareness	Preoperational (grades K–2)
Metacognition	Late preoperational/early concrete operational (grades 2–4)
Emotion perception	Concrete operational/early formal operational (grades 3–7)
Perspective taking	Formal operational (grades 7–12)

stages of preadolescent growth. In the following sections, four skills identified as relevant to 3C are presented alongside the Piagetian stage(s) at which their development may be most readily facilitated (Table 4.1). In addition to a discussion of these skills (and the reasons why the association with their corresponding Piagetian stage is merited), recommendations for developmental activities or experiences are provided such that educators may find ways to incorporate them into preexisting curricula. Again, as with the application of Piaget's framework, these recommendations do not guarantee that cross-cultural skills will be developed, nor do they presuppose that the development of every skill will be applicable within every classroom or to every student. Instead, they should be considered as one of many possible avenues by which educators can aid students in acquiring the skills that will prepare them for entering the 21st century workforce.

SELF-AWARENESS
(STAGE: PREOPERATIONAL—GRADES K–2)

The Ancient Greek maxim, "know thyself" (Plato, trans. 1980), emphasizes the basic but fundamental importance of self-awareness to overall self-development. Although not always acknowledged as a prerequisite of 3C, self-awareness is a critical first step toward the development of cross-cultural skills (Bennett, 1986; Stewart, 1966). In the present context, self-awareness, or more specifically, cultural self-awareness, refers to the recognition and understanding that one is a product of one's culture. At first glance, the notion that one is influenced by culture may seem rather obvious; however, most individuals are rarely conscious of the role culture plays in their day-to-day life and interactions with others. Furthermore, many training interventions aimed at increasing cultural awareness often focus exclusively on how other cultures are different while neglecting to address the fact that the trainees themselves think and behave according to cultural norms (Kraemer, 1973). Consequently, individuals are unlikely to see or understand how their values and behavioral tendencies influence their interactions with other people, especially when those people are members of different cultures.

Emphasizing the development of cultural self-awareness at an early stage in training or education is important for two reasons. First, cultural self-awareness helps individuals establish a baseline for better identifying and understanding cultural differences in others (Bennett, 1986). Research has consistently shown that people generally prefer to associate with those with whom they share common or familiar traits (e.g., gender, race/ethnicity, culture; Allport, 1954). Although this tendency to prefer similar others can help provide individuals with a sense of identity and social belonging, it can also widen the perceived gap between one's in-group and those belonging to the out-group (Tajfel & Turner, 1979; Turner, 1975). This gap becomes particularly problematic when members of the in-group perceive out-group members' attitudes and behavior to be abnormal or wrong (or in-group members' attitudes and behavior to be normal and right; Brewer, 1999). Such dichotomized "us versus them" thinking fosters a culturally insular or ethnocentric mindset, which makes it increasingly difficult for individuals to look beyond their differences when engaging with those who do not share their same cultural background.

Albeit not a guaranteed remedy, the development of cultural self-awareness is one means by which cultural distance between groups can be reduced (or, perhaps more accurately, reinterpreted). As individuals gain cultural self-awareness, they begin to understand that their own motivations, preferences, and behavioral tendencies are the product of the same force that influences others' motivations, preferences, and behavior as well. Not surprisingly, the development of cultural self-awareness is more likely to succeed in individuals who have yet to crystallize their view of themselves relative to other people. Some research has shown that social preferences are demonstrated in children as young as 2 or 3 years old (Jacklin & Maccoby, 1978; LaFreniere, Strayer, & Gauthier, 1984), with racial or ethnic preferences emerging between the ages of approximately 3 and 5 years (Kinzler & Spelke, 2011). As such, the development of cultural self-awareness should begin as early in a child's life as possible.

Another reason why self-awareness is important to develop at an early age is that it serves as a necessary precursor for other, more cognitively complex skills. Much in the same way that a basement provides the foundation for a house, self-awareness provides the foundation for processes that invoke cognitions specific or relevant to the self. Metacognition and perspective taking, for instance, are both higher-order processes that require an awareness of one's own knowledge or knowledge of others, respectively, to function effectively. Both skills, however, are extremely difficult (if not impossible) to develop without a previously established awareness and understanding of the self and/ or its role in social contexts. Thus, by focusing on developing cultural self-awareness early in children's lives, educators can better facilitate the mastery of more advanced cross-cultural skills as students progress through later stages of cognitive development. The preoperational stage is therefore an ideal point at which to begin exploration of the role and influence of culture because the focus of the child at this stage is predominantly egocentric and oriented toward matters of the self.

Recommendations

Many of the techniques used to develop cultural self-awareness in the professional populations discussed previously (e.g., social workers, clinicians, teachers, and lawyers; Bryant, 2001; Gay & Kirkland, 2003; Roysircar, 2004) are also applicable to the development of cultural self-awareness in children. Of these techniques, the self-interview or self-reflection method is perhaps the easiest to implement and most likely to be successful with preoperational children because it focuses exclusively on matters concerning the self without necessitating any direct self–other comparisons, which may be too complex for children at this stage to process. The self-interview method, when applied in a classroom context, involves students answering questions and/or engaging in activities that help them explore various elements of their self-concept or identity. A straightforward application of this method is to have teachers hand out sheets of paper that feature a number of personally relevant questions to which students can respond (e.g., "What is your name?" "What is your favorite color?", "What is your favorite hobby?"). These questions will help students begin to identify the elements of their environment they see as a reflection of themselves, which in turn will contribute to the development and maturation of their self-schema (Markus, 1977). The questions students are asked can vary in terms of their topical coverage and complexity, but they should ultimately be geared toward students' age and cognitive ability level so as not to be too difficult to answer. For example, it will likely be easier for younger students to answer questions about what they like and dislike as opposed to what they believe and why they believe it. In addition to the self-interview, teachers can also have students represent their identity through visual media. For example, teachers can have students draw a picture of themselves surrounded by the people, places, and/or things they find personally meaningful. Similarly, students can create a collage of images and words cut out from magazines or other print sources that they see as representative of themselves.

Culturally relevant adaptations of the questionnaire and/or visual-media activities can also be implemented to help students begin exploring how culture shapes their preferences, values, and beliefs about themselves (Markus & Kitayama, 1991). One of the most readily accessible lenses through which students can gain awareness of their own cultural background is by exploring how cultural elements are manifested within their family. For example, students can discuss how their family celebrates holidays, whether their family maintains traditions, how their family likes to spend its free time, and what things their family views as important (e.g., getting good grades, having a clean room, and being nice to others). With older or more cognitively advanced students, teachers can further this discussion by asking students to reflect on why they think their family views certain things as important (e.g., regarding getting good grades, "My family wants me to be smart") and how, in turn, those things affect what they do (e.g., "If my family wants me to get good grades, then I have to study more often"). By couching the discussion of culture within the familial unit, children will not only begin to develop an awareness of how family values influence their thoughts and behavior but also be better prepared to explore the ways in which culture manifests itself within other interpersonal contexts.

METACOGNITION (STAGE: LATE PREOPERATIONAL/ EARLY CONCRETE OPERATIONAL—GRADES 2–4)

If self-awareness is to know oneself, then metacognition is the knowledge that one knows oneself. Metacognition, often defined as "thinking about thinking," represents the awareness, processing, and regulation of one's knowledge (Dunlosky, Serra, & Baker, 2007; Flavell, 1976). Like self-awareness, metacognition involves knowing about or being aware of one's own cognitive processes. This component of metacognition, referred to as metacognitive knowledge, reflects information about the self that is stored in memory much in the same way that information about people, objects, or ideas is also stored in memory (Flavell, 1976). Unlike self-awareness, however, metacognition also encompasses the monitoring and evaluation of one's knowledge, a component known as metacognitive experiences. It is through metacognitive experiences that individuals are able to identify new information, use that information to revise or update their schemas, and evaluate those schemas for accuracy. In this sense, metacognitive experiences are akin to Piaget's notion of assimilation and accommodation, such that new knowledge or information prompts individuals to determine whether their existing schemas are sufficient (assimilation) or must be revised (accommodation) to more accurately represent the knowledge they have acquired (Piaget, 1952). By continuously attending to and revising the knowledge they acquire, individuals are, in turn, able to apply their knowledge in more useful and adaptive ways.

Research on metacognition arose several decades ago in the field of education, in which the primary focus was on exploring individual differences in children's memorization processes (Dunlosky et al., 2007; Flavell, 1979). Some of the first studies in this area demonstrated that children who performed better on memorization tasks did so because of their use of cognitive strategies when memorizing test material (Flavell, Friedrichs, & Hoyt, 1970; Markman, 1977). High performers were also more accurate in evaluating their readiness to recall test material and in predicting how well they would perform prior to being tested. These findings were later expanded on in studies that investigated how metacognition functioned to help children solve novel, complex tasks. Specifically, children with higher metacognitive skill were not only able to solve novel problems more efficiently but also did so irrespective of their cognitive aptitude (Swanson, 1990). These results suggest that metacognitive skill may serve a compensatory role in situations in which one's knowledge is absent or deficient.

This compensatory characteristic is what makes metacognition particularly essential in cross-cultural contexts. Often, and particularly in new or unfamiliar environments, individuals find that their knowledge of or information pertaining to culturally relevant norms and practices is incomplete, outdated, or altogether unknown. In these situations, attempting to apply cultural knowledge that is otherwise flawed or inaccurate may yield less than successful results. As such, individuals must find a way to supplant their insufficient cultural knowledge with some other cognitive mechanism that will allow them to navigate their environment more effectively. By relying on their metacognitive processes to "fill in the gaps," individuals are able to make more efficient use of their knowledge by continuously regulating and evaluating it as they interact with their environment. It is important to note that metacognition does not simply replace "wrong" knowledge with "right" knowledge—it is still very possible (in fact, likely) that an individual who has a high level of metacognitive skill will possess some knowledge that is flawed or inaccurate. The difference between individuals with high metacognitive skill and those with low metacognitive skill, however, is that the former are able to recognize that the knowledge is flawed, seek means by which to correct it, and update it for future use (Kruger and Dunning, 1999). Thus, as the utility, application, and accuracy of knowledge change, metacognition allows individuals to change (and adapt) with it.

Piaget (1976) noted that children in the concrete operational stage exhibited an awareness of their own knowledge and thought processes, a phenomenon he referred to as cognizance. Other neo-Piagetian theorists have identified similar processes (e.g., hypercognition) that reflect the monitoring, regulation, and evaluation of knowledge, which are thought to be present in varying degrees throughout the course of a child's cognitive development (Case, 1985; Demetriou, 1998, 2000). In either case, metacognition and its related cognitive processes are likely to emerge once children have near fully developed a sense of self-awareness and are able to begin thinking about information in a multidimensional fashion. According to Piaget's stages, this transition point occurs sometime between the last years of the preoperational stage and the early years of the concrete operational stage.

Recommendations

One important observation from early research on metacognition was that children differed markedly in the extent to which they utilized metacognitive processes to help them solve problems. As such, educators may notice that some students will already demonstrate a strong predilection toward using metacognition in the classroom to help with their studies, whereas other students may not. Fortunately, metacognition is a developable skill (Brown & DeLoache, 1978; Fisher, 1998) and one that can be readily incorporated into curricula that emphasizes critical thinking and the application of different problem-solving strategies (Darling-Hammond, Austin, Cheung, & Martin, 2003). Given that metacognition is composed of multiple subprocesses (i.e., awareness/monitoring, revising, and evaluating), developing it in students necessitates a multifaceted approach.

The first step toward developing metacognitive skill in students is to help them cultivate an awareness of their own knowledge. This can be accomplished by encouraging students to reflect on what they know and what they do not know. There are a variety of approaches that educators can use to facilitate the reflection process in students, one of which is through the use of KWL charts (Ogle, 1986). KWL charts are three-column tables wherein each column represents a different stage of students' knowledge or understanding of a topic. The first column represents what students already know about a topic (K), the second column represents what students want to know about a topic (W), and the third column represents what students have learned about a topic (L). KWL charts were originally developed to help students improve their reading comprehension; however, they may also be useful for developing metacognitive skill in general. For example, before introducing a new topic (e.g., exploring what life is like in Japan), educators can ask students to write down or verbalize what they already know (or think they know) about the topic (e.g., "Japanese cuisine relies heavily on seafood", "Japan is crowded"). This same exercise is then repeated, but students are now asked to list either what they do not know or what they would like to know about the topic as they progress through the lesson (e.g., "What does a Japanese house look like?" "How is school in Japan different than school in the United States?", "What do Japanese children do in their free time?"). Whereas the former activity helps students identify the knowledge they have acquired about a particular subject matter, the latter activity helps students identify what information is needed to comprehend it more fully. As the lesson evolves and more new information is presented, students should be encouraged to revisit their lists to determine what they learned and whether their initial assumptions about the topic were correct or if revisions and/or additional questions are merited.

In addition to exploring awareness of their own knowledge, students should also be asked to reflect on their own thinking patterns and learning preferences. For example, when studying for a test, what method or strategy do students like to employ and why? Do they find this strategy useful? Have they tried other strategies, and if so, what did they like or not like about those strategies? By asking students to identify how they are able to acquire knowledge most efficiently, educators can help students individually maximize their learning potential and apply it to contexts in which new or complementary information must be sought.

Fostering self-awareness of one's knowledge and learning strategies serves as a foundation for the next two steps in developing metacognitive skill—the planning and evaluation of one's knowledge. Equipped with an awareness of what they know, what they do not know, and the best means by which to go about improving both, students are well prepared to begin self-directing their own learning and enrichment pursuits. It is at this stage in the developmental process that students should be encouraged to adopt an investigative approach to knowledge acquisition similar to the scientific method that is employed by researchers. The first step in this approach is to identify the problem. In most cases, the problem will consist of the preidentified knowledge the student wishes to acquire, but it may also reflect more systemic questions or hypotheses the student is interested in exploring. Using the previous example of learning about life in Japan, a student may wish to learn more about the kinds of leisure activities in which Japanese people engage during their free time. Once the problem has been identified, the student must then consider various strategies by which the problem could be solved. Educators can help facilitate this part of the process by providing students with questions to ask themselves (e.g., "Which strategy would be most appropriate given the problem I'm trying to solve?", "How do I know the strategy is working?"), as well as any available resources that may influence how useful a strategy is likely to be. To answer the student's question about leisure activities in Japan, for instance, the teacher may suggest that the student consult the Internet, read a book about Japanese culture, watch a movie about Japan, or talk with a friend or family member who has had experience living in Japan. From here, students elect the strategy they think is most well-suited for solving the problem, apply it, and monitor its effectiveness. Sometimes the first chosen strategy provides an ideal solution to the problem; in other cases, the strategy proves to be less than effective, and a new strategy must be implemented until a solution is reached. Often, students may undergo several iterations of strategy selection. The student, in an effort to learn about Japan, may have found through an Internet search that *onsen*, or natural hot spring spas, are a popular destination for many locals. The student may then (mistakenly) assume that all Japanese people visit *onsen*. Through additional exploration, whether self-initiated, educator-initiated, or both, the student may eventually discover that there exists a diverse array of leisure activities in Japan, many of which are actually similar to those practiced in the United States. From here, the student's knowledge of Japanese culture can be updated accordingly, and the metacognitive cycle continues. As students grow more familiar with using their metacognitive skills to both acquire and adjust their knowledge of other cultures, they will be better suited to adapting and applying that knowledge in cross-cultural contexts.

Given that knowledge, in general, and cultural knowledge, in particular, often fluctuate or are imperfect, it is important for educators to emphasize that trial and error is a normal part of the problem-solving process and that students should not feel discouraged if the first strategy they choose is not the most optimal means by which to solve the problem. Perseverance is an extremely important lesson for students to learn, not only as it applies to the development of one's metacognitive skill but also with respect to one's ability to constructively cope with personal setbacks or failures (Dweck, 1999). By encouraging students early on to view problems as solvable challenges rather than insurmountable obstacles, educators can better prepare students to think more flexibly and react more adaptively when faced with real-world concerns.

EMOTION PERCEPTION (STAGE: CONCRETE OPERATIONAL/EARLY FORMAL OPERATIONAL—GRADES 3–6)

The ability to perceive emotions in oneself and in others is essential not only in cross-cultural interactions but also in any interpersonal interaction in which emotions play a vital role. Being able to perceive emotions in oneself means being able to identify the emotion(s) one is experiencing, as well as recognize the influence emotions have on one's thoughts and behavior (Bem, 1972; Ben-Ze'ev, 2001; Lane, Quinlan, Schwartz, Walker, & Zeitlin, 1990; Lane & Schwartz, 1987). Similarly, being able to perceive emotions in others means being able to identify the emotion(s) others are experiencing, as well as recognize the possible reasons for why those individuals are displaying particular emotions in a given situation (Mayer & Salovey, 1997; Salovey & Mayer, 1990). Emotion perception serves a number of important functions that make it both a useful and an adaptive skill. First, individuals who can identify emotions within themselves, whether occurring independent of or in response to a salient stimulus, gain access to valuable information about their own well-being and present state of mind. For example, individuals who can recognize that they are feeling angry (as opposed to sad or ashamed) may be moved to act or retaliate against the target who they believe is to blame for causing the feeling of anger in the first place. On the other hand, individuals who are not as in touch with their own emotions may fail to recognize that the fatigue and lack of motivation they are experiencing are a result of some deeper rooted sadness or grief that may have occurred in response to a loss, insult, or failure. In both scenarios, emotions are providing individuals with valuable feedback about their current state, but only in the first scenario are they moving individuals to react in response to them.

In addition to its adaptive value to the self, emotion perception also serves an important function in interpersonal contexts. Much in the same way emotion perception provides one with feedback on one's state of well-being, emotion perception can also communicate valuable information about the state and well-being of others (Ben-Ze'ev, 2001; Salovey & Mayer, 1990). Not surprisingly, emotion perception plays an extremely important role in cross-cultural contexts, particularly in situations in which individuals are unable to communicate directly with one another due to a lack of shared or common language. In these instances, individuals must rely on nonverbal means of communication, such as gesturing and emotional expressions, to effectively relay and interpret messages. Whereas language can vary tremendously across cultures (and even within cultures), decades of research have shown that facial expressions of emotions tend to be culturally universal (Ekman, 1973, 1993; Ekman, Friesen, & Ancoli, 1980; Izard, 1980; Matsumoto, 1990). Studies have demonstrated, for instance, that as many as seven fundamental emotions, including happiness, fear, disgust, and anger, can be recognized regardless of the cultural background of the individual displaying the emotion or the individual perceiving the emotion (Biehl et al., 1997; Matsumoto, 1992). As such, individuals who are otherwise unable to communicate with each other via verbal or written means may still be able to effectively interact through the use of emotional displays and signaling gestures that help contextualize those displays. If one is aware of the context, then the emotional expressions of others may provide sufficient information as to how those individuals are reacting to contextual stimuli and, in turn, how one should act or react accordingly (Aviezer et al., 2008; Knudsen & Muzekari, 1983).

Finally, emotion perception functions as a precursor to other relevant skills, such as emotion regulation. Like emotion perception, emotion regulation can occur within the self as well as toward other people (Gross, 2007; Mayer & Salovey, 1995; Salovey & Mayer, 1990). With regard to the self, being able to regulate one's emotions helps individuals cope with emotionally provocative stimuli or events, as well as control their reactions in situations in which strong emotional displays may not be appropriate or prudent (Mayer & Salovey, 1997; Saarni, 1997). Furthermore, emotion self-regulation can help facilitate problem solving, such that those who have greater control over their own emotions are better able to direct activity toward and remain focused on the task at hand (Goleman, 1995; Mayer, Roberts, & Barsade, 2008). Emotion regulation directed toward others, on the other hand, functions as an influential force wherein an individual either directly or indirectly manipulates the feelings, perceptions, or emotional reactions of others (Goffman, 1959; Rimé, 2007; Salovey & Mayer, 1990; Zaki & Williams, 2013). In cross-cultural contexts, interpersonal emotion regulation is often used to help build rapport and trust (Williams, 2007), as well as de-escalate conflicts by redirecting people's negative emotions (e.g., fear) into a more manageable state (Halperin, Sharvit, & Gross, 2010). Similarly, members of a team can use emotion regulation to refocus the team's performance, as well as their own performance, in the face of threats or challenges (Jordan & Troth, 2002, 2004; Schlaerth, Ensari, & Christian, 2013). Regardless of its application, emotion regulation is a powerful skill that affords individuals the potential not only to manage but also to exert control over their environment.

Prior research has suggested that the development of emotional awareness, in general, is hallmarked by a series of structural transformations not unlike those corresponding to the development of cognitive processes (Lane & Schwartz, 1987). Unlike the development of cognitive processes, however, which is gauged by changes in one's organization of knowledge about the external world, the development of emotional awareness reflects changes in one's knowledge of one's emotions and emotional experiences. Whereas the development of emotional awareness is believed to begin as early as the sensorimotor stage, the development of more complex emotional skills, including emotion perception and emotion regulation, occurs much later in a child's life (Cowan, 1978; Nannis & Cowan, 1987). This is largely because, in developing these skills, children need to be capable of identifying and articulating their emotional experiences in a way that others can understand. It is therefore suggested that the development of emotion self-perception begin at the onset of the concrete operational stage, with increasingly more complex skills (i.e., emotion self-regulation, interpersonal emotion perception, and interpersonal emotion regulation) being introduced throughout the progression of the concrete operational stage and into the formal operational stage.

Recommendations

As previously discussed, emotional perception most readily coincides with the early concrete operational stage of cognitive development in which children are beginning to grow out of their purely egocentric mindset and interact more meaningfully with their environment. Given that children, by this stage, are generally comfortable discussing their own perspectives, the application of an inquiry-based approach to exploring their emotions is ideal. An inquiry-based approach to developing emotional perception is a straightforward method wherein teachers ask students emotionally relevant questions (Perez, 2011). When first implementing this approach, the questions to be asked should be fairly simple. For example, teachers could inquire how many different feelings students can name or how students are feeling "right now." These questions, aside from being easily accessible to students, encourage the development of an emotional vocabulary, thereby making emotions themselves easier to iden- tify and discuss later in the developmental process (Joseph & Strain, 2003). Once emotions have become integrated as part of regular conversation in the classroom, teachers can begin increasing the complexity of the questions they ask. For example, teachers could present various hypothetical situations to which students would respond as if they were experiencing the situations themselves. Students could be asked to imagine that a younger sibling had bro- ken their favorite toy or that someone else had won an award for which they were competing. From here, students would be prompted with questions such as "How would you feel?" "How would you behave as soon as you found out?" and "What would you do after the fact?" By asking students to visualize their own emotional reactions to events, teachers can begin to help students develop and understand their own emotional repertoire, as well as the ways in which emotions influence their behavior, decision-making processes, and interactions with others.

Being able to identify emotions in the self facilitates the development of more complex skills, such as identifying emotions in others and emotion regu- lation. Developing an awareness of emotions in others follows a similar trajec- tory as the development of emotional awareness in the self with the exception that the cues signaling emotional expression are manifested externally as opposed to internally. Thus, students must learn to identify which observable characteristics are indicative of particular emotions and be able to interpret them accordingly. As with emotional self-perception, the development of inter- personal emotion perception can be facilitated through the application of an inquiry-based approach. In this case, however, teachers would ask students questions focused on how different emotions "look" and "sound." This could involve passive activities, such as having students identify emotions displayed on flashcards, in magazines, or in other visual media. Specifically, students would name the emotion and then articulate what it was about the face, body movement, and/or voice that led them to their conclusion (e.g., downturned eyebrows and a frown suggest the person is angry; Ekman, 1973). In contrast, a more active approach would involve students demonstrating emotions themselves for others to observe. For example, the teacher could ask students to show what happiness looks like and then discuss what the students see in one another as they look around the classroom. Teachers could also ask students to demonstrate their emotional expressions in response to different contexts (e.g., "Imagine you won a spelling contest versus imagine you found out you were going to have a baby sister"). Not only does this help students become better at identifying emotions in general but it also allows them to see how emotions can be expressed differently in different people and in response to different situations—a skill that is very useful in cross-cultural contexts in which the outward expression and intensity of some emotions may vary (Ekman et al., 1987; Matsumoto, 1993).

Once students are capable of identifying emotions in themselves and in others, they can use what they know about emotions to influence and regulate their own and others' emotional responses. The development of emotional self-regulation is akin to the development of coping strategies in that both help to mitigate the negative effects of stressors (Brenner & Salovey, 1997). Because stressors vary in terms of their controllability, however, different emotion regulation strategies can be more or less effective in meeting the demands of different stressors (Lazarus & Folkman, 1984). Furthermore, individual differences, such as age (Nolen-Hoeksema & Aldao, 2011), gender (Brenner & Salovey, 1997), and cultural background (Gross & John, 2003; John & Gross, 2004), influence the types of emotion regulation strategies individuals tend to employ. As such, there are a variety of approaches teachers can use to encourage the development of emotional self-regulation in their students, as well as help them identify which regulatory strategies are most effective in dealing with different stressors. One such approach is to discuss with students the ways in which they have handled various stressful situations in the past or would handle similar situations in the future (Webster-Stratton, 1992). To begin this discussion, the teacher would either present or ask students to generate a number of situations that they would find stressful or anxiety provoking (e.g., taking a test, giving a speech, being the new kid in school, getting lost in a store). The teacher would then prompt students to identify a number of different ways they could approach each situation. Teachers should encourage students to identify a wide range of strategies that vary in terms of their effectiveness, reliance on others (i.e., social support), and use of external (e.g., exercise, breathing deeply) versus internal (e.g., cognitive reframing) activities so that they can gain awareness of new strategies, as well as discuss which strategies are more or less effective across different situations. For example, in response to being teased by a friend, students could evaluate how ignoring the situation, talking to the friend about how being teased hurt their feelings, or yelling angrily at the friend would lead to different emotional outcomes and which, among those outcomes, would be most desirable. Teachers can also encourage students to implement emotion regulation strategies in response to stressors they are currently experiencing. For example, teachers can set aside a few minutes each day to allow students time for quiet reflection (Lantieri, 2008a, 2008b). During this time, students can practice stress-reduction techniques (e.g., deep breathing, progressive muscle relaxation) and/or reflect on what they are seeing, hearing, or feeling at that moment. By making reflection a part of students' daily routine, teachers can not only promote students' ability to control and regulate their emotions but also help them gain awareness of and actively manage ongoing stressors.

In contrast to emotional self-regulation, learning to regulate the emotions of others involves identifying what others are feeling, making inferences about why they are feeling that way, and determining what about the situation or individual can be changed in order to alter those feelings. Because this inferential process necessitates the use of perspective taking (discussed in the following section), interpersonal emotion regulation is decidedly more complex to develop in children and is therefore best suited to those who have reached the late concrete operational or early formal operational stage of development. Nevertheless, there are still a number of exercises teachers can use with students early on to help facilitate later, more advanced applications of this very influential interpersonal skill. Many of the exercises focusing on the development of interpersonal emotion regulation in children involve the modeling of empathic responses (Slaby, Roedell, Arezzo, & Hendrix, 1995). In these exercises, the teacher, often with the help of a teaching aid (e.g., a stuffed animal or a hand puppet) or student volunteer, demonstrates a situation in which someone is distressed (Adams & Baronberg, 2005). The teacher, for instance, can privately instruct the student volunteer to pretend to fall down and get hurt. The teacher then proceeds to ask students to identify what is going on in the situation based on the behavior they observed and the emotions the student volunteer is expressing. Asking questions such as "What just happened?" "How do you think he is feeling right now?" and "How would you feel if you were in the same situation?" will help students begin gathering the necessary details to inform their next steps. From here, the teacher prompts students to generate different means by which to make the student volunteer feel better (i.e., change the student's negative feelings into positive ones). The teacher or the students themselves present these approaches to the student volunteer, who would then react based on the effectiveness of each approach. When concluding the exercise, teachers should encourage students to apply the steps they learned in the classroom to situations they encounter outside of the classroom. In doing so, students will become increasingly more attentive and efficient consumers of situational and interpersonal knowledge, which in turn will make complex skills, such as perspective taking, easier for them to develop.

PERSPECTIVE TAKING (STAGE: FORMAL OPERATIONAL – GRADES 6–12)

As alluded to in the previous section, perspective taking is perhaps one of the most challenging skills to develop because it requires not only an understanding and awareness of one's own values, beliefs, and preferences but also the skill and willingness to perceive and understand the values, beliefs, and preferences of others. Simply stated, perspective taking is the ability to see the world from another's point of view (Galinsky, Ku, & Wang, 2005). The act of perspective taking involves taking into consideration the thoughts, feelings, and motivations of other people, often with the goal of reaching a clearer understanding as to why a particular individual behaved or reacted to a situation in a particular way. In some contexts, perspective taking can be used as a means to foster sympathy or empathy, two similar but distinct constructs that involve, respectively, the concern for another's well-being (Wispé, 1986) and the sharing in another's emotional experience (Duan & Hill, 1996; Eisenberg & Miller, 1987). Perspective taking can also influence stereotyping and in-group preferences, such that those who engage in perspective taking show decreased stereotypic biases and increased evaluations of out-groups relative to their in-group (Galinsky & Moskowitz, 2000).

In cross-cultural contexts, perspective taking is just as important, but it is also increasingly more complex because one must take into account the cultural influences that serve to shape the worldview and resulting behavior of others. Throughout the past decade, a great deal of research has been conducted that has explored perspective taking in groups of individuals who frequently work with diverse populations, such as soldiers (Rentsch, Gunderson, Goodwin, & Abbe, 2007; Rentsch, Mot, & Abbe, 2009) and medical professionals (Bentancourt, 2003; Hojat et al., 2002; Kumagai, 2008; Purnell, 2012). For these groups, perspective taking is critical in that it not only helps them accomplish their tasks more effectively but also allows them to work with others in accordance with their cultural norms—a consideration, in some situations, that can mean the difference between gaining an ally and creating an enemy.

The utility of perspective taking as a cross-cultural skill comes at the price of it being one of the most difficult skills to develop. The primary reason why it poses such a challenge is that it requires complete suspension of egocentric thought—a skill even many adults find both effortful and difficult to master (Epley, Keysar, Van Boven, & Gilovich, 2004; Epley, Morewedge, & Keysar, 2004; see also Gilovich, Medvec, & Savitsky, 2000). Perspective taking also requires a basic working knowledge of the cultural norms attributable to the individual or group whose perspective one is trying to take. In other words, the successful development of perspective taking requires that individuals have attained a certain level of cognitive maturity—in this case, a level that is reflective of individuals who are in the formal operational stage.

By the time children have reached the formal operational stage, they not only possess a more elaborate theory of mind but also are capable of applying deductive reasoning to solving problems (Inhelder & Piaget, 1958). Deductive reasoning, or the process of using general principles to predict specific outcomes, is a cornerstone of perspective taking, wherein cultural norms serve as the general principles that are used to predict or understand specific behavioral outcomes or responses. Although perspective taking does not ensure that every prediction one makes about the behavior of others will be accurate, it does help to refine one's schema of other cultures so that future interactions are likely to be more efficient and effective.

Recommendations

In this chapter's discussion of cross-cultural skills, perspective taking is presented last for one very important reason: Its development is contingent on the relative mastery of the three skills that precede it (i.e., self-awareness, metacognition, and emotion recognition). As such, the progressive steps leading toward the development of perspective taking closely mirror the order in which those three foundational skills are also developed. It naturally follows, then, that the first step toward developing perspective taking is to generate awareness that differences in perspective exist. There are a number of ways by which teachers can accomplish this with students. One method is simply to encourage discussion of a subjective topic and allow students to share their own opinions or perspectives on the matter. For example, students could be asked to explain what being a friend means to them. Although the topic of discussion does not need to be overly complex or divisive, it should illustrate the principle that it is possible for different people to have different viewpoints on the same issue. From here, teachers can advance the discussion by exploring topics that have greater real-world implications and consequences. Students can be asked to write two essays, for example, each arguing one side of a debatable topic, such as censorship or foreign aid and intervention. Similarly, students can discuss instances in the media in which different perspectives are given on a particular current event. Students can also be shown videos or articles that express one individual's or group's point of view on a subject and then be asked to generate a number of alternative perspectives that correspond to the other individuals or groups who may be implicated in the discussion of that subject. This latter activity, also referred to as a "lensperson assignment" (Colvin-Burque, Zugazaga, & Davis-Maye, 2007), is particularly beneficial in that it not only facilitates perspective taking but also helps students hone their critical thinking skills by emphasizing the importance of being a discerning consumer of information.

Once students are comfortable identifying and generating alternative perspectives across a variety of topics, teachers can begin to introduce the role of deductive reasoning as a means by which to predict the feelings, thoughts, and behaviors of the individuals who hold those perspectives. It is in the application of deductive reasoning that perspective taking assumes real utility in interpersonal interactions because it reflects not only the awareness that other perspectives exist but also the ability to hypothesize how those perspectives will influence future behavior and outcomes (Van Boven & Lowenstein, 2005). By predicting how others may respond to certain stimuli, one is afforded the potential to direct, manage, or, in some cases, completely alter the course of events. In cross-cultural contexts, the ability to accurately predict others' reactions could result in any number of outcomes, from successfully avoiding a faux pas to persuading members of another culture to make a decision or act in a particular way.

Like any other skill, predicting the thoughts, feelings, and behavior of others takes practice. In the classroom, students can begin exploring the method of prediction by watching a movie and deducing the ending based on what they have observed from the characters up until that point (Narvaez & Endicott, 2001). Essential to this exercise is the identification and elaboration of the characters' perspectives, emotions, and motives, with a particular focus on the reason(s) why the story would end the way the student predicted it would do so. Once students have shared their predictions, the class finishes the movie and discusses the actual ending and why it makes sense (or does not) with respect to the characters' motives and viewpoints. This same activity can be replicated using lesser known historical events or in-class role playing between students. In the latter case, the teacher would provide students with a scenario involving a number of characters, their characters' motives, and the scenario's end result. The students then act out the scenario as other students observe. This activity is mutually beneficial in that the students who are role playing are taking on the perspective of the characters they are portraying, whereas the rest of the class benefits by trying to deduce, through both verbal and nonverbal indicators, how the characters are feeling, thinking, and likely to respond. Through these activities, educators can encourage students to actively attend to and evaluate social information, both of which contribute to the overall development and successful application of perspective taking in interpersonal interactions, cross-cultural or otherwise.

IMPLICATIONS AND FUTURE DIRECTIONS

The skills discussed in the preceding sections reflect just four of the many skills and competencies employers view as important for individuals to develop prior to their entry into the 21st century workforce. Educational settings are, without a doubt, one of the most viable contexts in which to facilitate development of these skills; burgeoning demands for student and teacher time, however, make the implementation of independent training programs within the classroom largely impractical. The goal of this chapter was to address these challenges by providing recommendations for how educators can incorporate 3C-relevant skills training into preexisting curricula in such a way that, from a cognitive–developmental perspective, maximizes efficiency while minimizing interference.

Whereas the primary focus of this chapter was on the development of these skills as they relate to 3C, there are a number of other, non-cross-cultural contexts in which these skills are equally valuable. The development of self-awareness, for example, is important not only in helping individuals understand how culture influences their thoughts and behaviors but also in shaping their sense of identity and self-worth (Markus, 1977; Phinney, 1990). Research has shown that the exploration of one's cultural background or ethnic heritage can lead to greater self-acceptance, which in turn helps foster one's self-esteem and self-efficacy (Martinez & Dukes, 1997; Phinney, 1993). The development of metacognition, emotional awareness, and perspective taking also has important implications that extend beyond the cross-cultural domain. For example, metacognition is applicable to nearly any problem-solving context in which one's knowledge may be lacking or insufficient; likewise, emotional awareness and perspective taking play vital roles in nearly any interpersonal context in which judgments about others are necessitated. In other words, these four skills, although facilitative of cross-cultural performance in particular, are equally as important in facilitating interpersonal performance in general. Thus, time devoted to developing these skills in the classroom should not necessarily be thought of as focused exclusively on improving students' functioning in cross-cultural situations but, rather, improving students' overall functioning and performance across a wide range of contexts and settings.

It should also be noted that the development of these skills, although presented in this chapter as corresponding to specific Piagetian stages, is perhaps more accurately conceptualized as a continuous process that transcends age and cognitive–developmental level. Although it is still important that these skills be introduced at a young age so as to promote familiarity and encourage automaticity, individuals should constantly seek to improve the usage of their skills as they gather more information about their environment and encounter more situations in which they find their skills to be applicable. Fortunately, individuals can begin expanding the application and, in turn, generalizability of their skills well before they transition into adulthood. To promote skill generalization, teachers should encourage students to apply their newly learned skills to a variety of situations, both inside and outside the classroom. These situations can take place in familiar settings, such as in day-to-day interactions with peers and family members, but they should also take place, where possible, in contexts that are less familiar to students, such as those encountered during field trips or immersion experiences. By being given new, "real-world" opportunities in which to perform, students are able not only to demonstrate that they have sufficiently developed their skills such that they can effectively apply them to new situations but also to reinforce the skills they have learned by understanding their utility in novel contexts.

There is, of course, a caveat to this discussion, which is evident most notably in the lack of empirical research validating the effectiveness of the recommendations provided herein. At the beginning of the chapter, it was emphasized that these recommendations, aside from not constituting a one-size-fits-all approach, did not guarantee that 3C or 3C-relevant skills would be developed as a result of their implementation. The main justification for this qualifying remark is the fact that no formal studies have been conducted explicitly testing whether these recommendations impact one's level of 3C or cross-cultural performance. This is not to say, however, that these recommendations lack merit or should not be considered as potential means by which to help students advance their cognitive and interpersonal capabilities. Rather, expectations regarding the extent to which these recommendations are directly implicated in the development of 3C and 3C-relevant skills should be tempered. Provided that cross-cultural performance continues to be a top priority for both educators and employers, researchers should take measures to explore the validity of these and other recommendations as viable methods by which to develop 3C in educational contexts.

CONCLUSION

The nature of the 21st century workforce increasingly necessitates the development of skills that will aid organizations in meeting new and often unpredictable challenges. With globalization increasing at an unprecedented rate, the demand for employees capable of navigating such challenges within diverse, multicultural settings will undoubtedly increase as well. By prioritizing the development of cross-culturally relevant skills in the classroom, educators can help students address some of these challenges early in their careers so that they are adequately prepared to address them upon entering the workforce.

NOTE

1. For a more comprehensive list of skills, abilities, and other variables relevant to or comprising 3C, see Abbe, Gulick, and Herman (2007).

REFERENCES

Abbe, A., & Gouge, M. (2012, July–August). Cultural training for military personnel: Revisiting the Vietnam era. *Military Review*, 9–17.

Abbe, A., Gulick, L. M. V., & Herman, J. L. (2007). *Cross-cultural competence in Army leaders: A conceptual and empirical foundation* (Study Report 2008-01). Arlington, VA: US Army Research Institute for the Behavioral and Social Sciences.

Adams, S. K., & Baronberg, J. (2005). *Promoting positive behavior: Guidance strategies for early childhood settings*. Columbus, OH: Merrill.

Allport, G. W. (1954). *The nature of prejudice*. Cambridge, MA: Addison-Wesley.

Ang, S., & Van Dyne, L. (Eds.). (2008). *Handbook of cultural intelligence*. New York, NY: Sharpe.

Ang, S., Van Dyne, L., Koh, C., Ng, K. Y., Templer, K. J., Tay, C., & Chandrasekar, N. A. (2007). Cultural intelligence: Its measurement and effects on cultural judgment and decision making, cultural adaptation, and task performance. *Management and Organizational Review*, *3*, 335–371.

Aviezer, H., Hassin, R. R., Ryan, J., Grady, C., Susskind, J., Anderson, A., . . . Bentin, S. (2008). Angry, disgusted, or afraid? Studies on the malleability of emotion perception. *Psychological Science*, *19*, 724–732.

Baddeley, A. D. (1990). *Human memory: Theory and practice*. Boston, MA: Allyn & Bacon.

Baddeley, A. D., & Longman, D. J. A. (1978). The influence of length and frequency of training session on the rate of learning to type. *Ergonomics*, *21*, 627–635.

Baldwin, T. T., & Ford, J. K. (1988). Transfer of training: A review and directions for future research. *Personnel Psychology*, *41*, 63–105.

Banks, J. (1994). *Multiethnic education: Theory and practice*. Needham Heights, MA: Allyn & Bacon.

Bee, H. L., & Boyd, D. (2010). *The developing child*. Boston, MA: Allyn & Bacon.

Bem, D. J. (1972). Self-perception theory. *Advances in Experimental Social Psychology, 6*, 1–62.

Bennett, J. M. (1986). Modes of cross-cultural training: Conceptualizing cross-cultural training as education. *International Journal of Intercultural Relations, 10*, 117–134.

Ben-Ze'ev, A. (2001). *The subtlety of emotions*. Cambridge, MA: MIT Press.

Betancourt, J. R. (2003). Cross-cultural medical education: Conceptual approaches and frameworks for evaluation. *Academic Medicine, 78*, 560–569.

Biehl, M., Matsumoto, D., Ekman, P., Hearn, V., Heider, K., Kudoh, T., & Ton, V. (1997). Matsumoto and Ekman's Japanese and Caucasian Facial Expressions of Emotion (JACFEE): Reliability data and cross-national differences. *Journal of Nonverbal Behavior, 21*, 3–21.

Blake, B. F., & Heslin, R. (1983). Evaluating cross-cultural training. In D. Landis & R. W. Brislin (Eds.), *Handbook of intercultural training* (pp. 203–223). New York, NY: Pergamon.

Brainerd, C. (1978). The stage question in cognitive–developmental theory. *Behavioral and Brain Sciences, 2*, 173–213.

Brenneman, M. W., Klafehn, J. L., Burrus, J., Roberts, R. D., & Kochert, J. (2016). Assessing cross-cultural competence: A Working Framework and Prototype Measures for Use in Military Contexts. In J. L. Wildman, R. L. Griffith, & B. K. Armon (Eds.), *Critical issues in cross-cultural management* (pp. 103–131). Cham, Switzerland: Springer.

Brenner, E. M., & Salovey, P. (1997). Emotion regulation during childhood: Developmental, interpersonal, and individual considerations. In P. Salovey & D. J. Sluyter (Eds.), *Emotional development and emotional intelligence: Educational implications* (pp. 168–195). New York, NY: Basic Books.

Brewer, M. B. (1999). The psychology of prejudice: Ingroup love or outgroup hate? *Journal of Social Issues, 55*, 429–444.

Briggs, G. E., & Naylor, J. C. (1962). The relative efficiency of several training methods as a function of transfer task complexity. *Journal of Experimental Psychology, 64*, 505–512.

Broughton, J. (1981). Piaget's structural developmental psychology: 4. Knowledge without a self and without history. *Human Development, 24*, 320–346.

Brown, A. L., & DeLoache, J. S. (1978). Skills, plans, and self-regulation. In R. S. Siegler (Ed.), *Children's thinking: What develops?* (pp. 3–36). Hillsdale, NJ: Erlbaum.

Bruner, J. (1966). *Toward a theory of instruction*. Cambridge, MA: Belknap.

Brux, J., & Fry, B. (2009). Multicultural students in study abroad: Their interests, their issues, and their constraints. *Journal of Studies in International Education, 20*, 1–20.

Bryant, S. (2001). The five habits: Building cross-cultural competence in lawyers. *Clinical Law Review, 8*, 33–107.

Carlson, J. S., Burns, B. B., Useem, J., & Yachimowicz, D. (1990). *Study abroad: The experience of American undergraduates in western Europe and the United States*. New York, NY: Greenwood Press.

Case, R. (1985). *Intellectual development. Birth to adulthood*. New York, NY: Academic Press.

Casner-Lotto, J., & Barrington, L. (2006). *Are they really ready to work? Employers' perspectives on the knowledge and applied skills of new entrants to the 21st century U.S. workforce.* New York, NY: The Conference Board, Corporate Voices for Working Families, Partnership for 21st Century Skills, and Society for Human Resource Management. Retrieved from https://www.conference-board.org/pdf_free/BED-06-Workforce.pdf

Chua, R. Y. J., Morris, M. W., & Mor, S. (2012). Collaborating across cultures: Cultural metacognition and affect-based trust in creative collaboration. *Organizational Behavior and Human Decision Processes, 118,* 116–131.

Cohen, D. (1983). *Piaget: Critique and assessment.* London, England: Croom Helm.

Colvin-Burque, A., Zugazaga, C. B., & Davis-Maye, D. (2007). Can cultural competence be taught? Evaluating the impact of the SOAP model. *Journal of Social Work Education, 43,* 223–242.

Cowan, P. A. (1978). *Piaget: With feeling: Cognitive, social, and emotional dimensions.* New York, NY: Holt Rinehart & Winston.

Darling-Hammond, L., Austin, K., Cheung, M., & Martin, D. (2003). *Session 9: Thinking about thinking: Metacognition* [Course materials]. Retrieved from http://www.learner.org/courses/learningclassroom/support/09_metacog.pdf

Deardorff, D. K. (2006). Identification and assessment of intercultural competence as a student outcome of internationalization. *Journal of Student International Education, 10,* 241–266.

Demetriou, A. (1998). Cognitive development. In A. Demetriou, W. Doise, & K. F. M. van Lieshout (Eds.), *Life-span developmental psychology* (pp. 179–269). London, England: Wiley.

Demetriou, A. (2000). Organization and development of self-understanding and self-regulation. In M. Boekaerts, P. R., Pintrich, & M. Zeidner (Eds.), *Handbook of self-regulation* (pp. 209–251). New York, NY: Academic Press.

Duan, C., & Hill, C. E. (1996). The current state of empathy research. *Journal of Counseling Psychology, 43,* 261–274.

Dunlosky, J., Serra, M. J., & Baker, J. M. C. (2007). Metamemory. In F. Durso (Ed.), *Handbook of applied cognition* (2nd ed., pp. 137–160). Hoboken, NJ: Wiley.

Dweck, C. S. (1999). *Self-theories: Their role in motivation, personality and development.* Philadelphia, PA: Psychology Press.

Earley, P. C., & Ang, S. (2003). *Cultural intelligence: Individual interactions across cultures.* Stanford, CA: Stanford University Press.

Eisenberg, N., & Miller, P. A. (1987). The relation of empathy to prosocial and related behaviors. *Psychological Bulletin, 101,* 91–119.

Ekman, P. (1973). *Darwin and facial expression: A century of research in review.* Oxford, England: Academic Press.

Ekman, P. (1993). Facial expression and emotion. *American Psychologist, 48,* 384–392.

Ekman, P., Friesen, W. V., & Ancoli, S. (1980). Facial signs of emotional experience. *Journal of Personality and Social Psychology, 39,* 1125–1134.

Ekman, P., Friesen, W. V., O'Sullivan, M., Chan, A., Diacoyanni-Tarlatzis, I., Heider, K., . . . Tzavaras, A. (1987). Universals and cultural differences in the judgments of facial expressions of emotion. *Journal of Personality and Social Psychology, 53,* 712–717.

Ennis, R. (1978). Conceptualization of children's logical competence: Piaget's proposi-tional logic and an alternative proposal. In L. Siegel & C. Brainerd (Eds.), *Alternatives to Piaget* (pp. 201–260). New York, NY: Academic Press.

Epley, N., Keysar, B., Van Boven, L., & Gilovich, T. (2004). Perspective taking as ego-centric anchoring and adjustment. *Journal of Personality and Social Psychology, 87,* 327–339.

Epley, N., Morewedge, C. K., & Keysar, B. (2004). Perspective taking in children and adults: Equivalent egocentrism but differential correction. *Journal of Experimental Social Psychology, 40,* 760–768.

Ericsson, K. A., Krampe, R. T., & Tesch-Römer, C. (1993). The role of deliberate practice in the acquisition of expert performance. *Psychological Review, 100,* 363–406.

Fisher, R. (1998). Thinking about thinking: Developing metacognition in children. *Early Child Development and Care, 141,* 1–15.

Flavell, J. H. (1976). Metacognitive aspects of problem solving. In L. B. Resnick (Ed.), *The nature of intelligence* (pp. 231–235). Hillsdale, NJ: Erlbaum.

Flavell, J. H. (1979). Metacognition and cognitive monitoring: A new area of cognitive–developmental inquiry. *American Psychologist, 34,* 906–911.

Flavell, J. H., Friedrichs, A. G., & Hoyt, J. D. (1970). Developmental changes in memo-rization processes. *Cognitive Psychology, 1,* 324–340.

Fowler, S. M., & Mumford, M. G. (Eds.). (1995). *Intercultural sourcebook: Cross-cultural training methods* (Vol. 1). Yarmouth, ME: Intercultural Press.

Fowler, S. M., & Mumford, M. G. (Eds.). (1999). *Intercultural sourcebook: Cross-cultural training methods* (Vol. 2). Yarmouth, ME: Intercultural Press.

Fry, G. W., Paige, R. M., Jon, J. E., Dillow, J., & Nam, K. A. (2009). *Study abroad and its transformative power* (Occasional Paper No. 32). New York, NY: Council on International Education Exchange.

Galinsky, A. D., Ku, G., & Wang, C. S. (2005). Perspective-taking and self–other over-lap: Fostering social bonds and facilitating social coordination. *Group Processes & Intergroup Relations, 8,* 109–124.

Galinsky, A. D., & Moskowitz, G. B. (2000). Perspective-taking: Decreasing stereotype expression, stereotype accessibility, and in-group favoritism. *Journal of Personality and Social Psychology, 78,* 708–724.

Gallus, J. A., Gouge, M. C., Antolic, E., Fosher, K., Jasparro, V., Coleman, S., . . . Klafehn, J. L. (2014). Cross-cultural competence in the Department of Defense: An annotated bibliography (SR-71). Arlington, VA: US Army Research Institute for the Behavioral and Social Sciences.

Gay, G., & Kirkland, K. (2003). Developing cultural critical consciousness and self-reflection in preservice teacher education. *Theory into Practice, 42,* 181–187.

Gilovich, T., Medvec, V. H., & Savitsky, K. (2000). The spotlight effect in social judg-ment: An egocentric bias in estimates of the salience of one's own actions and appear-ance. *Journal of Personality and Social Psychology, 78,* 211–222.

Goffman, E. (1959). *The presentation of self in everyday life.* Garden City, NY: Doubleday.

Goleman, D. (1995). *Emotional intelligence: Why it can matter more than IQ.* New York, NY: Bantam Books.

Gross, J. J. (Ed.). (2007). *Handbook of emotion regulation.* New York, NY: Guilford.

Gross, J. J., & John, O. P. (2003). Individual differences in two emotion regulation processes: Implications for affect, relationships, and well-being. *Journal of Personality and Social Psychology, 85,* 348–362.

Groves, K. S., & Feyerherm, A. E. (2011). Leader cultural intelligence in context: Testing the moderating effects of team cultural diversity on leader and team performance. *Group & Organization Management, 36,* 535–566.

Gudykunst, W. B., & Hammer, M. R. (1983). Basic training design: Approaches to intercultural training. In D. Landis & R. W. Brislin (Eds.), *Handbook of intercultural training: Issues in theory and design* (pp. 118–154). New York, NY: Pergamon.

Halford, G. (1989). Reflections on 25 years of Piagetian cognitive developmental psychology, 1963–1988. *Human Development, 32,* 325–357.

Halperin, E., Sharvit, K., & Gross, J. J. (2010). Emotion and emotion regulation in intergroup conflict: An appraisal based framework. In D. Bar-Tal (Ed.), *Intergroup conflicts and their resolution: Social psychological perspectives* (pp. 83–104). New York, NY: Psychology Press.

Hammer, M. R., & Bennett, M. J. (1998). *The Intercultural Development Inventory (IDI) manual.* Portland, OR: Intercultural Communication Institute.

Hammer, M. R., Bennett, M. J., & Wiseman, R. (2003). Measuring intercultural sensitivity: The Intercultural Development Inventory. *International Journal of Intercultural Relations, 27,* 421–443.

Hart Research Associates. (2013). *It takes more than a major: Employer priorities for college learning and student success.* Washington, DC: Association of American Colleges and Universities.

Hojat, M., Gonnella, J. S., Nasca, T. J., Mangione, S., Veloksi, J. J., & Magee, M. (2002). The Jefferson Scale of Physician Empathy: Further psychometric data and differences by gender and specialty at item level. *Academic Medicine, 77,* S58–S60.

Inhelder, B., & Piaget, J. (1958). *The growth of logical thinking from childhood to adolescence: An essay on the construction of formal operational structures.* New York, NY: Basic Books.

Institute of International Education. (2014). Profile of U.S. study abroad students, 2000/01–2012/13. *Open Doors Report on International Educational Exchange.* Retrieved from http://www.iie.org/opendoors

Izard, C. E. (1980). Cross-cultural perspectives on emotion and emotion communication. *Handbook of Cross-Cultural Psychology, 3,* 185–221.

Jacklin, C. N., & Maccoby, E. E. (1978). Social behavior at 33 months in same-sex and mixed-sex dyads. *Child Development, 49,* 557–569.

Jacobs, M. S. (1997). People from the footnotes: The missing element in client-centered counseling. *Golden Gate UL Review, 27,* 345–422.

John, O. P., & Gross, J. J. (2004). Healthy and unhealthy emotion regulation: Personality processes, individual differences, and life span development. *Journal of Personality, 72,* 1301–1334.

Jordan, P. J., & Troth, A. C. (2002). Emotional intelligence and conflict resolution: Implications for human resource development. *Advances in Developing Human Resources, 4,* 62–79.

Jordan, P. J., & Troth, A. C. (2004). Managing emotions during team problem solving: Emotional intelligence and conflict resolution. *Human Performance, 17,* 195–218.

Joseph, G. E., & Strain, P. S. (2003). Enhancing emotional vocabulary in young children. *Young Exceptional Children, 6,* 18–26.

Kealey, D. J., & Protheroe, D. R. (1996). The effectiveness of cross-cultural training for expatriates: An assessment of the literature on the issue. *International Journal of Intercultural Relations, 20,* 141–165.

Kinzler, K. D., & Spelke, E. S. (2011). Do infants show social preferences for people differing in race? *Cognition, 119,* 1–9.

Kitsantas, A. (2004). Studying abroad: The role of college students' goals on the development of cross-cultural skills and global understanding. *College Student Journal, 38,* 441–452.

Klein, G., Klein, H. A., Lande, B., Borders, J., & Whitacre, J. C. (2015). Police and military as good strangers. *Journal of Occupational and Organizational Psychology, 88,* 231–250.

Knudsen, H. R., & Muzekari, L. H. (1983). The effects of verbal statements of context on facial expressions of emotion. *Journal of Nonverbal Behavior, 7,* 202–212.

Kraemer, A. (1973). *Development of a cultural self-awareness approach to instruction in intercultural communication* (Technical Report 73-17). Arlington, VA: HumRRO.

Kruger, J., & Dunning, D. (1999). Unskilled and unaware of it: How difficulties in recognizing one's own incompetence lead to inflated self-assessments. *Journal of Personality and Social Psychology, 77,* 1121–1134.

Kumagai, A. K. (2008). A conceptual framework for the use of illness narratives in medical education. *Academic Medicine, 83,* 653–658.

LaFreniere, P., Strayer, F., & Gauthier, R. (1984). The emergence of same-sex affiliative preferences among preschool peers: A developmental/ethological perspective. *Child Development, 55,* 1958–1965.

Lane, R. D., Quinlan, D. M., Schwartz, G. E., Walker, P. A., & Zeitlin, S. B. (1990). The Levels of Emotional Awareness Scale: A cognitive–developmental measure of emotion. *Journal of Personality Assessment, 55,* 124–134.

Lane, R. D., & Schwartz, G. E. (1987). Levels of emotional awareness: A cognitive–developmental theory and its application to psychopathology. *American Journal of Psychiatry, 144,* 133–143.

Lantieri, L. (2008a). *Building emotional intelligence: Techniques for cultivating inner strength in children.* Boulder, CO: Sounds True.

Lantieri, L. (2008b). Nurturing inner calm in children. *ENCOUNTER: Education for Meaning and Social Justice, 21,* 32–37.

Lazarus, R. S., & Folkman, S. (1984). *Stress, appraisal, and coping.* New York, NY: Springer.

Le, H., Schmidt, F. L., Harter, J. K., & Lauver, K. J. (2010). The problem of empirical redundancy of constructs in organizational research: An empirical investigation. *Organizational Behavior and Human Decision Processes, 112,* 112–125.

Leung, K., Ang, S., & Tan, M. L. (2014). Intercultural competence. *Annual Review of Organizational Psychology and Organizational Behavior, 1,* 489–519.

Little, J. W. (1993). Teachers' professional development in a climate of educational reform. *Educational Evaluation and Policy Analysis, 15,* 129–151.

Lourenço, O., & Machado, A. (1996). In defense of Piaget's theory: A reply to 10 common criticisms. *Psychological Review, 103,* 143–164.

Lubinski, D. (2004). Introduction to the special section on cognitive abilities: 100 years after Spearman's (1904) "'General Intelligence,' Objectively Determined and Measured." *Journal of Personality and Social Psychology, 86,* 96–111.

Maiworm, F., & Teichler, U. (1996). *Study abroad and early careers: Experiences of former Erasmus students.* London, England: Kingsley.

Markman, E. M. (1977). Realizing that you don't understand: A preliminary investigation. *Child Development, 48,* 986–992.

Markus, H. (1977). Self-schemata and processing information about the self. *Journal of Personality and Social Psychology, 35,* 63–78.

Markus, H. R., & Kitayama, S. (1991). Culture and the self: Implications for cognition, emotion, and motivation. *Psychological Review, 98,* 224–253.

Martinez, R. O., & Dukes, R. L. (1997). The effects of ethnic identity, ethnicity, and gender on adolescent well-being. *Journal of Youth and Adolescence, 26,* 503–516.

Matsumoto, D. (1990). Cultural similarities and differences in display rules. *Motivation and Emotion, 14,* 195–214.

Matsumoto, D. (1992). American–Japanese cultural differences in the recognition of universal facial expressions. *Journal of Cross-Cultural Psychology, 23,* 72–84.

Matsumoto, D. (1993). Ethnic differences in affect intensity, emotion judgments, display rule attitudes, and self-reported emotional expression in an American sample. *Motivation and Emotion, 17,* 107–123.

Mayer, J. D., Roberts, R. D., & Barsade, S. G. (2008). Human abilities: Emotional intelligence. *Annual Review of Psychology, 59,* 507–536.

Mayer, J. D., & Salovey, P. (1995). Emotional intelligence and the construction and regulation of feelings. *Applied and Preventative Psychology, 4,* 197–208.

Mayer, J. D., & Salovey, P. (1997). What is emotional intelligence? In P. Salovey & D. Sluyter (Eds.), *Emotional development and emotional intelligence: Educational implications* (pp. 3–31). New York, NY: Basic Books.

McAllister, G., & Irvine, J. J. (2000). Cross cultural competency and multicultural teacher education. *Review of Educational Research, 70,* 3–24.

Mendenhall, M. E., Stahl, G. K., Ehnert, I., Oddou, G., Osland, J. E., & Kühlmann, T. M. (2004). Evaluation studies of cross-cultural training programs: A review of the literature from 1988 to 2000. In D. Landis, J. M. Bennett, & M. J. Bennett (Eds.), *Handbook of intercultural training* (3rd ed., pp. 129–145). Thousand Oaks, CA: Sage.

Merrill, D. M. (2002). First principles of instruction. *Educational Technology Research and Development, 50,* 43–59.

Mor, S., Morris, M., & Joh, J. (2013). Identifying and training adaptive cross-cultural management skills: The crucial role of cultural metacognition. *Academy of Management Learning & Education, 12,* 453–475.

Nannis, E. D., & Cowan, P. A. (1987). Emotional understanding: A matter of age, dimension, and point of view. *Journal of Applied Developmental Psychology, 8,* 289–304.

Narvaez, D., & Endicott, L. (2001). *Nurturing character in the middle school classroom: Ethical sensitivity.* St. Paul, MN: Department of Children, Families & Learning.

Noe, R. A., & Colquitt, J. A. (2002). Planning for training impact: Principles of training effectiveness. In K. Kraiger (Ed.), *Creating, implementing, and maintaining effective training and development: State-of-the-art lessons for practice* (pp. 53–79). San Francisco, CA: Jossey-Bass.

Nolen-Hoeksema, S., & Aldao, A. (2011). Gender and age differences in emotion regulation strategies and their relationship to depressive symptoms. *Personality and Individual Differences, 51*, 704–708.

Ogle, D. M. (1986). KWL: A teaching model that develops active reading of expository text. *The Reading Teacher, 39*, 564–570.

Orahood, T., Kruze, L., & Pearson, D. E. (2004). The impact of study abroad on business students' career goals. *Frontiers: The Interdisciplinary Journal of Study Abroad, 10*, 117–130.

Perez, L. M. (2011). Teaching emotional self-awareness through inquiry-based education. *Early Childhood Research and Practice, 13*(2). Retrieved from http://ecrp.uiuc.edu/v13n2/perez.html

Phinney, J. S. (1990). Ethnic identity in adolescents and adults: A review of research. *Psychological Bulletin, 108*, 499–514.

Phinney, J. S. (1993). A three-stage model of ethnic identity development in adolescence. In M. E. Bernal & G. P. Knight (Eds.), *Ethnic identity: Formation and transmission among Hispanics and other minorities* (pp. 61–79). New York, NY: State University of New York Press.

Piaget, J. (1952). *The origins of intelligence in children.* New York, NY: International Universities Press.

Piaget, J. (1976). *The grasp of consciousness: Action and concept in the young child.* Cambridge, MA: Harvard University Press.

Plato. (trans. 1980). *The laws of Plato* (T. Pangle, Trans.). New York, NY: Basic Books.

Potts, D. (2015, April). Understanding the early career benefits of learning abroad programs. *Journal of Studies in International Education, 19*(5).

Puck, J. F., Kittler, M. G., & Wright, C. (2008). Does it really work? Re-assessing the impact of pre-departure cross-cultural training on expatriate adjustment. *International Journal of Human Resource Management, 19*, 2182–2197.

Purnell, L. D. (2012). *Transcultural health care: A culturally competent approach.* Philadelphia, PA: Davis.

Rentsch, J. R., Gunderson, A., Goodwin, G. F., & Abbe, A. (2007). *Conceptualizing multicultural perspective taking skills* (Technical Report 1216). Arlington, VA: US Army Research Institute for the Behavioral and Social Sciences.

Rentsch, J. R., Mot, I., & Abbe, A. (2009). *Identifying the core content and structure of a schema for cultural understanding* (Technical Report 1251). Arlington, VA: US Army Research Institute for the Behavioral and Social Sciences.

Rimé, B. (2007). Interpersonal emotion regulation. In J. J. Gross (Ed.), *Handbook of emotion regulation* (pp. 466–485). New York, NY: Guilford.

Roysircar, G. (2004). Cultural self-awareness assessment: Practice examples from psychology training. *Professional Psychology: Research and Practice, 35*, 658–666.

Saarni, C. (1997). Emotional competence and self-regulation in childhood. In P. Salovey & D. J. Sluyter (Eds.), *Emotional development and emotional intelligence: Educational implications* (pp. 35–69). New York, NY: Basic Books.

Salisbury, M. H., Umbach, P. D., Paulsen, M. B., & Pascarella, E. T. (2009). Going global: Understanding the choice process of the intent to study abroad. *Research in Higher Education, 50*, 119–143.

Salovey, P., & Mayer, J. D. (1990). Emotional intelligence. *Imagination, Cognition, & Personality, 9*, 185–211.

Schlaerth, A., Ensari, N., & Christian, J. (2013). A meta-analytical review of the relationship between emotional intelligence and leaders' constructive conflict management. *Group Processes & Intergroup Relations, 16,* 126–136.

Secretary's Commission on Achieving Necessary Skills. (1991). *What work requires of schools: A SCANS report for America 2000.* Washington, DC: US Department of Labor. Retrieved from https://wdr.doleta.gov/SCANS/whatwork

Siegel, L., & Brainerd, C. (Eds.). (1978). *Alternatives to Piaget.* New York, NY: Academic Press.

Slaby, R. G., Roedell, W. C., Arezzo, D., & Hendrix, K. (1995). *Early violence prevention: Tools for teachers of young children.* Washington, DC: National Association for the Education of Young Children.

Stewart, E. (1966). The simulation of cultural differences. *Journal of Communication, 16,* 291–304.

Sue, D. W. (1981). *Counseling the culturally different: Theory and practice.* New York, NY: Wiley.

Sue, D. W., Bernier, Y., Durran, A., Feinberg, L., Pedersen, P. B., Smith, E. J., & Vasquez-Nuttal, E. (1982). Position paper: Cross-cultural counseling competencies. *The Counseling Psychologist, 10,* 45–52.

Swanson, H. L. (1990). Influence of metacognitive knowledge and aptitude on problem solving. *Journal of Educational Psychology, 82,* 306–314.

Tajfel, H., & Turner, J. C. (1979). An integrative theory of intergroup conflict. In W. Austin & S. Worchel (Eds.), *The social psychology of intergroup relations* (pp. 33–47). Monterey, CA: Brooks/Cole.

Thomas, D. C., Elron, E., Stahl, G., Ekelund, B. Z., Ravlin, E. C., Cerding, J.-L., ... Lazarova, M. B. (2008). Cultural intelligence: Domain and assessment. *International Journal of Cross Cultural Management, 8,* 123–143.

Turner, J. C. (1975). Social comparison and social identity: Some prospects for intergroup behaviour. *European Journal of Social Psychology, 5,* 1–34.

US Bureau of Economic Analysis. (2013). *Summary estimates for multinational companies: Employment, sales, and capital expenditures for 2011* [News release]. Retrieved from https://www.bea.gov/newsreleases/international/mnc/mncnewsrelease.htm

Van Boven, L., & Loewenstein, D. (2005). Empathy gaps in emotional perspective taking. In S. Hodges & B. Malle (Eds.), *Other minds: How humans bridge the divide between self and others* (pp. 284–297). New York, NY: Guilford.

van der Zee, K. I., & van Oudenhoven, J. P. (2000). The Multicultural Personality Questionnaire: A multidimensional instrument of multicultural effectiveness. *European Journal of Personality, 14,* 291–309.

van Oudenhoven, J. P., & van der Zee, K. I. (2002). Predicting multicultural effectiveness of international students: The Multicultural Personality Questionnaire. *International Journal of Intercultural Relations, 26,* 679–694.

Vygotsky, L. S. (1978). Interaction between learning and development. In M. Cole, V. John-Steiner, S. Scribner, & E. Souberman (Eds.), *Mind in society: The development of higher psychological processes* (pp. 79–91). Cambridge, MA: Harvard University Press.

Ward, C., & Fischer, R. (2008). Personality, cultural intelligence, and cross-cultural adaptation. In S. Ang & L. Van Dyne (Eds.), *Handbook of cultural intelligence* (pp. 159–176). New York, NY: Sharpe.

Webster-Stratton, C. H. (1992). *The incredible years: A trouble-shooting guide for parents of children aged 3–8*. Toronto, Ontario, Canada: Umbrella Press.

Weng, C. (2004). Multicultural lawyering: Teaching psychology to develop cultural self-awareness. *Clinical Law Review, 11*, 369–403.

Williams, M. (2007). Building genuine trust through interpersonal emotion management: A threat regulation model of trust and collaboration across boundaries. *Academy of Management Review, 32*, 595–621.

Wispé, L. (1986). The distinction between sympathy and empathy: To call forth a concept, a word is needed. *Journal of Personality and Social Psychology, 50*, 314–321.

Wrenn, C. G. (1962). The culturally encapsulated counselor. *Harvard Educational Review, 32*, 444–449.

Yamakazi, Y., & Kayes, D. C. (2004). An experiential learning approach to cross-cultural learning: A review and integration of competencies for successful expatriate adaptation. *Academy of Management Learning and Education, 3*, 362–379.

Zaki, J., & Williams, W. C. (2013). Interpersonal emotion regulation. *Emotion, 13*, 803–810.

Rethinking How We Define and Measure 21st Century Skills

Commentary[1]

PATRICK C. KYLLONEN ■

As a college student, I had a part-time job that required me to drive early in the morning to the office of a Midwestern power company in rural Minnesota, pick up a computer printout, and then continue driving to deliver it to the power company's downtown office in Minneapolis 60 miles away. At that time, there was no more cost-effective way to transport that information from one office to another. Today, that job is done by e-mail at a tiny fraction of the time (roughly 3 hours there and back vs. less than 1 second) and cost (minimum wage × 3 hours vs. less than $.01) it took for me to do it. So the job I had that helped put me through school no longer exists.

There are many jobs from that time or longer ago that no longer exist or have been greatly reduced in number. Examples include travel agent, secretary typist, assembly line worker, and switchboard operator. Although there are many reasons for the reduction of these jobs, automation and changing task demands are in part responsible for these changes in the workforce. Autor, Levy, and Murnane (2003) systematically examined changes in occupations in the United States and changes within occupations of the duties performed based on listings in the *Dictionary of Occupational Titles* (DOT), comparing years between 1960 and 1998. They found that computer technology was *substituting* for workers performing routine tasks (ones that could be programmed) but *complementing* workers engaged in "nonroutine tasks demanding flexibility, creativity, generalized problem-solving capabilities, and complex communications" (p. 1322). Somewhat similar but more recent analyses, using either the DOT or the Department of Labor's O*NET database of jobs, concluded that jobs requiring high levels of both cognitive and social skills, such as lawyer, were growing faster than any other job category (Deming, 2015; Weinberger, 2014). With some exceptions (Tetlock & Gardner, 2015), we are notoriously poor at predicting the future (Levin, 2015), and these analyses look back rather than forward, but perhaps there are hints from those trend lines of what the workforce of the future might be like.

Another way to determine what constitutes a 21st century skill is to ask employers what they look for when hiring today. As noted in two of the previous chapters, employer surveys, such as "Are They Really Ready to Work?" (Casner-Lotto & Barrington, 2006) or the more recent National Association of Colleges and Employers (NACE) survey (2014), converge on the skills of communication, teamwork, leadership, work ethic, and problem solving as top priorities.

I next discuss each of the three previous chapters in turn and finish with some concluding remarks.

WORKPLACE READINESS AND PERSONNEL SELECTION: SETTING THE STAGE

The chapter by Sackett and Walmsley (Chapter 2) considers the issues of future job skills but in addition provides so much more to help us think about what it means to be *workforce ready*. In their encyclopedic overview, they lay out a comprehensive and considered treatment of the surrounding issues. It begins with a definition, and here, as throughout their chapter, they find that there are many—perhaps too many for the concept of *workforce readiness*—to have much value for its myriad applications. These include informing educational policy, helping individuals assess their own readiness, and contributing to professional development and job preparedness offerings given by universities and adult learning centers. These are the natural audiences for the concept, as the authors note. One problem is the diversity of opinions on which skills or competencies are important in today's workforce. Various methodologies can be brought to bear—employer surveys, predictive validity studies, the opinions expressed by experts or expert panels—but these all have their limitations.

Surveys and panels are affected by the zeitgeist, today's education and workplace jargon, and whatever happens to appear this week in the *New York Times* or on National Public Radio. Four years ago, no one knew about grit or growth mindsets, but today these are essential skills for all children: Has the world changed or just the terminology? The tower of Babel inhibits progress. Predictive validity studies especially as summarized in meta-analyses can help standardize terminology by identifying factors that by whatever name consistently predict workforce outcomes. One such factor so identified is *conscientiousness*—the tendency, skill, or disposition to show up, work hard, and be organized. By now, we have overwhelming evidence that this is a key—if not the key—factor associated with both educational and workforce success.

The authors also raise two critical points that suggest fertile future research areas. One is the construct–measurement distinction, which is central but often ignored. It is clear that significant progress in our ability to understand the importance of 21st century skills, as well as to teach them, will follow improvement in our ability to measure them (Kyllonen, 2013, 2015). Relying on our ability to describe skills in words is limiting; consider the difference between achievement and self-descriptions of achievement[2] as measured in PISA—the correlation is quite modest (Organization for Economic Co-operation and Development (OECD), 2013; see also Paulhus, Lysy, & Yik, 1998). Our ability to reveal our skills through performance rather than evaluate them through Likert scales is key to growth in this area. Efforts in the area of collaborative skills (von Davier, Zhu, & Kyllonen, 2017) represent significant first steps along this path.

Another important distinction made in the chapter is between options for achieving high performance in the workplace, where employee selection is one, but employee training, performance incentives, and engineering the performance environment are potentially viable alternatives. From an employer's perspective, this is a bottom-line consideration, and the alternatives differ in cost. Imagine selecting a worker who can speak Korean versus training him or her to do so, versus providing a translation machine, versus providing a budget that would enable outsourcing translation services. All could be viable depending on cost and requirements.

I have only a minor quibble with this excellent chapter. Citing another study, the authors suggest that human resource (HR) managers might not be aware of or appreciate the value of certain research findings, such as the superiority of cognitive ability over conscientiousness in predicting job performance, or the value of integrity tests for predicting workplace malfeasance despite their apparent susceptibility to faking (who would ever admit on a job application to having stolen something from their previous employer?). These may be education problems, as the authors suggest, but they also could reflect HR managers' accurate assessment of the data available to them. Theoretically, a latent cognitive ability factor is the best predictor of a latent job performance factor in an unrestricted, unselected population of potential applicants. However, in the make-a-decision world of an HR manager, there might be severe restriction of the range of cognitive ability observed in an applicant pool (e.g., due to self-selection or screening by education, institution, and major) such that the predictor–outcome relation comparison does favor a personality measure. Or, performance in an interview is more highly valued than some unreliable, future outcome of questionable validity such as a supervisor's performance rating. There are many circumstances in which a decision maker might acknowledge the general rule suggested by academic studies but at the same time respond rationally to local circumstances that might appear as being at odds with the general rule.

CRITICAL SKILLS FOR THE 21ST CENTURY WORKFORCE

The approach taken in Chapter 3 by Whorton, Casillas, Oswald, and Shaw is first to define skill as proficiency on a task or set of tasks requiring abilities and then to outline its parameters—its generality, nature, dependence on environment, entailed effort, and quantifiability/measurability. This establishes skill as a kind of intermediate level of description, between a basic ability or disposition such as spatial ability, fluid ability, openness, or conscientiousness on the one hand and performance of a task or set of tasks on the other hand. Psychometrically, skill under this scheme might be understood as a formative latent variable (Y), which predicts task performance (Z) but is a composite of (or predicted by) more basic abilities (X) (Edwards & Bagozzi, 2000) so that $X \to Y \to Z$.

A question that arises in the formative variable literature is, Are they necessary? If abilities predict skills and skills predict performance, why not just skip the middle (i.e., skills) layer—that is, $X \to Z$? Skills (the Y variable in this scheme) are troublesome constructs, conceptually and statistically (Howell, Breivik, & Wilcox, 2007; Jonas & Markon, 2016; Lee, Cadogan, & Chamberlain, 2013). What are they? And do we need them? Are skills simply arbitrary sums of a set of ability measures, or are they composites of ability measures weighted to predict performance on some defined set of tasks or performance outcomes? What exactly is the function of a skill, so defined?

I think the answer to the question of whether they are necessary is yes, there is value to the concept of skill as the authors define it, for two reasons. Skills represent constructs such as the authors' suggested leadership, teamwork, and creativity, at the level that consumers of this kind of information—students, HR managers, and program evaluators—would like to hear about. Information about more basic abilities, such as conscientiousness and fluid ability, might be too basic for reporting and might not be as useful to those consumers. Second, broad, general abilities by their nature as broad, general abilities are difficult to change. Project Intelligence attempted to change general cognitive ability for an entire nation, but it was abandoned (Herrnstein, Nickerson, Sanchez, & Swets, 1986; Nickerson, 2011). Abilities and personality are remarkably rank stable over the lifespan (Gow et al., 2011; Roberts & DelVecchio, 2000). However, parts of skills may be more amenable to instruction. A formative latent variable is a composite of, or is caused by, its component indicators, or causal indicators ($X \rightarrow Y$). If the causal model is true, that means that one can change the formative latent variable by changing level standing on the indicators. One can raise students' leadership levels by teaching components of leadership, such as in Rice University's new leadership development program, which teaches students how to wield influence, be confident, and be effective team members (Wermund, 2015). Amenability, or at least perceived amenability, to instruction is a key feature of the concept of skills as the authors define them.

The authors also propose a set of three dimensions (people-oriented, situation-oriented, and thinking skills) characterizing what they nominate as the nine key 21st century skills (leadership, customer service, teamwork, safety, creativity, critical thinking, metacognition, cross-cultural knowledge and competencies, and ethics and integrity). For example, leadership is a people-oriented skill, critical thinking is a thinking skill, teamwork and safety are both people- and situation-oriented, and cross-cultural competence and ethics and integrity are all three. They provide good motivations for the skills they chose for their list, and certainly there are overlaps between the skills they identify and those identified in other such exercises (e.g., a summary and crosswalk with several such exercises is provided by the National Research Council, 2012), although safety and customer service are somewhat idiosyncratic.

What I missed in this fine review was a discussion of measurement. Measurement is where the abstract work of defining skills gets put to the test. Creativity can be measured with a fluency test (Fredericksen & Ward, 1978) or it can be indicated as the number of libraries in a city (Florida, 2002)—these are very different measures. A great deal of our understanding of the kinds of constructs discussed here is bound up with how we measure them. Certainly, there is a need for better measures, but we may have to make do with what we can collect for evaluating the importance of the kinds of skills mentioned here.

CROSS-CULTURAL COMPETENCE AS A 21ST CENTURY SKILL

Unlike Chapters 2 and 3, which serve as overviews, Chapter 4 by Klafehn makes the case for one particular 21st century skill, cross-cultural competence (3C). It is difficult to argue with the general idea that due to the global economy, multinational corporations, free trade agreements, inexpensive international telephone service and air travel (compared to 30 years ago; Thompson, 2013), and multimedia technologies ranging from Skype to Cisco's TelePresence, the world is flatter. This lowers the cost and increases the demand for communicating with others from different cultural backgrounds. Over time, these changes may lead to a certain homogenization of culture. This is happening to some extent with the adoption of English as the world's second language. In the meantime, however, a skill that will be valued is that of being able to successfully navigate in cross-cultural contexts. Klafehn suggests that this is not accomplished through "do's and don'ts" crash courses, which have not proven very effective. Rather, she suggests that 3C is a broad construct itself, consisting of the component skills of cultural self-awareness, metacognition, emotion regulation, and perspective taking, among others.

Although in the literature there are some "multifaceted" (i.e., ability) models (most notably the theory of cultural intelligence, designated CQ, akin to emotional intelligence's EQ), and some process models, Klafehn, drawing on joint work between the Educational Testing Service and the Army Research Institute (Brenneman, Klafehn, Burrus, Roberts, & Kochert, 2016), proposes an alternative—a hybrid ability–process model. The model comprises four "steps" in cultural interactions: *recognize* (invoking self-awareness and cultural awareness), *hypothesize* (invoking emotion recognition and metacognition), *decide* (invoking either automatic Type 1 processes or deliberate Type 2 processes, depending on the person and context), and *behave* (invoking communication, persuasion, and emotional management). Klafehn thus frames 3C as essentially a problem-solving activity (Bransford & Stein, 1993; OECD, 2014; Pólya, 1957), which certainly makes sense (although as such, a fifth step of reflecting might also be worth including, as is the case in the previously cited references). The chapter is not explicit on how one might go about evaluating the model. However, given the four processing steps, and the associated abilities, one can imagine experimental tasks designed to isolate the steps and measures of the invoked abilities that would predict performance on the steps. Together, these might enable testing the degree to which the abilities account for performance on the respective steps of the cultural problem-solving episode. One could also examine the dimensionality of the steps (e.g., one vs. four dimensions) and the structural invariance of the prediction model across steps. Similar approaches for conceptualizing constructs such as Information Technology and Communications Literacy (Educational Testing Service, 2002) have tended to support low- or single-dimension variables underlying seemingly diverse processing steps, such as define, access, evaluate, and manage, or the problem-solving dimensions of exploring and understanding, representing and formulating, planning and executing, and monitoring and reflecting (OECD, 2014). However, whether or not the steps represent separate dimensions, they are useful devices for specifying the task.

Klafehn also makes the argument that although much of the research on 3C has focused on adult professionals, it is important to put some focus on the development of 3C skills in students, the ones who are preparing to enter the global workforce. She draws on Piaget's stage theory to help structure how a 3C curriculum might sensibly be laid out. Throughout this chapter, there are good ideas on how 3C might be introduced in school, and one could imagine developing learning progressions based on these ideas (Achieve, 2015).

CONCLUSION

Today's workplace is in some ways similar and in some ways very different from the workplace of the 1980s. Back then, there was no Internet, Google, Outlook, Amazon, iPhone, or LinkedIn. There were no app developers and no social media analysts. What will the workplace look like 15, 20, or 30 years from now when today's preschoolers enter the workforce? What should the schools be teaching to prepare those students for the future skill demands that will be required then? The National Research Council (2008) conducted a workshop on "future skill demands" with at least one theme being that "broad skills" such as interpersonal, written communication, teamwork in a diverse setting, social perceptiveness, and the ability to give and receive advice would be increasingly important (R. Murnane, p. 85). Another comment was that broad skills would be increasingly important as a "self-defense mechanism" in a rapidly changing and uncertain world (K. Kay, p. 88), suggesting the growing importance of flexibility and adaptability (Levin, 2015).

Presented as a set, Chapters 2–4 do an excellent job of laying out the issues that must be addressed for us to prepare students for the future workplace. They include thoughtful discussions of what skills will likely be most valued and what we must do to teach those skills and monitor their development. The only constant is change, and preparing students to cope with never-ending change is increasingly being recognized as an important function of school.

NOTES

1.   Writing of this chapter was supported in part by funding from ETS R&D, Center for Academic and Workforce Readiness and Success.

2. In PISA 2012, self-descriptions of achievement were measured in the Mathematics self-concept scale by items such as "I learn mathematics quickly" and "In my mathematics class, I understand even the most difficult work" (OECD, 2013, p. 95).

REFERENCES

Achieve. (2015). *The role of learning progressions in competency-based pathways* (CC BY-NC 4.0 Achieve). Retrieved from http://www.achieve.org/files/Achieve-LearningProgressionsinCBP.pdf

Autor, D. H., Levy, F., & Murnane, R. J. (2003). The skill content change of recent technological change: An empirical exploration. *Quarterly Journal of Economics, 118*(4), 1279–1333.

Bransford, J. D., & Stein, B. S. (1993). *The IDEAL problem solver* (2nd ed.). New York, NY: Freeman.

Brenneman, M. W., Klafehn, J., Burrus, J., Roberts, R. D., & Kochert, J. (2016). Assessing cross-cultural competence: A working framework and prototype measures for use in military contexts. In J. L. Wildman, R. L. Griffith, & B. K. Armon (Eds.), *Critical issues in cross cultural management* (pp. 103–131). Cham, Switzerland: Springer.

Casner-Lotto, J., & Barrington, L. (2006). *Are they really ready to work? Employers' perspectives on the basic knowledge and applied skills of new entrants to the 21st century U.S. workforce.* New York, NY: The Conference Board, Corporate Voices for Working Families, Partnership for 21st Century Skills, and Society for Human Resource Management.

Deming, D. (2015). *The growing importance of social skills in the labor market* (NBER Working Paper Series, Working Paper 21473). Cambridge, MA: National Bureau of Economic Research. Retrieved from http://www.nber.org/papers/w21473

Educational Testing Service. (2002). *Digital transformation. A framework for ICT literacy: A report of the International ICT Literacy Panel.* Princeton, NJ: Author. Retrieved from https://www.ets.org/Media/Tests/Information_and_Communication_Technology_ Literacy/ictreport.pdf

Edwards, J., & Bagozzi, R. (2000). On the nature and direction of relationships between constructs and measures. *Psychological Methods, 5*(2), 155–174.

Florida, R. (2002). *The rise of the creative class. And how it's transforming work, leisure and everyday life.* New York, NY: Basic Books.

Fredericksen, N., & Ward, W. C. (1978). *Measures for the study of creativity in scientific problem-solving* (ETS Research Report GREB-78-01SR). Princeton, NJ: Educational Testing Service. Retrieved from https://www.ets.org/Media/Research/pdf/GREB-78-01SR.pdf

Gow, A. J., Johnson, W., Pattie, A., Brett, C. E., Roberts, B., Starr, J. M., & Deary, I. J. (2011). Stability and change in intelligence from age 11 to ages 70, 79, and 87: The Lothian Birth Cohorts of 1921 and 1936. *Psychology of Aging, 26*(1), 232–240.

Herrnstein, R. J., Nickerson, R. S., Sanchez, M., & Swets, J. A. (1986). Teaching thinking skills. *American Psychologist, 41*, 1279–1289.

Howell, R. D., Breivik, E., & Wilcox, J. B. (2007). Reconsidering formative measurement. *Psychological Methods, 12*(2), 205–218.

Jonas, K., & Markon, K. E. (2016). A descriptivist approach to trait conceptualization and inference. *Psychological Review, 123*(1), 90–96.

Kyllonen, P. C. (2013). Soft skills for the workplace. *Change, 45*(6), 16–23.

Kyllonen, P. C. (2015). Designing tests to measure personal attributes and noncognitive skills. In S. Lane, M. R. Raymond, & T. M. Haladyna (Eds.), *Handbook of test development* (2nd ed., pp. 190–211). New York, NY: Routledge.

Levin, H. (2015). The importance of adaptability for the 21st century. *Society, 52*(2), 136–141.

National Association of Colleges and Employers. (2014). *Job Outlook 2015. The skills/ qualities employers want in new college graduate hires.* Retrieved from http://www. naceweb.org/about-us/press/class-2015-skills-qualities-employers-want.aspx

National Research Council. (2008). *Research on future skill demands: A workshop summary.* Washington, DC: National Academies Press.

National Research Council. (2012). *Education for life and work: Developing transferable knowledge and skills in the 21st century.* Washington, DC: National Academies Press.

Nickerson, R. (2011). Developing intelligence through instruction. In R. J. Sternberg & S. B. Kaufman (Eds.), *The Cambridge handbook of intelligence* (pp. 107–129). Cambridge, England: Cambridge University Press.

Organization for Economic Co-operation and Development. (2013). *PISA 2012 results: Ready to learn: Students' engagement, drive and self-beliefs (Volume III), PISA.* Paris, France: Author.

Organization for Economic Co-operation and Development. (2014). *PISA 2012 results: Creative problem solving: Students' skills in tackling real-life problem (Volume V), PISA.* Paris, France: Organization for Economic Co-operation and Development.

Paulhus, D. L., Lysy, D. C., & Yik, M. S. M. (1998). Self-report measures of intelligence: Are they useful proxies as IQ tests? *Journal of Personality, 66,* 525–554.

Pólya, G. (1957). *How to solve it.* Garden City, NY: Doubleday.

Roberts, B. W., & DelVecchio, W. F. (2000). The rank-order consistency of personality from childhood to old age: A quantitative review of longitudinal studies. *Psychological Bulletin, 126,* 3–25.

Tetlock, P. E., & Gardner, D. (2015). *Superforecasting: The art and science of prediction.* New York, NY: Crown.

Thompson, E. (2013, February 28). How airline ticket prices fell 50% in 30 years (and why nobody noticed). *The Atlantic.* Retrieved from http://www.theatlantic.com/ business/archive/2013/02/how-airline-ticket-prices-fell-50-in-30-years-and-why-nobody-noticed/273506

von Davier, A., Zhu, M., & Kyllonen, P. (Eds.) (2017). *Innovative assessment of collaboration.* New York, NY: Springer.

Weinberger, C. J. (2014). The increasing complementarity between cognitive and social skills. *Review of Economics and Statistics, 96*(5), 849–861.

Wermund, R. (2015, May 13). Rice to launch leadership institute with historic gift. *Houston Chronicle.* Retrieved from http://www.houstonchronicle.com/news/ houston-texas/houston/article/Rice-to-launch-leadership-institute-with-historic-6262247.php

Rethinking How We Prepare Students for the Workforce

Preparing Students for Workplace Diversity

Some Research Implications

JAIME LESTER, DAVID A. KRAVITZ,
AND CARRIE N. KLEIN ■

As Weissberg clearly argued in the foreword of this book, work and life success and the satisfaction of today's students will be profoundly affected by their social and emotional development. In this chapter, we focus on the social and emotional challenges posed by the increasing globalization of business as well as the increasing diversity of the workforce and in higher education. These changes have accelerated in recent years and are likely to grow further in the future. Because Klafehn discussed the growing need for diversity and cross-cultural skills in detail in Chapter 4, we are brief here.

We define diversity as the mixture of social, cultural, and individual attributes that affect an individual's attitudes and behaviors, as well as how others react to and interact with that individual. Narrower definitions of diversity normally focus on demographic attributes including race, ethnicity, gender, sexual orientation, religion, age, and disability. Although the broadest definition is relevant to the workplace and higher education, the research literature concentrates on a subset of demographic dimensions.

Attention to the increased diversity of the US workforce was stimulated by *Workforce 2000* (Johnston & Packer, 1987), which predicted that most new entrants to the US workforce would be women and racial/ethnic minorities.

We have now experienced the changes predicted in *Workforce 2000* (Toossi, 2002, 2007). The US Bureau of Labor Statistics (BLS) reports that in the decade from 2002 to 2012, only 28.9% of labor force entrants were non-Hispanic White males (BLS, 2013, Table 5). Between 1992 and 2012, the proportion of the labor force consisting of non-Hispanic White males decreased from 42.1% to 35.1% (BLS, 2013, Table). It is clear that the US workforce diversity will continue to increase as the US economy becomes more globally integrated.

According to the International Monetary Fund (2000, para. 6), globalization "refers to the increasing integration of economies around the world, particularly through trade and financial flows. The term sometimes also refers to the movement of people (labor) and knowledge (technology) across international borders." That global trade has increased dramatically during the past few decades is inarguable (International Monetary Fund, 2011). Although the recent recession led to a temporary drop in international trade, in the long term it is clear that business will be increasingly global. The growing trade and movement of people across borders imply a need for business, in general, and employees, in particular, to cultivate a global mindset in which they are able to "perceive, analyze, and decode behaviors and situations in multiple cultural contexts and to use that insight to build productive relationships with individuals and organizations across cultural boundaries" (Cabrera & Unruh, 2012, p. 33).

It is argued that one of the benefits of diversity, both domestically and via globalization, is that it provides additional resources that can enhance organizational performance (Thomas, 1990). Although this argument is correct, performance will be enhanced only if the organization successfully leverages the additional resources provided by diversity. Unfortunately, there is ample evidence that humans are prone to in-group favoritism and out-group biases such as prejudice, stereotypes, and discrimination (Dipboye & Colella, 2005; Hewstone, Rubin, & Willis, 2002; Pager & Shepherd, 2008). These biases may limit effective use of the additional resources and benefits that diversity provides. For example, McKay, Avery, and Morris (2008) report results that imply both the problems with diversity and the elimination of those problems when diversity is well managed. They studied employee sales performance in a large national retail organization and found that in stores with poor diversity climates, White employees had higher sales than either Hispanic or Black employees. However, this effect was eliminated or reversed in stores with positive diversity climates. Thus, organizations and their employees must understand both the benefits and the challenges of leveraging diversity and its associated resources to maximize desired outcomes.

To this end, organizational leaders are motivated to hire and to retain employees who are not affected by diversity-related biases and who can work well with others. Fortunately for organizations, many members of this new workforce are exposed to diversity while in college. Colleges and universities graduate approximately 2.5 million undergraduate students per year (National Center for Education Statistics (NCES), 2012), with increasing numbers of students from racial and ethnic minority (non-White) backgrounds. In 2010, the number of undergraduate degrees earned by racial minority students dramatically increased: Hispanic and Black students earned 27% of associate's degrees and 19% of bachelor's degree, representing a significant increase of 118% in a single decade (NCES, 2012). The US Department of Labor (2001) projects that half the population in the United States will be designated as racial/ethnic minority by 2050, suggesting that the racial diversity of higher education enrollment and degree completion will continue to rise. Thus, the role of higher education in exposing and educating students in diversity and in global and multicultural competencies becomes vital, both during their collegiate experience and in preparation for diverse workplaces. When today's students enter the workforce, their ability to work well with those who differ in socially significant demographic characteristics (e.g., gender, race, ethnicity, religion, sexual orientation, and (dis)ability) and with those who operate under different cultural assumptions (e.g., power distance and directness of communication) will be an important skill.

In this chapter, we draw from a variety of research areas to offer suggestions about the interventions that colleges and universities can use to better prepare students for the diverse world they will enter upon graduation. Importantly, the focus of diversity research in higher education has been largely across academic experiences and student affairs programming (i.e., student groups, housing programs, orientations, classrooms, etc.). This is contrary to the long history in higher education of separation of academic and student affairs with the perception that learning only occurs in the classroom (Benjamin & Hamrick, 2011; Lester, 2011). A movement toward acknowledgment of learning outside the classroom led to defining co-curricular experiences as follows (Benjamin & Hamrick, 2011):

> The co-curriculum serves as an applied curriculum that often presents student with the opportunity to put into action what they learn in the classroom, whether that learning is content based (e.g., accounting major serving as student government treasurer) or interpersonally based (e.g., students availing themselves of cultural knowledge that may be taught or alluded to in class by interaction with a diverse group of peers). (p. 28)

Our focus draws on the definition of co-curricular activities as the programmatic, noncognitive inventions that prepare students, including minority students, for diverse workplaces. We refer to research on informal interaction diversity—research that captures the quantity and quality of students' interaction with diverse peers outside the classroom, such as in residence halls, sporting activities, social activities, and other campus events (Gurin, Dey, Hurtado, & Gurin, 2002). We also include the more formal nonclassroom experiences that occur in student affairs, such as diversity training. However, we note that the research literature often combines these two conceptually distinct domains, so we cannot always separate them. Although we describe some conceptualizations that underlie these interventions (e.g., intergroup contact theory), our focus is on the interventions themselves and the empirical support they have (or have not) obtained.

CONCEPTUAL UNDERPINNINGS OF DIVERSITY RESEARCH IN BUSINESS AND HIGHER EDUCATION

A key question in both business and higher education domains is how diversity is related to individual and organizational performance, broadly construed. As noted previously, humans tend to respond negatively to those who differ from themselves. Thus, it is important to explore approaches to decreasing these negative reactions. Paluck and Green (2009) provide a research-focused review of interventions intended to reduce prejudice. They conclude that the strongest support is for intergroup contact and cooperation, although even for these areas, more solid experimental work is needed. The conceptual underpinnings of intergroup contact research derive from work conducted more than 70 years ago, with Allport (1954) providing a keystone text. Allport argued that contact with a member of an out-group should decrease prejudice toward that individual and the out-group when three conditions are met: (1) The groups have equal status; (2) they are cooperating—pursuing some common goal(s); and (3) the contact has institutional support (e.g., by authorities and/or social norms). Hundreds of studies designed to test and elaborate on this model have been published.

Pettigrew and Tropp (2006) provide a meta-analysis of the contact–prejudice literature based on 713 independent samples drawn from 515 studies. They found clear support for the relationship, with a mean correlation of −.21. The effect was particularly strong when Allport's (1954) ideal conditions were met (−.29); it was smaller (−.20) but still statistically significantly when those conditions were not met. When the sample of studies was categorized by methodological strength, the effect was larger among the stronger studies. In addition, the negative contact–prejudice relation was found in research on many different target groups, among respondents of many ages, and among both men and women. Tropp and Pettigrew (2005), however, found that the effect was larger for majority (–.23) than for minority (–.18) status individuals. In addition, they found that the significant effect of contact conditions on effect size was present for majority but not minority status individuals. In short, there is very strong evidence for an inverse relation between interpersonal contact with out-group members and prejudice toward the out-group.

An important question is the extent to which the effect generalizes—from interaction partner to the out-group overall and from the specific out-group involved in the contact to other out-groups (secondary transfer). Tausch et al. (2010) report a set of studies that clearly demonstrates secondary transfer, controlling for contact with the secondary out-group and using longitudinal designs to eliminate the possibility of reverse causation. For example, in Study 4, they gathered data from Irish Catholics and Protestants on two occasions, separated by slightly more than 1 year. They found that contact with members of the other religion at Time 1 predicted Time 2 attitudes toward racial minorities (the secondary group), controlling for both Time 1 contact with and attitudes toward racial minorities. Supplementary analyses revealed that the effect on attitudes toward racial minorities (the secondary out-group) was mediated by attitudes toward the religious (primary) out-group. Tests for reverse secondary transfer (contact with racial minorities predicting attitudes toward religious out-group) revealed nonsignificant effects.

The question of causal order, mentioned in the previous paragraph, is of key importance. Indeed, the order must be from contact to prejudice if interventions based on contact are to be successful. Much of the research on the contact effect, however, has involved cross-sectional designs. Fortunately, a few longitudinal studies have been performed (Binder et al., 2009; Swart, Hewstone, Christ, & Voci, 2010; Tausch et al., 2010). This work has supported the assumed direction of causation, although some studies reveal reverse order exists as well. This makes sense, given the normal human tendency to avoid those we dislike. However, that tendency does pose a challenge. Fortunately, Hodson (2011) reports that when prejudice-prone people experience increased contact or friendship with an out-group member, even they have fewer negative attitudes toward that group.

In the higher education literature, the contact hypothesis underpins much of the research that focuses on the impact of minority student populations on student success, which is often measured in terms of outcomes— retention and graduation. The benefits of diversity on college campuses have been widely researched, and there is overwhelming evidence that racial/ ethnic diversity has a positive benefit on student learning and educational outcomes. This research was motivated primarily by the court cases in the early 1990s challenging affirmative action. It sought to provide empirical evidence of the impact of contact with minority students on all students, both minority and White. Much of the groundbreaking work on diversity notes that interacting across racial groups among college students is positively associated with such student outcomes as graduation, confidence, critical thinking, and openness to diversity (Chang, 1996; Hurtado, 2001; Hurtado, Engberg, Ponjuan, & Landreman, 2002; Pascarella, Edison, Nora, Hagedorn, & Terenzini, 1996; Pascarella, Palmer, Moye, & Pierson, 2001). Gurin and colleagues (2002) found that cross-racial interaction increases active thinking, intellectual engagement, academic skills, citizenship engagement, racial/cultural engagement, and perspective taking. Chang (1999) noted similar findings in increasing intellectual and social self-confidence in addition to retention and overall college satisfaction. Other studies note similar gains in pluralistic orientation—a construct reflecting the extent to which students are able to see and accept other perspectives rather than being rigidly limited to their own point of view (Jayakumar, 2008), openness to diversity, democratic outcomes, and cognitive development (Chang, Astin, & Kim, 2004; Chang, Denson, Saenz, & Misa, 2006).

A significant theme in the literature on diversity in higher education is the role of peer interactions inside classrooms. Gurin and colleagues (2002) "contend that the impact of racial/ethnic diversity on educational outcomes comes primarily from engagement with diverse peers in the informal campus environment and in college classrooms" (p. 333). Often measured in engagement in diversity-related courses (e.g., women's and gender studies, ethnic studies, and multicultural education), research finds that participation in these courses has a positive and consistent effect on sociohistorical thinking, critical thinking, racial understanding, and reducing prejudice (Chang, 2002; Gurin, 1999; Hurtado, 2001). Other studies that look within disciplines find similar results. Engberg (2004) found that positive cross-racial peer interactions affect intergroup learning and pluralistic orientation.

Importantly, the benefits are not consistent across racial groups. Antonio (2004) found that interactions across racial groups had a positive impact on minority students but did not reach statistical significance in predictive multivariate regressions among White students. Recent research found that more than 60% of students in their fourth year of college reported that their friendship groups were primarily from similar races (Martin, Tobin, & Spenner, 2014). This suggests that students often remain isolated within their racial identity groups, often spending time in and outside of class with those peers who have similar identities, thereby limiting opportunities for cross-racial interactions. This is particularly troubling because cross-race interactions have a positive impact on minority students (Antonio, 2004). Thus, the quality of the interactions and the campus climate related to diversity has an impact on the outcome of these interactions (Jayakumar, 2008).

Why does interpersonal contact decrease prejudice? Three mediators have received strong support: interpersonal anxiety, empathy and perspective taking, and knowledge of the other (Pettigrew & Tropp, 2008). Perhaps the strongest mediator is interpersonal anxiety. Anticipation of interacting with members of a different or unknown group leads to intergroup anxiety, presumably due to uncertainty about whether the interaction will go well or not. Anxiety is threatening and motivates protective actions, including withdrawal and negative thoughts and feelings (including prejudice) toward the source of anxiety (Stephan & Stephan, 1985). Positive interactions decrease that anxiety and thus decrease prejudice (Binder et al., 2009; Swart et al., 2010; Tredoux & Finchilescu, 2010). A second significant mediator is empathy and perspective taking (Swart et al., 2010). It is easier to "walk a mile in another's shoes" if one knows the other. The third mediator, which appears to be less important than the other two, is simple knowledge about the out-group. Wagner and Hewstone (2012) review this and other work and conclude that "direct contact improves out-group attitudes by reducing anxiety, threat, and negative intergroup emotions, and by promoting positive emotions, empathy, perspective-taking, and self-disclosure" (p. 197). Aberson and Haag (2007) report a cross-sectional study that explored relations and sequencing among the mediators. They found that contact predicted perspective taking, which predicted anxiety, which in turn predicted both stereotypes and explicit bias.

In higher education research, why contact reduces prejudice has not been systematically examined through more rigorous experimental designs. Extrapolating from more relational studies of self-report survey data, contact with minority student populations apparently expands individual student perspectives or worldviews and promotes continued interactions. In one of the few empirical studies to examine the impact of diversity in college on cross-cultural workforce competencies, Jayakumar (2008) found that White students who experience structural diversity—having a large proportion of students of color within an institution—experience long-term benefits on two outcomes measures: pluralistic orientation and leadership skills. The leadership skills construct reflects students' self-ratings of various aspects of leadership, including their ability to discuss and negotiate controversial issues. Jayakumar (2008) found that campus structural diversity had a positive, indirect effect on cross-racial interaction, with the effect being mediated by racial climate. Cross-racial interactions, in turn, predicted pluralistic orientation after college. Furthermore, cross-racial interactions in college predicted continued socializing across race post-college. In short, White students who do not interact with minority groups in college are less prepared for a global workforce than are those White students who experience cross-racial interaction in college. In general, these effects were more pronounced among the

White students who had grown up in segregated neighborhoods and had gone to majority White schools than among those with more pre-college racial diversity experience. Jayakumar (2009) continued her research on sexual prejudices, finding that taking diversity courses and experiencing cross-racial interactions in college predicted decreased prejudice against gays, with lasting effects through college. This is an example of the secondary transfer effect discussed previously.

A few other studies report results similar to those of Jayakumar (2008). Denson and Bowman (2013), in a study of Australian college students, found that high-quality engagement with minority peers and groups predicted positive intergroup attitudes and civic engagement, such as volunteerism and voting. Importantly, negative diversity interactions were associated with less interaction engagement, less respect for cultural differences, and less civic engagement. Bowman, Brandenberger, Hill, and Lapsley (2011) conducted a longitudinal study on college students 13 years after graduation. Controlling for prosocial orientation in freshman year, positive engagement with racial/ethnic diversity in college indirectly predicted positive personal growth, recognition of racism, and increased volunteer work. In short, the literature on cross-racial interactions is robust. Although it is not possible to randomly assign students to colleges or college experiences, structural modeling and longitudinal studies are consistent with the conclusion that positive cross-racial interaction can help prepare students for diverse workplaces, reduce prejudice, and increase civic engagement long after college graduation.

Although the research reviewed previously is encouraging, some limitations and potential problems with intergroup contact have been demonstrated. Perhaps most important, there is evidence for a negative bias. Paolini, Harwood, and Rubin (2010) found that negative contact increases the individual's awareness of the other's out-group identity and tends to increase prejudice toward that out-group. Barlow et al. (2012) found that negative contact increased prejudice more than positive contact decreased it. In addition, contact quality interacted with contact quantity so that the impact of increased negative contact was greater than the impact of increased positive contact. In short, contact is a two-edged sword. Similar findings exist in the higher education literature with inconclusive findings on the impact across racial/ethnic groups. As Antonio (2004) notes, the impact of interaction with racially different students tends to be more pronounced among minority student groups than among majority groups. Other studies, particularly those related to global experiences, find that study abroad can reinforce discriminatory stereotypes (Vande Berg, Paige, & Lou, 2012). Thus, any interventions based on increased contact between groups should ensure that the contact is positive and provide appropriate reflection in order to challenge student beliefs, not reinforce prejudicial ideas.

As stated at the beginning of this chapter, a diverse workforce poses a challenge for many employees because their biases regarding out-groups inhibit their ability to work well with members of those out-groups. Thus, a key question is how to decrease such prejudices and increase the ability to work with diverse others. Our discussion to this point has focused on work dealing with bias and the effects of various experiences on that bias. Conceptually, the contact hypothesis has garnered the most attention and support. In the remainder of this chapter, we review a number of interventions designed to decrease biases and increase students' ability to work with out-groups. Some of the empirical reviews we discuss include research done both on students and workers, whereas other reviews are limited to one population or the other. We include all this work because we believe human nature does not suddenly alter when students graduate. Approaches that work in the workplace are likely to work on campus as well.

Research on reducing racial bias among students in higher education has focused on several areas: diversity courses; intercultural education; formal training workshops; and student celebrations, safe spaces, and housing. Some studies (Chang, 2002; Whitt, Nora, Edison, Terenzini, & Pascarella, 1999) note small but significant changes, whereas others (Henderson-King & Kaleta, 2000) do not show any effect. In addition, even if the interventions reduce prejudice, intentional practice may be needed to meaningfully affect cross-racial interactions. The impact of interventions also varies by race, with racial minority students receiving the larger gains compared to White students (Antonio, 2004).

DIVERSITY COURSES

Some research attention has been given to diversity courses, including stand-alone courses focused on specific identity groups (i.e., women and gender studies courses), multiple courses that combine for a certificate or academic concentration, and multicultural education infused across a college curriculum similar to Writing Across the Curriculum. Studies of courses in women studies, African American studies, and the like consistently find positive effects of course participation on student understanding and engagement with diversity. Martin (2014) meaningfully expanded the criteria in an examination of the effects of participation in a single one-semester multicultural course. The criteria included cultural identity, intergroup understanding and contact, democratic participation, and academic outcomes. Students in the multicultural course showed an increase in the first three criteria but not in academic outcomes. Martin concluded that participation in diversity courses compliments the research on structural diversity (Gurin et al., 2002). Unfortunately, strong causal conclusions are impossible due to the lack of random assignment to the class and the use of a weak control group (an elective class in a different discipline—psychology rather than sociology). Watt and Linley (2014) argue that multicultural education presumes that cultural identity as a part of college student development plays a role in supporting college student learning. The exploration and infusion of identity into academic work creates a connection between the material being presented in a course and the lived experience of the student; simply, they have greater identification with the course material. In addition, multicultural education is found to promote a greater capacity for complex thinking, assisting with academic and interpersonal success (Bowman, 2009).

The impact on multicultural education varies across racial/ethnic groups. Multiple studies confirm that White students obtain a greater benefit from multicultural education than do non-White students (Bowman, 2009; Denson, 2009; Gurin et al., 2002; Kuklinski, 2006), contrary to the work of Antonio (2004). Explanations for the greater impact on White students focus on the contact hypothesis and support the need to recruit more minority students to achieve structural diversity. White students are less likely than non-White students to have experienced substantial contact with members of racially different groups pre-college. Multicultural education provides some of the first opportunities for some White students to engage in intergroup education and, therefore, they reap the largest benefits from what is termed "acquaintance potential" (Sidanius, Levin, van Laar, & Sears, 2008). Moreover, multicultural education can promote a valuing of diversity and a rejection of oppression, perspectives that are more likely to be preexisting for non-White than for White students.

Underlying diversity courses and multicultural education are intentional curricular strategies that motivate college students from varied groups to move away from simply sitting in the same classroom together to interaction and reflection. The literature consistently finds that interventions that include learning about other groups decrease racial bias, but larger effects on bias are provided by interventions that include positive intergroup contact (Denson, 2009). As mentioned previously, Pettigrew and Tropp (2008) found in a meta-analysis that knowledge is the least effective mediator of intergroup contact and prejudice. Prejudice is more effectively reduced by knowledge coupled with reducing anxiety and increasing empathy.

INTERCULTURAL EDUCATION

Another important intervention in higher education involves intercultural and cross-cultural interactions, which are historically facilitated in classrooms and through co-curricular on-campus experiences. Intercultural research concerns cognitive knowledge (i.e., learning) and the ability to adapt to new environments with different values (Byram, 1997; Deardorff, 2006). As Hammer (2012) explains, intercultural or cross-cultural competence building involves "increasing cultural self-awareness; deepening understanding of the experiences, values, perceptions, and behaviors of people from diverse cultural communities; and expanding the capability to shift cultural perspective and adapt behavior to bridge across cultural differences" (p. 116). Inter- and cross-cultural competency development occurs over the course of time and can be facilitated through increased contact with diverse individuals and through interactions both inside and outside the classroom. Faculty are important in facilitating intercultural interactions because research shows that intercultural encounters "can even reinforce stereotypes and prejudices," which tends to happen "if the experiences of critical incidents in intercultural contexts are not evaluated on cognitive, affective, and behavioral levels" (Otten, 2003, p. 15). In other words, encountering differences can lead to individuals feeling superior rather than encouraging their growth and development (Hurtado, 2001), unless those critical incidents (and associated behaviors, thought patterns, and actions) can be thoughtfully processed by the individuals involved, via faculty or staff facilitation (Otten, 2003).

The previous paragraph dealt with intercultural experiences that occur on campus. More extensive cross-cultural interactions are provided by study abroad programs, which provide unique opportunities for students to engage in meaningful learning away from their home campus (Passarelli & Kolb, 2012). Astin, Astin, and Lindholm (2011) point to the power that study abroad has for enlarging students' perspectives by exposing them to a diversity of cultures, peoples, and ideas. They write that study abroad encourages students "to consider the 'other,' to develop an understanding of differences and of how the self and others are interconnected" (Astin et al., 2011, p. 130). When they study and live in a new culture, college students must make sense of the ambiguity and unfamiliarity with which they are repeatedly confronted (Passarelli & Kolb, 2012). In these moments of sense-making, students often assume new ways of thinking and behaving (Passarelli & Kolb, 2012). However, immersion in another culture does not guarantee significant learning, and similar to on-campus intercultural experience, it can reaffirm stereotypes and create a feeling of superiority (Vande Berg et al., 2012).

For both intercultural and cross-cultural interactions, providing structured opportunities for reflection is essential to moving students beyond a mindset of polarized superiority toward one of adaptation—which involves shifting cultural perspectives and behaviors in a genuine and appropriate manner (Hammer, 2012). Vande Berg et al. (2012) note that "only when students are learning within a context informed by experiential/constructivist perspectives—only when they are immersed in another culture and receive meaningful intercultural mentoring and opportunities for reflection on meaning-making—do most students develop to an impressive degree" (p. 21). Hammer (2012) recommends "cultural mentoring, learning about patterns of cultural differences, reflection on intercultural experiences, active involvement in the cultural setting, pre-departure and re-entry preparation, and onsite intercultural interventions" (p. 133) to successfully facilitate learning during study abroad experiences. Many of these factors involve curricular design and involvement from instructors who can create structured reflection opportunities and mentoring.

DIVERSITY TRAINING WORKSHOPS

Many college campuses provide diversity training workshops for student, faculty, and staff audiences. These training sessions are typically offered through the student affairs division in offices on diversity; multiculturalism; women and gender studies; lesbian, gay, bisexual, transgender, and queer or questioning (LGBTQ); and the like; they differ from diversity courses in that they are often shorter, more interactive, and intentionally bridge academic and student affairs. Trainings are often peer-facilitated (especially for student groups, which also include a professional staff member as facilitator), interactive with collaborative techniques, and include intergroup dialogues (Watt & Linley, 2014). Training content often focuses on both individual and community development in relation to dominant social and institutional structures. Research finds that such diversity training and workshops have only a moderate effect on reducing racial bias overall (Watt & Linely, 2014). One study that examined drama-based diversity training found that student perception of diversity changed through the 1-day workshop and helped students to visualize situations and increase emotional intelligence around equity and diversity (Hayat & Walton, 2013). Bezrukova, Jehn, and Spell (2012), in their narrative review, found that a majority of the campus studies they unearthed focused on curricular rather than on co-curricular interventions and suggest that using multiple training activities and integrating diversity training with a larger scale diversity management initiative is most likely to be effective.

Although the question of interracial relations has dominated higher education research on diversity and conflict, a scattering of studies addresses other dimensions. For example, Safe Zone training is designed to increase understanding and support for sexual minority (LGBTQ) students and faculty (Poynter & Tubbs, 2007). Such programs can include a variety of activities, such as a discussion of stereotypes and terminology, presentations by gay and trans-gendered individuals about their experiences, role-play exercises about how to respond to bigoted comments, and provision of written resources for allies. The program may provide signs or symbols for display, in many cases only to those who have completed the training. Such displays indicate that the individual is a safe contact for individuals with minority gender or sexual orientations. This visibility is thought to help create a more inclusive campus climate. Finkel, Storaasli, Bandele, and Schaefer (2003) investigated the effects of Safe Zone training on graduate psychology students' self-reported attitudinal and behavioral changes. The authors interpret the results as promising, but the lack of a control group makes it difficult to interpret the results with confidence.

Religion is another demographic dimension that can stimulate bias. Clark, Brimhall Vargas, Schlosser, and Allmo (2002) introduce the issue of Christian privilege and offer some thoughts about how to increase awareness of the issue—approaches that might be applied to students. Clark (2003) then provides a case study of how one higher education unit attempted to build a religiously inclusive community. Note that neither report provides any data regarding what actually works. Hage, Hopson, Siegel, Payton, and DeFanti (2006) surveyed counseling programs and found that even these programs, for which an understanding of religious differences would seem to be important, provide very little instruction on religion and spirituality.

In short, although both religious and sexual orientation diversity address important dimensions of human differences both on and off campus, there are significant problems in both cases. Although there appear to be many Safe Zone training programs on college campuses, solid research on their efficacy appears to be missing. The problem with religious diversity appears even more basic; with little evidence for any on-campus training, much less research on training efficacy exists. These points highlight the need to prepare students for diversity on dimensions other than race and the need for research on the efficacy of such training.

Within the business domain, there is a substantial literature on diversity and cross-cultural training, in particular, when used to prepare expatriates for overseas assignments (Litrell, Salas, Hess, Paley, & Riedel, 2006; Nam, Cho, & Lee, 2014). Because cross-cultural competence was covered by Klafehn in Chapter 4, we do not discuss this literature here. A survey of 674 randomly selected HR professionals revealed that the existence of a diversity training budget in 2010 varied greatly with organization size, ranging from 5% among organizations with fewer than 100 employees to 52% among organizations with at least 25,000 employees (Society for Human Resources Management, 2011). Anand and Winters (2008) review the changes in how diversity training has been implemented throughout the decades. Contemporary approaches are likely to include course offerings on specific demographic dimensions (e.g., sexual orientation) and issues (e.g., intercultural communication). In addition, trainers can take a wide variety of approaches, including e-learning and intact work group sessions. In short, there is no doubt that many different approaches are taken to diversity training. To explore the relevance of this work for students in higher education, we must answer two questions. First, what are the effects of diversity training? Specifically, does it decrease employee bias and increase the inclusive culture of the organization? Second, if it has a positive effect, what aspects of the training have that effect? Unfortunately, neither of these questions can be answered with confidence.

In their massive review of research on prejudice reduction, Paluck and Green (2009) could not find a single example of a field experiment on diversity training from which causal conclusions could be drawn. In a 30-year study of diversity management, Kalev, Dobbin, and Kelly (2006) found that diversity training had negative effects on the representation of Black women in managerial ranks. A more detailed analysis found that the effect was positive for Black and White women among federal contractors but had the opposite effect among noncontractors.

Kalinoski et al. (2013) report a meta-analysis of the diversity training literature. Over all studies, diversity training was significantly related to affective-based, cognitive-based, and skill-based criteria. Consistent with the emphasis on intergroup contact, they report that the effects on affective and cognitive criteria were larger for training procedures that facilitated social interaction than for those that did not. Directly relevant to this chapter, they found larger effect sizes (for both affective and cognitive criteria) for research on employees than for research on student participants. Related to this, although apparently inconsistent, the effect sizes for affective-based outcomes were larger for diversity education than for diversity training. Finally, effect sizes were smaller for objective measures than for self-report on cognitive-based outcomes and for control group designs than for repeated-measures designs. They do not specifically group studies that used strong control group designs with students in educational settings, but they list 30 independent groups studies of students, and the results summarized previously suggest a positive effect, at least on attitudes and knowledge.

CELEBRATIONS, SAFE SPACES, AND STUDENT HOUSING

As stated previously, student affairs units are often the hub for diversity training programs on campus. These units are also often responsible for creating non-academic and nonformal teachable moments related to diversity through celebrations, safe spaces, and housing initiatives and programming. Typical student affairs diversity celebrations and events are often centered on Black History Month, Asian American History Month, Women's History Month, Pride Week, and so on. At our institution, George Mason University, International Week—a showcase of diverse countries, cultures, and cuisines—has been celebrated for more than 30 years, and it is one of the most popular and anticipated student events on campus. From a student affairs perspective, celebrations such as this bolster more formal trainings and courses on campus by creating an inclusive environment in which race, ethnicity, internationality, and identity can be explored in a creative, nonthreatening, and engaging way.

Creating visible spaces for exploration of this kind is vital on campuses. Again, this work is primarily done by student affairs professionals, who work to both support and challenge students learning in the area of diversity by ensuring that safe spaces on campus are available for free speech, reflection, and connection. Furthermore, these spaces allow for organic interactions, such as those espoused in contact theory, that can work to further integrate a diverse perspective into the students who experience them. Examples of this work are manifold and can be found throughout campuses. They include establishing free speech zones and negotiating respectful student protests; providing veteran "green spaces," campus ministry spaces, and meditation rooms for reflection; working with facilities to build foot baths for adherence to prayer rituals and establish rooms for students who are nursing mothers; working with recreation centers to allow women-only swimming times; and ensuring access for students with differing abilities. By establishing visible spaces on campus, diversity is thus made more visible, and students are able to engage with difference in tangible ways.

Among the most important spaces in which diversity can be made visible and be explored is campus student housing. Shook and Fazio (2008) report a study in which White freshmen were randomly assigned to a White or an African American roommate. They completed a survey and test of implicit racism during the first and last 2 weeks of the autumn quarter. Those with interracial roommates reported less satisfaction and less involvement with their roommates at both times than did those with same-race roommates. On the other hand, the general decline in relationship satisfaction over the quarter was smaller or even reversed among interracial roommates as compared to same-race roommates, with some of those differences being statistically significant. Implicit bias toward African Americans decreased significantly more among White students with African American roommates than among those with White roommates. Finally, intergroup anxiety decreased significantly only among White students with African American roommates. It is significant to note that this study lasted only a single quarter; one wonders about the longer term effects.

RECOMMENDATIONS

Positive gains in attitudes and knowledge that can be leveraged through increased opportunities for education and training are key to developing both diversity-aware college students and a globally prepared workforce. The varied contexts of higher education institutions (student demographics and campus location, resources, governance, mission, etc.) create complications in recommending specific practices for individual campuses. For example, a campus with the designation of a Minority Serving Institution has different diversity challenges and opportunities than a campus with a majority Caucasian population. Therefore, we focus our recommendations on more macro-level or organizational considerations that can be implemented using a variety of practices that suit the needs of the individual campuses.

Diversity Training and Programming for Faculty and Staff

College faculty and staff must have the relevant training and tools to provide meaningful learning opportunities for students in the area of global and multicultural competence and to support student-focused interventions. This training is particularly important for student affairs staff. Student affairs professionals, given their historical role of enriching college student experiences by attending to campus environments and student development, are well poised to integrate multiculturalism in higher education. To address changing student needs, Pope, Reynolds, and Muller (2004) recommend that all student affairs practitioners become multiculturally competent by integrating multicultural awareness, knowledge, and skills into the core competencies of student affairs practice.

Although there is much confusion regarding the terminology of multicultural competence, with many terms being used interchangeably (e.g., multiculturalism, cross-cultural awareness, global competence, and cross-cultural competency), the model most adopted in student affairs practice is that of Pope, Miklitsch, Mueller, and Weigand (2008). Pope et al. begin with the premise that colleges are increasingly complex organizations with more diverse student bodies that have significant challenges related to race, gender, physical disability, and other differences. Since the 1990s, scholars have argued that student affairs practitioners need to reflect on their own race and understand themselves as racial beings in order to effectively work with diverse student groups (McEwen & Roper, 1994). Landreman, Rasmussen, King, and Jiang (2007) found that establishing multicultural competence within university educators, inclusive of faculty and student affairs professionals, required exposure to diversity and one or more critical incidents combined with reflection. Critical incidents refer to significant events that simulated reflection and include such events as watching a movie about race, revealing one's sexual identity to friends and family, and traveling to other countries. For example, one participant met his Latina grandmother for the first time in a hotel, where she was mistaken by a guest for a housekeeper. Landreman and colleagues note,

> Further exposure, critical incidents, and reflection resulted in continued meaning making. These eventually led to intentional decisions to develop intergroup relationships and build coalitions, resulting in the development of a critical consciousness whereby participants intentionally pursued— rather than passively received—additional intercultural learning experiences. (p. 292)

Although some colleges and universities have training and education geared specifically for faculty and staff (special Safe Zone sessions, small group identity workshops, diversity trainers for classrooms, etc.), education and training for faculty and staff are not usually a requirement, nor are they consistent across campuses. This inconsistency can create a disconnect between the experiences students need to be prepared for a changing workforce and faculty and staff's ability to provide those experiences (Pope et al., 2008). Thus, higher education organizations need to capitalize on critical incidents for staff and students as reflective opportunities to promote multicultural competence and diversity on campus.

Campus Climate Surveys and Bias Reports

For staff and faculty to provide useful and informed support of diversity on their campuses through safe spaces and an inclusive climate, it is important for them to know what diversity issues are prevalent in their communities. Campus climate surveys have become increasingly useful in this respect because they ask students, faculty, and staff about the environments in which they live and work, and they should be a regular and ongoing part of campus assessments (Hurtado, Griffin, Arellano, & Cuellar, 2008). Campus climate surveys are useful in that they help construct a clearer picture of the state of diversity at an institution so that administrators, faculty, and staff can make evidence-based assessments and take actions to remedy and improve the campus climate (Hurtado et al., 2008). In particular, these surveys incorporate the use of bias incident reports, a helpful way for students to report incidents of discrimination or prejudice on campus. If there is no formal process for students to report bias incidents, one should be established by collaborative efforts between diversity offices, ombudsman offices, and faculty, staff, and student senates. Results from these resources can help craft approaches to training and educational programs on campus.

Collaboration via Diversity in the Co-curriculum and Core Curriculum

Historically, diversity training and programming has been the work of women and gender studies centers and diversity and LGBTQ offices (or officers) on campus. Although diversity and associated competencies are often woven into aspects of other student affairs programming, services, and events on campus (through housing staff training, housing programs, student involvement events, etc.), diversity is not necessarily a focus of these efforts. Greater connection and collaboration between diversity-focused offices and their student affairs colleagues has the potential to broaden the number of students exposed to diversity-related benefits and competencies.

There are a number of areas throughout the college experience in which this collaboration could provide useful competency-based education and integration that can benefit students, faculty, staff, and employers. Orientation programs often offer common read programs, which help students make connections with faculty, staff, and other incoming freshman. Diversity and multicultural competency could easily be a focus of common read programming, providing a platform of introduction and processing of diversity issues by all members of the campus community. Opportunities for multi-stakeholder education and training are also possible through common university courses geared toward the first-year experience. These courses often highlight the diversity of campus, but they could be leveraged to not just highlight diversity but also provide cooperative learning opportunities on its importance. Paluck and Green (2009) report that cooperative learning receives relatively strong support. In cooperative learning interventions, students must both learn from and teach one another. This is based on Deutsch's (1949) theory of social interdependence and is frequently operationalized as a "jigsaw" group.

This approach is clearly consistent with the intergroup contact theory—the mutual teaching and learning implies the presence of authority-supported intergroup contact with equal status and a common goal. By having students teach students in freshman and transfer transition courses, their development, as it relates to diversity, will allow them to make connections not just to life on campus but also to life after college and in their careers. Finally, there is an often-untapped opportunity for career centers on campus to specifically connect diversity training and programming to the work that they do in connecting students to employers and careers. Career centers should work with diversity offices and employers to incorporate diversity and multicultural/global competency as key components of career readiness.

Finally, as core curriculums are developed on campuses, administrators and faculty should make diversity, including global and multicultural competence, integral to student learning. Specifically, core curriculum diversity experiences should move beyond required course-taking by asking students to participate in diversity programming, training, and internship opportunities during their undergraduate experience. Furthermore, diversity and global/multicultural competence should be incorporated as a key component into capstone curriculum.

Consider Nontraditional and Graduate Student Needs

Much of the research done on diversity exposure and competency at the undergraduate level has focused on traditional students and small, private, liberal arts colleges. However, traditional students are no longer the majority on most college campuses, as they make up only 16% of enrollments (Stokes, 2006). Increasingly, the college undergraduate student body is composed of part-time, older, transfer, and returning students (Stokes, 2006). This change in the student body implies an increase in diversity in terms of age and life experiences, both of which can contribute to diversity-related programing and conversations. In addition, to leverage learning related to diversity on campus, faculty, staff, and administration should craft development opportunities that are geared toward nontraditional students, perhaps by taking advantage of their lived experiences and current off-campus employment. Many colleges have developed off-campus student offices to reach out to nonresidential and nontraditional students. These offices are primed to connect nontraditional students with diversity learning opportunities and support on campus. In addition, nontraditional and international students make up a large portion of the graduate student population and current and future workforce. Given their roles, often as graduate teaching assistants, it is important that graduate students participate in the diversity training and programming opportunities to which other students, faculty, and staff have access.

Research and Recognize Multiple Diversity Forms on Campus

As evidenced in this chapter, traditional research related to diversity on campus and in the marketplace has focused on racial and ethnic difference. Although newer research has begun to explore diversity as it relates to LGBTQ populations, there are still areas of diversity on campus that require greater investigation and promotion. Colleges and universities should incorporate multiple forms of diversity, including age, ability, religion, spirituality, and veteran status, and they should expand research and conversation in these areas. Further research should investigate the intersection of multiple identities, with potential research questions to include the following: How do race, gender, and socioeconomic status impact the college student diversity experience? Does the focus of racial diversity or cross-cultural competency training in college have the same outcomes for students who only partially identify as part of an underrepresented group? What impact do multiple and intersecting identities have on workforce choice and outcomes? In what ways can programs, courses, and co-curricular programs meet, support, and challenge the diverse needs of students from all backgrounds? Better understanding of the aspects, interests, and needs of these community members will help integrate effective climate questions, training, and courses. The outcome of garnering new and more information in these less-researched areas of diversity will be a more diverse and inclusive campus.

REFERENCES

Aberson, C. L., & Haag, S. C. (2007). Contact, perspective taking, and anxiety as predictors of stereotype endorsement, explicit attitudes, and implicit attitudes. *Group Process & Intergroup Relations, 10*(2), 179–201.

Allport, G. W. (1954). *The nature of prejudice*. New York, NY: Addison-Wesley.

Anand, R., & Winters, M.-F. (2008). A retrospective view of corporate diversity training from 1964 to the present. *Academy of Management Learning & Education, 7*(3), 356–372.

Antonio, A. L. (2004). The influence of friendship groups on intellectual self-confidence and educational aspirations in college. *Journal of Higher Education, 75*(4), 446–471.

Astin, A. W., Astin, H. S., & Lindholm, J. A. (2011). *Cultivating the spirit: How college can enhance students' inner lives*. San Francisco, CA: Jossey-Bass.

Barlow, F. K., Paolini, S., Pedersen, A., Hornsey, M. J., Radke, H. R. M., Harwood, J., . . . Sibley, C. G. (2012). The contact caveat: Negative contact predicts increased prejudice more than positive contact predicts reduced prejudice. *Personality and Social Psychology Bulletin, 38*(12), 1629–1643.

Benjamin, M., & Hamrick, F. A. (2011). Expanding the learning environment. In P. M. Magolda & M. B. Baxter Magolda (Eds.), *Contested issues in student affairs: Diverse perspectives and respectful dialogue* (pp. 23–34). Sterling, VA: Stylus.

Bezrukova, K., Jehn, K. A., & Spell, C. S. (2012). Reviewing diversity training: Where we have been and where we should go. *Academy of Management Learning and Education*, *11*(2), 207–227.

Binder, J., Zagefka, H., Brown, R., Funke, F., Kessler, T., Mummendey, A., ... Leyens, J. P. (2009). Does contact reduce prejudice or does prejudice reduce contact? A longitudinal test of the contact hypothesis among majority and minority groups in three European countries. *Journal of Personality and Social Psychology*, *96*(4), 843–856.

Bowman, N. A. (2009). College diversity courses and cognitive development among students from privileged and marginalized groups. *Journal of Diversity in Higher Education*, *2*, 182–194.

Bowman, N. A., Brandenberger, J. W., Hill, P. L., & Lapsley, D. K. (2011). The long-term impact of college diversity experiences: Well-being and social concerns 13 years after graduation. *Journal of College Student Development*, *52*, 729–739.

Byram, M. (1997). *Teaching and assessing intercultural communicative competence*. Philadelphia, PA: Multilingual Matters.

Cabrera, A., & Unruh, G. (2012). *Being global: How to think, act, and lead in a transformed world*. Cambridge, MA: Harvard Business Press.

Chang, M. J. (1996). *Racial diversity in higher education: Does a racially mixed student population affect educational outcomes?* Unpublished doctoral dissertation, University of California at Los Angeles.

Chang, M. J. (1999). Does racial diversity matter? The educational impact of racially diverse undergraduate population. *Journal of College Student Development*, *40*, 377–395.

Chang, M. J. (2002). The impact of an undergraduate diversity course requirement on students' racial views and attitudes. *Journal of General Education*, *51*(1), 21.

Chang, M. J., Astin, A. W., & Kim, D. (2004). Cross-racial interaction among undergraduates: Some consequences, causes, and patterns. *Research in Higher Education*, *45*, 529–553.

Chang, M. J., Denson, N., Saenz, V., & Misa, K. (2006). The educational benefits of sustaining cross-racial interaction among undergraduates. *Journal of Higher Education*, *77*, 430–455.

Clark, C. (2003). Diversity initiatives in higher education: A case study of multicultural organizational development through the lens of religion, spirituality, faith, and secular inclusion. *Multicultural Education*, *10*(3), 48–54.

Clark, C., Brimhall Vargas, M., Schlosser, L., & Allmo, C. (2002). It's not just "secret Santa" in December: Addressing educational and workplace climate issues linked to Christian privilege. *Multicultural Education*, *10*(2), 52–57.

Deardorff, D. K. (2006). Identification and assessment of intercultural competence as a student outcome of internationalization. *Journal of Studies in International Education*, *10*(3), 241–266.

Denson, N. (2009). Do curricular and co-curricular diversity activities influence racial bias? A meta-analysis. *Review of Educational Research*, *79*, 805–838.

Denson, N., & Bowman, N. A. (2013). University diversity and preparation for a global society: The role of diversity in shaping intergroup attitudes and civic outcomes. *Studies in Higher Education*, *38*, 555–570.

Deutsch, M. (1949). A theory of co-operation and competition. *Human Relations*, *2*(2), 129–152.

Dipboye, R. L., & Colella, A. (2005). *Discrimination at work: The psychological and organizational bases.* Mahwah, NJ: Erlbaum.

Engberg, M. E. (2004). Improving intergroup relations in higher education: A critical examination of the influence of educational interventions on racial bias. *Review of Educational Research, 74,* 473–524.

Finkel, M. J., Storaasli, R. D., Bandele, A., & Schaefer, V. (2003). Diversity training in graduate school: An exploratory evaluation of the Safe Zone project. *Professional Psychology: Research and Practice, 34*(5), 555–561.

Gurin, P. (1999). Expert report of Patricia Gurin. In: The compelling need for diversity in higher education, presented in *Gratz, et al. v. Bollinger, et al. and Grutter, et al. v. Bollinger, et al.* Washington, DC: Wilmer, Cutler, and Pickering.

Gurin, P., Dey, E. L., Hurtado, S., & Gurin, G. (2002). Diversity and higher education: Theory and impact on educational outcomes. *Harvard Educational Review, 72,* 330–366.

Hage, S. M., Hopson, A., Siegel, M., Payton, G., & DeFanti, E. (2006). Multicultural training in spirituality: An interdisciplinary review. *Counseling and Values, 50*(3), 217–234.

Hammer, M. (2012). The Intercultural Development Inventory: A new frontier in assessment and development of intercultural competence. In M. Vande Berg, R. M. Paige, & K. H. Lou (Eds.), *Student learning abroad: What our students are learning, what they're not, and what we can do about it* (pp. 115–136). Sterling, VA: Stylus.

Hayat, K., & Walton, S. (2013). Delivering equality and training within a university setting through drama-based training. *Journal of Psychological Issues in Organizational Culture, 3*(S1), 290–305.

Henderson-King, D., & Kaleta, A. (2000). Learning about social diversity: The undergraduate experience and intergroup tolerance. *Journal of Higher Education, 71,* 142–164.

Hewstone, M., Rubin, M., & Willis, H. (2002). Intergroup bias. *Annual Review of Psychology, 53*(1), 575–604.

Hodson, G. (2011). Do ideologically intolerant people benefit from intergroup contact? *Current Directions in Psychological Science, 20*(3), 154–159.

Hurtado, S. (2001). Linking diversity and educational purpose: How diversity affects the classroom environment and student development. In G. Orfield (Ed.), *Diversity challenged: Evidence on the impact of affirmative action* (pp. 187–203). Cambridge, MA: Harvard Education.

Hurtado, S., Engberg, M. E., Ponjuan, L., & Landreman, L. (2002). Students' precollege preparation for participation in a diverse democracy. *Research in Higher Education, 43*(2), 162–186.

Hurtado, S., Griffin, K. A., Arellano, L., & Cuellar, M. (2008). Assessing the value of climate assessments: Progress and future directions. *Journal of Diversity in Higher Education, 1*(4), 204.

International Monetary Fund. (2000, April 12). *Globalization: Threats or opportunity.* Retrieved from http://www.imf.org/external/np/exr/ib/2000/041200to.htm

International Monetary Fund. (2011, June 15). *Changing patterns of global trade.* Retrieved from http://www.imf.org/external/np/pp/eng/2011/061511.pdf

Jayakumar, U. M. (2008). Can higher education meet the needs of an increasingly diverse global society? Campus diversity and cross-cultural workforce competencies. *Harvard Educational Review, 78,* 615–651.

Jayakumar, U. M. (2009). The invisible rainbow in diversity: Factors influencing sexual prejudice among college students. *Journal of Homosexuality, 56*(6), 675–700.

Johnston, W. B., & Packer, A. E. (1987). *Workforce 2000: Work and workers for the 21st century.* Indianapolis, IN: Hudson Institute.

Kalev, A., Dobbin, F., & Kelly, E. (2006). Best practices or best guesses? Assessing the efficacy of corporate affirmative action and diversity practices. *American Sociological Review, 71,* 589–617.

Kalinoski, Z. T., Steele-Johnson, D., Peyton, E. J., Leas, K. A., Steinke, J., & Bowling, N. A. (2013). A meta-analytic evaluation of diversity training outcomes. *Journal of Organizational Behavior, 34*(8), 1076–1104.

Kuklinski, J. (2006). Review: The scientific study of campus diversity and students' educational outcomes. *Public Opinion Quarterly, 70*(1), 99–120.

Landreman, L. M., Rasmussen, C. J., King, P. M., & Jiang, C. X. (2007). A phenomenological study of the development of university educators' critical consciousness. *Journal of College Student Development, 48,* 275–295.

Lester, J. (2011). Supporting intragroup and intergroup dialogues: A model for collaborative campuses. In M. Magolda & M. Baxter Magolda (Eds.), *Contested issues in student affairs: Diverse perspectives and respectful dialogue.* Sterling, VA: Stylus.

Litrell, L. N., Salas, E., Hess, K. P., Paley, M., & Riedel, S. (2006). Expatriate preparation: A critical analysis of 25 years of cross-cultural training research. *Human Resource Development Review, 5*(3), 355–388.

Martin, D. (2014). Good education for all? Student race and identity development in the multicultural classroom. *International Journal of Intercultural Relations, 39,* 110–123.

Martin, N. D., Tobin, W., & Spenner, K. I. (2014). Interracial friendships across the college years: Evidence from a longitudinal case study. *Journal of College Student Development, 55*(7), 720–725.

McEwen, M. K., & Roper, L. D. (1994). Incorporating multiculturalism into student affairs preparation programs: Suggestions from the literature. *Journal of College Student Development, 35,* 46–53.

McKay, P. F., Avery, D. R., & Morris, M. A. (2008). Mean racial–ethnic differences in employee sales performance: The moderating role of diversity climate. *Personnel Psychology, 61*(2), 349–374.

Nam, K.-A., Cho, Y., & Lee, M. (2014). West meets East? Identifying the gap in current cross-cultural training research. *Human Resource Development Review, 13*(1), 36–57.

Otten, M. (2003). Intercultural learning and diversity in higher education. *Journal of Studies in International Education, 7*(1), 12–26.

Pager, D., & Shepherd, H. (2008). Racial discrimination in employment, housing, credit, and consumer markets. *Annual Review of Sociology, 34,* 181–209.

Paluck, E. L., & Green, D. P. (2009). Prejudice reduction: What works? A review and assessment of research and practice. *Annual Review of Psychology, 60,* 339–368.

Paolini, S., Harwood, J., & Rubin, M. (2010). Negative intergroup contact makes group memberships salient: Explaining why intergroup conflict endures. *Personality and Social Psychology Bulletin, 36*(12), 1723–1738.

Pascarella, E. T., Edison, M., Nora, A., Hagedorn, L. S., & Terenzini, P. T. (1996). Influence on students' openness to diversity and challenge in the first year of college. *Journal of Higher Education, 67,* 174–195.

Pascarella, E. T., Palmer, B., Moye, M., & Pierson, C. T. (2001). Do diversity experiences influence the development of critical thinking? *Journal of College Student Development, 42,* 257–271.

Passarelli, A. M., & Kolb, D. A. (2012). Using experiential learning theory to promote student learning and development in programs of education abroad. In M. Vande Berg, R. M. Paige, & K. H. Lou (Eds.), *Student learning abroad: What our students are learning, what they're not, and what we can do about it* (pp. 137–161). Sterling, VA: Stylus.

Pettigrew, T. F., & Tropp, L. R. (2006). A meta-analytic test of intergroup contact theory. *Journal of Personality and Social Psychology, 90*(5), 751–783.

Pettigrew, T. F., & Tropp, L. R. (2008). How does intergroup contact reduce prejudice? Metaanalytic tests of three mediators. *European Journal of Social Psychology, 38,* 922–934.

Pope, R. L., Miklitsch, T. A., Mueller, J. A., & Weigand, M. J. (2008, March). *Transforming practice through multicultural competence.* Papter presented at the meeting of the American College Personnel Association, Atlanta, GA.

Pope, R. L., Reynolds, A. L., & Mueller, J. A. (2004). *Multicultural competence in student affairs.* San Francisco, CA: Jossey-Bass.

Poynter, K. J., & Tubbs, N. J. (2007). Safe Zones: Creating LGBT safe space ally programs. *Journal of LGBT Youth, 5*(1), 121–132.

Shook, N. J., & Fazio, R. H. (2008). Interracial roommate relationships: An experimental field test of the contact hypothesis. *Psychological Science, 19*(7), 717–723.

Sidanius, J., Levin, S., van Laar, C., & Sears, D. O. (2008). *The diversity challenge.* New York, NY: Russell Sage.

Society for Human Resources Management. (2011). *SHRM survey findings: An examination of organizational commitment to diversity and inclusion.* Alexandria, VA: Author.

Stephan, W. G., & Stephan, C. W. (1985). Intergroup anxiety. *Journal of Social Issues, 41*(3), 157–175.

Stokes, P. J. (2006). *Hidden in plain sight: Adult learners forge a new tradition in higher education.* The Secretary of Education's Commission on the Future of Higher Education. Retrieved from https://www2.ed.gov/about/bdscomm/list/hiedfuture/reports/stokes.pdf

Swart, H., Hewstone, M., Christ, O., & Voci, A. (2010). The impact of crossgroup friendships in South Africa: Affective mediators and multigroup comparisons. *Journal of Social Issues, 66*(2), 309–333.

Tausch, N., Hewstone, M., Kenworthy, J. B., Psaltis, C., Schmid, K., Popan, J. R., . . . Hughes, J. (2010). Secondary transfer effects of intergroup contact: Alternative accounts and underlying processes. *Journal of Personality and Social Psychology, 99*(2), 282–302.

Thomas, R. R., Jr. (1990). From affirmative action to affirming diversity. *Harvard Business Review, 90*(2), 107–117.

Toossi, M. (2002). A century of change: The U.S. labor force, 1950–2050. *Monthly Labor Review, 125*(5), 15–28.

Toossi, M. (2007). Labor force projections to 2016: More workers in their golden years. *Monthly Labor Review, 130*(11), 33–52.

Tredoux, C., & Finchilescu, G. (2010). Mediators of the contact–prejudice relation among South African students on four university campuses. *Journal of Social Issues, 66*(2), 289–308.

Tropp, L. R., & Pettigrew, T. F. (2005). Relationships between intergroup contact and prejudice among minority and majority status groups. *Psychological Science, 16*(12), 951–957.

US Bureau of Labor Statistics (BLS). (2013). *Labor force projections to 2022: The labor force participation rate continues to fall.* Retrieved from https://www.bls.gov/opub/mlr/2013/article/labor-force-projections-to-2022-the-labor-force-participation-rate-continues-to-fall.htm

US Department of Education, National Center for Education Statistics. (2013). *The condition of education 2013* (NCES 2013-037). Washington, DC: Author.

Vande Berg, M., Paige, R. M., & Lou, K. H. (Eds.). (2012). *Student learning abroad: What our students are learning, what they're not, and what we can do about it.* Sterling, VA: Stylus.

Wagner, U., & Hewstone, M. (2012). Intergroup contact. In L. Tropp (Ed.), *Oxford handbook of intergroup conflict* (pp. 193–209). Oxford, England: Oxford University Press.

Watt, S. K., & Linley, J. L. (Eds.). (2014). *Creating successful multicultural initiatives in higher education and student affairs: New directions for student services* (no. 144). San Francisco, CA: Wiley.

Whitt, E. J., Nora, A., Edison, M., Terenzini, P. T., & Pascarella, E. T. (1999). Interactions with peers and objective and self-reported cognitive outcomes across 3 years of college. *Journal of College Student Development, 40*, 61–78.

Entrepreneurial, Professional, and Leadership Career Aspiration Survey

Toward Holistic Career Development of University Students in the 21st Century[1]

OLEXANDER S. CHERNYSHENKO, KIM-YIN CHAN,
RINGO HO MOON-HO, MARILYN UY, AND
EMMA YOKE LOO SAM ■

THE 21ST CENTURY CONTEXT OF WORK AND CAREERS

For many individuals in developed nations, a career is more than just a vocation or occupation; it concerns meaning created over an unfolding set of experiences and the lessons of a lifetime (Savickas, 2002; Super, 1957, 1980). More than just choosing a job, vocation, or occupation, youth throughout the world today expect to unfold a career over a lifetime, shaped by environmental opportunities and constraints, personal aspirations (including motivations, efficacies, and intentions), abilities, and experiences. In this context, it is useful to distinguish the act of making a vocational choice—typically associated with selecting a postsecondary or high school education program—from shaping and developing a career over a lifetime, which should be a constant work in progress. Although there is a clear framework for understanding vocational interests—namely Holland's (1959, 1997) Realistic, Investigative, Artistic, Social, Enterprising, Conventional (RIASEC) model (discussed in Chapter 8)—there is no well-accepted framework for representing the subjective space in which careers unfold over time.

Along with the shift in work and career attitudes, the range of career options available to youth entering the workforce has substantially widened. Most formal education systems are still designed to produce specialized vocationalists and professionals to supply the workforce needed to support a national economy (a legacy of the 19th century Industrial Revolution). However, in today's work environments, these specialists are increasingly asked to handle managerial and commercial challenges that often lie outside of their functional training. In this work environment of entrepreneurial, professional, and leadership career opportunities, important questions concern the career aspirations of youth, especially in the postsecondary or tertiary education system, who are being prepared to join the workforce: How do they make sense of their future work and careers given the typically specialized professional and/or vocational education and training that they receive? To what extent do students hold boundaryless versus single-track notions of their future careers? Do they view entrepreneurial, professional, and (organizational) leadership careers as competing or mutually reinforcing options for the future?

The 21st century workplace has also become increasingly reliant on entrepreneurism and innovation as the means for economic survival as well as continued expansion. Public and private companies throughout the world strive to recruit and retain "talent," which is defined as employees capable of initiating and leading business development initiatives. On the other hand, the status of many professionals, individuals with a deep technical expertise in particular fields, has deteriorated as their knowledge base has either become obsolete or readily accessible by non-experts (Evetts, 2011; Falconbridge & Muzio, 2007).

However, most modern universities in developed economies, which were designed for highly professional faculties, continue training students for mostly professional careers. It is not surprising, therefore, that the dominant mindset of university graduates today is to prepare for a particular profession, enter the workforce, and rise up the ranks within the safety and security of an organization. Under this model, development of entrepreneurial and, to some extent, leadership capabilities is left to the environment, to the "school of life," and to some chance encounters with role models or market opportunities. As we progress through the 21st century, one might wonder when universities will face the realities of today's workplace and take a more active role in shaping students' careers not just along professional but also along entrepreneurial and leadership paths.

The NTU Career Aspiration Survey

As a research-based university with subject-defined colleges and programs that aim to produce highly qualified professionals and experts for society, the

Nanyang Technological University (NTU) in Singapore has launched several initiatives aimed at imbuing its professionally minded students with the culture and capacity for leadership, enterprise, and innovation. Given that career aspirations can affect individuals' initial career decisions, how they move from one job to another, and even how individuals view themselves in relation to previous work experiences (Derr & Laurent, 1989), NTU decided to launch the Career Aspiration Survey (CAS) to gain a better understanding of the factors that affect students' career aspirations and the extent to which these career aspirations change over the course of their tertiary education.

The NTU CAS was designed on the basis of a new, person-centered framework for more "boundaryless" careers called entrepreneurship, professionalism, and leadership (EPL; Chan et al., 2012). The survey encompassed a number of domains, constructs, and factors affecting student career aspirations. The survey data collected across the entire student population offered insights on how best to refine and augment NTU's educational and innovation/enterprise programs to ensure that the university provides balanced and holistic education for its students. This chapter offers readers an introduction to the NTU CAS, its framework, and key observations from the first 4 years of survey data. It also presents examples of how the survey is used to provide career feedback to students and how it is used to evaluate the effectiveness of career development courses.

The Value of Understanding Student Career Aspirations

With the exception of McClelland's (1961, 1963) research conducted during the height of the "Industrial Age" that examined the motivation of managers and entrepreneurs and, to a more limited extent, professionals, most research has studied various career aspirations in relative isolation and within different academic disciplines or fields of study. Relatively recently, organizational researchers such as Cogliser and Bingham (2004) and Vecchio (2003) have also noted how leadership and entrepreneurship are studied as separate domains when they can in fact benefit from greater exchange of ideas. As a result, existing scientific knowledge—for example, of "who chooses an entrepreneurial career" or "how to train and educate entrepreneurs"—is largely based on research and theory focusing solely on the study of entrepreneurs' motivation, careers, and performance, independent of alternative or even competing career or work options such as professions or leadership/managerial paths. Although such an approach may help clarify what makes certain people choose entrepreneurial work, it fails to appreciate how those who choose professional or leader/managerial paths think about entrepreneurship or, specifically, why they may shun or simply not consider entrepreneurial work.

Studying career aspirations or motivation is important because they affect an individual's initial career decisions, how one moves from one job to another, and even how one views oneself in relation to his or her work experiences (Derr & Laurent, 1989). As nations become more developed, necessity or survival-based entrepreneurship also becomes replaced by the security of organizational careers and working life. Today, most modern universities are designed for highly professional "professors" to train future "professionals." The 21st century, however, has witnessed the rise of a new, knowledge-based globalized economy that demands a significant change in the models of work, education, and careers in many societies. Meeting these changes calls for a new mindset whereby entrepreneurship, professionalism, and leadership (EPL) are not viewed as different career paths but, rather, as a lifelong developmental career space in which individuals can and should grow and apply themselves in all three domains. Such a mindset is also necessary in an age of the "protean or boundaryless career" (Arthur, 1994; Arthur & Rousseau, 1996; Hall & Associates, 1996) in which people are increasingly adopting a personal values-driven, self-directed attitude toward career management, resulting in greater mobility and a more "whole-life perspective" in their careers. In this case, it becomes increasingly more meaningful to think of individuals' careers in terms of a trajectory evolving in a multidimensional (EPL) career space rather than developing along a single vocational domain.

EPL as a Broad Framework for Careers in the 21st Century

In 1989, the renowned organizational strategist, Rosabeth Moss Kanter (1989), wrote a chapter in the *Handbook of Career Theory* titled "Careers and the Wealth of Nations," in which she called for a better understanding of the connections between careers and economic, social, and political issues in societies, beyond the individual psychological or organizational perspectives. Kanter presented a framework of "three principal forms"—bureaucratic (or leader/managerial), professional, and entrepreneurial careers—as a way to think about career at the macro-organizational, socioeconomic level. She argued that each of these career forms was defined by its own "logic," as summarized in Table 7.1.

Whereas Kanter (1989) described the three career forms as three different "types," each with its own "logic," Chan et al. (2012) contended that it may be more beneficial to think of the three forms as dimensions of career space such that all individual careers can be defined as vectors in a three-dimensional (EPL) career space originating from a particular vocational domain/subject (Figure 7.1). In this sense, the EPL framework may be especially relevant at the tertiary education level: Students starting their university education in the knowledge era are faced with many choices and opportunities, among which

Table 7.1 THE THREE PRINCIPAL CAREER FORMS OF KANTER (1989)

	Leader	**Professional**	**Entrepreneur**
Logic defined by . . .	Advancement	Craft or skill and reputation	Creation of new value
Key resources for individual	Rank and position in organizational hierarchy	Monopolization of socially valued knowledge and reputation	Capacity to create valued outputs
"Growth" involves . . .	"Moving up" in the hierarchy	Increased cross-organizational mobility	Organizational growth
Essence of career	Security	Rarity and quality of one's skill and expertise	Risk
Nature of career	Predictable; but can get stuck in hierarchy (cannot move until others leave) . . .	Freedom, independence, and control over one's tasks	Freedom, independence, and control over one's tasks and organizational context; also more uncertainty about the future

the pursuit of expert knowledge and skills (i.e., professional career path with a particular vocational subject) is only one potential alternative. For example, a starting engineer might be initially reliant on in-depth knowledge of a field (professional) but might later be promoted to management level (leadership)

- **Career vision & passion**
  - Next question is how they would like to apply their discipline specific knowledge/skills as a "career"

- Vocational choice:
  - Assuming people have "chosen" their topic, subject or discipline, e.g., Engineering, Teaching, Accounting.

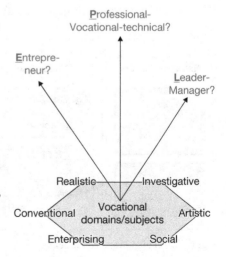

Figure 7.1 EPL "career vectors."

and, as his responsibilities evolve, tasked with the creation of new products or services to capture a new sector of a market (entrepreneurial). On the other hand, a young entrepreneur may initially rely on her entrepreneurial skills to take advantage of market opportunities by creating a company but, in time, may find herself in a senior leadership role dealing with the day-to-day pains of business expansion.

The ultimate question is therefore whether university education should continue to emphasize the professional path or should encourage and provide opportunities for students to gain skills more evenly across the three dimensions, which in turn may equip them for more fruitful and successful careers in the future. The NTU CAS effort incorporated the EPL framework for a more comprehensive and holistic view of students' careers. It drew a picture of their current career aspirations as well as helped in understanding how these three career paths are interrelated. The longitudinal data collection also provided an opportunity to see how students' career motivations changed during the course of their studies and how these were affected by university experiences.

NTU CAS MEASUREMENT MODEL

Design of the NTU CAS Survey: EPL Intent, Motivation, and Efficacy

As a tool designed to guide university student development policy, the NTU CAS has seven core fixed components: personal background, entrepreneurial climate perceptions, nascent entrepreneurial activity, career choice, as well as career aspirations as measured via EPL career intent, EPL efficacy, and EPL career motivation (Figure 7.2). All items and scales for the seven core

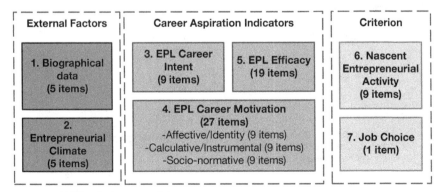

Figure 7.2 NTU CAS core model.

components were developed and validated in a pilot study involving 304 students in June and July, 2010. The function of each component in the survey is discussed in turn. Unless otherwise stated, all scales are measured on a 5-point Likert scale, where 1 corresponds to strongly disagree and 5 to strongly agree. The content of all survey items is shown in Appendix 1.

External Factors

BIOGRAPHICAL DATA

In an effort to determine whether individual or familial work experience influenced student career aspirations, five items soliciting biographical data were included. Items covered previous work experience of the individual and work experience of immediate family members (parents and siblings) in a small or medium-sized enterprise. Duration of employment in these enterprises was also measured. Past research had shown biographical data to predict a variety of outcomes related to objective and subjective career success (Ng, Eby, Sorensen, & Feldman, 2005).

ENTREPRENEURIAL CLIMATE

To take into account the sociopolitical influence of the environment in Singapore on student entrepreneurial career aspirations, the CAS included an 8-item scale on entrepreneurial climate. The scale covered both the perceived level of social respect (3 items) and negative support for entrepreneurs (5 items) at the national level. Students responded by stating the extent to which they agreed or disagreed with eight statements of entrepreneurship in Singapore. The following is an example: "Being a career entrepreneur is a very respected occupation in this society." In their study of more than 4000 Singapore workers, Lee, Wong, Foo, and Leung (2001) demonstrated that work environments with unfavorable climates influence entrepreneurial intentions.

Career Aspiration Indicators

The CAS attempts to draw a comprehensive picture of student career intentions by examining them concurrently with other factors that may contribute to an individual's career aspirations, providing quantifiable insight into this concept. At the core are the motivational aspects that influence an individual's attitudes toward a particular career path. Motivation for a career path should not be confused with intent. In the CAS, intent is operationalized as the readiness of an individual to pursue a particular career path, whereas motivation is based on factors such as personal identification with a career path and the norms of the immediate social environment that affect the direction, intensity, and persistence to achieve the chosen career aspiration. Efficacy is another critical component of career aspirations in the CAS survey. It is thought that individuals seldom pursue a career path in which they possess no skill. Efficacy is operationalized as how capable or competent individuals perceive themselves to be at performing the various proficiencies associated with a particular career path.

EPL CAREER INTENT

In this subscale, students reported the extent to which they agreed or disagreed with statements regarding their career goals and preferences on a 5-point scale, where 5 is "strongly agree" and 1 is "strongly disagree." The following is an example of an entrepreneurial intent item: "I have a viable business idea and intend to start my own business soon after graduation."

EPL CAREER MOTIVATION

The measurement of EPL career motivation in the CAS model is based on earlier work on the motivation to lead by Chan and Drasgow (2001). Their scale examines EPL motivation via affective/identity, calculative/instrumental, and socio-normative factors. The affective/identity factor takes into consideration an individual's preference for a certain career. This subscale examines an individual's valence toward a career path as well as how much the individual identifies with that career path. An example of an entrepreneurial affective/identity item is the following: "Ever since I was a kid I have dreamed about opening my own business." The calculative/instrumental factor examines the individual's beliefs and evaluation of costs and benefits of a particular career track. The following is an example of an entrepreneurial calculative/instrumental item: "The rewards and satisfaction of starting and running a business far outweigh the risks and sacrifices needed." Last, the socio-normative factor assesses the prevailing attitudes and opinions of each career path in an individual's immediate social environment. An example of an entrepreneurial socio-normative item is the following: "I feel I ought to live up to my parents' expectations to work in an entrepreneurial business environment."

EPL EFFICACY

Students' perceptions of their efficacy in entrepreneurial, professional, and leadership domains was examined via 19 items. Efficacy was operationalized as the extent to which students believed they would be confident in performing certain proficiencies associated with a particular career path. An example of an entrepreneurial efficacy item is the following: "How confident would you be in identifying opportunities to start-up viable businesses?" The following is an example of a professional proficiency item: "How confident would you be to constantly keep up with advancing knowledge and skills in your area of expertise, specialization, or profession?" Lastly, an example of a leadership item is the following: "How confident would you be to plan, direct, organize, and prepare others on what they need to do?"

Criteria

NASCENT ENTREPRENEURIAL ACTIVITY

In addition to investigating the various perceptions and attitudes that students have about entrepreneurship, the CAS model included a behavioral measure of entrepreneurship, which was labeled nascent entrepreneurial activities and operationalized as behaviors associated with and/or antecedent to setting up a new enterprise. This behavioral component serves an important role in understanding how various perceptions and attitudes translate into actual behavior. On a list of nine nascent entrepreneurial activities, students reported which they had engaged in previously. The following is an example of a nascent entrepreneurial activity: "I have a business idea that I think could be viable."

JOB CHOICE (INTENDED OCCUPATION)

The final career aspiration subcomponent in the CAS model considers the preferred job students intend to pursue after graduation. Students chose one specific job type from a list adapted from the Singapore Standard Occupational Classification (Singapore Department of Statistics, 2010). To integrate the EPL framework within this scale, an additional job, entrepreneur, was added to the list. Other examples of jobs on this list include legal professional, librarian, archivist, curator, hospitality, retail or related services manager, and senior public sector official.

Since its inception in 2010, the CAS has been refined and expanded beyond core components to include a broader range of factors thought to influence the career aspirations of students. In the 2012 CAS, an additional scale was added to measure the impact of social influence (e.g., family members, relatives, friends, and role models) on students' career aspirations in each of the EPL career domains. Reasons for not starting a business were added in 2013.

WHAT WE KNOW FROM NTU CAS

Students' Immediate and Long-Term Career Intentions

Results from the 4 years of surveying NTU students have been remarkably similar. As expected, entrepreneurship was the least preferred career option

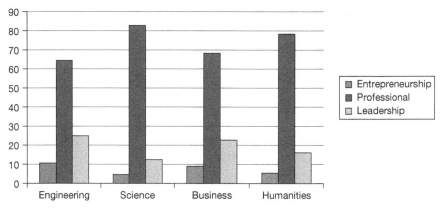

Figure 7.3 NTU undergraduate desired job (job choice), by college.

immediately upon graduation (2013, 8%; 2012, 7%; 2011, 8%; 2010, 9%) relative to professional (2013, 69%; 2012, 68%; 2011, 69%; 2010, 71%) and leadership (2013, 24%; 2012, 25%; 2011, 23%; 2010, 21%).

As can be seen from Figure 7.3, which shows 2010 preferred job choice preferences across different NTU colleges, science (83%) and humanities (76%) students are keener to join a professional career path. On the other hand, compared to other students, more engineering and business school students (9–10%) prefer to pursue entrepreneurship. Also, more business and engineering school students (23–25%) show interest in joining leadership positions compared to students from other colleges. Not surprisingly, postgraduate business school students showed nearly equal career preferences between professionalism and leadership career paths. When provided a time frame, however, approximately 30% of survey participants expressed the intention to start a business within the next 10 years.

Furthermore, approximately one-third of NTU students have reported having engaged in up to two (out of a checklist of nine) nascent entrepreneurship-related activities, such as developing a business idea, developing business plans, or searching for financing (Figure 7.4). Thus, although an entrepreneurial career path was not an immediate priority for many NTU students, it was a part of many students' lifelong career plan.

Relationships Between Entrepreneurial, Professional, and Leadership Intentions and Motivations

Table 7.2 presents correlations between EPL motivations, intent, and entrepreneurial activities for the 10,140 students from the 2010 NTU CAS. It can

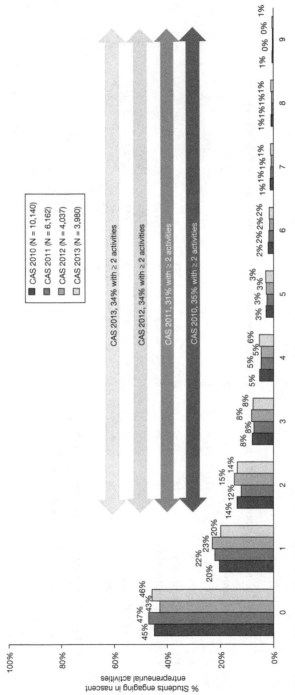

Figure 7.4 Percentage of students engaging in nascent entrepreneurial activities.

Table 7.2 Descriptive Statistics and Correlations Between EPL Motivations and Intent[a]

	CAS Component	Mean	SD	1	2	3	4	5	6	7
1	ENT activities	1.41	1.84	(.75)						
2	ENT motivation	3.09	0.65	.435**	(.82)					
3	PROF motivation	3.74	0.52	−.042**	.089**	(.75)				
4	LEAD motivation	3.56	0.49	.162**	.245**	.189**	(.72)			
5	ENT intent	2.69	0.87	.500**	.689**	.032**	.201**	(.78)		
6	PROF intent	3.72	0.67	−.227**	−.200**	.505**	.051**	−.249**	(.74)	
7	LEAD intent	3.64	0.73	.113**	.206**	.191**	.478**	.164**	.184**	(.74)

[a]Values in bold are internal consistency reliabilities.

ENT, entrepreneurial; LEAD, leadership; PROF, professional.

be seen that the correlation between entrepreneurial and professional intent was negative (–.25), whereas the correlations between leader/managerial intent and entrepreneurial intent and professional intent were positive (i.e., r = .16 and .18, respectively); entrepreneurial and professional motivations were also uncorrelated. Entrepreneurial activities had positive correlations with entrepreneurial/leadership motivations and intents but negative correlations with professional motivations and intent. This suggests that NTU students tend to think of entrepreneurial and professional jobs as competing/opposing career options, whereas leader/managerial jobs potentially complement either entrepreneurial or professional work. Hence, the major question from the university education perspective is how to encourage professionally motivated students to consider entrepreneurship and associated activities as complementing rather than competing.

Sustaining Career Aspirations: The "Rope" of Exposure

One important finding from NTU CAS was that high exposure to career-related activities enables a person to sustain, or even intensify, his or her career aspirations over time. This is especially true for entrepreneurship, for which it was observed that the entrepreneurial career aspirations of students in the high-exposure (to entrepreneurship activities in NTU) group remained relatively stable over time, whereas those in low- or medium-exposure groups showed gradual declines. This can be seen in Figure 7.5, which shows changes in entrepreneurial aspirations from 2010 to 2014 for students who had various levels of exposure to entrepreneurship activities.

Effects of exposure were particularly evident for formal university courses. Between January 2012 and January 2013, we collected valid surveys from 102

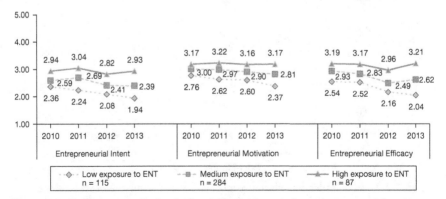

Figure 7.5 Average scores for level of exposure with regard to entrepreneurial careers.

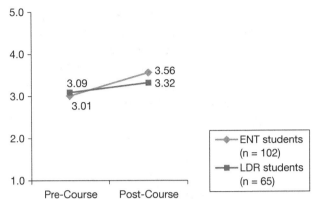

Figure 7.6 Level of entrepreneurial efficacy before and after the course. Note that all the increases in entrepreneurial and leadership efficacy are significant at the 0.01 level.

students from four classes in the "Introduction to Entrepreneurship" course and 65 students from two classes in the "Leadership in Organizations" course. Both courses were electives and taken by students from different NTU colleges. Both courses focused on the development of entrepreneurial and leadership skills, and they had virtually no content devoted to students' actual majors. The students were provided the same EPL career questionnaire twice, at the start of their courses and toward the end of their courses approximately 12 weeks later. The students were also asked to rate their learning experience during the second survey at the end of their courses.

Figure 7.6 and Figure 7.7 show levels of self-reported entrepreneurial and leadership efficacy among the students before and after the courses. There was a significant increase in entrepreneurial efficacy for students from both

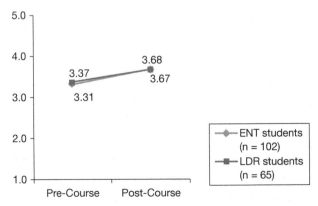

Figure 7.7 Level of leadership efficacy before and after the course. Note that all the increases in entrepreneurial and leadership efficacy are significant at the 0.01 level.

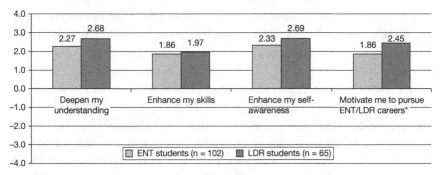

Figure 7.8 Students' ratings on their learning experience. *The rating shown for students from the entrepreneurship course refers to ENT careers, whereas that for students from the leadership course refers to LDR careers. ENT, entrepreneurship; LDR, leadership.

entrepreneurship and leadership courses, indicating that both courses are effective in improving students' perceptions of skills and knowledge for entrepreneurship. The increase in the level of entrepreneurial efficacy is even higher for students from the entrepreneurship course, from a score of 3.01 to 3.56 (see Figure 7.6). This was probably because of the course's higher relevance and knowledge application with regard to starting a business. Both entrepreneurship and leadership courses also helped students improve perceptions of their leadership skills and abilities; the increase in leadership efficacy was similar for both courses (see Figure 7.7).

The students from both courses also rated their learning experience positively, especially those from the leadership course. Figure 7.8 shows that on a 9-point scale ranging from –4 to +4, students in general believe that the course they attended had deepened their understanding, enhanced their skills and self-awareness, and increased their motivation to pursue their career interests. Together, these results provided evidence that entrepreneurship and leadership courses were effective in fostering a balanced development of students' career aspirations.

Career Adaptability, Boundarylessness, and EPL Career Aspirations

The field of career guidance and counseling is witnessing a paradigmatic change, with "career adaptability" fast replacing "career maturity" as a central construct in both research and practice (Goodman, 1994; Savickas, 1997; Savickas & Porfeli, 2011, 2012). If the goal of career development in the past century was to help individuals to be more ready (i.e., "mature") to decide on a job, occupation, or career (i.e., a question of career maturity or readiness), the focus today is shifting toward assessing and strengthening individuals' abilities to manage occupational transitions in an uncertain and changing job market.

Our early research reported in Chan et al. (2012) showed that the EPL framework can be used to operationalize the boundaryless (not confined to a specific organization) and protean (driven by an individual) career concepts. By categorizing students into eight "profile" groups on the basis of whether their E, P, and L motivation scores were above or below the mean obtained for the large sample of 10,326, we observed that individuals concurrently high in E, P, and L career motivations and those high in E and L career motivations were also highest in boundaryless and protean career attitude. In contrast, those with only high P or low EPL career motivations were lowest on these career attitudes.

To further examine the relevance of our EPL framework in relation to 20th versus 21st century career attitudes, we included with the 2012 and 2013 NTU CAS established measures of career maturity (i.e., Savickas & Porfeli, 2011; revised Career Maturity Index) and career adaptability (i.e., Savickas & Porfeli, 2012; Career Adapt Abilities Scale). Analysis of the relationship between students' EPL profiles and (20th century) "career maturity" and (21st century/future) "career adaptability" revealed that students who were highest in E, P, and L (i.e., most "multidimensional" in career aspirations) were also highest in "career adaptability" (Figure 7.9). In contrast, students highest in "career maturity or readiness" were highest in P and L motivations, intentions, and efficacies, which suggested that exposure to the EPL framework and entrepreneurial careers may have the potential to help prepare NTU students to be more adaptable (rather than "matured" or "locked in") in their future careers (Chan et al., 2015).

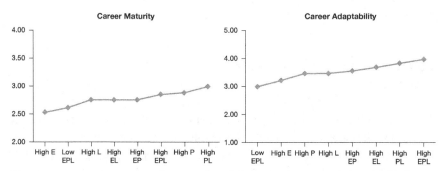

Figure 7.9 Career maturity and career adaptability. E, entrepreneurship; L, leadership; P, professionalism.

EPL Career Motivations and Individual Differences

In developing the EPL career framework, we began by recognizing the distinction between *career* (which has a dynamic, temporal aspect) and *vocation* and also the possibility of multidirectional (as opposed to linear; Baruch, 2004) models of careers in which an individual's career vector can move in any direction. In other words, in our framework, entrepreneurship (E), professionalism (P), and leadership (L) were conceptualized as dimensions of *career* space in which individual careers could be viewed as vectors in a three-dimensional subjective career space—independent of Holland's (1959, 1997) RIASEC vocational interests. We believed that by representing the elements of time, direction, and strength (including career speed, clarity, etc.) in the form of vectors, the EPL career framework could help young people who face many options, among which the pursuit of expert knowledge and skills (i.e., a professional career path) is only one alternative. Instead of thinking of E, P, and L as alternative career paths, we hoped that students would take a more holistic view of their lifelong career development by considering a three-dimensional EPL career space in which their careers may evolve over time.

To confirm the distinction between the EPL constructs and Holland's vocational interests, we reported empirical research (Chan et al., 2012) showing that our EPL measures were independent of vocational interests measured using a 48-item brief public domain RIASEC marker scale (Armstrong, Allison, & Rounds, 2008).

Recently, we also reported correlational analyses from two of our student samples that showed that personality traits seem to have more similar relationships with both entrepreneurial and leadership motivations than with professional work-role motivations (Chan et al., 2015). Specifically, we observed that traits accounted for the greatest variance in leadership motivation, followed by entrepreneurial motivation and then professional motivation. Although the Big Five personality traits low risk aversion and proactive personality seem to correlate with and explain variance in both entrepreneurial and leadership motivations, it was mainly high-risk aversion that correlated with the motivation for more vocationally based, professional work. In addition, proactive personality and extraversion were positively related to both entrepreneurial and leadership motivations, and conscientiousness seemed to predict leadership, whereas low risk aversion and openness correlated with entrepreneurial motivation.

Overall, our studies of traits and EPL suggest that it may be useful to go beyond the Big Five in explaining the difference between the motivation for entrepreneurship, professional work, and leadership. Further research should also examine how other individual-difference factors such as social values (e.g., individualism–collectivism, power distance, and uncertainty avoidance) and career attitudes (e.g., boundarylessness and self-directedness) may distinguish entrepreneurial, professional, and leadership motivations. Research is also needed to understand the role of environmental influences, including personal history and family and social influences, in shaping career motivations.

NEXT PHASE: FROM SURVEY TO DEVELOPMENTAL TOOL

Preliminary NTU CAS Developmental Feedback Report

Following the initial results of the NTU CAS, a decision was made to transform the survey into a university-wide system for entrepreneurial promotion and career development. We thus embarked on a pilot effort to provide students with feedback on the EPL career aspirations. Providing feedback to students regarding their career aspirations can help them with their career decision-making process. Such feedback can highlight their current EPL motivation, intent, and perceived efficacy relative to those of other students, so they can focus on what they may desire but are lacking. For example, the EPL report might inform a student of his or her high entrepreneurship intent and motivation but low entrepreneurship efficacy. In response to this feedback, the student may choose to enroll in more entrepreneurship courses or intern at a start-up to address the lack of entrepreneurial skills. As such, the report can inform and facilitate the actualization of career aspirations.

A preliminary EPL feedback report was developed and administered at the start and end of three courses during the first semester of the 2011–2012 academic year: two entrepreneurship courses with a total of 61 entrepreneurship students and one leadership course with 29 leadership students. A total of 90 students from all three courses completed both surveys. Student EPL aspirations were examined using a survey given at the beginning of the course, and a 5-page EPL feedback report was generated based on their scores. Students were also asked to give comments and suggestions based on the report they received after the end-of-course survey. In general, the reaction was positive, with 75% expressing that it was useful to them and beneficial to their future career (Table 7.3).

Student suggestions for improving the EPL feedback report centered around two main themes. First, many students wanted to understand the methodology and rationale behind the scores reported as well as be offered an extended interpretation of their EPL profile (e.g., a list of jobs that matched the profile). Second, students suggested that we report their EPL aspirations along with other variables relevant to their career interests (e.g., personality). Other notable

Table 7.3 FREQUENCY OF RESPONSES: POST FEEDBACK REACTIONS[a]

Theme	Strongly Disagree/ Disagree (%)	Neither (%)	Strongly Agree/ Agree (%)
1. Accuracy	7.88	34.37	67.54
2. Usefulness	7.47	18.68	74.95
3. Benefit future career	6.59	19.23	75.27
4. Positive feelings about the feedback report	4.95	31.32	64.83

[a]For a full breakdown of frequency of responses by scale item, see Appendix.

suggestions for the feedback report included providing information as to how they could ameliorate their deficits in certain areas (e.g., a low leadership efficacy) or capitalize on their strengths (e.g., a high entrepreneurial intent).

A University-wide System for Entrepreneurial Promotion and Career Development

In 2014, the university embarked on a multiyear project to enhance the NTU CAS from being only a university survey to a system to support holistic career development of students. The university will have an information technology system (including website/portal, database, and computational engine) that will enable the automated production of a CAS Feedback Report for all student participants over time. Relevant entrepreneurial, professional, and leadership career coaching content will also be developed to guide students in their career development by providing useful information on entrepreneurial, professional, and leadership development opportunities and resources offered by the university. The aim is to incorporate the NTU CAS Feedback Report and new instructional content into various career-related courses in the university. The vision is for the NTU CAS to become a one-stop gateway to connect all individuals in NTU to information and opportunities related to entrepreneurial, professional, and leadership development opportunities in the university.

Our hope is that eventually the NTU CAS will be offered to NTU students throughout the period of their studies and also beyond (e.g., when they become alumni) to help them "construct" more holistic (as opposed to single-tracked) careers with entrepreneurial alongside professional and/or leadership dimensions over a lifetime. In this long-term vision, all freshmen will be invited to participate in the NTU CAS upon joining the university, and students will also be invited to participate in it 6–9 months before graduating from NTU. All participants will receive an NTU CAS Feedback Report, in which they can compare their EPL career aspiration profile to that of the larger student population, and they will be encouraged to participate more actively in the many developmental opportunities in the E, P, and L aspects during their time at NTU. The report will link them to an online career and educational advising website at NTU that will point them to the many educational, curricula, and co-curricula (e.g., student life) opportunities to develop their leadership and entrepreneurial potential while at NTU and beyond. Specific programs or "ecosystems" within NTU (e.g., general elective courses on career development and entrepreneurship and/or leadership) can also use this system to measure "change" in the students. This system can even be enhanced with social networking tools and "apps" to help students build networks both within and across E, P, and L developmental communities at NTU and beyond (e.g., alumni). This system may even be integrated with the university's career office system for job placements to point students to the many E, P, and L opportunities (and variants) in the job market.

CONCLUSION

The first 4 years of the NTU CAS project (2010–2013) provided NTU with a stable and consistent picture of the entrepreneurial, professional, and leadership aspirations among its students and of the university's entrepreneurship landscape. The important and unique contribution is that rather than focusing on vocational choices of university students and their immediate career prospects, the project deliberately takes a more holistic, long-term view of student careers by tracking their aspirations in a three-dimensional EPL career space.

The NTU CAS is currently being transformed from an annual university-wide survey exercise into a system to support students' long-term career planning and development through feedback and career guidance. The vision is to develop students along all three EPL dimensions as they progress through their studies and beyond. The hope is that by doing so, students will be boundaryless and better prepared to meet the emerging demands of the 21st century workplace. The extent to which this vision can be achieved will depend on a whole-university approach (e.g., involving the individual schools, career office, alumni office, etc.), patience, and NTU leadership support.

The framework also connects well to the "T-shaped professional" metaphor, which has been promoted by IBM for the workforce of the future (http://tsummit.org/t) and has gained some traction in university circles (see http://www.ceri.msu.edu/t-shaped-professionals). T-shaped professionals are believed to possess breadth of transferrable skills and depth of professional skills. Such people are highly valued in today's workplace for their ability to contribute in multiple areas while staying resilient to drastic changes in technology and market conditions. Entrepreneurship (E) and leadership (L) seem to correspond to the arm of the "T" that represents opposing ends of a breadth of skills ranging from business acumen to social influence, respectively. In comparison, the leg of the "T" represents possession of deep professional skills specialized in at least one discipline. The T-shaped movement aims to ready students to develop the breadth and depth of skills at the university level in order to better prepare them as part of the 21st century workforce.

NOTE

1. This chapter presents the views of the authors and does not represent the official views of Nanyang Technological University.

REFERENCES

Armstrong, P. I., Allison, W., & Rounds, J. (2008). Development and initial validation of brief public domain RIASEC marker scales. *Journal of Vocational Behavior, 73*(2), 287–299.

Arthur, M. B. (1994). The boundaryless career: A new perspective for organizational inquiry. *Journal of Organizational Behavior, 15*(4), 295–306.

Arthur, M. B., & Rousseau, D. M. (Eds.). (1996). *The boundaryless career: A new employment principle for a new organizational era.* New York, NY: Oxford University Press.

Baruch, Y. (2004). Transforming careers: From linear to multidirectional career paths—Organizational and individual perspectives. *Career Development International, 9*(1), 58–73.

Chan, K. Y., & Drasgow, F. (2001). Toward a theory of individual differences and leadership: Understanding the motivation to lead. *Journal of Applied Psychology, 86*(3), 481–498.

Chan, K. Y., Ho, M.-H. R., Chernyshenko, O. S., Bedford, O. A., Uy, M. A., Gomulya, D. M., . . . Phan, J. W. (2012). Entrepreneurship, professionalism, leadership: A framework and measure for understanding boundaryless careers. *Journal of Vocational Behavior, 81*, 73–88.

Chan, K. Y., Uy, M. A., Moon-ho, R. H., Sam, Y. L., Chernyshenko, O. S., & Yu, K. Y. T. (2015). Comparing two career adaptability measures for career construction theory: Relations with boundaryless mindset and protean career attitudes. *Journal of Vocational Behavior, 87*, 22–31.

Cogliser, C. C., & Brigham, K. H. (2004). The intersection of leadership and entrepreneurship: Mutual lessons to be learned. *Leadership Quarterly, 15*(6), 771–799.

Derr, C. B., & Laurent, A. (1989). The internal and external career: A theoretical and cross-cultural perspective. In M. B. Arthur, D. T. Hall, & B. S. Lawrence (Eds.), *The handbook of career theory* (pp. 454–471). Cambridge, England: Cambridge University Press.

Evetts, J. (2011). A new professionalism? Challenges and opportunities. *Current Sociology, 59,* 406–422.

Falconbridge, J., & Muzio, D. (2007). Reinserting the professional into the study of globalizing professional service firms: The case of law. *Global Networks, 7,* 249–270.

Goodman, J. (1994). Career adaptability in adults: A construct whose time has come. *Career Development Quarterly, 43,* 74–84.

Hall, D. T., & Associates. (1996). *The career is dead—Long live the career: A relational approach to careers.* San Francisco, CA: Jossey-Bass.

Holland, J. L. (1959). A theory of vocational choice. *Journal of Counseling Psychology, 6*(1), 35–45.

Holland, J. L. (1997). *Making vocational choices: A theory of vocational personalities and work environments* (3rd ed.). Odessa, FL: Psychological Assessment Resources.

Kanter, R. M. (1989). Careers and the wealth of nations: A macro-perspective on the structure and implications of career forms. In M. Arthur, D. Hall, & B. Lawrence (Eds.), *Handbook of career theory* (pp. 506–522). Cambridge, England: Cambridge University Press.

Lee, L., Wong, P. K., Foo, M. D., & Leung, A. (2001). Entrepreneurial intentions: The influence of organizational and individual factors. *Journal of Business Venturing, 26,* 124–136.

McClelland, D. C. (1961). *The achieving society.* New York, NY: Appleton-Century-Crofts.

McClelland, D. C. (1963). The achievement motive in economic growth. In B. F. Hoselitz & W. E. Moore (Eds.), *Industrialization and society* (pp. 74–96). Paris, France: UNESCO.

Ng, T., Eby, L. T., Sorensen, K. L., & Feldman, D. C. (2005). Predictors of objective and subjective career success: A meta-analysis. *Personnel Psychology, 58,* 367–409.

Savickas, M. L. (1997). Career adaptability: An integrative construct for life-span, life-space theory. *Career Development Quarterly, 45,* 247–259.

Savickas, M. L. (2002). Reinvigorating the study of careers. *Journal of Vocational Behavior, 61,* 381–385.

Savickas, M. L., & Porfeli, E. J. (2011). Revision of the Career Maturity Inventory: The adaptability form. *Journal of Career Assessment, 19*(4), 335–374.

Savickas, M. L., & Porfeli, E. J. (2012). Career Adapt-Abilities Scale: Construction, reliability, and measurement equivalence across 13 countries. *Journal of Vocational Behavior, 80,* 661–673.

Super, D. E. (1957). *The psychology of careers.* New York, NY: Harper & Row.

Super, D. E. (1980). A life-span, life space approach to career development. *Journal of Vocational Behavior, 16,* 282–298.

Vecchio, R. P. (2003). Entrepreneurship and leadership: Common trends and common threads. *Human Resource Management Review, 13*(2), 303–328.

APPENDIX: CORE NTU CAS SURVEY

Background Experience

1. Do you have any employment/working experience? ☐ Yes ☐ No
   [Note: *work = received income/pay; please *exclude* National Service).

2. Have you ever been self-employed or the owner of a Small or Medium-sized Enterprise (SME)?

Never	Less than 1 year	1–3 years	3–5 years	5–10 years	More than 10 years
☐	☐	☐	☐	☐	☐

3. Have your parents or siblings ever been **self-employed** or **the owner of a Small or Medium-sized Enterprise (SME)**?

	Never	Less than 1 year	1–3 years	3–5 years	5–10 years	More than 10 years
Father	☐	☐	☐	☐	☐	☐
Mother	☐	☐	☐	☐	☐	☐
Brother or Sister*	☐	☐	☐	☐	☐	☐

*If you have more than one sibling, choose the one with the most self-employed/SME experience

4. Have your parents or siblings ever held **professional positions** (e.g., teacher/lawyer/ accountant/ engineer, doctor)?

	Never	Less than 1 year	1–3 years	3–5 years	5–10 years	More than 10 years
Father	☐	☐	☐	☐	☐	☐
Mother	☐	☐	☐	☐	☐	☐
Brother or Sister*	☐	☐	☐	☐	☐	☐

*If you have more than one sibling, choose the one with the most professional work experience

5. Have your parents or siblings ever held **leadership/managerial positions in an organization**?

	Never	Less than 1 year	1–3 years	3–5 years	5–10 years	More than 10 years
Father	☐	☐	☐	☐	☐	☐
Mother	☐	☐	☐	☐	☐	☐
Brother or Sister*	☐	☐	☐	☐	☐	☐

*If you have more than one sibling, choose the one with the most leadership/managerial work experience

How Are Entrepreneurs Perceived And Supported?

To what extent do you agree/disagree with the following statements?

Scale:

1	2	3	4	5
Strongly Disagree	Disagree	Neither	Agree	Strongly Agree

1   I am the kind of person who strives to be highly specialized in my field of study.

2   If I am nominated to be in charge of a project or a group, I feel it is an honor and privilege to accept such a role.

3   The easiest and fastest way to make lots of money is to start my own business

4   If I stick to becoming a professional in my field of study, I am guaranteed to make a good living.

5   I am definitely more of a follower by nature, so I am happy to pass leadership responsibilities to others.

6   I feel I ought to live up to my parents' expectations to work in an entrepreneurial business environment.

7   It is a privilege and honor for me to excel in my chosen area of study.

8   If I agree to lead a group I would never expect any advantages or special benefits.

Your Motivations

Please read each statement carefully and indicate the extent to which you disagree or agree with it.
Scale:

1	2	3	4	5
Strongly Disagree	Disagree	Neither	Agree	Strongly Agree

1   I am the kind of person who strives to be highly specialized in my field of study.

2   If I stick to becoming professional in my field of study, I am guaranteed to make a good living.

3   It is a privilege and honor for me to excel in my chosen area of study.

4   The best way to increase my country's competitiveness is for people like me to become highly skilled professionals in my field of study.

5   I doubt that becoming a skilled professional in my field would result in sizable monetary or social status gains.

6	Being a highly specialized professional in my chosen field will assure me of a steady income.
7	I like to be highly specialized and experienced in a specific area of expertise.
8	My parents hope that I will be a highly skilled professional in my chosen area of expertise.
9	I like others to depend on me for my highly specialized knowledge, skills and experience.
10	If I am nominated to be in charge of a project or a group, I feel it is an honor and privilege to accept such a role.
11	I am definitely more of a follower by nature, so I am happy to pass leadership responsibilities to others.
12	If I agree to lead a group I would never expect any advantages or special benefits.
13	I am only interested to lead a group if there are clear advantages for me.
14	I agree to lead whenever asked or nominated by the other group members.
15	I don't expect to get any privileges if I agree to lead or be responsible for a project.
16	I've always enjoyed leading others and would assume leadership roles whenever I could.
17	I am the kind of person who likes influencing and managing people more than doing anything else.
18	I feel that I have a duty to lead others if I am asked.
19	I am the kind of person who constantly has ideas about making money.
20	The easiest and fastest way to make lots of money is to open my own business.
21	I feel I ought to live up to my parents' expectations to work in an entrepreneurial business environment.
22	The rewards and satisfactions of starting and running a business far outweigh the risks and sacrifices needed.
23	I see working for myself as the best way to escape the rigidity and routines of organizations.
24	Ever since I was a kid I dreamed about opening my own business.
25	This country needs more entrepreneurs and I feel obliged to "give it a go."
26	I have a strong sense of duty to take over a family-related business.
27	I like thinking about ways to create new products and services for the market.

Your Skills Now

How confident are you in performing the following tasks successfully?

Scale:

1	2	3	4	5
Not At All Confident	A Little Confident	Moderately Confident	Fairly Confident	Extremely Confident

1   Come up with ideas for products and services that may be needed in a market.

2   Plan a business (including market analysis, pricing, finances/costs, marketing/sales).

3   Build a network of contacts or partners who will support my business.

4   Manage the financial assets and performance of a company or firm.

5   Start a firm and keep it growing.

6   Identify opportunities to start-up viable businesses.

7   Design an effective campaign for marketing a new product or service.

8   Create and/or build a vision that will inspire others.

9   Align and rally people towards a common goal.

10   Motivate others working with me to do more than they dreamed they could do.

11   Take charge of decisions needed for a group or organization.

12   Plan, direct, organize and prepare others as to what they need to do.

13   Use rewards and punishments to get people working harder.

14   Develop and train future leaders for an organization.

15   Become one of the best experts or professionals in my field of specialization.

16   Constantly keep up with the advancing knowledge and skills in my area of expertise, specialization, or profession.

17   Teach or share with others my knowledge, experience, and expertise in my chosen area of work specialization.

18   Conduct research to further advance knowledge in my area of expertise, specialization, or profession.

19   Write research papers/books and make presentations at professional meetings.

Entrepreneurship Activities

Have you ever been or are you currently engaged in any of the following entrepreneurship activities?

YES	NO	
☐	☐	I have a business idea that I think could be viable.
☐	☐	I've sought information on how to start a business.
☐	☐	I've started talking to potential partners and customers for my future business.
☐	☐	I've started doing financing planning for my business.
☐	☐	I have a prototype of the products/services that my future business will provide.
☐	☐	I have written down an initial business plan for my idea.
☐	☐	I am in the process of legalizing/registering my business and securing any intellectual protections.
☐	☐	I have started or taken over a business that is still active today.
☐	☐	I've had my own business in the past, but it is no longer active.

What Career do You Intend to Pursue After Graduation?

To what extent do you agree/disagree with the following statements?

Scale:

1	2	3	4	5
Strongly Disagree	Disagree	Neither	Agree	Strongly Agree

1   My main career goal is to be a technical expert, specialist or professional in my field of study.

2   I am definitely going to be an entrepreneur after my studies and am prepared to do anything to achieve that goal.

3   I plan to become a general leader or manager in the near future.

4   I do not see myself as a leader or manager—in charge of others—in my future working life.

5   I'd much prefer a career as a specialized expert or professional in a large and stable organization.

6   My main career goal is to rise up the ranks as a leader or manager, in charge of others, in organizations.

7   I see myself continuously furthering or advancing in my specialization and professional/technical expertise throughout my working life.

8   I have a viable business idea and intend to start my own business soon after graduation.

9   I definitely don't see myself working as a professional or a technical expert after graduation.

Your Most Desired Job After Graduation Is:

Choose ONE category only:

☐	Senior public sector official (incl. legislator, senior official in a statutory board, political parties, non-profit organisations, etc)
☐	Director, managing director, Chief Executive/Operating Officer, General Manager of a company or business
☐	Entrepreneur
☐	Administrative or business manager
☐	Production or specialized service manager
☐	Hospitality, retail or related services manager
☐	Science or Engineering Professional (e.g., chemist, statistician, biologist, engineer, etc)
☐	Health Professional (e.g., doctor, TCM professional, vet, dentist, pharmacist, etc)
☐	Teaching Professional
☐	Business Professional (e.g., accountant, finance, HR, marketing, PR, IT professional)
☐	Legal Professional
☐	Librarian, Archivist, curator
☐	Social science professional (e.g., economist, psychologist, sociologist, social worker, counsellor, political scientist, historian, etc)
☐	Author, journalist or editor
☐	Creative or performing artist.
☐	Other professional (e.g., religious)

Interests and Person–Environment Fit

A New Perspective on Workforce Readiness and Success

RONG SU AND CHRISTOPHER D. NYE ■

In the past two decades, psychological and educational research on academic and workforce success has undergone a movement from primarily focusing on studying cognitive abilities to recognizing the importance of "noncognitive" skills and incorporating them into the prediction of educational and labor market outcomes (Borghans, Duckworth, Heckman, & ter Weel, 2008; Brunello & Schlotter, 2011; Heckman & Rubinstein, 2001; Roberts, Kuncel, Shiner, Caspi, & Goldberg, 2007). This transition has brought new insights into additional contributing factors for success in school and work, such as personality traits and motivation, and has enabled exciting opportunities for new interventions that can enhance students' college and workforce readiness (Heckman & Kautz, 2013). Nonetheless, these recent efforts have largely excluded an essential domain in individuals' educational and career development: interests. In this chapter, we present a new perspective on workforce readiness and success, from the angle of individual differences and person–environment (P–E) fit, and provide evidence that interests and the fit between individual interests and their environments predict job performance (broadly defined), extrinsic and intrinsic career success, as well as educational achievement.

INTERESTS DEFINED: FROM INDIVIDUAL
DIFFERENCES TO PERSON–ENVIRONMENT FIT

Interests are defined as relatively stable preferences for activities, contexts in which activities occur, or outcomes associated with preferred activities that orient individuals toward certain environments and motivate goal-oriented behaviors (Rounds & Su, 2014). Interests have been studied as one of the major domains of individual differences[1] (Ackerman & Heggestad, 1997; Chamorro-Premuzic, von Stumm, & Furnham, 2011; Lubinski, 2000; Savickas & Spokane, 1999). Lubinski (2000) discussed interests along with cognitive abilities and personality as critical dimensions in structuring important human behaviors and outcomes (e.g., achieved socioeconomic status, educational choices, work performance, delinquency, health risk behaviors, and income). In education, interest has long been studied as a critical antecedent of motivation, attention, selective persistence, and knowledge acquisition (Renninger, Hidi, & Krapp, 1992). In career counseling, interests have been shown as a core predictor of individuals' career choice, adjustment, and change and are traditionally deemed one of the "big three" constructs (along with abilities and needs/values) to be assessed in guiding individuals' career development (Brown & Lent, 2005). Although early pioneers in interest research termed interests "vocational personalities" and conceptualized interests as "downstream" constructs or workplace instantiations of basic personality traits (Holland, 1997; McCrae & Costa, 1990), recent research has suggested that the rank-order stability of interests is higher than that of personality traits (Low, Yoon, Roberts, & Rounds, 2005) and that the average levels of genetic effects on broad interest domains are similar to those on personality traits (Kandler, Bleidorn, Riemann, Angleitner, & Spinath, 2011). This evidence highlights interests as a relatively stable domain of individual differences distinct from personality traits and useful for academic and career guidance and prediction (for a more detailed discussion on the nature of interests, see Rounds & Su, 2014).

Interests are typically measured as the degree of liking or disliking of certain work activities or environments (e.g., a college major or an occupation). When responding to an interest inventory, individuals are asked to indicate how they feel about each type of work activity or environment, such as doing scientific research or managing a business, either on a scale from "strongly like" to "strongly dislike" or in comparison to each other. Contrary to the common misunderstanding among laypeople and even among some individual difference researchers that interests are just feelings of enjoyment, interests are not necessarily characterized by a sense of pleasure. Instead, interests are more strongly associated with curiosity and promote prolonged engagement in tasks and experiences, even when they are complex and perplexing (Silvia, 2008;

Turner & Silvia, 2006). As such, interests serve as a source of intrinsic motivation that drives the direction, effort, and persistence of human behaviors and their consequences (Rounds & Su, 2014).

Understanding the motivational functions of interests is crucial because motivation is a direct determinant of performance (Campbell, 1990) and one of the most important pathways through which interests predict workforce readiness and success. Specifically, there are three ways interests can influence behaviors through motivation (Nye, Su, Rounds, & Drasgow, 2012; Rounds & Su, 2014). First, interests can influence the direction of behaviors by driving activities and goals toward specific domains. For example, students with strong interests in mathematics may seek out learning opportunities in math, choose to major in math, and eventually go into an occupation in a relevant field. Second, interests can influence the vigor of behaviors by energizing goal-striving efforts. Third, interests can influence the persistence of behaviors by providing a context that helps sustain efforts on a goal until the objective is achieved. For example, when interested, students are more engaged in math activities and persist longer in solving a challenging math problem. Figure 8.1 illustrates the motivational functions of interests as one mechanism of predicting performance behaviors and performance outcomes.

Importantly, interests promote learning and exploration through the previously mentioned motivational functions. Interest in a particular activity leads to intrinsic motivation that drives individuals to learn more about it. As a result, interests are linked to performance through the acquisition of declarative and procedural job knowledge, which are the other direct determinants of job performance (Campbell, 1990). When individuals are interested in the work that

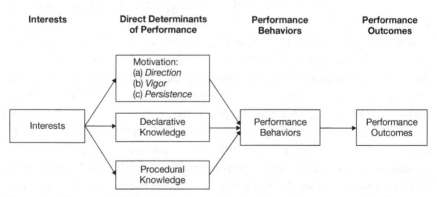

Figure 8.1 Theoretical relationships among interests, direct determinants of performance, performance behaviors, and performance outcomes.

SOURCE: Adapted from Rounds and Su (2014).

they are doing, they are likely to develop the knowledge, skills, and experiences needed to perform well in the job (Silvia, 2008; also see Ackerman, 1996; Schmidt, 2014). This mechanism provides an indirect pathway for interests to influence performance on the job through knowledge acquisition. Similarly, a large volume of research in educational psychology has shown that interested students "persist longer at learning tasks, spend more time studying, read more deeply, remember more of what they read, and get better grades in their classes" (Silvia, 2008, p. 58; also see Hidi & Harackiewicz, 2000; Silvia, 2006). The dynamic and reciprocal relationship among interests, knowledge acquisition, and ability development is often overlooked and yet is key to the link between interests and academic achievement and job performance. We elaborate on this point later in the chapter.

The predictive power of interests derives not only from the degree of liking something, or how strong interests are for certain work activities or environments, but also from the degree of P–E fit, or how similar an individual's profile of interests is to the characteristics of his or her environments. P–E fit theories stemmed from early work of researchers including Kurt Lewin (1935) and Henry Murray (1938) that propose behaviors as a function of individuals in their environment, and they have been developed to explain various work outcomes, including performance and satisfaction (Pervin, 1968, 1987), work adjustment (Dawis & Lofquist, 1984), job stress and strain (French, Caplan, & Harrison, 1982), career choice and turnover (Schneider, 1987), and organizational tenure and commitment (Chatman, 1989, 1991). The P–E fit approach to interests falls under this overarching framework and is best summarized in Holland's (1959, 1997) theory of vocational personalities and work environments: The degree of similarity between a person's interest type and his or her work environment (also referred to as interest congruence) affects a person's work attitudes and behaviors; higher levels of interest congruence lead to greater satisfaction, success, and persistence.

Unlike cognitive abilities or most personality traits, in which case a greater amount of a desirable trait tends to result in more positive outcomes (e.g., the more intelligent and the more conscientious, the better grades in college or job performance), interests do not always follow the rule of "the more the better." Interest has an object, be it conducting research, teaching high school students, or engaging in business negotiations. The predictive validity of interests is maximized when an individual's interests fit an environment. In other words, the characteristics of an environment interact with the interest profile of an individual and moderate its effect, such that individuals' interests most strongly predict their performance in a "matching" environment. For example, although interests in science and research are generally beneficial for knowledge acquisition, which in turn contributes to job performance (main effect), strong research interests are likely to be most predictive of performance in a research position because of the high level of congruence between interests and the work tasks compared to performance in a sales position, in which interests and work tasks are much less compatible (interaction effect). Therefore, individuals' interests are always *in relation to* their environments. This relationship between a person's interests and his or her environment, captured by interest congruence or "fit," is predictive of work outcomes over and above individual interests alone (Su, Murdock, & Rounds, 2014). This feature of interests, termed the contextualization of interests, sets interests apart from other individual difference variables and provides another mechanism for interests to predict work outcomes (Rounds & Su, 2014).

Overall, the concept of P–E fit has consistently demonstrated predictive validity. Two meta-analyses in organizational research (Kristof-Brown, Zimmerman, & Johnson, 2005; Verquer, Beehr, & Wagner, 2003) documented the effect of fit for an array of critical work outcomes, including some very strong relationships with attitudinal outcomes (e.g., $r = .56$ for person–job fit and job satisfaction). As a form of P–E fit, interest congruence is expected to be positively related to work outcomes. We argue that a modern perspective on workforce readiness and success should not only take into account individual differences in interests but also consider and examine the fit between profiles of interests for both the person and the environment, based on the premise that greater fit enhances work outcomes. In the next sections of the chapter, we discuss the predictive power of interest congruence in addition to that of interest scores for job performance, extrinsic and intrinsic career success, and workforce preparation.

INTERESTS AND PERFORMANCE ON THE JOB

Job performance is central to the evaluation of workplace success. It is a broad construct that encompasses several interrelated but different criteria, including task performance (i.e., how well work tasks are done on the job), organizational citizenship behaviors (OCB), and (the absence of) counterproductive work behaviors (CWB) (Motowidlo, 2003). In the organizational literature, one of the most widely cited theories of job performance was proposed by John Campbell (Campbell, 1990; Campbell, Gasser, & Oswald, 1996). In this model, Campbell suggested that declarative knowledge (knowledge about facts and things), procedural knowledge (i.e., knowing how to perform a task), and motivation to perform the task are direct determinants of performance on the job. In other words, employees will perform well if they know what they need to do (declarative knowledge), how to do it (procedural knowledge), and are motivated to perform the task. As discussed previously, interests can affect each of these determinants of performance.

First, interests can affect the acquisition of declarative and procedural job knowledge. Although the role of interests in learning has been widely studied in the educational psychology literature (Hidi & Harackiewicz, 2000; Silvia, 2006), research in the organizational literature has focused on cognitive ability as the primary precursor to the acquisition of job knowledge (Schmidt & Hunter, 1998). Recently, Schmidt (2014) attempted to integrate these two perspectives and suggested an integrative theory linking both interests and cognitive ability to the acquisition of the knowledge, skills, and aptitudes needed to perform well at work and in school. According to Cattell's (1987) investment theory of intelligence, individuals have a certain level of innate fluid intelligence that they invest in activities and that helps them to develop crystallized intelligence, which Cattell defined as knowledge and skills. Building on this framework, Schmidt (2014) suggested that individuals will choose which activities to invest in based on their interest in those activities. In other words, an individual's cognitive ability will provide the capacity to acquire knowledge and skills in a particular area, but interests will direct and focus his or her attention on specific tasks. Other theories have proposed similar relationships between interests, intelligence, and knowledge acquisition (Ackerman, 1996).

Although interests may affect job performance by motivating the acquisition of knowledge, skills, and experience, interests may also influence performance by motivating behavior directly. As described previously and illustrated in Figure 8.1, interests can affect the direction, vigor, and persistence of behaviors, and these motivational components are direct determinants of job-related behavior (Nye et al., 2012). As a result, individuals who are interested in their work will be more likely to focus on work tasks, work hard to achieve work goals, and persist to complete their work even when it becomes difficult.

In summary, interests have direct relationships with the primary determinants of job performance. As such, we would expect interests to predict job performance, and theoretical models of vocational interests have noted this relationship for several decades (Holland, 1963; Strong, 1943). However, the research evidence for this relationship has been mixed, with some studies finding substantial relationships and others finding only negligible results. For example, Strong (1943) reviewed the results of several studies on the relationship between interests and sales positions and found correlations around .37–.40 in samples of job incumbents. In addition, Wiggins and Weslander (1979) found correlations of .64 between supervisor ratings of performance and both Social and Artistic interest scales. In contrast, a number of other studies have found negligible correlations less than .10 between interest scales and performance at work or in school (Dik, 2006; Kieffer, Schinka, &

Curtiss, 2004; Lent, Brown, & Larkin, 1987; Schmitt, Oswald, Friede, Imus, & Merritt, 2008).

To address the inconsistencies in these findings, Hunter and Hunter (1984) published an influential meta-analysis that examined the relationship between interests and job performance. These authors found that the meta-analytic correlation between interests and performance was just .10. This paper has been widely cited in the organizational literature and has been used by subsequent studies to suggest that interests are not effective predictors of performance on the job (Barrick & Mount, 2005; Schmidt & Hunter, 1998). Possibly as a result of these findings, interests have been excluded from recent reviews of the employee selection literature (Cortina & Luchman, 2013; Ployhart, 2006; Sackett & Lievens, 2008; Schmitt, Cortina, Ingerick, & Weichmann, 2003) and have seemingly been ignored as potential predictors of performance on the job.

Two recent meta-analyses re-examined the relationship between interests and performance. Van Iddekinge, Roth, Putka, and Lanivich (2011) conducted an updated meta-analysis and found that interests had much stronger validities for predicting performance outcomes including job performance, training performance, turnover intentions, and actual turnover, with corrected correlations ranging from .14 to .26 for performance criteria and from –.15 to –.19 for turnover outcomes. In a separate study, Nye et al. (2012) also examined this issue and found meta-analytic corrected correlations of .14 for task performance, .21 for OCB (e.g., helping others with their jobs, supporting the organization, or volunteering for work duties), and .20 for persistence on the job. These studies suggest that the relationship between interests and performance outcomes may be stronger than previously reported by Hunter and Hunter (1984). Importantly, these results also indicate that interests can predict the broader construct of job performance, with correlations for the most widely used interest inventories ranging from .14 to .26 for these criteria.

One of the primary limitations of previous research on the interest–performance relationship is that many authors examined this association without considering P–E fit. Again, Holland's (1997) theory emphasized the match or congruence between an individual and his or her environment. As described previously, the effects of interests on the determinants of job performance (i.e., the acquisition of job knowledge and the motivation to perform) are only realized when an individual is in a job that he or she is interested in. Therefore, we would expect interests to be related to job performance but only when there is P–E fit (Holland, 1997). Consequently, the extent of P–E fit should be a better predictor of workplace behavior than interest scores alone.

In addition to reviewing the correlations for interest scores alone, Nye et al. (2012) coded studies that used congruence indices to predict performance. Of the 60 studies that they included in their meta-analysis, 76% examined interest level rather than congruence. This means that the vast majority of the studies in this literature administered an interest inventory and simply correlated scores on an interest scale with some measure of performance, without first considering the match between the person and the environment. Although Nye et al. found a moderate baseline correlation between interests scores and performance (.20), results indicated that correlations with congruence indices were, on average, .16 higher than for interest scores alone in the work domain (.09 higher in academic samples). In other words, the baseline correlation between congruence indices and performance was .36, which suggests that the predictive validity of interest congruence is as high as or higher than the validity of other noncognitive predictors of performance (Barrick & Mount, 1990; Dudley, Orvis, Lebiecki, & Cortina, 2006; Hurtz & Donovan, 2000). These results support Holland's (1997) theory and emphasize the need to consider P–E fit in interest research.

In the interest literature, P–E fit is often operationalized using congruence indices that compare the profile of interest scores for both the individual and the environment. Although a number of indices have been proposed (for reviews, see Brown & Gore, 1994; Camp & Chartrand, 1992), Holland's (1963) original conceptualization of congruence simply compared the highest interest scores (also called the first-letter code) in both the individual and the environmental profiles. Using this conceptualization of fit, Holland (1997) described several degrees of congruence between six types of interests and corresponding work environments—Realistic, Investigative, Artistic, Social, Enterprising, and Conventional—collectively referred to as the RIASEC model and arranged in a hexagonal structure following the previously presented sequence (Figure 8.2). Specifically, Realistic interests refer to preferences in working with one's hands, working with things and gadgets, and working outdoors; Investigative interests refer to preferences in science and research; Artistic interests refer to preferences in activities that allow creative expression; Social interests refer to preferences in working with and helping people; Enterprising interests refer to preferences in persuading and influencing people; and Conventional interests refer to preferences in well-organized, structured work. It was proposed that interest (and work environment) types closer to each other in the hexagonal model (e.g., Realistic and Investigative) are more similar than those that are farther apart (e.g., Realistic and Artistic or Realistic and Social). These levels of congruence are shown in Figure 8.2. If the first-letter codes in individual and environmental profiles match, then the individual is congruent with the environment and is likely to be interested in the work that he or she will be doing. However, if the individual's dominant interest is adjacent to the primary occupational interest type, this is considered a close fit but a less satisfactory match between individual and environment. In contrast, occupations with an

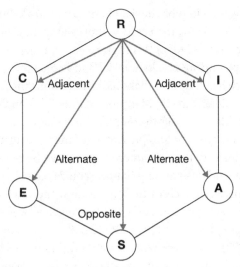

Figure 8.2 Holland's RIASEC model of interests and work environments and degrees of interest congruence.
SOURCE: Adapted from Nye et al. (2014).

alternate Holland type would be a poor fit for the individual, whereas occupations with opposite Holland types represent the worst fit and an unsatisfactory match for the individual's interests. Due to the simplicity of this approach, this conceptualization of congruence is one of the most widely used in the interest literature (Spokane, 1985).

Nye et al. (2012) also conducted supplemental analyses to examine the validity of this form of congruence. Results showed that even matching just the dominant interest types in the individual and occupational profiles could improve validity. Specifically, the meta-analytic baseline correlation between interests and performance when the dominant interest types for the individual and the occupation matched was .27. Even adjacent individual and occupational interest types had moderate validity (.23) for predicting performance on the job. However, the meta-analytic correlation for opposite scores was only .06. Again, these results support Holland's (1997) theory that similarities between the individual and the environment are important for predicting success on the job.

Interestingly, neither interest scores alone nor congruence indices predicted CWB (deviant behavior at work, such as stealing, yelling at coworkers, avoiding work, etc.). However, the supplemental analyses did indicate that opposite interest types do have moderate validity (.22) for predicting this behavior. In other words, although fit between the person and the environment may result in higher performance, more OCB, and longer tenure with the company, misfit (in the form of opposing interests and occupational requirements) may result in individuals engaging in more deviant behavior at work due to boredom, dissatisfaction with the job, or increased withdrawal from everyday work activities. More research is needed on this topic to explore this issue further.

Despite these promising results for Holland's conceptualization of congruence, this approach has several limitations. First, it limits the amount of information that is used to determine fit. Many jobs are complex and require employees to perform many different tasks to complete their work. Therefore, it is unlikely that a single interest type could represent all of the tasks that are performed in a particular job. Instead, multiple interest types may be required to describe a single occupation, and determining fit may require considering the similarities (or differences) between each of these types and the individual interest profile. A second limitation of this approach to congruence is that focusing on a single interest type can maximize sex differences in vocational interests (Camp & Chartrand, 1992). There are well-established differences between men and women on Holland's six interest types (Su, Rounds, & Armstrong, 2009), and these differences could result in the differential selection of male and female applicants in an employee selection context. However, these differences could potentially be mitigated if a broader range of interest scores with differences in opposite directions (e.g., conventional and investigative interests) is considered (Sackett & Ellingson, 1997).

As a result of these limitations, a number of congruence indices have been proposed as alternatives to Holland's original conceptualization of congruence (Gati, 1985; Iachan, 1984; Kwak & Pulvino, 1982). Although a full review of the available indices is outside the scope of this chapter, congruence is generally operationalized by quantifying the similarities between individual and occupational interest profiles. In addition, many of these indices were developed in reference to Holland's hexagon model and quantify similarities by examining the distances between these profiles on the exterior of the hexagon. In the first step, each entry in the individual and occupation profile would be compared to determine similarities. Next, weights are assigned based on distances between each interest type in Holland's hexagon. Although the way that these weights are assigned varies with each index, matching interests are generally assigned the highest weights (i.e., most congruent), followed by adjacent, alternate, and opposite interests. By assigning points to each of these categories, a single index of congruence or fit can be calculated.

Despite the theoretical importance of congruence indices and the positive results found by Nye et al. (2012), the limitations of congruence indices more broadly have been recognized for several decades (Cronbach & Gleser, 1953; Edwards, 1993). For example, congruence indices combine different constructs into a single index, making the overall score conceptually ambiguous; provide only limited information about differences (e.g., exclude information about the level of each constituent construct); do not provide information about the source of incongruence; and place unnecessary constraints on the comparisons (Edwards, 1993). Given these limitations, it is worth considering alternative approaches to indexing fit. One potential alternative is to create simple linear regression composites of interest scores for predicting performance in an occupation. Van Iddekinge, Roth, et al. (2011) explored this approach in their meta-analysis and found that the validity of these composites was stronger than for interest scores alone. A more sophisticated approach to indexing congruence would be to use polynomial regression, which has received a substantial amount of attention as an alternative to congruence indices (Edwards, 1993; Edwards & Shipp, 2007). However, we are unaware of any studies that have used this approach to index congruence in the interest–performance literature. Clearly, more research is needed on alternative approaches to calculating interest congruence.

INTERESTS AND EXTRINSIC CAREER SUCCESS

Career success is defined as the work-related achievements and positive psychological outcomes accumulated from one's work experiences (Judge, Cable, Boudreau, & Bretz, 1995; Seibert & Kraimer, 2001). As indicated by this definition, there are two conceptually distinct aspects of career success: Extrinsic career success, also referred to as objective career success, includes instrumental rewards from the job or occupation that are objectively observable, such as salary, promotions, and occupational status; intrinsic career success, or subjective career success, refers to factors inherent in the job or occupation itself that depend on incumbents' subjective evaluation relative to their own goals and expectations, typically measured in terms of career satisfaction. A core feature of career success, and its key distinction from job performance, is that it measures outcomes that are *accumulated* over an incumbent's career or a sequence of jobs rather than behavioral effectiveness on a specific job. As we discuss workforce readiness and success, both on-the-job performance and long-term, accumulated career success are important criteria for evaluating individuals' work-related accomplishments, and both can eventually contribute to organizational success.

Compared to the literature on interests and job performance, studies on the relationship between interests and career success are less abundant. Traditionally, research on the antecedents of career success primarily focused on three groups of variables: demographic backgrounds, including gender, race, age, and marital status; human capital (Becker, 1964), including level of education, training, and work experiences; and organizational resources, such as organization size, type of industry, and development opportunities within an organization (Ng, Eby, Sorensen, & Feldman, 2005; Seibert & Kraimer, 2001). Relatively recently, marked by Howard and Bray's (1994) classic study on the career advancement of AT&T managers, researchers turned their attention to relatively stable individual difference factors, primarily personality traits and cognitive ability (Judge et al., 1995; Judge, Higgins, Thoresen, & Barrick, 1999; Seibert & Kraimer, 2001; Strenze, 2007). However, interests have been largely overlooked in the investigation of the predictors of career success. Only a handful of studies to date examined the relationship between interests and extrinsic career success, despite early evidence supporting this link (Strong, 1943). We review evidence on the relationship between interests and extrinsic career success in this section, and we continue our discussion of interests and intrinsic career success in the next section.

In his classic contribution, *Vocational Interests of Men and Women*, E. K. Strong (1943) proposed that occupations may be arranged in a hierarchy in terms of their income (or socioeconomic status) and prestige, which can be meaningfully differentiated by the interests of individuals working in them. Based on this idea, Strong developed the Occupational Level (OL) interest scale by empirically contrasting the interests of unskilled workers who earned a low salary with business and professional workers whose income was in the top one-seventh of the nation. Items on the OL scale include interest in "meeting and directing people" and interest in being "corporation lawyers." It was expected that individuals who had high scores on the OL scale should also be found in occupations with higher status and higher income. As he showed in a series of 5 studies, the correlations between interest scores on the OL scale and individuals' income ranged from .12 and .77, with a median of .61. These values were in the same range as the correlations between intelligence and income found in another set of 15 studies conducted by Strong and colleagues. After considering these findings, Strong (1943) concluded that "interests are equally significant (as intelligence) for determining occupational success" (p. 213).

It is not surprising that interests are associated with income, given the well-established evidence that interests are strong predictors of occupational membership (Campbell, 1971; Savickas & Spokane, 1999) and that income differs at the occupational level (Huang & Pearce, 2013). Here, the mechanism for interests to predict income and occupational prestige lies in the motivational function of interests for directing individuals' career choices *across* occupations. Moreover, interests are also associated with income and occupational status because interests influence individuals' career advancement *within* an occupation. In several additional studies, Strong (1946, 1949, 1955) showed that interests were related to the level of responsibility or managerial role within various occupational groups, including administrators and accountants. For example, senior administrators, compared to junior administrators, had significantly higher interest scores in business and professional types of occupational scales, including the President, Lawyer, Advertiser, and Sales Manager scales, as well as the OL scale. These early findings provided preliminary evidence for the link between certain kinds of interests, particularly those of an enterprising nature, and indicators of extrinsic success.

Additional evidence for the link between interests and career success came from a longitudinal study on the career development of approximately 400,000 high school students from more than 1,000 schools throughout the nation (Su, 2012). This study found participants' interests measured in high school to be strong predictors of their income and occupational prestige 11 years after high school graduation. Collectively, six interest factors (Things, Artistic, Science, People, Business, and Leadership) had a multiple correlation of .49 with income, explaining 24% of its variance. Specifically, Science interests and Business interests were the strongest predictors of income ($r = .13$ and $.16$, respectively). Some interest factors negatively predicted income ($r = -.11$ for Artistic interests and $r = -.41$ for People interests). Similarly, the six interest factors had a multiple correlation of .46 with occupational prestige, explaining 21% of its variance. Science interests, Artistic interests, and Business interests stood out as important predictors for occupational prestige ($r = .30$, $.10$, and $.10$, respectively). Things interests and People interests had negative effects on occupational prestige ($r = -.36$ and $-.29$, respectively). Furthermore, Su operationalized the congruence between participants' interests and their occupations using polynomial regressions (Edwards, 1993, 2002) and showed it to be an even stronger predictor of income with a multiple correlation of .60.

Importantly, interests predicted extrinsic career success above and beyond other individual difference domains and human capital. Su (2012) found that, after controlling for the effect of cognitive ability and personality, the six interest factors explained an additional 16% of variance in income and 7% of variance in occupational prestige. In another study, Neumann, Olitsky, and Robbins (2009) examined 93,229 college alumni throughout the United States from the ACT Alumni Outcomes Survey and demonstrated the effect of interest congruence on income over the effect of education and academic achievement (ACT scores). Neumann and colleagues operationalized interest congruence as Euclidean distances (lower scores represent greater fit between individuals and their jobs) and showed that one standard deviation decrease in interest congruence scores resulted in a 5.0% increase in income. This effect was of the same order of magnitude as the effect of education (one standard deviation increase in years of education resulted in 6.9% increase in income) and exceeded that of ACT scores. In this sample, interest congruence contributed to 1% of the variance explained in addition to education and ACT scores.

In summary, existing evidence supports the link between interests and extrinsic career success. Interests are powerful predictors of income, with effects comparable to that of education and stronger than that of cognitive ability. In addition, interests substantially contribute to career attainment both across occupations (i.e., occupational prestige) and within an occupation (i.e., job level). The relationship between interest congruence and extrinsic career success, however, is complex. Because some interests have negative effects on income and occupational prestige (e.g., People interests), the positive effects of interest congruence may be overshadowed. That constitutes one possible explanation for why a few studies did not support the link between interest congruence and extrinsic career success. For example, Schwartz, Andiappan, and Nelson (1986) examined a sample of 1,053 accountants and found a negative relationship between their Conventional interest scores (supposedly congruent with the accounting profession) and annual income. Findings like this, again, bring back the question of how to best operationalize interest congruence. A single Holland interest type is too limited to capture the complexity of any job and thus is not the optimal representation of interest congruence. Furthermore, it confounds the effect of interest level (e.g., the Conventional interest score) and that of interest congruence (e.g., the fit between the Conventional interest type and the accounting profession). More studies are needed to examine the relationship between interest congruence and extrinsic career success, and future research on this topic should consider using more sophisticated approaches to measuring interest congruence, such as polynomial regression (Edwards, 1993, 2002).

INTERESTS AND INTRINSIC CAREER SUCCESS

In addition to job performance, income, and promotion—the most direct indicators of success in the workplace—we also consider job and career satisfaction as a coherent part of the criteria for workplace success. Individuals who are dissatisfied with their jobs or careers are unlikely to consider themselves to be successful at work. Moreover, the lack of job and career satisfaction can affect individuals' job performance and persistence at work. Previous research has demonstrated a strong association between satisfaction and job performance (Judge, Thoresen, Bono, & Patton, 2001), particularly when withdrawal behaviors such as lateness, absenteeism, turnover intentions, and actual turnover behavior are included (Harrison, Newman, & Roth, 2006; Tett & Meyer, 1993).

Holland (1996, 1997) proposed that interest congruence implies satisfaction, such that people flourish in their work environment when there is a good fit between their personality (vocational interest) type and the characteristics of the environment. Lack of congruence between personality (vocational interest) and environment leads to dissatisfaction, unstable career paths, and lowered performance. (Holland, 1996, p. 397)

However, earlier findings on the association between interest congruence and job satisfaction revealed only modest relationships, and the confidence intervals usually included zero (Assouline & Meir, 1987; Tranberg, Slane, & Ekeberg, 1993; Tsabari, Tziner, & Meir, 2005), leading some researchers to conclude that interest congruence based on Holland's RIASEC model is not a valid predictor of job satisfaction (Tinsley, 2006; see also Tinsley, 2000).

Updated and more comprehensive reviews with advanced meta-analytic techniques pointed out the methodological issues in prior studies that led to inconsistent results and provided more positive evidence. For example, Morris (2003) re-examined 93 studies with 51,091 employed adults and estimated interest congruence and job satisfaction to be moderately correlated (corrected for sampling error and unreliability) at .24 (95% confidence interval [CI] = .03–.45; fail safe N = 287). Importantly, Morris identified several moderators of the interest congruence–satisfaction relationship. Specifically, the predictive validity of interest congruence depended on the type of satisfaction measured. The interest congruence–satisfaction relationship is stronger for satisfaction with work itself, supervisor, and coworker (mean r = .17, .17, .21, respectively) than for satisfaction with pay and promotion (mean r = .06 and .08, respectively). This result is unsurprising because interests are the preferences for the intrinsic characteristics pertaining to work environments, including the type of work activities and people that comprise the work environment, rather than the extrinsic aspects of work such as pay and promotion. In addition, echoing what we have discussed previously in this chapter, the predictive validity of interest congruence depended on the type of congruence index used. However, existing studies (Assouline & Meir, 1987; Camp & Chartrand, 1992; Morris, 2003) did not fully agree on the magnitude of predictive validity for different congruence indices and diverged in their conclusions on which congruence indices are superior. Moreover, we are not aware of any studies that use the polynomial regression approach (Edwards, 1993, 2002) to examine the link between interest congruence and job satisfaction, which may be a fruitful direction for future research.

Satisfaction seems to be the most proximal, natural consequence of interest congruence, as predicted by P–E fit theories (Dawis & Lofquist, 1984; Holland, 1997), and one may expect job attitudes to have a stronger relationship with interest congruence than more distal outcomes of performance behaviors and extrinsic career success. Thus, it is perplexing why the reported interest congruence–satisfaction relationship was not higher than, or nearly as high as, the interest–performance relationship or the interest–income relationship. A potential explanation is that interests primarily affect behavioral outcomes, such as learning and knowledge acquisition, through the pathways highlighted in Figure 8.1, rather than attitudinal outcomes. Several other issues may have dampened the interest congruence–satisfaction relationship. For example, the Cornell model of job attitudes (Hulin, Roznowski, & Hachiya, 1985) identified two boundary conditions for job satisfaction: opportunity costs and frame of reference. When the local unemployment rate is high and competition for the few job vacancies available is fierce, the opportunity costs for switching jobs are greater. As a result, individuals' job satisfaction may depend less on whether their job matches their interests than on factors such as job security or extrinsic rewards from the job. Similarly, individuals' satisfaction with their current job is a subjective evaluation and depends on their experiences in their previous jobs (frame of reference), making interest congruence less relevant. It is important for future research to move beyond the question of whether interest congruence predicts job satisfaction and identify moderators and boundary conditions for the interest congruence–satisfaction relationship (Su et al., 2014).

INTERESTS AND WORKFORCE PREPARATION

Academic achievement and educational attainment comprise the human capital one needs to be successful in the workplace and are essential antecedents of labor market outcomes (Becker, 1964). A student who is doing poorly academically and decides to drop out of college is less likely to embark on a successful career, whereas students with higher high school grade point averages and eventual degree attainment have substantially higher income and occupational status (French, Homer, Popovici, & Robins, 2014). Therefore, as we consider the predictors of workforce readiness and success, it is equally important to consider the predictors of workforce preparation—that is, academic performance, persistence in school, and degree attainment.

As discussed previously, interests provide intrinsic motivation for learning and exploration. By motivating people to learn for its own sake, interests ensure that people will develop a broad set of knowledge, skills, and experiences (Silvia, 2008). More important, by directing people to set goals and initiate activities in specific domains (e.g., mathematics), interests contribute to knowledge acquisition and skill and ability development (e.g., quantitative ability) that prepares individuals for their pursuits in specific educational and occupational fields (e.g., mathematics, sciences, and engineering). The accumulation of knowledge, skills, and abilities increases individuals' probability of success in a particular field and, in turn, reinforces individual interests and contributes to interest development in that field.

This dynamic and reciprocal relationship between interests, knowledge acquisition, and ability development is supported by empirical evidence. Ackerman (1996; also see Ackerman & Heggestad, 1997), for example, proposed the Process, Personality, Interests, and Knowledge (PPIK) theory of adult intellectual development and presented meta-analytic findings that demonstrated that interests are critically related to the development of adult intelligence across the life span: Realistic and Investigative interests had substantial correlations with quantitative abilities, Artistic interests were closely aligned with verbal abilities, and Conventional interests were linked to clerical/perceptual speed abilities. Armstrong, Day, McVay, and Rounds (2008) also provided evidence for overlapping interests and cognitive abilities using Holland's RIASEC model as an integrative framework. In addition, Denissen, Zarrett, and Eccles (2007) examined the longitudinal development of approximately 1,000 students between grades 1 and 12 (ages 6–17 years) and found that interests were positively associated with students' self-concept of ability and academic achievement; more important, the within-person correlations among interests, self-concept of ability, and academic achievement increased across time. The increasing association between interests and abilities starts from an early age and continues throughout the life span. Therefore, individual interests have profound influences on their academic achievement, educational attainment, and the ongoing development of knowledge and skills that ensure their readiness for and success in an ever-changing world of work.

Nye et al. (2012) meta-analyzed 18 studies on the relationship between interests and academic achievement and found interests to be significantly correlated with both grades and persistence in school ($r = .21$ and $.25$, respectively). Moreover, interest congruence had even stronger relationships with these outcomes ($r = .30$ and $.34$, respectively). Furthermore, Su (2012) showed that interests predicted college grades, persistence in college, and degree attainment 11 years after high school graduation, even after controlling for cognitive ability and personality traits. Collectively, six interest factors (Things, Artistic, Science, People, Business, and Leadership) had multiple correlations of $r = .26$ with overall grades in college and $r = .50$ with degree attainment. Consistent with previous findings (Ackerman & Heggestad, 1997; Armstrong et al., 2008), Su found Science and Artistic interests to be the single best predictors of college grades ($r = .09$ and $.16$, respectively) and degree attainment ($r = .30$ and $.16$, respectively). Individuals with higher Science and Artistic interests were also more likely to persist in college rather than drop out ($\exp(B) = 1.39$ and 1.24, respectively). Interest congruence, operationalized using polynomial regressions (Edwards, 1993, 2002), explained 9% of the variance in college grades and 12% of the variance in college persistence, consistent with the effects reported by Nye et al. (2012). Importantly, in all cases, the effects of interests were comparable to, or stronger than, the effects of personality traits.

In summary, interests contribute to individuals' workforce readiness and success through multiple pathways. Interests motivate performance behaviors and behaviors that are linked to extrinsic career success. Moreover, interests prepare individuals for entering the occupational fields to which they aspire by influencing their knowledge acquisition and ability development and by ensuring their academic success. The empirical evidence we reviewed suggests that interests and cognitive development are closely linked. Although typically considered to be in the "noncognitive" domain, interests have a profound influence on workplace success that is tied to cognition and learning.

USING INTEREST ASSESSMENTS FOR EDUCATIONAL AND CAREER GUIDANCE

The use of interest assessments for educational and career guidance has enjoyed a long and prosperous history during the past century (Parsons, 1909). Many of the most widely administered interest inventories are used to help high school and college students make better school and career decisions. For example, the ACT Interest Inventory (American College Testing Program, 1995) is administered to more than 1 million middle school and high school students annually in the United States, and the Strong Interest Inventory (Harmon, Hansen, Borgen, & Hammer, 1994) is used by more than 70% of US colleges and universities to assist students in their career planning. Interest inventories are also used in career counseling to help clients with career transition and adjustment. The Self-Directed Search (Holland, Fritzsche, & Powell, 1994), for example, has been used by more than 30 million people worldwide and has been translated into more than 25 different languages (Psychological Assessment Resources, 2009). There is an abundance of literature discussing the use of interest assessments to prepare and readjust individuals for the workforce. Instead of reinventing the wheel on this topic, we refer interested readers to Strong (1943), Savickas and Spokane (1999), Harmon et al. (1994), and Holland et al. (1994) for more information.

We see the future of interest assessment in educational and career guidance as becoming increasingly accessible to the public and increasingly integrated with assessments of other individual differences domains as well as occupational information systems to assist individuals in their career decision-making. For example, under the sponsorship of the US Department of Labor (DOL), the

National Center for O*NET Development provides the O*NET Interest Profiler (Short Form) online for free as a career exploration tool for students and job-seekers (Rounds, Su, Lewis, & Rivkin, 2010). This interest measure is linked to DOL's Occupational Information Network (O*NET; Peterson, Mumford, Borman, Jeanneret, & Fleishman, 1999) database and can be used in combination with other public-domain assessments of abilities and work values to facilitate users' career exploration and choice. A key area for future research is the development of P–E fit models that fully integrate various domains of individual differences. Rather than using information from each domain of individual differences alone, more effective educational and career guidance systems can be developed based on integrated models of P–E fit that help individuals navigate educational and work environments using the full range of individual differences, including interests, values, work styles, skills, and abilities (for an extended discussion, see Su et al., 2014).

The close link between interests and cognitive development reviewed in this chapter has important implications for potential interventions targeting interests. If interests motivate learning and the acquisition of new knowledge, researchers and educators may design curricula and help generate environments that appeal to students' interests, which would in turn promote engagement in academic activities and contribute to academic performance. Such interventions are particularly relevant for math and science learning, which has received substantial attention due to its importance for the development of a competitive workforce (National Science Board, 2014). For example, it has been demonstrated that teaching high school science courses by highlighting the societal relevance of the material and appealing to students' Social interests improved attitudes toward science, particularly for female students (Bennett, Lubben, & Hogarth, 2007). Although evidence of the effectiveness of these interventions is still preliminary, this research suggests a promising approach to using interests to improve academic achievement. Future research needs to examine the best methods, timing, as well as boundary conditions for interventions targeting students' interests (for a discussion regarding potential interventions targeting interest and cognitive development, see Su & Rounds, 2015).

IMPLICATIONS OF USING INTEREST ASSESSMENTS FOR PERSONNEL SELECTION

The research described in this chapter also suggests the potential use of interests for selecting high-quality employees. Existing evidence indicates that employees who are interested in the work that they do will be more likely to perform better on the job, engage in more OCB, feel more satisfied with their work, and remain on the job longer (i.e., lower attrition). More important, interests have been shown to predict these work outcomes over and above cognitive ability and personality traits (Dyer, 1987; Gellatly, Paunonen, Meyer, Jackson, & Goffin, 1991; McHenry, Hough, Toquam, Hanson, & Ashworth, 1990; Van Iddekinge, Putka, & Campbell, 2011), suggesting that interest assessments have value and utility for personnel selection in addition to the ability and personality measures that are already used in organizations. Nonetheless, the role of interests for employee selection has largely been overlooked in past research. Given the predictive power and incremental validity of interests for workplace outcomes, more research is needed to understand the potential implications of using interests to hire employees.

A key area for future research is the development of interest measures specifically for the purpose of selection. The assessment of interests has a long and distinguished history, dating back to a seminar conducted by C. S. Yoakum at the Carnegie Institute of Technology in 1919. Since that time, a number of well-known interest measures have been developed and widely used (e.g., Strong Interest Inventory, Kuder Preference Record, and Holland's Self-Directed Search). However, the majority of these measures were developed specifically for the purpose of career counseling and not with the employee selection process in mind. More research is needed to determine the generalizability of interest measures primarily used for career counseling to operational employment settings. Specifically, the most widely used interest measures were frequently developed using classical test theory (CTT) techniques, which often result in the exclusion of negative or neutral items during the test development process (Chernyshenko, Stark, Drasgow, & Roberts, 2007; Stark, Chernyshenko, Drasgow, & Williams, 2006). Although CTT techniques are commonly employed to construct psychological measures, the exclusion of negative or neutral items can limit the accuracy of trait estimates and, therefore, affect the rank order of high- and low-scoring individuals and reduce the precision of employee selection decisions. In contrast, modern psychometric models that incorporate item response theory have been developed to address this issue, and recent research suggests that these models may provide a more accurate description of the response process for interest measures (Tay, Drasgow, Rounds, & Williams, 2009). These modern methods of scoring and constructing psychological tests may benefit interest assessment and make it more suitable for use in high-stakes selection settings.

Issues with faking may be another potential concern with the measurement of interests in employee selection settings. Concerns about faking in personality assessment have received substantial attention in the organizational literature (Morgeson et al., 2007) but have received very little attention in the interest literature. One potential reason for this omission is that issues with faking are less of a concern when interest measures are used for career counseling. When using interest measures for making educational or career choices, individuals may have little motivation to distort their responses to reflect an ideal rather than their actual interest profile. However, in high-stakes settings such as the employee selection process, individuals may be more likely to provide inaccurate responses if it will help them to get a job that they want or even need. For example, college students applying for a summer job may be more interested in getting an extrinsically rewarding job rather than getting a job that they will be interested in long term. Similarly, individuals may apply for jobs for many reasons other than pursuing their actual interests, such as availability, location, perceived social pressure, short-term family needs, or lack of alternatives. In all these cases, getting the job may take priority over actual interests, and individuals may distort their responses in order to get the position. Therefore, more research is needed to determine whether the validity of interests is affected under operational conditions and how it can be maintained.

In addition, it is important to consider the level of specificity at which interests are measured. General interest scales (also referred to as "general occupational themes"), such as the RIASEC interest types, are designed to describe broad occupational preferences and include a heterogeneous set of work activities or occupations. Although these scales can provide a concise conceptual model of interests, the lack of specificity makes them less optimal for pinpointing individuals' interests. On the other hand, occupational interest scales are designed to measure the similarity of a person's interests to the interests of typical individuals within a specific occupation. Although these scales can describe interests at a refined level, they were most useful at a time when employees remained in a job or at a company for their entire career but are much less useful for understanding the current workforce, which is characterized by frequent job/occupation changes and increased overall mobility (Day & Rounds, 1997). As a result, some researchers have suggested assessing basic interests as an alternative to using the general interest or occupational interest scales (Jackson, 1977; Liao, Armstrong, & Rounds, 2008). Basic interests are specific, homogeneous dimensions of interests that group together work activities that may be relevant to a number of occupations. These narrow interest dimensions are analogous to trait facets in personality research. Assessing basic interests can provide both the content specificity and the flexibility required to more accurately select and classify individuals into a range of occupations. Therefore, more research is needed to examine the utility of basic interest scales in employment settings.

Finally, more research is needed to address the observed sex differences in interest measures (Su et al., 2009). Because these differences may result in adverse impact, the use of interests for employee selection could potentially result in the disproportionate selection of some groups of applicants and legal issues for organizations employing interest assessments. One potential solution to this issue may be to use targeted recruitment. Newman and Lyon (2009) showed that targeted recruitment efforts to attract highly qualified minority applicants for jobs could reduce the adverse impact of a selection measure. Similarly, Jones, Newman, and Jung (2013) found that targeted recruiting based on interests could reduce their potential adverse impact on African American applicants. Although Jones and colleagues did not examine the effects of targeted recruiting based on gender, a similar result is expected to occur for male and female applicants. For example, an organization that is hiring employees for a things-oriented job may want to actively recruit qualified female applicants who are interested in these types of positions. Future research needs to examine the effectiveness of recruiting strategies and other psychometric techniques for reducing potential adverse impact when using interest measures during the selection process.

CONCLUSION

Interests play a critical role in individuals' educational and career development. In this chapter, we reviewed research evidence that demonstrated the links between interests and job performance, career success, and successful preparation for the workforce. The most important message from this line of research, particularly recent studies on the relationship between interests and job performance, is that interests matter—not just for individuals' career choices before they enter the workforce but also for individuals' success at work. Therefore, interest assessment can help improve organizations' selection and staffing decisions.

Often misunderstood and thought of as "downstream" constructs of personality traits or yet another "noncognitive" domain, interests are in fact very unique in nature and have distinct psychological pathways for predicting human behaviors. Interests as an individual difference domain serve as a source of intrinsic motivation and are closely tied to learning and cognitive development. The contribution of interests to knowledge acquisition—in formal education, informal learning environments, or work settings—drives academic and job performance. Furthermore, interests, as a mechanism of person–environment fit, provide an interface for individuals to constantly relate to and interact with their environments. In the short term, the fit between an individual's interests and an academic major, an occupational field, an organization, a job, or a work task on a job influences the individual's performance behaviors and efforts. In the long term, these behaviors cumulate and determine the individual's career success. In this chapter, we highlighted these two aspects of interests in the hope of providing a new perspective for understanding workforce readiness and success.

In the long history of interest research, the focus has primarily been on the structure of human interests, the use of interest assessment for guiding educational and career decision-making, and the prediction of occupational memberships. Despite the renewed attention to and the accruing evidence on the relationship between interests and organizational behaviors, our knowledge about the use of interest assessment in organizational setting for making high-stakes decisions is still limited. It was our goal in this chapter to summarize recent advances and challenges in interest research and, in the meantime, call for future research in these new fronts.

NOTE

1. Traditionally, interest has been studied from either a situational perspective or a dispositional perspective (Silvia, 2006). The field of education examines situational interest as the context-specific state of emotional experience and curiosity; the field of vocational psychology examines interests as dispositions. In this chapter, we discuss interests primarily from the dispositional perspective because dispositional measures of interest are frequently used in applied settings for guiding individuals who are making education- and career-related decisions. Nonetheless, we also integrate findings and insights from research on situational interest.

REFERENCES

Ackerman, P. L. (1996). A theory of adult intellectual development: Process, personality, interests, and knowledge. *Intelligence, 22*, 227–257.

Ackerman, P. L., & Heggestad, E. D. (1997). Intelligence, personality, and interests: Evidence for overlapping traits. *Psychological Bulletin, 121*(2), 219–245.

American College Testing Program. (1995). *Technical manual: Revised Unisex Edition of the ACT Interest Inventory (UNIACT)*. Iowa City, IA: Author.

Armstrong, P. I., Day, S. X., McVay, J. P., & Rounds, J. (2008). Holland's RIASEC model as an integrative framework for individual differences. *Journal of Counseling Psychology, 55*, 1–18.

Assouline, M., & Meir, E. I. (1987). Meta-analysis of the relationship between congruence and well-being measures. *Journal of Vocational Behavior, 31*, 319–332.

Barrick, M. R., & Mount, M. K. (2005). Yes, personality matters: Moving on to more important matters. *Human Performance, 18*, 359–372.

Becker, G. (1964). *Human capital: A theoretical and empirical analysis with special reference to education*. New York, NY: Columbia University Press.

Bennett, J., Lubben, F., & Hogarth, S. (2007). Bringing science to life: A synthesis of the research evidence on the effects of context-based and STS approaches to science teaching. *Science Education, 91*, 347–370.

Borghans, L., Duckworth, A. L., Heckman, J. J., & ter Weel, B. (2008). The economics and psychology of personality traits. *Journal of Human Resources, 43*(4), 972–1059.

Brown, S. D., & Gore, P. A., Jr. (1994). An evaluation of interest congruence indices: Distribution of characteristics and measurement properties. *Journal of Vocational Behavior, 45*(3), 310–327.

Brown, S. D., & Lent, R. W. (Eds.). (2005). *Career development and counseling: Putting theory and research to work.* New York, NY: Wiley.

Brunello, G., & Schlotter, M. (2011). *Non cognitive skills and personality traits: Labour market relevance and their development in education and training systems* (Discussion Paper Series No. 5743). Bonn, Germany: Institute for the Study of Labor.

Camp, C. C., & Chartrand, J. M. (1992). A comparison and evaluation of interest congruence indices. *Journal of Vocational Behavior, 41*(2), 162–182.

Campbell, D. P. (1971). *Handbook for the Strong Vocational Interest Blank.* Stanford, CA: Stanford University Press.

Campbell, J. P. (1990). Modeling the performance prediction problem in industrial organizational psychology. In M. D. Dunnette & L. M. Hough (Eds.), *Handbook of industrial and organizational psychology* (Vol. 1, 2nd ed., pp. 687–732). Palo Alto, CA: Consulting Psychologists Press.

Campbell, J. P., Gasser, M. B., & Oswald, F. L. (1996). The substantive nature of job performance variability. In K. R. Murphy (Ed.), *Individual differences and behavior in organizations* (pp. 258–299). Hillsdale, NJ: Erlbaum.

Cattell, R. B. (1987). *Intelligence: Its structure, growth, and action.* New York, NY: Elsevier.

Chamorro-Premuzic, T., von Stumm, S., & Furnham, A. (Eds.). (2011). *Handbook of individual differences.* Oxford, England: Wiley-Blackwell.

Chatman, J. A. (1989). Improving interactional organizational research: A model of person–organization fit. *Academy of Management Review, 14*, 333–349.

Chatman, J. A. (1991). Matching people and organizations: Selection and socialization in public accounting firms. *Administrative Science Quarterly, 36*, 459–484.

Chernyshenko, O. S., Stark, S., Drasgow, F., & Roberts, B. W. (2007). Constructing personality scales under the assumption of an ideal point response process: Toward increasing the flexibility of personality measures. *Psychological Assessment, 19,* 88–106.

Cortina, J. M., & Luchman, J. N. (2013). Personnel selection and employee performance. In N. W. Schmitt, S. Highhouse, & I. B. Weiner (Eds.), *Handbook of psychology: Industrial and organizational psychology* (Vol. 12, 2nd ed., pp. 143–183). Hoboken, NJ: Wiley.

Cronbach, L. J., & Gleser, G. C. (1953). Assessing the similarity between profiles. *Psychological Bulletin, 50*, 456–473.

Dawis, R. V., & Lofquist, L. H. (1984). *A psychological theory of work adjustment.* Minneapolis, MN: University of Minnesota Press.

Day, S. X., & Rounds, J. (1997). "A little more than kin, less than kind": Basic interests in vocational research and career counseling. *The Career Development Quarterly, 45,* 207–220.

Denissen, J. J. A., Zarrett, N. R., & Eccles, J. S. (2007). I like to do it, I'm able, and I know I am: Longitudinal couplings between domain-specific achievement, self-concept, and interest. *Child Development, 78*, 430–447.

Dik, B. J. (2006). Moderators of the Holland-type congruence–satisfaction and congruence–performance relations. *Dissertation Abstracts International: Section B: The Sciences and Engineering, 66*(8-B), 4520.

Dudley, N. M., Orvis, K. A., Lebiecki, J. A., & Cortina, J. M. (2006). A meta-analytic investigation of conscientiousness in the prediction of job performance: Examining the intercorrelations and the incremental validity of narrow traits. *Journal of Applied Psychology, 91*(1), 40–57.

Dyer, E. D. (1987). Can university success and first-year job performance be predicted from academic achievement, vocational interest, personality and biographical measures? *Psychological Reports, 61*(2), 655–671.

Edwards, J. R. (1993). Problems with the use of profile similarity indices in the study of congruence in organizational research. *Personnel Psychology, 46*(3), 641–665.

Edwards, J. R. (2002). Alternatives to difference scores: Polynomial regression analysis and response surface methodology. In F. Drasgow & N. Schmitt (Eds.), *Measuring and analyzing behavior in organizations: Advances in measurement and data analysis* (pp. 350–400). San Francisco, CA: Jossey-Bass.

Edwards, J. R., & Shipp, A. J. (2007). The relationship between person–environment fit and outcomes: An integrative theoretical framework. In C. Ostroff & T. A. Judge (Eds.), *Perspectives on organizational fit* (pp. 209–258). San Francisco, CA: Jossey-Bass.

French, J. R. P., Jr., Caplan, R. D., & Harrison, R. V. (1982). *The mechanisms of job stress and strain.* New York, NY: Wiley.

French, M. T., Homer, J. F., Popovici, I., & Robins, P. K. (2014, May 19). What you do in high school matters: High school GPA, educational attainment, and labor market earnings as a young adult. *Eastern Economic Journal.*

Gati, I. (1985). Description of alternative measures of the concepts of vocational interest: Crystallization, congruence, and coherence. *Journal of Vocational Behavior, 27*, 37–55.

Gellatly, I. R., Paunonen, S. V., Meyer, J. P., Jackson, D. N., & Goffin, R. D. (1991). Personality, vocational interest, and cognitive predictors of managerial job performance and satisfaction. *Personality and Individual Differences, 12*(3), 221–231.

Harmon, L. W., Hansen, J. C., Borgen, F. H., & Hammer, A. L. (1994). *Strong Interest Inventory applications and technical guide.* Stanford, CA: Stanford University Press.

Harrison, D. A., Newman, D. A., & Roth, P. L. (2006). How important are job attitudes? Meta-analytic comparisons of integrative behavioral outcomes and time sequences. *Academy of Management Journal, 49*, 305–325.

Heckman, J. J., & Kautz, T. (2013). *Fostering and measuring skills: Interventions that improve character and cognition* (NBER Working Paper No. 19656).

Heckman, J. J., & Rubinstein, Y. (2001). The importance of noncognitive skills: Lessons from the GED testing program. *American Economic Review, 91*(2), 145–149.

Hidi, S., & Harackiewicz, J. M. (2000). Motivating the academically unmotivated: A critical issue for the 21st century. *Review of Educational Research, 70*, 151–179.

Holland, J. L. (1959). A theory of vocational choice. *Journal of Counseling Psychology, 6*, 35–45.

Holland, J. L. (1963). Explorations of a theory of vocational choice and achievement: II. A four-year prediction study. *Psychological Reports, 12,* 547–594.

Holland, J. L. (1996). Exploring careers with a typology: What we have learned and some new directions. *American Psychologist, 51,* 397–406.

Holland, J. L. (1997). *Making vocational choices: A theory of vocational personalities and work environments* (3rd ed.). Odessa, FL: Psychological Assessment Resources.

Holland, J. L., Fritzsche, B., & Powell, A. (1994). *Self-directed search: Technical manual.* Odessa, FL: Psychological Assessment Resources.

Howard, A., & Bray, D. W. (1994). Predictions of managerial success over time: Lessons from the management progress study. In K. E. Clark & M. B. Clark (Eds.), *Measures of leadership* (pp. 113–130). West Orange, NJ: Leadership Library of America.

Huang, J. L., & Pearce, M. (2013). The other side of the coin: Vocational interests, interest differentiation and annual income at the occupation level of analysis. *Journal of Vocational Behavior, 83*(3), 315–326.

Hulin, C. L., Roznowski, M., & Hachiya, D. (1985). Alternative opportunities and withdrawal decisions: Empirical and theoretical discrepancies and an integration. *Psychological Bulletin, 97,* 233–250.

Hunter, J. E., & Hunter, R. F. (1984). Validity and utility of alternative predictors of job performance. *Psychological Bulletin, 96,* 72–98.

Hurtz, G. M., & Donovan, J. J. (2000). Personality and job performance: The Big Five revisited. *Journal of Applied Psychology, 85,* 869–879.

Iachan, R. (1984). A measure of agreement for use with the Holland classification system. *Journal of Vocational Behavior, 24,* 133–141.

Jackson, D. N. (1977). *Manual for the Jackson Vocational Interest Survey.* Port Huron, MI: Research Psychologists Press.

Jones, K. S., Newman, D. A., & Jung, S. (2013). Targeted recruiting on vocational interests: An initial investigation. In R. Su (Chair), *Interests: New frontier for personnel selection.* Symposium presented at the 29th annual conference of the Society for Industrial and Organizational Psychology, Honolulu, HI.

Judge, T. A., Cable, D. M., Boudreau, J. W., & Bretz, R. D. (1995). An empirical investigation of the predictors of executive career success. *Personnel Psychology, 48,* 485–519.

Judge, T. A., Higgins, C. A., Thoresen, C. J., & Barrick, M. R. (1999). The Big Five personality traits, general mental ability, and career success across the life span. *Personnel Psychology, 52,* 621–652.

Judge, T. A., Thoresen, C. J., Bono, J. E., & Patton, G. K. (2001). The job satisfaction-job performance relationship: A qualitative and quantitative review. *Psychological Bulletin, 127,* 376–407.

Kandler, C., Bleidorn, W., Riemann, R., Angleitner, A., & Spinath, F. M. (2011). The genetic links between the Big Five personality traits and general interest domains. *Personality and Social Psychology Bulletin, 37,* 1633–1643.

Kieffer, K. M., Schinka, J. A., & Curtiss, G. (2004). Person–environment congruence and personality domains in the prediction of job performance and work quality. *Journal of Counseling Psychology, 51,* 168–177.

Kristof-Brown, A. L., Zimmerman, R. D., & Johnson, E. C. (2005). Consequences of individuals' fit at work: A meta-analysis of person–job, person–organization, person–group, and person–supervisor fit. *Personnel Psychology, 58,* 281–342.

Kwak, J. C., & Pulvino, C. J. (1982). A mathematical model for comparing Holland's personality and environmental codes. *Journal of Vocational Behavior, 21,* 231–241.

Lent, R. W., Brown, S. D., & Larkin, K. C. (1987). Comparison of three theoretically derived variables in predicting career and academic behavior: Self-efficacy, interest congruence, and consequence thinking. *Journal of Counseling Psychology, 34,* 293–298.

Lewin, K. (1935). *Dynamic theory of personality.* New York, NY: McGraw-Hill.

Liao, H.-Y., Armstrong, P. I., & Rounds, J. (2008). Development and initial validation of public domain Basic Interest Markers. *Journal of Vocational Behavior, 73,* 159–183.

Low, K. S. D., Yoon, M., Roberts, B. W., & Rounds, J. (2005). The stability of vocational interests from early adolescence to middle adulthood: A quantitative review of longitudinal studies. *Psychological Bulletin, 131,* 713–737.

Lubinski, D. (2000). Scientific and social significance of assessing individual differences: "Sinking shaft at a few critical points." *Annual Review of Psychology, 51,* 405–444.

McCrae, R. R., & Costa, P. T. (1990). *Personality in adulthood.* New York, NY: Guildford.

McHenry, J. J., Hough, L. M., Toquam, J. L., Hanson, M. A., & Ashworth, S. (1990). Project A validity results: The relationship between predictor and criterion domains. *Personnel Psychology, 43,* 335–354.

Morgeson, F. P., Campion, M. A., Dipboye, R. L., Hollenbeck, J. R., Murphy, K., & Schmitt, N. (2007). Reconsidering the use of personality tests in personnel selection contexts. *Personnel Psychology, 60,* 683–729.

Morris, M. A. (2003). *A meta-analytic investigation of vocational interest-based job fit, and its relationship to job satisfaction, performance, and turnover.* Doctoral dissertation. Retrieved from ProQuest Dissertations and Theses database (UMI No. 3089788).

Motowidlo, S. J. (2003). Job performance. In W. C. Borman, D. R. Ilgen, & R. J. Klimoski (Eds.), *Handbook of psychology: Industrial and organizational psychology* (Vol. 12, pp. 39–53). Hoboken, NJ: Wiley.

Murray, H. A. (1938). *Explorations in personality.* New York, NY: Oxford University Press.

National Science Board. (2014). *Science and engineering indicators 2014* (NSB 14-01). Arlington, VA: National Science Foundation.

Neumann, G. R., Olitsky, N. H., & Robbins, S. B. (2009). Job congruence, academic achievement, and earnings. *Labour Economics, 16*(5), 503–509.

Newman, D. A., & Lyon, J. S. (2009). Recruitment efforts to reduce adverse impact: Targeted recruiting for personality, cognitive ability, and diversity. *Journal of Applied Psychology, 94,* 298–317.

Ng, T. W. H., Eby, L. T., Sorensen, K. L., & Feldman, D. C. (2005). Predictors of objective and subjective career success: A meta-analysis. *Personnel Psychology, 58,* 367–408.

Nye, C. D., Su. R., Rounds, J., & Drasgow, F. (2012). Vocational interests and performance: A quantitative summary of over 60 years of research. *Perspectives on Psychological Science, 7,* 384–403.

Parsons, C. K. (1909). *Choosing a vocation.* Boston, MA: Houghton-Mifflin.

Pervin, L. A. (1968). Performance and satisfaction as a function of individual–environment fit. *Psychological Bulletin, 69,* 56–68.

Pervin, L. A. (1987). Person–environment congruence in the light of the person–situation controversy. *Journal of Vocational Behavior, 31,* 222–230.

Peterson, N. G., Mumford, M. D., Borman, W. C., Jeanneret, P., & Fleishman, E. A. (1999). *An occupational information system for the 21st century: The development of O* NET.* Washington, DC: American Psychological Association.

Ployhart, R. E. (2006). Staffing in the 21st century: New challenges and strategic opportunities. *Journal of Management, 32,* 868–897.

Psychological Assessment Resources. (2009). Publisher website. Retrieved from http://www.self-directed-search.com

Renninger, K. A., Hidi, S., & Krapp, A. (Eds.). (1992). *The role of interest in learning and development.* Hillsdale, NJ: Erlbaum.

Roberts, B. W., Kuncel, N. R., Shiner, R., Caspi, A., & Goldberg, L. R. (2007). The power of personality: The comparative validity of personality traits, socio-economic status, and cognitive ability for predicting important life outcomes. *Perspectives in Psychological Science, 2,* 313–345.

Rounds, J., & Su, R. (2014). The nature and power of interests. *Current Directions in Psychological Science, 23*(2), 98–103.

Rounds, J., Su, R., Lewis, P., & Rivkin, D. (2010). *O*NET Interest Profiler Short Form Psychometric Characteristics: Summary and supporting evidence.* Washington, DC: US Department of Labor, National O*NET Resource Center. Retrieved from http://www.onetcenter.org/dl_files/IPSF_Psychometric.pdf

Sackett, P. R., & Ellingson, J. E. (1997). The effects of forming multi-predictor composites on group differences and adverse impact. *Personnel Psychology, 50,* 707–721.

Sackett, P. R., & Lievens, F. (2008). Personnel selection. *Annual Review of Psychology, 59,* 1–32.

Savickas, M., & Spokane, A. (Eds.). (1999). *Vocational interests: Their meaning, measurement and use in counseling.* Palo Alto, CA: Davies-Black.

Schmidt, F. L. (2014). A general theoretical integrative model of individual differences in interests, abilities, personality traits, and academic and occupational achievement: A commentary on four recent articles. *Perspectives on Psychological Science, 9,* 211–218.

Schmidt, F. L., & Hunter, J. E. (1998). The validity and utility of selection methods in personnel psychology: Practical and theoretical implications of 85 years of research findings. *Psychological Bulletin, 124*(2), 262–274.

Schmitt, N., Cortina, J. M., Ingerick, M., & Weichmann, D. (2003). Personnel selection and employee performance. In R. J. Klimoski, W. C. Borman, & D. R. Ilgen (Eds.), *Handbook of psychology: Industrial and organizational psychology* (Vol. 12, pp. 77–105). Hoboken, NJ: Wiley.

Schmitt, N., Oswald, F. L., Friede, A., Imus, A., & Merritt, S. (2008). Perceived fit with an academic environment: Attitudinal and behavioral outcomes. *Journal of Vocational Behavior, 72,* 317–335.

Schneider, B. (1987). The people make the place. *Personnel Psychology, 40,* 437–453.

Schwartz, R. H., Andiappan, P., & Nelson, M. (1986). Reconsidering the support for Holland's congruence–achievement hypothesis. *Journal of Counseling Psychology, 33,* 425–428.

Seibert, S. E., & Kraimer, M. L. (2001). The five-factor model of personality and career success. *Journal of Vocational Behavior, 58*, 1–21.

Silvia, P. J. (2006). *Exploring the psychology of interest*. New York, NY: Oxford University Press.

Silvia, P. J. (2008). Interest—The curious emotion. *Current Directions in Psychological Science, 17*(1), 57–60.

Spokane, A. 1985. A review of research on person–environment congruence in Holland's theory of careers. *Journal of Vocational Behavior, 26*, 306–343.

Stark, S., Chernyshenko, O. S., Drasgow, F., & Williams, B. A. (2006). Examining assumptions about item responding in personality assessment: Should ideal point methods be considered for scale development and scoring? *Journal of Applied Psychology, 91*, 25–39.

Strenze, T. (2007). Intelligence and socioeconomic success: A meta-analytic review of longitudinal research. *Intelligence, 35*, 401–426.

Strong, E. K., Jr. (1943). *The vocational interests of men and women*. Stanford, CA: Stanford University Press.

Strong, E. K., Jr. (1946). Interests of senior and junior public administrators. *Journal of Applied Psychology, 30*, 55–71.

Strong, E. K., Jr. (1949). Vocational interests of accountants. *Journal of Applied Psychology, 33*, 474–481.

Strong, E. K., Jr. (1955). *Vocational interests eighteen years after college*. Minneapolis, MN: University of Minnesota Press.

Su, R. (2012). *The power of vocational interests and interest congruence in predicting career success*. Unpublished doctoral dissertation, University of Illinois at Urbana–Champaign. Retrieved from http://hdl.handle.net/2142/34329

Su, R., Murdock, C. D., & Rounds, J. (2014). Person–environment fit. In P. Hartung, M. Savickas, & B. Walsh (Eds.), *APA handbook of career intervention* (pp. 81–98). Washington, DC: American Psychological Association.

Su, R., & Rounds, J. (2015). All STEM fields are not created equal: People and things interests explain gender disparities across STEM fields. *Frontiers in Psychology, 6*, 189.

Su, R., Rounds, J., & Armstrong, P. I. (2009). Men and things, women and people: A meta-analysis of sex differences in interests. *Psychological Bulletin, 135*, 859–884.

Tay, L., Drasgow, F., Rounds, J., & Williams, B. A. (2009). Fitting measurement models to vocational interest data: Are dominance models ideal? *Journal of Applied Psychology, 94*, 1287–1304.

Tett, R. P., & Meyer, J. P. (1993). Job satisfaction, organizational commitment, turn-over intention, and turnover: Path analyses based on meta-analytic finding. *Personnel Psychology, 46*, 259–293.

Tinsley, H. E. A. (2000). The congruence myth: An analysis of the efficacy of the person–environment fit model. *Journal of Vocational Behavior, 56*, 147–179.

Tinsley, H. E. A. (2006). A pig in a suit is still a pig: A comment on "Modifying the C Index for use with Holland codes of unequal length." *Journal of Career Assessment, 14*, 283–288.

Tranberg, M., Slane, S., & Ekeberg, S. E. (1993). The relation between interest congruence and satisfaction: A meta-analysis. *Journal of Vocational Behavior, 42*, 253–264.

Tsabari, O., Tziner, A., & Meir, E. I. (2005). Updated meta-analysis of the relationship between congruence and satisfaction. *Journal of Career Assessment, 13*, 216–232.

Turner, S. A., Jr., & Silvia, P. J. (2006). Must interesting things be pleasant? A test of competing appraisal structures. *Emotion, 6*, 670–674.

Van Iddekinge, C. H., Putka, D. J., & Campbell, J. P. (2011). Reconsidering vocational interests for personnel selection: The validity of an interest-based selection test in relation to job knowledge, job performance, and continuance intentions. *Journal of Applied Psychology, 96*(1), 13–33.

Van Iddekinge, C. H., Roth, P. L., Putka, D. J., & Lanivich, S. E. (2011). Are you interested? A meta-analysis of relations between vocational interests and employee performance and turnover. *Journal of Applied Psychology, 96*(6), 1167–1194.

Verquer, M. L., Beehr, T. A., & Wagner, S. H. (2003). A meta-analysis of relations between person–organization fit and work attitudes. *Journal of Vocational Behavior, 63*, 473–489.

Wiggins, J. D., & Weslander, D. L. (1979). Personality characteristics of counselors rated as effective or ineffective. *Journal of Vocational Behavior, 15*, 175–185.

The Sourdough Model
of Conscientiousness

BRENT W. ROBERTS AND PATRICK L. HILL ■

Conscientiousness is a spectrum of constructs that describe individual differences in the propensity to be self-controlled, responsible to others, hardworking, orderly, and rule abiding (Roberts, Jackson, Fayard, Edmonds, & Meints, 2009). Conscientiousness predicts most of the major preventative and risky behaviors for physical health (Bogg & Roberts, 2004). Conscientiousness also predicts physical health (Hampson, Goldberg, Vogt, & Dubanoski, 2007; Moffitt et al., 2011), the onset of Alzheimer's disease (Wilson, Schneider, Arnold, Bienias, & Bennett, 2007), as well as longevity (Kern & Friedman, 2008). In addition, conscientiousness predicts outcomes such as relationship quality and duration (Roberts, Kuncel, Shiner, Caspi, & Goldberg, 2007). In the case of school, conscientiousness is the most important factor after cognitive abilities when examining school performance (Poropat, 2009). Succinctly, conscientiousness is a personality trait that promotes better health, wealth, relationships, and school success (Roberts et al., 2007).

Given the increasing awareness of the importance of conscientiousness, it is becoming increasingly common for people to want to understand how an individual arrives at adulthood possessing some adequate level of conscientiousness. This is a question on the minds of both parents and societies throughout the world. Most parents and social communities are invested in having their children become responsible, hard-working, and appropriately self-controlled adults. As evidence of the promoted nature of conscientiousness, facets of the trait (e.g., industrious and reliable) appear in lay conceptions of the "good person" from multiple countries throughout the world (Smith, Smith, & Christopher, 2007).

Answering the introductory question is the central focus of this chapter. In order to address this overarching question, we unpack it into more manageable, smaller questions. Specifically, we attempt to answer the following: (1) What is conscientiousness? (2) How does conscientiousness develop across childhood and into adulthood? and (3) What are the necessary ingredients for fostering conscientiousness in today's youth? In addressing these questions, we invoke existing developmental and personality theory and in so doing elaborate on these theoretical structures to arrive at a set of conjectures that, it is hoped, is constructive for future research.

WHAT IS CONSCIENTIOUSNESS?

We consider conscientiousness to be a system of interrelated constructs that can be assessed on several levels—that is, it is a domain and not simply a unitary entity. A conscientious person generally can be counted on by others to fulfill prosocial obligations created by social groups and societies (Roberts, Lejuez, Krueger, Richards, & Hill, 2014). Historically, constructs associated with the domain of conscientiousness have been studied for more than 100 years. In the time between Freud and the Big Five personality traits, related constructs were studied under terms such as impulsivity, super-ego strength, social confor- mity, and ego control (Block & Block, 1980). Many decades of clinical research has focused on components of psychopathology manifest in tests such as the Minnesota Multiphasic Personality Inventory that reflect low conscientious- ness or disconstraint (Harkness, Finn, McNulty, & Shields, 2012; Sellbom, Ben- Porath, & Bagby, 2008).

Conscientiousness, like all other personality traits, is a hierarchically struc- tured system. In terms of the hierarchy, traits can be ordered from broad to narrow. When conceptualized at the level of the broad conscientiousness domain, the trait-eliciting contexts are multifaceted because they aggregate across the component parts of the broader conscientiousness spectrum. When narrow facets of conscientiousness are examined, the contextual aspects of the specific elements of the broader domain become apparent. For example, when one assesses self-control, the items typically refer to situations in which one faces temptation (e.g., rash purchases or eating too much). Likewise, industriousness measures typically refer to contexts manifest in achievement or work settings.

A number of studies have examined personality descriptors and produced information on the lower-order structure of the conscientiousness domain. We recently reviewed all of the studies that have contributed to our understanding of the domain of conscientiousness (Roberts et al., 2014). We found that the two most common domains identified as key components of conscientiousness are orderliness and industriousness. Orderliness encompasses the overarching tendency to be "prepared," which includes tendencies toward neatness, cleanliness, and planfulness on the positive side and disorderliness, disorganization, and messiness on the negative end of the spectrum. Industriousness captures the tendency to work hard, aspire to excellence, and persist in the face of challenge. Several studies have identified a separate persistence factor (de Raad & Peabody, 2005; MacCann, Duckworth, & Roberts, 2009), which can be thought of as a construct that bridges conscientiousness and ambition, a facet of extraversion. Given that the facet of industriousness also correlates with components of extraversion (Roberts, Bogg, Walton, Chernyshenko, & Stark, 2004), it might be appropriate to categorize persistence as a form of industriousness.

The next two most common facets identified are self-control and responsibility. Self-control represents the propensity to control impulses or to inhibit a pre-potent response. On the negative end of this facet, one finds the tendency to be reckless, impulsive, and out of control. Responsibility reflects the tendency to follow through with promises to others and to follow rules that make social groups work more smoothly. On the low end, it reflects the tendency to be an unreliable partner in achievement settings and to break one's promises. Although identified as a conscientiousness facet in most of the listed studies, responsibility measures also tend to correlate quite highly with agreeableness (Roberts, Chernyshenko, Stark, & Goldberg, 2005); therefore, its placement may shift depending on the content of the measures used to tap this facet.

Most of the remaining facets of conscientiousness have been found at least twice. Conventionality (or traditionality) reflects a tendency to endorse and uphold societal rules and conventions. Decisiveness subsumes the propensity to act firmly and consistently. Formalness reflects a tendency to follow rules of decorum, such as keeping one's appearance neat and clean, holding doors for others, and shaking hands. Punctuality reflects the simple tendency to show up on time to scheduled appointments. Interestingly, of all the facets of conscientiousness, punctuality appears to be most strongly correlated with all the remaining facets of conscientiousness (Jackson et al., 2010). That is, being punctual appears to be important when considering one's ability to plan (orderliness), work hard toward goals (industriousness), avoid temptations that might lead one to be late (self-control), care enough to meet other people on time (responsibility), and understand the rules and conventions surrounding one's social group (conventionality).

The findings for punctuality go to a fundamental question: Why are these traits a family of constructs? Or, to a point, why are they all strongly positively correlated? According to Costantini et al. (2015), the core of conscientiousness is the anticipation of future consequences of one's actions manifest in the explicit or implicit goal to plan. This is obvious in a facet such as orderliness, in which planning is a key feature. One can identify similar markers of anticipation of future consequences in each of the remaining facets. Industriousness typically prepares the way for success at a later time. Self-control is the tendency to avoid immediate rewards and prefer delayed long-term rewards. Responsibility entails being a reliable social partner over time. Similarly, being traditional or rule abiding entails committing to the status quo so that things remain stable over time. As such, global measures of conscientiousness that combine these elements will, at their core, be assessing this long-term planning or anticipation of the future.

PATTERNS OF CONTINUITY AND CHANGE IN CONSCIENTIOUSNESS

To understand how to scaffold the development of conscientiousness, it is critical to discern the typical patterns of change in conscientiousness across the life course. Unfortunately, both because of the heterogeneity of the domain and because of keen data oversights on the part of developmental psychology, there is less direct evidence about the continuity and change in conscientiousness in children and adolescents. Ironically, we know more about what happens to conscientiousness in adults.

To understand what happens to conscientiousness in childhood and adolescence, we start with two meta-analyses that examined both continuity and change in both temperamental traits and personality traits. In terms of continuity, temperamental dimensions related to conscientiousness, such as effortful control, are surprisingly stable over relatively long periods of time (Roberts & DelVecchio, 2000). Starting at approximately age 3 years, the average test–retest correlations for temperament and trait dimensions range from .36 to .52 when focusing in childhood and early adolescence. Clearly, these levels of consistency are far from unity. On the other hand, correlations of approximately .5 would belie a level of continuity that bolsters the potential that temperamental dimensions have long-term influence over psychosocial functioning (Moffitt et al., 2011). As one moves through adulthood, conscientiousness and its facets appear to grow in consistency, although they never reach a level of consistency that would preclude the possibility of growth or change.

In terms of normative increases or decreases in dimensions related to conscientiousness, previous meta-analytic work has not examined childhood and has identified adolescence as a time during which there is no consistent pattern of increase or decrease (Roberts, Walton, & Viechtbauer, 2006). In contrast, dimensions that fall into the domain of conscientiousness show consistent increases starting in young adulthood that continue through old age. The lack of perfect stability and the existence of changes in adulthood highlight the fact that conscientiousness can change throughout the life course. Thus, focusing on the development and fostering of conscientiousness in younger age periods would not be undermined by any idea that personality is calcified by any specific juncture in the life course.

WHAT ARE THE INGREDIENTS AND CONDITIONS NECESSARY TO FOSTER CONSCIENTIOUSNESS? THE SOURDOUGH ANALOGY

Given this lack of calcification, we turn next to considering how best to promote conscientiousness by reference to a surprisingly analogous domain, namely baking sourdough bread. How does sourdough help us understand how and why conscientiousness develops? Sourdough bread is a deceptively simple creation. It is a combination of four basic ingredients: a starter (a combination of flour, water, yeast, and a *Lactobacillus* bacteria), flour, water, and salt. The quality of the bread is linked to the quality and amounts of the ingredients that go into making the bread. Different types and amounts of flour, water, salt, and starters result in dramatically different breads.

These ingredients are combined and exposed to a set of "environmental" features to create different forms and qualities of sourdough, including the ambient temperature, the containers in which the dough sits, and the humidity of the environment in which the dough "proofs." Once combined, the ingredients need time to "proof" in order to develop the flavor and character that are unmistakably found in sourdough bread. Proofing is the leveraging of context and time to help develop the qualities that make up sourdough bread. Many contextual factors can be varied during the process in order to change the texture and flavor of the bread. These contextual factors can also be varied in order to speed up, slow down, or even arrest the development of the bread. Early in the process, some recipes call for an "autolyse" where the flour, water, and starter sit for a time before adding the salt, all in an effort to improve the texture of the resulting bread. Add more heat and the entire process quickens, but the end product will not be as complex or flavorful. Put the proofing dough in a refrigerator and the process can be slowed to a crawl.

The length of time the dough proofs has a remarkable effect on the bread. The longer a sourdough proofs before baking, the more sour, complex, and hearty the flavor and texture. Timing also is critical. Bake the dough too soon and the bread will be bland and not very sour. Conversely, wait too long and the yeast consumes all of the sugars and then the dough collapses, resulting in something more akin to a brick than a loaf. Therefore, the baker must be diligent and monitor the proofing dough in order to catch it when it is in the optimal window of having proofed for as long as possible but not so long that it collapses. Finally, when it is time to bake, adding moisture to the oven can change the character of the loaf, as can different levels of heat.

Analogously, the development of conscientiousness begins with a set of basic ingredients that go into its creation combined with various environmental conditions that might help or hinder its development. Similar to sourdough bread, these basic ingredients need to be combined and "proofed" in order to achieve a reasonable facsimile of conscientiousness. Moreover, we believe two of the most critical environmental features for the development of psychological dimensions such as conscientiousness are time and timing. Finally, environmental variations can affect how those original ingredients come together and then coalesce to form something as complex and rich as conscientiousness.

The beauty of sourdough is that one can work with the ingredients in many different ways. In this case, the baker is analogous to the environment. In the hands of an amateur, even the best ingredients may never come together to form a good loaf of bread. In contrast, an expert baker can even make do with mediocre ingredients to make a beautiful loaf. Analogously, a psychological dimension such as conscientiousness may never develop in a context hostile to its growth. Conversely, a rich environment, like a skilled baker, may be able to produce a conscientious person despite not beginning with the ideal set of temperamental starting values. Next, we review factors of the ingredients and the environmental features, or "baking techniques," that we believe contribute to the development of conscientiousness.

The Ingredients That Make Up Conscientiousness

Like sourdough, conscientiousness begins with a composite of ingredients that need to be combined in order to move successfully down the path toward the adult version of the personality trait. It is clear from both behavior genetics and temperament research that children are not born blank slates (Krueger & Johnson, 2008). The key question, then, is whether the characteristics that children possess affect their development of conscientiousness over time. Longitudinal prospective studies have shown that precursors to the adult form of conscientiousness, often discussed as temperamental factors, play out over the long term, such that certain children are more likely to follow paths of development that will result in the development of a sense of conscientiousness (Moffitt et al., 2011). Accordingly, certain children have more optimal starting points for the development of conscientiousness. This is not to say that the remaining children are a lost cause; far from it. Rather, we simply note that there are robust selection effects that pervade development, which allow certain children to be more likely to develop specific attributes such as conscientiousness. In this section, we describe some of the qualities that we believe make it easier for some children to grow into adolescents who are more conscientious.

What are the key ingredients that are necessary for the development of conscientiousness? First, as alluded to previously, it appears that children with a stronger sense of effortful control early in life are more prepared to follow developmental paths that lead to higher levels of conscientiousness later in life. Effortful control entails the ability to delay gratification and inhibit the often powerful desire to give into temptation or impulse when appropriate in childhood. Effortful control appears to be the childhood dimension that differentiates into the two adult traits most strongly related to conscientiousness: agreeableness and conscientiousness (Deal, Halverson, Havill, & Martin, 2005). In childhood, higher levels of effortful control are related to a wide range of outcomes deemed positive by most societies, such as higher achievement in school (Blair & Razza, 2007) and fewer behavioral problems across contexts (Olson, Sameroff, Kerr, Lopez, & Wellman, 2005). Therefore, like good flour, effortful control appears to be a positive quality in childhood that makes the path to elevated conscientiousness in adolescence easier to follow.

Second, there appear to be additional cognitive precursors to conscientiousness that would ideally be combined with effortful control. Specifically, one must possess the cognitive faculties that plan for and adopt long-term goals (e.g., strong executive functioning). Because planning for future actions and prioritizing them above immediate, albeit less rewarding, actions is a core component of conscientiousness, this is an additional key ingredient.

Third, it would be ideal for children to possess regulatory systems that would make it more likely to adopt long-term goal setting and/or delay of gratification. Self-conscious emotions appear to be potential candidates for serving this function. On the promotional side of the ledger, positive self-conscious emotions such as authentic pride (Tracy & Robins, 2007) would clearly serve as a reward system for successfully delaying gratification. On the inhibitory side of the ledger, the capacity for negative self-conscious emotions such as guilt would help individuals avoid impulsive actions. For instance, conscientious individuals appear higher on guilt proneness (Fayard, Roberts, Robins, & Watson, 2012), which may actually prove adaptive insofar as it guides individuals away from activities that will induce negative self-conscious emotions in the future, such as deviating from one's long-term goals in favor of short-term benefits. Although individuals generally hold some capacity for both executive functioning and self-conscious emotions, it is clear that children differ in their starting points for both.

As children age, they develop stronger levels of cognitive control over their choices and the freedom to choose how to invest their time. Developmental research on volunteering in adolescence reveals how commitment—the cognitive pursuit of a goal to achieve some group or societally sanctioned activity—is another component of the suite of attributes that make conscientiousness more likely to develop. Specifically, if a child or teenager has bought into a set of shared goals that are prosocial in nature, he or she is more likely to develop a sense of conscientiousness (Wood, Larson, & Brown, 2009). On the other hand, adolescents who lack motivation or who do not care about an outcome will likely avoid the situations altogether or go through the motions when called on to act. This may be one reason why boot camps have such notoriously poor efficacy in fostering prosocial behavior (Hill et al., 2011): They are typically forced on a child or adolescent and take a severe authoritarian approach to work and discipline, which in turn can create a level of alienation between the student and the institution that undermines commitment. The other feature that might lead to the failure of boot camps is their typically short duration. Like proofing dough, developing conscientiousness takes time.

In terms of the ingredients that facilitate the development of conscientiousness—like the flour, water, starter, and salt of sourdough bread—we see the necessity for at least four ingredients. First, it would help if a child possesses some form of effortful control with which to begin life. Second, individuals should hold the cognitive capacities for long-term, future-oriented goal pursuit and planning. Third, some form of emotion-based regulatory system like that found in self-conscious emotions seems necessary. Finally, it appears beneficial to hold the motivational desire to commit to others and one's community, which would afford environments to have their potential effect on a person. Although it is unclear whether these ingredients are either necessary or sufficient (a point we consider in greater detail later), we suggest that in combination, they can constitute a "dough" for conscientiousness that may either rise or fall as an effect of the individual's environment.

Environmental Features That Lead to Conscientiousness

Just as sourdough is more than the sum of its ingredients, conscientiousness does not develop in a vacuum. As such, what then are the features of the environment that would contribute to teenagers acquiring increasing levels of conscientiousness as they age? Unlike sourdough, there appear to be a litany of contextual factors associated with its development or the development of analogous phenotypes. Although there is little direct evidence of the effects of different environments on the development of conscientiousness, it is clear from research on analogous dimensions, such as delinquency, that one should consider a range of environments from proximal to distal. For this purpose, one system valuable for organizing environmental factors is Bronfrenbrenner's (1979) ecological systems theory (EST). EST delineates the social environment from the most proximal, in the child's immediate relational environment (the microsystem), through the interrelations among immediate environments (e.g., home to school effects; mesosystem), through the ancillary environments that might impinge on a child's world (e.g., parents' work experiences; exosystem), and finally to the culture surrounding the child (macrosystem). These environments are analogous to the ones manipulated by a baker when making bread. From the proximal basket in which the dough proofs to the ambient temperature of the kitchen and the climate of the region in which it is baked (purportedly, the Bay Area in California is ideal for bread baking and storing), the baker has many levels of environments with which to work to make a loaf of bread.

The obvious and most commonly studied environment is parenting and family structure. As noted previously, children are less likely to grow up to engage in delinquent activities if their parents have a consistent disciplinary style (Rutter, Giller, & Hagell, 1998). Family factors that contribute to prosocial behaviors include being born into a small family, being born to older parents, and not experiencing divorce (Rutter et al., 1998). Children born into small families by older parents are more likely to experience better parenting, such as effective monitoring, consistent punishment, and responsiveness. In turn, positive, authoritative parenting is a strong predictor of prosocial outcomes (Patterson, 1982). Likewise, intact homes and warm, supportive family environments are also strongly related to prosocial traits and behaviors (Roberts, Jackson, Berger, & Trautwein, 2009).

One of the specific mechanisms that appears to promote the temperamental basis for conscientiousness concerns the type of relationship a child develops with his or her parents. For example, Kochanska and Murray (2000) identified the mutually reinforcing orientation (MRO) between a young child and his or her parent as a major factor in the acquisition of a conscience. The MRO is the positive relationship between parent and child in which the child comes to admire the parent. Children who have mutually reinforcing relationships with their parents are more likely to internalize parental values for moral behavior. According to Kochanska and Murray, children with MRO relationships with their parents do this because they like and admire their parents and experience positive emotions when they act in ways consistent with parental expectations and ideals.

The rationale behind MRO has far-reaching implications for the development of conscientiousness at later ages. Many people believe that adopting strict, authoritarian social structures is necessary for children, teenagers, and even adults to develop the discipline necessary to become conscientious. This is the implicit ideology behind boot camp interventions, for example, in which teenagers are forced to experience a demanding and highly structured environment for a short period of time in the hope that it will teach them "a lesson" (Hill, Roberts, Grogger, Guryan, & Sixkiller, 2011). The MRO research implies something quite different. It suggests that if a person likes and admires the individuals in his or her social settings who are communicating role expectations, and the person enjoys and is satisfied with his or her relationships, the person will be more likely to acquire and enact the expected role behaviors. For example, 4H experiences and summer camp may be far better for teaching conscientiousness than boot camp.

Moving beyond parents and immediate authority figures such as teachers, peer groups also play a significant role in the development of externalizing disorders and presumably then play a role in the development of conscientiousness. At a pragmatic level, many externalizing behaviors are undertaken in social groups (Reiss, 1988). Drug and alcohol use tends to occur in social groups, as do antisocial activities (Hirschi, 2002). The facilitating effects of peer groups can manifest externalizing behaviors through either selection or socialization effects (Rutter et al., 1998). In terms of selection, individuals may choose to associate with certain peer groups in order to manifest their externalizing tendencies in a social group. That is, people may choose to belong to a group that does drugs because they already do drugs themselves. On the other hand, individuals may join peer groups and be influenced to adopt new externalizing behaviors because of peer pressure. Through either mechanism, peer groups have been shown to maintain externalizing behaviors if they are made up of members who already participate in these behaviors (Farrington, 1986).

One then would assume that associating and identifying with peers prone to prosocial behaviors would facilitate the development of conscientiousness. Some data indirectly support this notion. For example, Jessor, Turbin, and Costa (1998) found that involvement in conventional social institutions, such as family, school, and church, was a protective factor against risky health behavior even when controlling for the effects of more proximal predictors of health behaviors, such as valuing health, internal health locus of control, and peer models of health behavior. Thus, adolescents who interact with peers in prosocial organizations tend to adopt behaviors that are viewed as more responsible by most societies.

Similarly, in research on volunteering in adolescence, social roles provided the context and contingencies that appeared to facilitate the development of conscientiousness because they allowed for something to be committed to (Wood, Larsen, & Brown, 2009). Adolescents who were more likely to experience challenging task demands in their volunteer activities reported increasing conscientiousness. Tasks that facilitated increasing conscientiousness tended to be demanding and required teenagers to exceed the expectations they had for themselves prior to volunteerism. Another feature of the experience related to increasing conscientiousness was roles within the volunteer activities. Adopting formal roles that carried responsibilities for others and the program (e.g., being a president, director, or committee chair) was associated with an increased sense of conscientiousness. Finally, high time demands were also described as facilitating conscientiousness. Teenagers who worked longer hours and more days than expected also viewed themselves as becoming more responsible.

These institutions that adolescents are capable of committing to can be viewed as analogous to the parental mutually reinforcing orientation. In this case, the child or adolescent would be willing to commit to such an institution. Their willingness to commit could be driven by the fact that they already possess the key ingredients for conscientiousness. It could also come about because they perceive the institution as supportive. An ancillary benefit of "MRO institutions" is the self-reinforcing nature of the connections that adolescents make to others and to social institutions. These institutions provide explicit rewards for continuing to express conscientious thoughts, feelings, and emotions. Also, the relationships with others embedded in these institutions bring a second layer of consequences if an adolescent quits an activity or social institution. Quitting a volunteer activity would entail severing ties to people with whom the adolescent has developed positive relationships. This might cause the feeling of guilt that would induce the teenager to continue with his or activities and thus "proof" for slightly longer.

The connection between individual and conventional social institutions appears to continue to exert influence over traits related to conscientiousness even in the transition from adolescence to young adulthood. For example, Sampson and Laub (1990; Laub, Nagin, & Sampson, 1998) showed that the development of bonds to social institutions reduced delinquent behavior in adulthood. Sampson and Laub defined social bonds as social investments made in work, marriage, and to one's community. They argued that simply receiving employment or getting married did not confer the salutary effect of these social contexts. Rather, the positive effect of these roles occurred when one became committed to a job or developed a strong attachment to a spouse. These social investments are thought to exact a form of social control through the role demands embedded in these contexts that call on individuals to act with more control, conscientiousness, and probity (i.e., act more conscientious). Sampson and Laub found that job stability and a strong emotional attachment to one's spouse significantly reduced delinquent and criminal activity in men.

Finally, at the broadest level, it appears reasonable to assume that if a community and broader society also had a "mutually reinforcing attitude" toward the individual, this would maximize the development of prosocial attributes such as conscientiousness. This idea has no clear test that we can identify, but it can be seen in its absence in descriptions of poor students trying their best to succeed (Tough, 2013). If the broader social milieu sends the message that the adolescent's efforts will not be rewarded or appreciated, even individuals with the most positive of ingredients may have difficulty building conscientiousness. Why invest in a path that will inevitably go unappreciated? Following the path of probity and delayed gratification relies heavily on a social contract with a culture or society that will provide the necessary rewards in the long term.

In terms of the environment, we have identified proximal, distal, and distant environmental factors and experiences that appear to be necessary for the successful fostering and development of conscientiousness. The experience of supportive, stable, consistent environments that send the unambiguous message that both the child and his or her efforts toward being conscientious are valued seems to be critical for the development of this attribute. We view these environmental features as analogous to those that contribute to better sourdough bread. Like good bread, conscientiousness requires a supportive environment that rewards thinking and behaving with the future and long-term outcomes in mind.

Time and Timing, the Final Conditions

Like sourdough, we believe that developing psychological traits such as conscientiousness takes time. For someone to meet a challenge, persist in the effort, and then overcome obstacles, he or she will clearly have to spend more than a few days or weeks on a task. Moreover, if the construct requires persistent effort in a time-consuming activity, by definition, a quick experience will not suffice. Challenges that are met easily and quickly would most likely be processed as easy and therefore not diagnostic of one's conscientiousness. Finally, overcoming failures clearly entails some long-term investment in an activity, the consequence of failure, and then the re-engagement in the activity and a subsequent success. It is difficult to imagine that these types of experiences can be manifest quickly.

Second, if the developmental process laid out previously is correct, then experiences early in life will help to create the scaffolding necessary for later experiences to take hold. This is analogous to the baker's actions, such as doing an autolyse with dough. Early actions in the proofing process have subtle but important effects on the quality and character of the dough. Early environmental conditions and developmental experiences may work similarly with conscientiousness. When handled well by supportive parents, peers, or mentors, the early ingredients of effortful control, planning, self-conscious emotions, and commitment may integrate better, making it easier to develop conscientiousness later in life. Implicit in this process is the idea that these lessons play out over years rather than days. Furthermore, as a child ages and becomes a self-reflecting adolescent, having more time to consider the lessons learned from one's experiences may help to deepen the meaning of the experiences and in turn solidify the perception that one has acquired a sense of conscientiousness.

Finally, the advantage that time brings is the opportunity to practice and re-experience relevant lessons. This may be critical for a characteristic such as conscientiousness because most conceptualizations of the construct clearly entail that people often sacrifice or experience discomfort in the short term in anticipation of long-term reward. Following through with obligations that entail working long hours and expending extraordinary effort becomes rewarding only in the long term when the subsequent, often larger rewards become apparent. With time and practice, the salience of the long-term rewards may begin to outweigh the aversive nature of the short-term costs. Thus, over time spans of years, someone may learn progressively to become more conscientious as these contingencies are made clearer with the simple passage of time coupled with experience.

Just like determining the optimal time to bake the sourdough loaf, timing may also be just as important as time for the development of conscientiousness. Some research has shown that structural variables may affect the timing of the increase in conscientiousness. Typically, conscientiousness begins to increase in young adulthood (Roberts et al., 2006). However, in societies in which the transition to adult roles begins earlier in the life course, so does the increase in conscientiousness (Bleidorn et al., 2013). Other studies indirectly support the idea that transitions that occur at the right time might facilitate change better than those that do not. For example, German students on the cusp of transitioning to adulthood who worked diligently for 1 year to study for the Abitur test showed marked gains in conscientiousness (Bleidorn, 2012). In contrast, students just 1 year younger who had no pressure to either work harder than normal or make a critical transition showed no signs of an increase in conscientiousness.

In contrast, developmental snares may catch people at critical times that interrupt the more common pattern of increasing conscientiousness. This would be like suddenly moving the proofing dough from an optimal, warm and humid environment to the refrigerator right before it was ready to bake. For example, the tendency for adolescent-limited delinquency to manifest right before the transition to adulthood could be extraordinarily poor timing (Moffitt, 1993). Although many teenagers participate in risky behaviors, doing so and getting caught right before making the transition to adulthood could adversely affect the development of conscientiousness. One study found that boys who were jailed as adolescents showed a much-delayed increase in traits related to conscientiousness (Morizot & Le Blanc, 2003). Similarly, people who continue to use and abuse alcohol in young adulthood, as in late adolescence, show evidence of "arrested development" such that they do not increase in conscientiousness like their peers (Littlefield, Sher, & Steinley, 2010; Roberts & Bogg, 2004). Conversely, mistakes made at younger ages may be easier to overcome as long as a person has a supportive, stable, and forgiving environment.

A TRANSACTIONAL MODEL OF THE DEVELOPMENT OF CONSCIENTIOUSNESS

We assert that conscientiousness emerges out of the coalescence of the person and environment factors described previously. In an effort to capture the process of developing conscientiousness, Table 9.1 outlines these critical ingredients, environments, and timing considerations. Although this table is by no means exhaustive, it provides a review of what the empirical literature suggests may be most critical for the development of conscientiousness. As seen in Table 9.1, we believe that the primary temperamental precursors to conscientiousness are early childhood effortful control, the ability to plan, and the self-conscious emotions linked to higher conscientiousness. In our conceptualization of conscientiousness, we do not equate it with temperament. Rather, we view temperamental dimensions as something akin to starting values. Children are clearly not blank slates but, rather, come to the world with tendencies that are genetically preprogrammed. These tendencies are starting values in the sense that they are prone to develop and change with experience. The path between one's starting value and what would be construed as conscientiousness entails the dynamic interplay between temperament and context, at least early on, and then in the future the interplay of context and the eventual trait of conscientiousness.

In terms of context, we believe it is constructive to identify developmentally sequenced childhood contexts. These contexts are divided into parental, sibling, friend, and societal categories, reflecting what we believe to be the most developmentally and evolutionarily relevant contexts for the development of

Table 9.1 Critical Ingredients, Environments, and Timing Issues for the
Development of Conscientiousness

Ingredient	Environment	Time and Timing
Effortful control or the ability to delay gratification and control impulses	Well-structured, predictable family environment	Early supportive environments that reinforce conscientiousness
Long-term planning capacity, such as being able to visualize and anticipate long-term successes	Supportive relationship with at least one parental figure	Continuous supportive environments in the transition from childhood to adolescence (e.g., schools)
Self-conscious emotions, such as the capacity to feel shame, guilt, and pride in relation to supporting or failing the expectations of others	Affiliating and preferring conscientious peers	Opportunities to practice conscientiousness
Prosocial commitment, such as being willing to invest in volunteer roles that bring expectations for facets of conscientiousness such as responsibility and punctuality	Acquiring social roles that afford the opportunities to be conscientious, such as work and relationship roles Societal norms that reward conscientiousness, such as those found in most religious systems	Avoiding poorly timed pitfalls, such as adolescent snares

conscientiousness. Our hypothesis is that children develop context-specific patterns of thoughts, feelings, and behaviors that initially reflect a combination of early childhood temperament and the demands of the social context in each of these categories. Thus, as Kochanska, Murray, and Harlan (2000) have shown, children with specific temperamental starting points will respond differentially to parental influence to manifest the intervening cognitive and emotional scaffolding necessary for conscientiousness.

These stable patterns that develop within the context of social roles and relationships represent intermediary points between temperament and the manifestation of conscientiousness. That is, children will develop consistent patterns of conscientiousness precursors that reflect both their temperament and the press of the environment within specific social relationships (Su & Costigan, 2009). Children will have different experiences with their parents and with society (often through their interactions with teachers and mentors) that will prove variable presses for conscientiousness. For example, parents may provide a less demanding press for conscientiousness than elementary school teachers because parents do not have the task of managing 25–35 children simultaneously. The latter demands will result in differential patterns of thoughts, feelings, and behaviors across these contexts. The unruly child at home might be the star pupil in class because of the differential demands of the environments. The effects of these environments will be tempered by early temperament, such that children who are extremely undercontrolled will have a difficult time responding effectively to the demands of either environment.

We hypothesize that the experiences within each role, which reflect a mix of temperament and environmental demands, are eventually combined and generalized. This is a fundamental idea taken from learning generalization models of social development (Kohn & Schooler, 1982). Experiences will integrate into the cognitive, emotional, and behavioral components of conscientiousness that develop throughout childhood. Learning to delay gratification, work hard toward goals, and persist in the face of failure all appear to be critical features to develop on the path to being a conscientious adult.

The resulting generalized trait of conscientiousness then acts in a reciprocal manner with social roles and social environments as the child grows into an adolescent. For example, adolescents who are less impulsive tend to choose friends and activities that are less delinquent in orientation and thus create new social relationships that reinforce their development levels of conscientiousness (Jessor et al., 1998). Alternatively, children who never showed any signs of incivility in the past may acquire a new set of unruly habits because of the friendships that they develop during adolescence. Thus, as Moffitt (1993) notes, life course persistent delinquents become social leaders in adolescence. In turn, many adolescents who previously showed no signs of delinquency acquire a newfound antisocial attitude through their association with delinquent peers. In terms of our model, this means that inputs from friends could override previously developed patterns in social relations with parents, teachers, and siblings. However, adolescent-limited delinquent adolescents tend to possess lower levels of effortful control as children (Moffitt, 1993), making them more susceptible to the potential pull of the delinquent peer leaders they take up with.

These initial forms of conscientiousness merge with a supportive environment to create the motivations to invest and commit to life paths that would reward higher levels of conscientiousness. This is where the initial ingredients for conscientiousness prove critical as higher levels of them will increase the probability that a child will not be caught in snares that would derail the developmental process. Moreover, this is where community-level support may be critical. If the community or society communicates its support for individuals— its willingness to invest in and support individuals—it may be more likely that they develop the motivations necessary to follow paths that reward and advance conscientiousness.

Applying the Transactional Model of the Development of Conscientiousness to the Goal of Developing Students

The resulting transactional model that emerges out of observational studies of the development of conscientiousness leads to a set of research hypotheses and questions that resonate with the goal of helping students succeed. The first, and most fundamental, is whether one needs all of the ingredients in place for the development of conscientiousness. This is a critical question for those who wish to design interventions to help students be more conscientious. Often, programs focus on eliminating problematic behaviors, teaching teachers and parents how to behave differently, or modifying rewards in the school environment. Inevitably, these interventions tend to focus on (at best) one or two of the ingredients or environmental features present in the model discussed previously. If each of the components of the model plays a small but critical role in the development of conscientiousness, then we hypothesize that these types of interventions will have very limited effects.

This basic question also motivates related questions, including whether conscientiousness develops in the absence of one or more of these ingredients. There are many stories of children who experienced incredible deprivation or abuse in childhood only to grow up to be upstanding, conscientious adults. Conversely, there are stories of children born to affluent, conscientious parents who end up demonstrably maladaptive adults and engage in serious crimes. The existence of these anecdotes seems to answer the question with an affirmative—that no one ingredient is necessary and sufficient. Moreover, they exemplify an underlying principle of several lifespan theories of development (Cicchetti & Rogosch, 1996), namely that individuals can proceed to a similar endpoint (e.g., levels of conscientiousness) from very different paths (equifinality), as well as how similar ingredients or starting points can lead to a wide array of outcomes (multifinality). However, it is still important for us to understand the relative contribution of these factors. If a person is born into poverty and experiences disproportionate hardships while young, what is his or her chance of becoming a conscientious adult? These are research questions that have not yet been asked or answered.

A related series of questions concerns the relative importance of each of the elements. Developmental and educational science, for good reasons, focuses on parents and teachers. But are parents and teachers the most important environmental factors for the development of conscientiousness? It may be that peers and communities are much more important than parents and teachers. For example, in a massive intervention study designed to help at-risk children avoid a delinquent adolescence, the most important factor was not parents or teachers but, rather, peers; associating with more delinquent peers undermined years of strenuous interventions (Dishion, McCord, & Poulin, 1999).

Other questions concerning time and timing also arise. Many interventions are predicated on a model of human nature that tends to diminish the importance of "starting values" or temperament. Thus, short-term interventions are often prescribed and implemented but seldom succeed. One reason may simply be that in the face of pervasive temperamental and environmental factors, a single mentoring experience or a semester-long classroom experience may fail to modify the underlying scaffolding necessary for the development of conscientiousness. It is also an open question of how much time and experience are necessary for the development of conscientiousness.

The most interesting timing question is whether, like language (Hensch, 2005), the development of conscientiousness has a critical period in childhood. Given the complex cocktail of factors that are in play, we doubt that any age period should be privileged, but admittedly there is little good data to inform a hypothesis. We could hypothesize that it will be easier to work with populations that have had more of the critical ingredients in place for a longer amount of time than with populations that are deprived. Therefore, intervening earlier may be more efficacious.

Extrapolating from two data points—the fact that conscientiousness tends to increase more in young adulthood and that this change is related to structural changes that communicate the demands of adulthood—we propose that if there is a critical period, it is when an adolescent is on the cusp of adulthood. This is when all of the ingredients are in place, the appropriate level of time has been spent "proofing" the ingredients, and the person is most responsive to the heat of the environment.

CONCLUSION

In this chapter, we attempted to both define conscientiousness and provide an overview of the critical ingredients—both psychological and environmental— necessary for its development. In this effort, we found it useful to think of the development of conscientiousness as analogous to that of a good loaf of rustic sourdough bread. The latter takes good ingredients, critical environmental supports, time, and timing to develop. Likewise, it appears that conscientiousness necessitates a similar set of factors to develop successfully. We hope that the resulting model can provide new testable hypotheses and also some perspective on the task of developing conscientiousness and similar attributes in young students. If our model is even partially correct, the modal approach to interventions, which tend toward the short term and punitive (Hill et al., 2011), would appear to be non-optimal. It would also indicate that no one factor, such as parents or teachers, should either be the focus of all efforts or shoulder the entire responsibility for the goal of developing satisfactory levels of conscientiousness in students.

REFERENCES

Blair, C., & Razza, R. P. (2007). Relating effortful control, executive function, and false belief understanding to emerging math and literacy ability in kindergarten. *Child Development, 78*(2), 647–663.

Bleidorn, W. (2012). Hitting the road to adulthood short-term personality development during a major life transition. *Personality and Social Psychology Bulletin, 38*(12), 1594–1608.

Bleidorn, W., Klimstra, T. A., Denissen, J. J., Rentfrow, P. J., Potter, J., & Gosling, S. D. (2013). Personality maturation around the world: A cross-cultural examination of social-investment theory. *Psychological Science, 24*(12), 2530–2540.

Block, J. H., & Block, J. (1980). The role of ego-control and ego-resiliency in the organization of behavior. In W. A. Collins (Ed.), *Development of cognition, affect, and social relations: The Minnesota symposia on child psychology* (Vol. 13, pp. 39–101). Hillsdale, NJ: Erlbaum.

Bogg, T., & Roberts, B. W. (2004). Conscientiousness and health behaviors: A meta-analysis of the leading behavioral contributors to mortality. *Psychological Bulletin, 130*, 887–919.

Bronfrenbrenner, U. (1979). The ecology of human development: Experiments by nature and design. Cambridge, MA: Harvard University Press.

Cicchetti, D., & Rogosch, F. A. (1996). Equifinality and multifinality in developmental psychopathology. *Development and Psychopathology, 8*, 597–600.

Costantini, G., Richetin, J., Borsboom, D., Fried, E. I., Rhemtulla, M., & Perugini, M. (2015). Development of indirect measures of conscientiousness: Combining a facets approach and network analysis. *European Journal of Personality, 29*(5), 548–567.

de Raad, B., & Peabody, D. (2005). Cross-culturally recurrent personality factors: Analyses of three factors. *European Journal of Personality, 19*, 451–474.

Deal, J. E., Halverson, C. F., Havill, V., & Martin, R. (2005). Temperament factors as longitudinal predictors of young adult personality. *Merrill–Palmer Quarterly, 51*(3), 315–334.

Dishion, T. J., McCord, J., & Poulin, F. (1999). When interventions harm: Peer groups and problem behavior. *American Psychologist, 54*(9), 755.

Farrington, D. P. (1986). Age and crime. *Crime and Justice, 7*, 189–250.

Fayard, J. V., Roberts, B. W., Robins, R. W., & Watson, D. (2012). Uncovering the affective core of conscientiousness: The role of self-conscious emotions. *Journal of Personality, 80*, 1–32.

Hampson, S. E., Goldberg, L. R., Vogt, T. M., & Dubanoski, J. P. (2007). Mechanisms by which childhood personality traits influence adult health status: Educational attainment and healthy behaviors. *Health Psychology, 26*, 121–125.

Harkness, A. R., Finn, J. A., McNulty, J. L., & Shields, S. M. (2012). The Personality Psychopathology–Five (PSY-5): Recent constructive replication and assessment literature review. *Psychological Assessment, 24*(2), 432.

Hensch, T. K. (2005). Critical period plasticity in local cortical circuits. *Nature Reviews Neuroscience, 6*(11), 877–888.

Hill, P. L., Roberts, B. W., Grogger, J. T., Guryan, J., & Sixkiller, K. (2011). Decreasing delinquency, criminal behavior, and recidivism by intervening on psychological factors other than cognitive ability: A review of the intervention literature. In P. J. Cook, J. Ludwig, & J. McCrary (Eds.), *Making crime control pay: Cost-effective alternatives to incarceration* (pp. 367–406). Chicago, IL: University of Chicago Press.

Hirschi, T. (2002). *Causes of delinquency.* New Brunswick, NJ: Transaction Publishers.

Jackson, J. J., Wood, D., Bogg, T., Walton, K. E., Harms, P. D., & Roberts, B. W. (2010). What do conscientious people do? Development and validation of the Behavioral Indicators of Conscientiousness (BIC). *Journal of Research in Personality, 44*, 501–511.

Jessor, R., Turbin, M. S., & Costa, F. M. (1998). Protective factors in adolescent health behavior. *Journal of Personality and Social Psychology, 75*, 788.

Kern, M. L., & Friedman, H. S. (2008). Do conscientious individuals live longer? A quantitative review. *Health Psychology, 27*, 505–512.

Kochanska, G., & Murray, K. T. (2000). Mother–child mutually responsive orientation and conscience development: From toddler to early school age. *Child Development, 71*(2), 417–431.

Kochanska, G., Murray, K. T., & Harlan, E. T. (2000). Effortful control in early childhood: Continuity and change, antecedents, and implications for social development. *Developmental Psychology, 36*(2), 220.

Kohn, M. L., & Schooler, C. (1982). Job conditions and personality: A longitudinal assessment of their reciprocal effects. *American Journal of Sociology, 87*(6), 1257–1286.

Krueger, R. F., & Johnson, W. (2008). Behavioral genetics and personality. In O. P. John, R. W. Robins, & L. A. Pervin (Eds.), *Handbook of personality: Theory and research* (3rd ed., pp. 287–310). New York, NY: Guilford.

Laub, J. H., Nagin, D. S., & Sampson, R. J. (1998). Trajectories of change in criminal offending: Good marriages and the desistance process. *American Sociological Review*, 225–238.

Littlefield, A. K., Sher, K. J., & Steinley, D. (2010). Developmental trajectories of impulsivity and their association with alcohol use and related outcomes during emerging and young adulthood I. *Alcoholism: Clinical and Experimental Research, 34*(8), 1409–1416.

MacCann, C., Duckworth, A. L., & Roberts, R. D. (2009). Empirical identification of the major facets of conscientiousness. *Learning and Individual Differences, 19*, 451–458.

Moffitt, T. E. (1993). Adolescence-limited and life-course-persistent antisocial behavior: A developmental taxonomy. *Psychological Review, 100*(4), 674.

Moffitt, T. E., Arseneault, L., Belsky, D., Dickson, N., Hancox, R. J., Harrington, H. L., . . . Caspi, A. (2011). A gradient of childhood self-control predicts health, wealth, and public safety. *Proceedings of the National Academy of Sciences of the USA*, *108*, 2693–2698.

Morizot, J., & Le Blanc, M. (2003). Continuity and change in personality traits from adolescence to midlife: A 25-year longitudinal study comparing representative and adjudicated men. *Journal of Personality*, *71*(5), 705–755.

Olson, S. L., Sameroff, A. J., Kerr, D. C., Lopez, N. L., & Wellman, H. M. (2005). Developmental foundations of externalizing problems in young children: The role of effortful control. *Development and Psychopathology*, *17*(1), 25–45.

Patterson, G. R. (1982). *Coercive family process* (Vol. 3). Eugene, OR: Castalia.

Poropat, A. E. (2009). A meta-analysis of the five-factor model of personality and academic performance. *Psychological Bulletin*, *135*(2), 322.

Reiss, A. J., Jr. (1988). Co-offending and criminal careers. *Crime and Justice*, *10*, 117–170.

Roberts, B. W., & Bogg, T. (2004). A 30-year longitudinal study of the relationships between conscientiousness-related traits, and the family structure and health-behavior factors that affect health. *Journal of Personality*, *72*, 325–354.

Roberts, B. W., Bogg, T., Walton, K., Chernyshenko, O., & Stark, S. (2004). A lexical approach to identifying the lower-order structure of conscientiousness. *Journal of Research in Personality*, *38*, 164–178.

Roberts, B.W., Chernyshenko, O., Stark, S. & Goldberg, L. (2005). The structure of conscientiousness: An empirical investigation based on seven major personality questionnaires. *Personnel Psychology*, *58*, 103–139.

Roberts, B. W., & DelVecchio, W. F. (2000). The rank-order consistency of personality from childhood to old age: A quantitative review of longitudinal studies. *Psychological Bulletin*, *126*, 3–25.

Roberts, B. W., Jackson, J. J., Berger, J., & Trautwein, U. (2009). Conscientiousness and externalizing psychopathology: Overlap, developmental patterns, and etiology of two related constructs. *Development and Psychopathology*, *21*, 871–888.

Roberts, B. W., Jackson, J. J., Fayard, J. V., Edmonds, G., & Meints, J. (2009). Conscientiousness. In M. Leary & R. Hoyle (Eds.), *Handbook of individual differences in social behavior* (pp. 369–381). New York, NY: Guilford.

Roberts, B. W., Kuncel, N., Shiner, R., N., Caspi, A., & Goldberg, L. R. (2007). The power of personality: The comparative validity of personality traits, socio-economic status, and cognitive ability for predicting important life outcomes. *Perspectives in Psychological Science*, *2*, 313–345.

Roberts, B. W., Lejuez, C., Krueger, R. F., Richards, J. M., & Hill, P. L. (2014). What is conscientiousness and how can it be assessed? *Developmental Psychology*, *50*(5), 1315–1330.

Roberts, B. W., Walton, K., & Viechtbauer, W. (2006). Patterns of mean-level change in personality traits across the life course: A meta-analysis of longitudinal studies. *Psychological Bulletin*, *132*, 1–25.

Rutter, M., Giller, H., & Hagel, A. (1998). Varieties of antisocial behaviour. In *Antisocial behaviour by young people* (pp. 95–126). Cambridge, England: Cambridge University Press.

Sampson, R. J., & Laub, J. H. (1990). Crime and deviance over the life course: The salience of adult social bonds. *American Sociological Review*, *55*(5), 609–627.

Sellbom, M., Ben-Porath, Y. S., & Bagby, R. M. (2008). Personality and psychopathology: Mapping the MMPI-2 Restructured Clinical (RC) scales onto the five factor model of personality. *Journal of Personality Disorders, 22*(3), 291–312.

Smith, K. D., Smith, S. T., & Christopher, J. C. (2007). What defines the good person? Cross-cultural comparisons of experts' models with lay prototypes. *Journal of Cross-Cultural Psychology, 38*(3), 333–360.

Su, T. F., & Costigan, C. L. (2009). The development of children's ethnic identity in immigrant Chinese families in Canada: The role of parenting practices and children's perceptions of parental family obligation expectations. *Journal of Early Adolescence, 29*(5), 638–663.

Tough, P. (2013). *How children succeed.* New York, NY: Houghton Mifflin.

Tracy, J. L., & Robins, R. W. (2007). The psychological structure of pride: A tale of two facets. *Journal of Personality and Social Psychology, 92*(3), 506.

Wilson, R. S., Schneider, J. A., Arnold, S. E., Bienias, J. L., & Bennett, D. A. (2007). Conscientiousness and the incidence of Alzheimer disease and mild cognitive impairment. *Archives of General Psychiatry, 64,* 1204–1212.

Wood, D., Larson, R. W., & Brown, J. R. (2009). How adolescents come to see themselves as more responsible through participation in youth programs. *Child Development, 80*(1), 295–309.

Rethinking How We Prepare Students for the Workforce

Commentary

INDAKO E. CLARKE, KIT S. DOUBLE, AND CAROLYN
MACCANN ■

The purpose of education defines a society in both social and economic terms. As President Obama noted, "The future belongs to the nation that best educates its citizens" (Obama, 2009). Fundamentally, the purpose of education is to prepare students for their life after graduation. This chapter considers what such preparation might consist of for life in the 21st century, focusing on four areas discussed in detail in previous chapters: respect for diversity (Chapter 6), entrepreneurship (Chapter 7), interest and person–environment fit (Chapter 8), and conscientiousness (Chapter 9).

John Locke believed that the purpose of education was more than "an accumulation of facts" (Ezell, 1983, p. 141), and we agree with this assertion. Educational institutions are more than repositories of knowledge that is passed on to students as they progress toward graduation. Students do not just acquire graduate knowledge but also develop graduate attributes—skills and qualities that make them desirable employees and contributors to society. These attributes are often called workforce readiness KSAs (knowledge, skills, and abilities), noncognitive skills, or 21st century skills. They extend beyond discipline-specific knowledge and skills to include widely applicable and easily transferable skills. It is clear that workplaces require more than just technical and professional training in the relevant disciplines. The large-scale US employer survey *Are They Really Ready to Work?* (Casner-Lotto & Barrington, 2006) reports that employers want graduates with attributes such as professionalism, teamwork, leadership skills, and workplace resilience.

Rapid changes in workplace characteristics pose both challenges and opportunities for employees and organizations. Globalization is drastically changing the nature of work and workplaces through increased global trade and the development of an international job market. Moreover, rapid technological change is redefining the ways that people communicate, with increased reliance on e-mail, multimedia conferencing, and other long-distance methods. Collectively, these ongoing changes to the workplace require workers who can rapidly adapt to change and can manage the social and emotional demands of working within a global workforce. Employees who have both the cognitive and the noncognitive skills needed to work effectively within modern working environments are likely to flourish within workplaces, whereas those who lack these skills will be at a disadvantage. Indeed, workplaces that embrace changes to work, particularly those that have been able to quickly adapt to changing market demands, outperform workplaces that are less willing or able to do this (Jayne & Dipboye, 2004; McMahon, 2010; Stevens, Plaut, & Sanchez-Burks, 2008). This chapter provides a summary of the ways in which institutions and organizations can prepare students to operate effectively within modern workplaces by managing the increasingly dynamic demands of the modern workforce.

DIVERSITY

What Is Diversity and Why Is It Important?

Perhaps one of the most significant ways in which the workplace has changed in terms of the requirements and expectations of graduates is through the changes prompted by increased diversity. Workplace diversity has been defined in many different ways by different organizations and individuals. Traditionally, definitions of workplace diversity were largely drawn from American experiences of diversity, particularly racial diversity, which has for a long time characterized its workplaces according to race (Barak, 2013). Narrow definitions stemming from this tradition rarely extend beyond the relevant legislative requirements (Barak, 2013; Wentling & Palma-Rivas, 1998).

How Can Students Be Prepared for the Workforce?

Increases in workplace diversity are accompanied by growing diversity within college and university campuses. Most educational institutions, both within the

United States and globally, are seeing increases in enrollments from students in minority groups and backgrounds. Recent projections from the National Center for Education Statistics show that tertiary enrollments are predicted to increase by at least 26% between 2011 and 2022 for Black and Hispanic students (Hussar & Bailey, 2013). Despite increased diversity in enrollments, persistent segregation in education and campus housing continues to result in campuses that have limited diversity in many respects (Orfield & Lee, 2006). As such, it is incumbent upon educational institutions to implement interventions that promote diversity in order to prepare students for the workplace. Early experiences with out-group members have been shown to shape latter out-group interactions. For example, the demographic makeup of an individual's school influences his or her out-group interactions in college, and their skill and competency when encountering diversity later in life (Gurin, Dey, Hurtado, & Gurin, 2002; Milem, Chang, & Antonio, 2005).

In Chapter 6, Lester et al. broadly summarize some of the interpersonal strategies that are available to individuals and organizations seeking to enhance diversity practices and competencies of their students. In particular, they focus on how the institutional environment can be modified by interventions that target graduates and current tertiary students and enhance their readiness for the workplace. As Lester et al. suggest, a significant body of relevant research can be found in the prejudice literature, which investigates the strategies and experiences that decrease prejudice and stereotyping. Broadly speaking, Lester et al. outline the contextual demands that reduce prejudice by drawing on Allport's (1979) seminal work, which argues for the need for group equality, cooperation, and institutional support above all else.

As Lester et al. outline, early interactions with out-group members have a large bearing on an individual's ability to develop the skills needed to operate in a diverse workplace. Reviews of hundreds of studies have shown the importance of intergroup relations for reducing prejudice by increasing empathy and knowledge while decreasing anxiety related to the out-group (Pettigrew & Tropp, 2006, 2008; Tropp & Pettigrew, 2005). Given that intergroup interaction has been established as one of the best predictors of later out-group attitudes, changing the demographic makeup of college campuses has a significant flow-on effect for educational outcomes and workplace readiness (Gurin et al., 2002). Campuses with large racial majorities provide limited opportunities for intergroup interaction and limit student experience with cultural diversity (Kanter, 1977). There is evidence that a lack of opportunities for face-to-face contact can be overcome through online contact. White, Abu-Rayya, and Weitzel (2014) found that an online text-based paradigm showed significant long-lasting reductions in prejudicial attitudes toward Muslim students by Christian students after speaking for short sessions over 9 weeks.

In addition to decreasing prejudice, improving the demographic diversity of college campuses benefits a wide range of outcomes. For instance, in two large-scale studies in the United States, the Michigan Student Study and a national study of diversity outcomes, Gurin et al. (2002) consistently found that campus diversity had a considerable positive effect on educational outcomes and intellectual engagement. Similarly, a meta-analysis conducted by Bowman (2010) found that college diversity experiences enhanced cognitive development. Campus diversity is also important for students' adjustment to college life (Hurtado et al., 2007). However, as Lester et al. note, although peer interaction tends to improve diversity readiness, the benefits may not be consistent across racial groups. For example, Antonio (2004) found that only non-White students benefited from friendship-group diversity in terms of academic confidence and educational aspirations. However, it is important to note that White students appear to benefit substantially from the process nonetheless (Jayakumar, 2008).

Another area for intervention reviewed by Lester et al. is the use of intercultural education and institutional changes. Training programs are generally well received within workplaces as an avenue to promote diversity (Wentling & Palma-Rivas, 1998), and much work has been done to develop and refine workplace educational programs (Barak, 2013). Similarly, college campuses have been successful at providing formalized diversity training workshops as well as safe spaces and celebrations of diverse groups. However, the objective outcomes of such programs have proven to be difficult to assess, particularly over the long term, and rarely use appropriate control groups (Paluck & Green, 2009). Despite this, such programs fulfill many of the criteria proposed by Allport (1979) as necessary for improvements in diversity relations. As Lester et al. note, formalized programs such as these "provide an opportunity for authority-supported intergroup contact with equal status and a common goal."

One issue that should be noted from reviewing the diversity literature is the dominance of race as one of the primary dimensions considered. Most of the studies in the current volume and, indeed, within the extant literature have focused on race and race relations, largely due to the contextual characteristics of the US educational and vocational systems. Although studying diversity through interracial issues, interventions, and outcomes provides significant insight, much of which is likely to generalize to other groups, there is a need to study the effects of the interventions proposed by the literature in a more complete representation of the groups that comprise diverse workplaces and colleges.

ENTREPRENEURSHIP

What Is Entrepreneurship and Why Is It Important?

Career development and progression in the 21st century represent a significant divergence from previous norms and expectations. The modern workforce offers a wider variety of jobs to graduates than ever before. However, despite educational training becoming in many ways increasingly specialized, graduates who are able to flexibly apply their knowledge and skills are more likely to succeed in the modern workforce (Birney, Beckmann, & Wood, 2012). In Chapter 7, Chernyshenko et al. note the gap between the manner in which universities train students for a particular career and the fact that students are increasingly undertaking so-called "boundaryless" careers. This raises the question of how universities and colleges can prepare students to operate in a workforce in which they are likely to change career direction, and careers no longer map onto traditional linear pathways.

Chernyshenko et al. provide an overview of a new measure of career aspirations that can be used to assess university students' career aspirations and the factors that determine their career pathways within a broad framework of modern boundaryless career development. Of particular interest to the survey is the role of entrepreneurial factors in determining the career aspirations of students. Due to the rapid rate at which skills and knowledge become obsolete, entrepreneurial competence and aspirations have become increasingly important in the 21st century. A large-scale implementation of the survey explored the role of entrepreneurial climate, career intent, entrepreneurial efficacy, and career motivation as predictors of career choice and entrepreneurial activity.

Higher value is now placed on "nontraditional" career paths, both by graduates and by their potential employers. Such nontraditional career paths lend themselves to the development of graduate attributes such as entrepreneurship and leadership ability. Traditionally, an entrepreneur was an industrialist—someone who had created a significant business venture. Nowadays, the term is more broadly used to describe anyone starting a business or testing a business idea. Colloquially, a "startup" is a business that is yet to be profitable or sustainable, and the people behind that startup are the entrepreneurs. Media representations of these entrepreneurs celebrate particular aspects of entrepreneurship—taking risks, rapid scaling of concepts, and disruption to traditional methods or established incumbents.

Contemporary views of business now call for entrepreneurial traits within large established organizations, from universities to corporations and nonprofit organizations, where workers in leadership or professional roles are also expected to embrace entrepreneurial behaviors such as taking risks, testing hypotheses, and rapid scaling. Entrepreneurial methodologies test assumptions and assume no fixed time period or set sequence of steps in creating new ventures. For this reason and others, entrepreneurship is touted as being essential to every profession, leading to the coining of the term "intrapreneur"—an entrepreneur who works within an existing organization rather than starting a new one (Pinchot, 1984). The result is that there are two paths for students with an interest in being an entrepreneur: create a new organization or join an existing one and apply entrepreneurial behaviors to it. The challenge for universities, nonprofits, and corporation is how to attract entrepreneurs to an existing organization and encourage entrepreneurial behaviors.

How Can Students Be Prepared for the Workforce?

Organizations struggle to determine whether entrepreneurship is an inherent quality or whether it is a teachable process. One organization, Founders Institute, believes entrepreneurship is both an inherent trait and a set of learned skills. Applicants to the Founders Institute program must complete an hour-long battery of personality and aptitude tests. Founders Institute claims that its test is 85% accurate in predicting entrepreneurial success, and it uses the results of the test as part of the application process for its program, which has produced more than 2,000 technology businesses (Founders Institute, 2016). However, Founders Institute also recognizes the gap in skills required to launch a new venture, so applicants to its program are put through an intense 12-week training program.

Some traits of an entrepreneur are innate. For example, taking risks is considered to be one of the core traits of the entrepreneur; however, the work of Kahneman and Tversky (1984) has shown that, in general, individuals are risk adverse. Given the option of taking a risky action or not taking any action, the potential upside of the risky action needs to be as much as 1.5–3.5 times greater than the downside for most people to act. Finametrica, a company associated with the London School of Economics, measures risk tolerance in individuals, finding that an individual's risk tolerance profile is consistent over time, even after a major financial windfall or loss or after a major economic upturn or downturn.

If many elements of entrepreneurship are innate, the key to producing graduate entrepreneurs may be to identify potential entrepreneurs early and provide them with opportunities to develop. An expansion of this identification process could be to provide workplaces with the means of identifying entrepreneurs for key leadership roles. One recent possibility for identifying, displaying, and quantifying informal learning and skills is digital badging (The Mozilla Foundation, Peer 2 Peer University, & The MacArthur Foundation, 2011). Micro-credentials (e.g., entrepreneurship) can be quantified as a digital badge, earned based on demonstrable achievements or experiences. Digital badges are a relatively recent phenomenon. They are managed online and may be displayed on key social media platforms such as LinkedIn.

For many universities, fostering entrepreneurship is a hot topic. Typical approaches to fostering entrepreneurship include startup competitions, incubators, and internships. Many universities currently arrange startup internships, often unpaid work experience placements in which students are connected with a startup. The intent is to expose students to the type of entrepreneurial environment that they do not experience in their usual studies or in the typical paid work that is available to them. The danger here is a broad misuse of the term "startup," which is adopted by many new businesses regardless of whether or not they are applying best-practice entrepreneurial processes. The unfortunate reality is that most startups fail for the very reason that they did not apply entrepreneurial processes and practices. Because of this, internships on their own are not a complete solution for preparing students for an entrepreneurial workforce and should be used in conjunction with other methods, such as business incubation programs and startup competitions.

INTERESTS

What Are Interests and Why Are They Important?

In Chapter 8, Su and Nye examine interest as a disposition that precedes behaviors and motivations, especially in the domains of education and work. Similarly, Su and Nye discuss the importance of person–environment fit as an important predictor of outcomes such as job performance and satisfaction. These two factors are important considerations from the perspective of students who are entering the workforce, and they are increasingly more important to workplaces attempting to attract and retain potential workers. Despite interest having intrinsic appeal when considering personnel selection, with special appeal to potential workers, Hunter and Hunter (1984) found that the meta-analytic correlation between interests and on-the-job performance was just .10. Su and Nye argue, however, that this finding does not take into account the importance of person–environment fit. Interest alone cannot predict job performance if there is incongruence between an individual and his or her work environment. Specifically, Su and Nye are concerned with how similar an individual's interests are to the characteristics of their environment using the RIASEC model (Holland, 1997).

From the perspective of the student, degree of "interest" extends beyond enjoyment or preference for certain activities, additionally encompassing curiosity and persistence in tasks. However, interests are typically measured as the level of like or dislike for certain work activities or environments. Although interests are typically viewed as noncognitive, Su and Nye show the close links between interest and the development of cognitive ability in specific domains. However, greater interest alone does not necessarily predict additional or greater positive outcomes for job performance. As Su and Nye state, "The predictive validity of interests is maximized when an individual's interest fit an environment." Thus, there is a reciprocal and mutually beneficial relationship between worker and workplace. Although it could be argued that it is the role of the potential worker to only seek out jobs and workplaces that fit in with his or her interests, the benefits of considering workplace environments extend beyond the benefits of person–environment fit alone.

How Can Students Be Prepared for the Workforce?

From the perspective of the employer, considerations of worker interest and person–environment fit can reduce or eliminate counterproductive work behaviors and increase job performance. Interests motivate individuals to acquire knowledge, skills, and experiences, which, when teamed with person–environment fit, lead to better job performance (Nye, Su, Rounds, & Drasgow, 2012). It is important for employers to consider potential employee interests when selecting personnel; however, Su and Nye would advocate that this take place in the context of considering person–environment fit. This leaves room for a number of new tools and scales to be developed for personnel selection.

Beyond the workplace, Etzel and Nagy (2016) found that perceived person–environment fit in a tertiary context predicted academic satisfaction and academic performance. Although Su and Nye do not discuss how interest can be fostered or catered to by educational institutions, from the perspective of the educational institution, harnessing student interests may be critical to the retention and matriculation of well-rounded, motivated, skillful graduates who are attractive to potential employers. Certainly, interest motivates students to select particular subjects and particular majors, which in turn shape career pathways and job choices. However, Wijnia, Loyens, Derous, and Schmidt (2014) found that topic interest resulted in greater motivation, which in turn positively predicted test performance. This illustrates that interest predicts not only major educational and work outcomes such as job satisfaction but also smaller outcomes that together contribute to success in both the university and work context.

CONSCIENTIOUSNESS

What Is Conscientiousness and Why Is It Important?

The importance of conscientiousness is clear. A growing number of meta-analyses link conscientiousness with a range of positive life outcomes, including workplace performance, academic performance, health outcomes, and mortality (Barrick & Mount, 1991; Bogg & Roberts, 2004; Judge, Rodell, Klinger, Simon, & Crawford, 2013; Kern & Freidman, 2008; Poropat, 2009). Conscientious graduates are likely to be better workers, have graduated with better grades, and be in better health over the course of their careers. The definition of conscientiousness is less clear. In Chapter 9, Roberts and Hill define conscientiousness as a constellation of related noncognitive characteristics that broadly relate to an awareness of how one's actions influence future consequences. Although there are different models of conscientiousness, five core components appear in most models: industriousness (behavioral engagement with work), order (organization of one's time and tasks), persistence (maintaining motivation over time), self-control (delaying gratification of immediate rewards for long-term outcomes), and responsibility (meeting social obligations).

Although all components of conscientiousness predict workplace performance, components relating to industriousness generally show stronger prediction than those relating to order (Judge et al., 2013). However, job performance is often considered as two components: technical proficiency at one's job (known as task performance) versus performance on the social and psychological tasks implicit to maintaining a successful organization (known as contextual performance) (Borman & Motowidlo, 1997). Almost all components of conscientiousness relate more strongly to contextual performance than to task performance (Judge et al., 2013), and the component representing responsibility predicts more than twice as much variance in contextual performance than task performance. This difference in task versus contextual performance may be relevant when considering changes to the workplace landscape. Routine, technical tasks are increasingly being automated, whereas nonroutine tasks requiring initiative, communication skills, or rapid adjustment to change are becoming increasingly more common (see Chapter 5). Although not precisely the same, this distinction between routine and open-ended tasks echoes the distinction between task and contextual performance, suggesting that personality traits (and conscientiousness in particular) will be of increasing relevance to graduates and their employers due to the changing nature of the 21st century workplace.

Roberts and Hill provide a nuanced definition of conscientiousness that implies that conscientiousness may act as the personality trait underpinning engagement in metacognitive processes, particularly the regulation of cognition (Schraw, 1998). Specifically, Roberts and Hill propose that the defining feature of constructs in the conscientiousness umbrella is "the anticipation of future consequences of one's actions manifest in the explicit or implicit goal to plan." Unpacking this definition, we see conscientiousness instantiated as goal-driven processes that are engaged in with an awareness of how such processes will affect future outcomes. That is, conscientiousness is the set of noncognitive characteristics that motivate people to engage in metacognitive processes such as planning, monitoring, awareness, and evaluation.

Although this is a complex definition, we believe that there are several advantages to it. First, this definition links conscientiousness to a set of processes. Personality is traditionally conceived as a set of characteristics that people possess to greater or lesser degree. Although possessing these characteristics is associated with better outcomes across a range of domains (particularly for conscientiousness), the traditional conception of personality says nothing about the processes or mechanisms that translate personality into better outcomes. Second, this definition suggests both the possibility that conscientiousness can be improved and potentially how this might be done (through links to metacognitive training). Research on metacognition stems from a different tradition to personality research, and it focuses on the development of metacognitive functions through training and education. Again, traditional conceptions of personality propose that personality traits are more or less set in stone and impervious to environmental influences. Newer paradigms for conceptualizing personality (e.g., those proposed by Roberts and Hill in Chapter 9) instead consider personality in terms of a series of transactions between person and environment characteristics occurring over time (Fielden, Tiliopoulos, & MacCann, 2016). Defining conscientiousness as the set of traits that motivate particular metacognitive processes proposes a clear mechanism by which conscientiousness affects future outcomes. Specifically, conscientious people use more metacognitive strategies compared to their less conscientious counterparts.

How Can Students Be Prepared for the Workforce?

The essence of Roberts and Hill's chapter is that initial levels of conscientiousness can be changed, but this change is difficult. Environments must be altered at the right time, in the right ways, and for a substantial amount of time. Although we believe it is possible to develop interventions to improve conscientiousness or its components, we also believe that trying to change students' personality is not the only way that conscientiousness is useful in preparing students for the workforce. As with entrepreneurship, identification of conscientiousness and its components may also be an important process. Such identification serves multiple purposes. First, increasing students' self-knowledge allows them to develop compensatory strategies that use their strengths to compensate for weaknesses. For example, students high on responsibility but low on persistence may organize their study, work, or long-term projects as a collaborative effort with others, such that they will be motivated to complete their work in order to fulfill their obligations. Second, students can be informed of their particular strengths as well as the importance of these strengths in the workplace, and they can be taught to market or communicate these attributes as well as their technical skills to potential employers. Third (and relatedly), employers can identify conscientious graduates and explicitly advertise or recruit based on the elements of conscientiousness most relevant to the job.

Although we propose that identifying conscientious students is a useful undertaking in its own right, the potential for increasing students' conscientiousness (although difficult) is also a key way to build better students. Roberts and Hill summarize the research on which aspects of the school environment promote conscientiousness. The primary drivers appear to be participation in volunteer work and in positions of responsibility or leadership. To produce conscientious graduates requires that students are given autonomous tasks with real responsibility and consequences. We previously suggested that conscientiousness motivates the uptake of metacognitive strategies, and at least some of the predictive power of conscientiousness derives from increased use of such strategies. As such, interventions to increase self-regulatory processes may also increase conscientiousness, or at least some of the key behaviors associated with it. For example, Schraw (1998) suggests using regulatory checklists and training in self-monitoring, as well as the use of strategy evaluation matrices to aid academic tasks. Other researchers have designed interventions addressing a single specific component of conscientiousness, such as organization of time (Burrus, Jackson, Holtzman, Roberts, & Mandigo, 2013). This intervention consisted of three to five homework assignments on goal setting and time management techniques, and it was successful in increasing teacher ratings of high school students' time management and students' own ratings of their anxiety and stress. In summary, increasing conscientiousness among students as well as identifying conscientious students may help to produce better graduates for tomorrow's workforce.

CONCLUSION

In educating students for their future roles in society, one key task that institutions must grapple with is the notion of 21st century skills (also referred to as graduate attributes or noncognitive skills). The first step is identifying what these skills might be. Good progress has been made toward this end, with two recent employer surveys converging on key skills of creativity and innovation, professionalism, and ethics and social responsibility (Casner-Lotto & Barrington, 2006; National Association of Colleges and Employers, 2014). The graduate attributes discussed in this section mirror these desirable workplace skills and traits: Entrepreneurship encompasses creativity and innovation, conscientiousness leads to professionalism, and respect for and experience with diversity falls under ethics and social responsibility. The second step is developing accurate measures of these skills so as to identify the students who possess these skills. Such identification serves multiple purposes. First, star performers may be identified in cases in which traditional educational outcomes such as grades and test scores would overlook highly valuable workers. Second, providing students with self-knowledge of these skills can help them manage their own patterns of strengths and weaknesses, communicate or market their strengths to prospective employers, and match their profile of both soft and technical skills to future job roles. Third, identifying potential weaknesses may show areas in which individuals or cohorts need training to meet the needs of the future workplace. This brings us to the third step that institutions need to consider—educating their student body to develop 21st century skills. Although some of these constructs may require more time and greater effort to change than others, all can be changed to some extent, and the processes leading to change are surprisingly similar across constructs. Project-based work with positions of real responsibility (and real possibilities for failure) requiring collaboration across diverse groups seems to be the key to developing essential 21st century skills. In the end, we conclude that hard-won personal growth is as much a goal of education as is the transmission of technical skills and knowledge.

REFERENCES

Allport, G. W. (1979). *The nature of prejudice*. New York, NY: Addison-Wesley.

Antonio, A. L. (2004). The influence of friendship groups on intellectual self-confidence and educational aspirations in college. *Journal of Higher Education, 75*(4), 446–471.

Barak, M. E. M. (2013). *Managing diversity: Toward a globally inclusive workplace* (3rd ed.). Thousand Oaks, CA: Sage.

Barrick, M. R., & Mount, M. K. (1991). The Big Five personality dimensions and job performance: A meta-analysis. *Personnel Psychology, 44*, 1–26.

Birney, D. P., Beckmann, J. F., & Wood, R. E. (2012). Precursors to the development of flexible expertise: Metacognitive self-evaluations as antecedences and consequences in adult learning. *Learning and Individual Differences, 22*(5), 563–574.

Bogg, T., & Roberts, B. W. (2004). Conscientiousness and health-related behaviors: A meta-analysis of the leading behavioral contributors to mortality. *Psychological Bulletin, 130*(6), 887–919.

Borman, W. C., & Motowidlo, S. J. (1997). Task performance and contextual performance: The meaning for personnel selection research. *Human Performance, 10*(2), 99–109.

Bowman, N. A. (2010). College diversity experiences and cognitive development: A meta-analysis. *Review of Educational Research, 80*(1), 4–33.

Burrus, J., Jackson, T., Holtzman, S., Roberts, R. D., & Mandigo, T. (2013). Examining the efficacy of a time management intervention for high school students. *ETS Research Report Series, 2013*(2), 1–35.

Casner-Lotto, J., & Barrington, L. (2006). *Are they really ready to work? Employers' perspectives on the basic knowledge and applied skills of new entrants to the 21st US workforce.* New York, NY: The Conference Board, Corporate Voices for Working Families, Partnership for 21st Century Skills, and Society for Human Resource Management.

Etzel, J. M., & Nagy, G. (2016). Students' perceptions of person–environment fit: Do fit perceptions predict academic success beyond personality traits? *Journal of Career Assessment, 24*(2), 270–288.

Ezell, M. J. M. (1983). John Locke's images of childhood: Early eighteenth century response to *Some Thoughts Concerning Education. Eighteenth-Century Studies, 17*(2), 139–155.

Fielden, C., Tiliopoulos, N., & MacCann, C. (2016). A philosophical foundation for trait accounts of personality: Universal field theory. Submitted for publication.

Founders Institute. (2016). *Do you have entrepreneur DNA?* Retrieved from http://fi.co/dna

Gurin, P., Dey, E., Hurtado, S., & Gurin, G. (2002). Diversity and higher education: Theory and impact on educational outcomes. *Harvard Educational Review, 72*(3), 330–367.

Holland, J. L. (1997). *Making vocational choices: A theory of vocational personalities and work environments.* Odessa, FL: Psychological Assessment Resources.

Hunter, J. E., & Hunter, R. F. (1984). Validity and utility of alternative predictors of job performance. *Psychological Bulletin, 96*(1), 72–98.

Hurtado, S., Han, J. C., Sáenz, V. B., Espinosa, L. L., Cabrera, N. L., & Cerna, O. S. (2007). Predicting transition and adjustment to college: Biomedical and behavioral science aspirants' and minority students' first year of college. *Research in Higher Education, 48*(7), 841–887.

Hussar, W. J., & Bailey, T. M. (2013). *Projections of education statistics to 2022* (NCES 2014-051). Washington, DC: US Government Printing Office.

Jayakumar, U. (2008). Can higher education meet the needs of an increasingly diverse and global society? Campus diversity and cross-cultural workforce competencies. *Harvard Educational Review, 78*(4), 615–651.

Jayne, M. E., & Dipboye, R. L. (2004). Leveraging diversity to improve business performance: Research findings and recommendations for organizations. *Human Resource Management, 43*(4), 409–424.

Judge, T. A., Rodell, J. B., Klinger, R. L., Simon, L. S., & Crawford, E. R. (2013). Hierarchical representations of the Five-Factor model of personality in predicting job performance: Integrating three organizing frameworks with two theoretical perspectives. *Journal of Applied Psychology, 98*(6), 875–925.

Kanter, R. M. (1977). Some effects of proportions on group life: Skewed sex ratios and responses to token women. *American Journal of Sociology, 82*(5), 965–990.

Kahneman, D., & Tversky, A. (1984). Choices, values, and frames. *American Psychologist, 39*(4), 341–350.

Kern, M. L., & Friedman, H. S. (2008). Do conscientious individuals live longer? A quantitative review. *Health Psychology, 27*(5), 505–512.

McMahon, A. M. (2010). Does workplace diversity matter? A survey of empirical studies on diversity and firm performance, 2000–09. *Journal of Diversity Management, 5*(2), 37–48.

Milem, J. F., Chang, M. J., & Antonio, A. L. (2005). *Making diversity work on campus: A research-based perspective.* Washington, DC: Association of American Colleges and Universities.

National Association of Colleges and Employers. (2014). *Job outlook 2015.* Retrieved from http://www.naceweb.org/s11122014/job-outlook-skills-qualities-employers-want.aspx

Nye, C. D., Su, R., Rounds, J., & Drasgow, F. (2012). Vocational interests and performance: A quantitative summary of over 60 years of research. *Perspectives on Psychological Science, 7,* 384–403.

Obama, B. H. (2009, March 10). President Obama's remarks to the Hispanic Chamber of Commerce. *The New York Times.* Retrieved from http://www.nytimes.com/2009/03/10/us/politics/10text-obama.html

Orfield, G., & Lee, C. (2006). *Racial transformation and the changing nature of segregation.* Cambridge, MA: The Civil Rights Project at Harvard University.

Paluck, E. L., & Green, D. P. (2009). Prejudice reduction: What works? A review and assessment of research and practice. *Annual Review of Psychology, 60,* 339–367.

Pettigrew, T. F., & Tropp, L. R. (2006). A meta-analytic test of intergroup contact theory. *Journal of Personality and Social Psychology, 90*(5), 751–783.

Pettigrew, T. F., & Tropp, L. R. (2008). How does intergroup contact reduce prejudice? Meta-analytic tests of three mediators. *European Journal of Social Psychology, 38*(6), 922–934.

Pinchot, G. (1984). *Intrapreneuring: Why you don't have to leave the corporation to become an entrepreneur.* New York, NY: Harper & Row.

Poropat, A. E. (2009). A meta-analysis of the five-factor model of personality and academic performance. *Psychological Bulletin, 135*(2), 322–338.

Schraw, G. (1998). Promoting general metacognitive awareness. *Instructional Science, 26,* 113–125.

Stevens, F. G., Plaut, V. C., & Sanchez-Burks, J. (2008). Unlocking the benefits of diversity: All-inclusive multiculturalism and positive organizational change. *Journal of Applied Behavioral Science, 44*(1), 116–133.

The Mozilla Foundation, Peer 2 Peer University, and the MacArthur Foundation. (2011). *Open badges for lifelong learning.* Retrieved from https://wiki.mozilla.org/images/b/b1/OpenBadges-Working-Paper_092011.pdf

Tropp, L. R., & Pettigrew, T. F. (2005). Relationships between intergroup contact and prejudice among minority and majority status groups. *Psychological Science, 16*(12), 951–957.

Wentling, R. M., & Palma-Rivas, N. (1998). Current status and future trends of diversity initiatives in the workplace: Diversity experts' perspective. *Human Resource Development Quarterly, 9*(3), 235–253.

White, F. A., Abu-Rayya, H. M., & Weitzel, C. (2014). Achieving twelve-months of intergroup bias reduction: The dual identity-electronic contact (DIEC) experiment. *International Journal of Intercultural Relations, 38,* 158–163.

Wijnia, L., Loyens, S. M., Derous, E., & Schmidt, H. G. (2014). Do students' topic interest and tutors' instructional style matter in problem-based learning? *Journal of Educational Psychology, 106*(4), 919–933.

Bridging the Gap Between College and Workforce Readiness

Linking Education and Employment

A Foundational Competency Framework for Career Success

HOPE CLARK ■

There is much debate within higher education and workforce development about the value of input-oriented measures of work readiness, such as measuring the expected amount of time students spend in class (i.e., seat time) and out of class on coursework, to outcome-based performance measurements such as measuring what students know and are able to do as a result of their coursework (i.e., competency-based measures) (Schneider, 2012). This debate has spurred a renewed interest in competency-based learning and assessments led by industry-driven efforts that value experiential learning and employer-validated credentials. There is also expanded interest by local, state, and national workforce development stakeholders to fund the use of competency-based credentials. However, there is no national evidence-based framework for developing and validating these credentials.

This chapter presents an overview of various frameworks for organizing and measuring *foundational academic* and *workplace competencies* that are needed for broad career success, and it expands on recently published research on work readiness standards and benchmarks (Clark, 2012). Foundational competencies and career success are thoroughly defined, with discussion about blending and assessing the combination of knowledge, cognitive and noncognitive skills, and behaviors important for success. Definitions of foundational competencies are based on job analysis methods and reference the US Department of Labor's industry competency models. Work/career success construct definitions are based on criterion validation research linking assessments of foundational competencies to outcome-based performance at the individual, organizational, state, and national levels.

Finally, examples of how foundational competencies are used in the workplace and in educational settings are highlighted with recommendations on building a common language between educators and employers. To support this common language, linking foundational competency assessments and credentials to labor market outcomes, such as successful education and training program completion, employment, and higher wages, is critical. These frameworks can be used by education-to-career continuum stakeholders to develop authentic learning experiences that incorporate work-based foundational competencies into kindergarten through grade 12 (K–12) and postsecondary education programs.

A HOLISTIC APPROACH TO CAREER SUCCESS: MOVING BEYOND TRADITIONAL MEASURES OF COLLEGE AND CAREER READINESS

Efforts to better align the transition between secondary and postsecondary education have gained momentum in recent years with a universal goal of preparing students to be both college and career ready. Former US Department of Education Secretary Arne Duncan (2011) stated, "It is the responsibility of K–12 educators to prepare all students for both college and a career." At the same time, workforce development stakeholders are focused on ensuring that both secondary and postsecondary education are aligned with job skill requirements that reflect trends in the global economy. This effort has been backed by various national initiatives, such as the President's Council on Jobs and Competitiveness, to ensure that students will graduate with the knowledge, skills, and industry-relevant education needed to get on a pathway to a successful career (President's Job Council, 2011).

Among education and workforce development circles, much has been discussed about how to ensure that individuals are "college," "career," and "work" ready in order to prepare them for career success. As a result, there is a great deal of confusion in the education and workforce market about what these terms really mean with regard to readiness. There is a recent movement to provide clarity around these concepts and to further develop broader definitions of college and career readiness that move beyond traditional indicators of core academic skills such as high school grade point average, class rank, scores on college readiness assessments, and classroom rigor. These expanded definitions also include reference to noncognitive skills and workplace competencies that are not addressed in traditional academic settings (Mattern et al., 2014). Framed by this expanded view of college and career readiness, the next step is to examine the inclusion of foundational workplace competencies, both cognitive and noncognitive, that are important above and beyond just core academic skills as potential additional measures of career success.

UNIQUE CONTRIBUTIONS OF COLLEGE, CAREER, AND WORK READINESS FOR SUCCESS

This section reviews current definitions of *college readiness* and presents workable, policy-relevant definitions of *career readiness* and *work readiness* with respect to how they are different and how they intertwine throughout an individual's journey through the world of education and work. A proposed framework is presented to clarify how these concepts uniquely contribute and interact to achieve successful outcomes in both education and workplace settings.

College Readiness

Unlike career readiness and work readiness, there has been less ambiguity around the concept of *college readiness* and the types and levels of skills that are needed for an individual to successfully transition from secondary to postsecondary education (ACT, 2006).

> *College readiness* is currently defined as the level of achievement a student needs to be ready to enroll and succeed—without remediation—in credit-bearing first-year postsecondary courses.

ACT's definition of college readiness is well known and has been accepted by the educational community, and it was the basis for the definition adopted by the Common Core State Standards initiative. Delving further into the definition of college readiness, the level of achievement needed for college success can be determined through a combination of college education standards and college readiness benchmarks. College education standards are defined as precise descriptions of the essential skills and knowledge that students need to become ready for college. College readiness standards are validated by student academic performance data through their alignment with benchmarks set for college readiness (ACT, 2008a).

College readiness benchmarks are often defined by scores on college readiness assessments and represent the level of achievement required for students to have a high probability of success in postsecondary education (e.g., attainment of a specific grade level in corresponding credit-bearing first-year college courses) (ACT, 2008b). When based on nationally representative samples, benchmarks are intended to be median course placement values for postsecondary institutions and as such represent a typical set of expectations. The combination of both college readiness standards and benchmarks represents a consistent set of academic expectations for all graduating high school students to be ready to succeed in postsecondary education.

ACT is among several leading research institutions that propose expanding the definition of college readiness to include noncognitive behaviors in addition to the traditional academic knowledge and skills (Mattern et al., 2014). Research has shown that the path to academic and workplace success also requires emphasis on the "whole person" and includes nonacademic factors such as behavioral tendencies, vocational interests, motivation, and self-beliefs. Teachers, researchers, and policymakers alike are realizing the need to focus not only on academics but also on engagement and motivation to enhance learning and performance outcomes (Sparks, 2014).

Career Readiness

To date, "career ready" is most often used to describe the K–16 student population, which largely excludes individuals who have already proceeded through and exited the traditional K–12 education pathway. This has led to an assumption that career readiness is static—that it describes a single universal benchmark to be achieved once, at a particular point in time. This static view of career readiness disregards the likelihood that most individuals in today's workforce will have multiple jobs over their lifetime and will likely need to complete more than one type of post-high school credential (e.g., postsecondary degree, occupational certification, and workplace certification) in order for their skills to continue to be relevant in the workplace. ACT proposes that *career readiness* be defined in a way that accounts for a broader population and supports the dynamic nature of career pathways.

Career readiness is defined as the level of "foundational skills" an individual needs for success in a career pathway or career cluster, coupled with the level of "career planning skills" needed to advance within a career path or transition to other career paths.

The combination of foundational cognitive and noncognitive skills, along with career planning skills, provides a framework for career readiness that has been proposed previously, and all three have been shown to contribute to career success (ACT, 2007). Two types of foundational skills make up career readiness. First, *cognitive skills* include both academic and workplace domains. The necessary level of cognitive skills is contingent on the career path and an individual's location on that path at any point during an individual's career. Examples include reading, math, critical thinking, and problem solving. Second, *noncognitive skills*, also known as personal effectiveness or soft skills, are personal characteristics and behavioral skills applicable across a broad range of settings. Examples include adaptability, communication skills, cooperation, discipline, and integrity.

These skills are *foundational skills*: They are the fundamental, portable skills that are critical to training and workplace success. These skills are fundamental in that they serve as a basis—the foundation—for supporting more advanced skill development. Also, they are portable because rather than being job specific, they can be applied at some level across a wide variety of occupations. Individuals who develop these skills are more likely to be successful in training and in the workforce and are more competitive in the job market. Reading a technical manual, listening to instructions, showing up to work on time, writing a memo, putting forth extra effort, and giving an oral presentation are all examples of using foundational skills on the job.

Career planning skills are used to engage in informed exploration and make effective education and career choices. Research shows that the degree to which career interests fit a planned choice of college major or career impacts measures of success, such as academic success and persistence, job satisfaction and performance, and earnings (Neumann, Olitsky, & Robbins, 2009). In the K–12, postsecondary, and workforce arenas, there should be an understanding of how to obtain information on career opportunities, how to assess interests, and how to interpret the information to help individuals develop a viable career pathway.

Work Readiness

Within the context of career pathways, *work readiness* describes the skill needs and demands of a specific occupation or job. "Work ready" describes what it takes for an individual to be considered a viable applicant for a given job. Although the level of foundational skills varies between career paths, the mix and level of foundational skills required for a specific occupation are even more diverse.

Work readiness is defined as the level of "foundational skills" an individual needs to be minimally qualified for a specific occupation/job as determined through an occupational profile or job analysis.

Similar to foundational skills for career readiness, *work readiness* includes both workplace cognitive and noncognitive skills. The difference is that foundational skills needed for career readiness are portable across all occupations (e.g., reading for information, applied mathematics, problem solving, and critical thinking). The foundational skills needed for work readiness (1) are occupation specific—they vary both in importance (i.e., the percentage of job tasks that require a specific skill) and level (i.e., degree of difficulty or complexity of the skill) for different occupations; (2) may include more and different skills than just the foundational cognitive skills; and (3) depend on the critical tasks identified via occupational or job profiles. Furthermore, an individual must achieve a level of career readiness needed for a career path before he or she can be considered ready to work in a specific occupation.

Occupational profiles are descriptions of the key skill areas and levels of skills required to enter an occupation and successfully perform tasks. Occupational profiles are usually developed via job analysis, or the process of identifying in detail the particular job duties and requirements and the relative importance of these duties for a given job (Cascio & Aguinis, 2005). One source of occupational profiles is the Occupational Information Network (O*NET), which identifies and describes the key knowledge, skills, and abilities for more than 1,100 occupations (US Department of Labor, n.d., "Occupational Information Network"). ACT also publishes occupational profiles based on the WorkKeys system that contain the combination and level of skills needed to be successful in target occupations (ACT, n.d.). The occupational profiles were developed by combining information from the job profiles for groups of jobs that share the same identification numbers in the O*NET database.

Much like college readiness, the level of achievement needed for work success can be determined via a combination of work readiness standards and benchmarks (Clark, 2012). Work readiness standards, as determined by the level of foundational skills profiled for a nationally representative sample of jobs in a given occupation, could serve as precise descriptions of the essential skills and knowledge that individuals need to become ready for an occupation. Likewise, work readiness benchmarks should be defined by scores on work readiness assessments that would represent the level of skill achievement required for individuals to have a high probability of success in a job.

THE INTERPLAY OF COLLEGE, CAREER, AND WORK READINESS FOR SUCCESS

Although the terms college, career, and work readiness are distinct, they are also complementary. For example, in order for an individual to be work ready for a specific occupation, he or she will also need to satisfactorily meet the levels of career readiness needed for that occupation's career pathway. Without the necessary education and training credentials needed for a career (including academic degree, occupational certificates, and workforce certifications), most jobseekers would not be considered to be fully qualified to enter a job or to be able to successfully perform on-the-job duties. Individuals will need to achieve different levels of career readiness for a given career pathway as they enter and exit education and workforce development systems throughout their lifetime— a pathway that at some point will likely necessitate the need to achieve college readiness.

Figure 11.1 provides a framework for how college, career, and work readiness are necessary for career and work success and expands on past models that are limited to measures of only academic and workplace cognitive skills, as opposed to competencies, which take into account knowledge, skills, abilities, and behaviors that are important for career success. Although the terms are complimentary, they also uniquely contribute to career and work success.

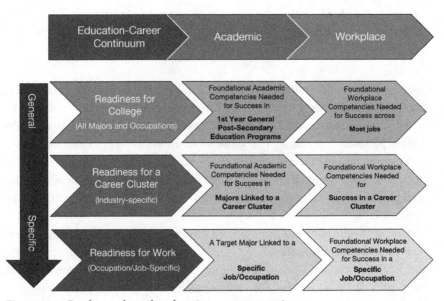

Figure 11.1 Readiness along the education to career continuum.

Readiness for college and readiness for career are similar in that an individual needs to acquire certain academic foundational skills and competencies to be successful in a first-year general postsecondary education program as well as workplace competencies needed to be successful across most occupations. Although the majority of new jobs created in the United States will require at least some form of postsecondary education or training, US employers have indicated that a substantial percentage of college graduates are not adequately prepared to perform in entry-level jobs that require postsecondary education. As a result, it is important to recognize the value of acquiring both foundational academic and workplace competencies needed for workplace success.

Once an individual identifies a career cluster or pathway to pursue, the type and level of academic and workplace competencies required become more specific to the requirements of those academic majors and occupations within the target career cluster. Within the career cluster, an individual may identify a specific occupational target, and the skill level and requirements become even more specific to a target major linked to a specific occupation. This model provides the basis for identifying academic and workplace competencies needed to acquire stackable credentials that will support an individual's career progression. Stackable credentials are part of a sequence of credentials that can be accumulated over time to build up an individual's qualifications and help him or her to move along a career pathway or move up a career ladder to different and potentially higher paying jobs (US Department of Labor, 2010).

FOUNDATIONAL ACADEMIC AND WORKPLACE COMPETENCIES IMPORTANT FOR WORK AND CAREER SUCCESS

There are common indicators between college and workplace success. For example, research has shown that cognitive ability is the strongest predictor for both job performance and academic success (Mattern et al., 2014). In addition, certain personality traits, such as conscientiousness and emotional stability, as well as motivational factors such as goal setting, also predict both college and work outcomes. Although there are some commonalities among academic and workplace success indicators, there are differences in how these indicators are measured.

A report by the National Assessment Governing Board found that measuring reading and math for academic settings does not equate to measuring reading and math for applied workplace settings. Although some overlap was found, the results of the study did not support using only academic assessments to measure career readiness (HumRRO, 2014). These findings provide further support for incorporating both foundational academic and workplace competencies into secondary and postsecondary education programs so that the targets of instruction are aligned with general job skill requirements.

In summary, research shows that college and career success is multidimensional and needs to be assessed using a variety of indicators. How we measure these important indicators depends on the context (academic vs. workplace), and there is value in combining these indicators to create a more holistic view of an individual's potential for career success. Table 11.1 provides examples of common predictors and outcomes that underlie the various domains of readiness for college and work (Mattern et al., 2014).

EXPANDING THE CURRENT READINESS FRAMEWORK: MOVING BEYOND ASSESSING JUST SKILLS TO MEASURING COMPETENCIES

This section provides an overview of various definitions of competencies and the concepts of knowledge, skills, abilities, and behaviors that are important for career and workplace success.

Skills Versus Competencies

There is much confusion in the human capital marketplace regarding whether it is more appropriate to develop and measure competencies versus skills as part of an organization's talent management and development process. A review of the literature on the use of competencies versus skills in the workplace yields different interpretations of these terms. For example, the US Department of Labor (USDOL) defines basic skills as "developed capacities that facilitate learning or the more rapid acquisition of knowledge" (USDOL, n.d., "Occupational Information Network"). Examples of basic skills include reading comprehension, mathematics, and active listening. Social skills are defined as "developed capacities used to work with people to achieve goals." Examples include social perceptiveness, negotiation, and service orientation. On the other hand, the US Office of Personnel Management (OPM) defines a competency as "a measurable pattern of knowledge, skills, abilities, behaviors, and other characteristics that an individual needs to perform work roles or occupational functions successfully" (OPM, n.d., "What Is a Competency and Competency-Based Assessment?"). According to OPM, competencies represent a "whole-person" approach to assessing individuals and specify the "how" of performing job tasks, or what the person needs to do the job successfully.

Table 11.1 PREDICTORS AND OUTCOMES OF READINESS FOR COLLEGE AND WORK

Domain	Cognitive	Noncognitive	Traditional	Nontraditional
Career	Critical thinking Collaboration skills Information and communication skills Cognitive ability Degrees/credentials Work samples	Fit (person–job, person–organization) Integrity Interests Personality (notably conscientiousness) Self-efficacy Self-esteem Values	Job performance Job training performance	Counterproductive work behavior Employment Fired Intention to quit Job satisfaction Job tenure Obtaining a job in one's desired field Organizational citizenship behavior Promotion/advancement Salary Turnover/quit job
College	Cognitive ability High school grade point average Test scores (ACT/SAT/GRE/MAT)	Absenteeism Academic self-efficacy Academic/grade goals Achievement Needs Behavioral problems Fit (interest–major) Goal orientation Interests Motivation Personality (notably conscientiousness) Self-regulation Social engagement Study skills Test anxiety	First-year grade point average Course grades Credentials/licensure	Dropped out Engagement Expelled Graduation Persistence Retention Satisfaction Timely degree completion

SOURCE: Adapted from Mattern et al. (2014).

OPM also breaks out competencies into general or technical categories. *General competencies* reflect the cognitive and social capabilities (e.g., problem-solving and interpersonal skills) required for job performance in a variety of occupations. On the other hand, *technical competencies* are more specific because they are tailored to the particular knowledge and skill requirements necessary for a specific job. A job analysis can be used to identify job tasks that are then linked to both competencies and skills.

According to a technical assistance guide on competency models developed for USDOL, a competency is "the capability to apply or use a set of related knowledge, skills, and abilities required to successfully perform critical work functions or tasks in a defined work setting" (USDOL, 2012). Competency is not to be confused with "competence," which describes a level of performance. For example, competencies often serve as the basis for skill standards that specify the *level* of knowledge, skills, and abilities required for success in the workplace, as well as potential measurement criteria for assessing competency attainment. To document competencies, a competency model can be used to specify what is essential to select for or to train and develop individuals for specific jobs and job clusters or across organizations and industries.

Within human resource (HR) circles, such as the Ohio HR Roundtable, discussions regarding competencies versus skills center on how they are used during the talent management process (HR Roundtable, 2011). For example, skills are "tangible," and competencies are the effective "application of skills." HR professionals state that skills are easier to define; job candidates either have them or they do not. Competencies are broader, subject to interpretation, and more difficult to measure. As a result, when employers are in hiring mode, they prefer to use measures of skills and work experience, which are easier to validate than competencies.

Within the field of industrial and organizational psychology, competencies are viewed as encompassing knowledge, skills, abilities, and behaviors (Harris, 1998). In essence, a competency is a broader construct than a skill and has a wider application within the talent management process. Specifically, competency modeling aims at identifying skills and abilities that are important for a variety of jobs in the same organization and across organizations and industries. For example, one may be able to create a list of competencies that might be used for selection, performance appraisal, compensation, and training purposes. In contrast to competency modeling, a job analysis examines the tasks performed in a job, the competencies required to perform those tasks, and the connection between the tasks and competencies.

HOW ARE COMPETENCIES ORGANIZED AND MEASURED?

This section provides a framework for documenting competencies that are important for work and career success, such as competency modeling and job analysis.

Competency models can take a variety of forms and typically include the following elements:

- *Competency names and detailed definitions*: For example, a competency model could include a competency called "teamwork," defined as working cooperatively with others to complete work assignments.
- *Descriptions of activities or behaviors associated with each competency*: For example, the following behaviors could be associated with the competency "teamwork":
  - Abiding by and supporting group decisions
  - Facilitating team interaction and maintaining focus on group goals
  - Handling differences in work styles effectively when working with coworkers
  - Capitalizing on strengths of others on a team to get work done
  - Anticipating potential conflicts and addressing them directly and effectively
  - Motivating others to contribute opinions and suggestions
  - Demonstrating a personal commitment to group goals
- *A diagram of the model*: Competency models may include additional information about skills and abilities required for different levels of mastery or information about the level of competence required at different occupational levels. Figure 11.2 provides an example of an industry competency model.

Although a traditional job analysis can result in the documentation of competencies and/or knowledge, skills, abilities, and behaviors that are important for the job, it is usually used to define a narrower, more specific set of skills and abilities for personnel selection purposes. Job analysis data are used to

- establish and document competencies required for a job;
- identify the job-relatedness of the tasks and competencies needed to successfully perform the job; and
- provide a source of legal defensibility of assessment and selection procedures (OPM, n.d., "Assessment and Selection").

Information from a job analysis can also be used to determine job requirements, training needs, position classification and grade levels, and inform other personnel actions, such as promotions and performance appraisals.

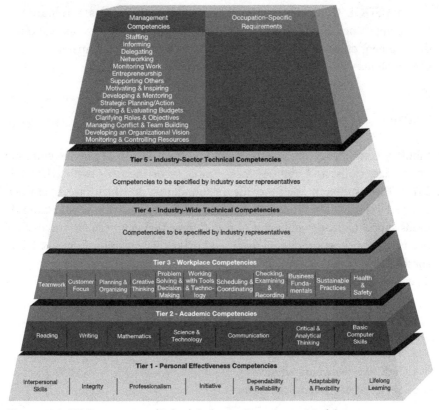

Figure 11.2 US Department of Labor's Industry Competency Model.

HOW CAN COMPETENCY MODELS BE USED FOR WORKFORCE DEVELOPMENT?

This section provides an overview of how competencies are used for workforce development and introduces the USDOL's industry competency models and associated measures of identified foundational, occupational, and industries competencies.

Competency models are developed as a resource for multiple uses, such as the following:

- Career exploration and guidance
- Developing career pathways
- Workforce program planning and labor pool analysis
- Curriculum evaluation, planning, and development
- Certification, licensure, and assessment development
- Industry models and registered apprenticeships

The USDOL Competency Model Clearinghouse provides a resource on how competency models have been used to support the various workforce development efforts described previously (USDOL, n.d., "Competency Model Clearinghouse").

Industry Competency Models

Industry competency models developed by the USDOL depict the common knowledge, skills, and abilities in an industry or industry sector (USDOL, 2012). The resulting models provide the foundation on which career pathways can be developed. The articulation of broad industry-wide knowledge and skill needs supports the development of a workforce that can perform successfully in a variety of cross-functional teams and make the transition from one job to another. These models are called "building blocks" and consist of key competencies and behaviors; they are grouped into the following tiers:

1. Personal effectiveness competencies
2. Academic competencies
3. Workplace competencies
4. Industry-wide competencies
5. Sector-specific competencies

The pyramid-shaped graphic shown in Figure 11.2 depicts how competencies become more specific as one moves up the tiers. The tiers are divided into blocks representing skills, knowledge, and abilities essential for successful performance in an industry or occupation. Each competency is described by key behaviors or by examples of the critical work functions or technical content common to an industry.

Each USDOL industry competency model is built on a series of tiers. At the base, Tiers 1–3 represent foundational academic and workplace competencies that form the foundation for success in educational settings as well as in the workplace. Foundational competencies are portable across many occupations and are important for career success (USDOL, n.d., "Competency Model Clearinghouse"). An example of a national layered credentialing system is the Manufacturing Skills Certification System, endorsed by the National Association of Manufacturers. This system of using industry-recognized credentials to certify competencies and skills begins with the ACT National Career Readiness Certificate at the foundation, followed by increasingly targeted occupation and job-specific skills credentials (Manufacturing Institute, n.d.).

A CROSS-INDUSTRY APPROACH TO FOUNDATIONAL SKILLS: COMMON EMPLOYABILITY SKILLS

The National Network for Business and Industry Associations (NNBIA) brought together organizations that represent employers from major economic sectors, representing leaders in manufacturing, retail, health care, energy, construction, hospitality, transportation, and information technology sectors, to identify a core set of fundamental skills that potential employees need in the workplace and a common vocabulary to describe these skills (NNBIA, 2014). They presented a model outlined in Figure 11.3 that serves as the foundation for all industries to map skill requirements to credentials and career paths. It provides a road map for educators and learning providers on specific foundational skills they should teach that employers value. Although the NNBIA describes a framework for specific "employability skills," when viewed holistically, the model actually describes competencies that are important for workplace

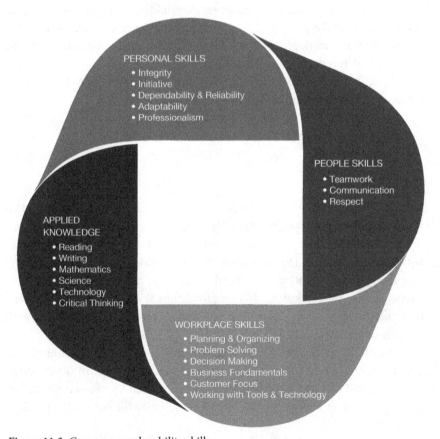

Figure 11.3 Common employability skills.

success. Employability skills can be acquired in traditional and nontraditional educational environments, such as through military service, work experiences, and community service.

Table 11.2 provides more detailed descriptions for constructs that make up each of the four domains of employability skills.

INTEGRATING EMPLOYABILITY SKILLS: A FRAMEWORK FOR ALL EDUCATORS

According to the American Institutes of Research, employability skills are the general skills necessary for success in the labor market at all employment levels and in all sectors (Center on Great Teachers and Leaders, 2014). The Employability Skills Framework, an online resource from the USDOL designed to support the instruction and assessment of employability skills, is based on a crosswalk of existing employability skills standards and assessments. The framework takes into account various employability skill initiatives for which existing skills overlapped on many dimensions, despite differences in terminology. The framework groups the skills and competencies into an organizing structure, which is depicted in Figure 11.4.

These skills can be taught through education and workforce development systems and fall into three broad categories:

- Effective relationships
- Workplace skills
- Applied knowledge

Effective relationships are the interpersonal skills and personal qualities that enable individuals to interact effectively with clients, coworkers, and supervisors. *Workplace skills* are the analytical and organizational skills and understandings that employees need to successfully perform work tasks. *Applied knowledge* is the thoughtful integration of academic knowledge and technical skills, put to practical use in the workplace. The Employability Skills Framework includes a source matrix that crosswalks various assessment frameworks and tools to each of the three categories (Table 11.3).

Employability skills are often integrated into academic and technical skill instruction and are not intended to be taught on their own. In other words, teachers are not asked to add employability skills to their list of teaching responsibilities but merely to seek opportunities to emphasize the skills when possible.

Table 11.2 DOMAINS OF EMPLOYABILITY SKILLS

 Applied Knowledge

 Workplace Skills

Reading: *Understanding written sentence and paragraphs in work-related documents*
- Read and comprehend work-related instructions and policies, memos, bulletins, notices, letters, policy manuals, and governmental regulations
- Read and comprehend documents ranging from simple and straightforward to more complex and detailed
- Attain meaning and comprehend core ideas from written materials
- Integrate what is learned from written materials with prior knowledge
- Apply what is learned from written material to work situations

Writing: *Using standard English to clearly communicate thoughts, ideas, and information in written form*
- Prepare written materials that are easy to understand using correct wording
- Communicate thoughts, ideas, information, messages, and other written information in a logical, organized, and coherent manner
- Use correct grammar, spelling, punctuation, and capitalization
- Write in a factual manner in a tone appropriate for the target audience in multiple formats

Mathematics: *Using mathematics to solve problems*
- Add, subtract, multiply, and divide whole numbers, fractions, decimals, and percents
- Convert decimals to fractions; convert fractions to percents
- Calculate averages, ratios, proportions, and rates
- Take measurement of time, temperature, distance, length, width, height, and weight; convert one measurement to another
- Translate practical problems into useful mathematical expressions

Planning and organizing: *Planning and prioritizing work to manage time effectively and accomplish assigned tasks*
- Able to plan and schedule tasks so that work is completed on time
- Ability to prioritize various competing tasks
- Demonstrate the effective allocation of time and resources efficiently
- Will take necessary corrective action when projects go off track

Problem solving: *Demonstrating the ability to apply critical thinking skills to solve problems by generating, evaluating, and implementing solutions*
- Able to identify and define the problem
- Will communicate the problem to appropriate personnel
- Capable of generating possible solutions
- Ability to choose and implement a solution

Decision-making: *Applying critical thinking skills to solve problems encountered in the workplace*
- Identify and prioritize the key issues involved to facilitate the decision-making process
- Anticipate the consequences of decisions
- Involve people appropriately in decisions that may impact them
- Quickly respond with a backup plan if a decision goes amiss

(continued)

Table 11.2 CONTINUED

 Applied Knowledge

 Workplace Skills

Science: *Knowing and applying scientific principles and methods to solve problems*
- Understand basic scientific principles
- Understand the scientific method (i.e., identify problem, collect information, form opinion, and draw conclusion)
- Apply basic scientific principles to solve problems and complete tasks

Technology: *Using information technology and related applications to convey and retrieve information*
- Navigation and File Management
- Understand common computer terminology
- Use scroll bars, a mouse, and dialog boxes to work within the computer's operating system
- Access and switch between applications and files of interest
- Adhere to standard conventions for safeguarding privacy and security
- Internet and e-mail
- Navigate the Internet to find information
- Open and configure standard browsers
- Use searches, hypertext references, and transfer protocols (enter URL, send and retrieve e-mail)

Business fundamentals: *Having fundamental knowledge of the organization and the industry*
- Understand the importance of one's role in the functioning of the company and the potential impact one's performance can have on the success of the organization
- Recognize the importance of maintaining privacy and confidentiality of company information, as well as that of customers and coworkers, and comply with intellectual property laws
- Understand the significance of maintaining a healthful and safe environment and report any violations/discrepancies to appropriate personnel

Customer focus: *Actively look for ways to identify market demands and meet customer or client needs*
- Understand and anticipate customer needs
- Provide personalized service with prompt and efficient responses to meet the requirements, requests, and concern of customers or clients
- Be pleasant, courteous, and professional when dealing with internal and external customers or clients
- Evaluate customer or client satisfaction

(*continued*)

Table 11.2 CONTINUED

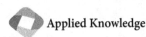 **Applied Knowledge**

 Workplace Skills

Critical thinking: *Using logical thought processes to analyze and draw conclusions*
- Identify inconsistent or missing information
- Critically review, analyze, synthesize, compare, and interpret information
- Draw conclusions from relevant and/or missing information.
- Test possible hypotheses to ensure the problem is correctly diagnosed and the best solution is found

Working with tools and technology: *Selecting, using, and maintaining tools and technology to facilitate work activity*
- Identify, select, and use appropriate tools and technological solutions to frequently encountered problems
- Carefully consider which tools or technological solutions are appropriate for a given job, and consistently choose the best tool or technological solution for the problem at hand
- Operate tools and equipment in accordance with established operating procedures and safety standards
- Seek out opportunities to improve knowledge of tools and technologies that may assist in streamlining work and improving productivity

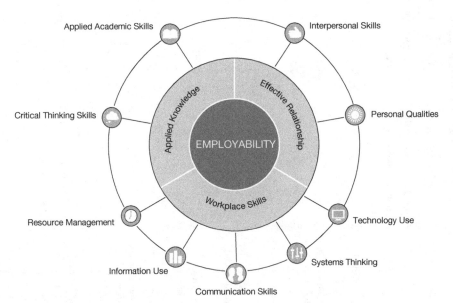

Figure 11.4 Employability skills framework.

Table 11.3 Employability Skills Framework: Source Matrix

Resource	Applied Knowledge		Effective Relationships		Resource Management	Information Use	Workplace Skills		
	Applied Academic Skills	Critical Thinking Skills	Interpersonal Skills	Personal Qualities			Communications Skills	Systems Thinking	Technology Use
21st Century Skills for Workplace Success; NOCTI	X	X	X	X			X	X	X
Arizona's New Workplace Skills; Arizona Department of Education		X	X	X	X		X	X	X
Assessing 21st Century Skills; Board on Testing and Assessment, the National Research Council		X	X	X	X		X		
Assessment and Teaching of 21st Century Skills; Cisco, Intel, and Microsoft		X	X	X	X				X
Career Clusters Framework; National Association of State Directors of Career Technical Education Consortium	X	X	X	X	X	X	X	X	X
Citizenship Foundation Skills and Knowledge Clusters; US Citizenship and Immigration Services						X	X		
Common Employability Skills; National Network of Business and Industry Associations	X	X	X	X	X	X	X	X	X
Comparative Analysis of Soft Skills: What Is Important for New Graduates? US Department of Agriculture		X	X	X	X		X	X	X

Framework	Col 1	Col 2	Col 3	Col 4	Col 5	Col 6	Col 7	Col 8
Employability Assessment Rubric; Chicago Public Schools	X	X		X	X		X	
Employability Skills 2000+; Conference Board of Canada	X	X		X	X			X
Employability Skills Blueprint; Skills USA	X	X	X	X	X		X	
Equipped for the Future; Center for Literacy Studies, University of Tennessee	X	X		X	X		X	X
Industry Competency Models; Employment and Training Administration, US Department of Labor	X	X	X	X	X	X	X	X
Maryland Skills for Success; Maryland State Department of Education	X	X	X	X	X		X	
National Career Readiness Certificate; ACT	X	X		X	X			X
National Work Readiness Credential; National Work Readiness Council	X	X		X	X	X	X	
O*NET; Employment and Training Administration, US Department of Labor	X	X	X	X	X	X	X	
Partnership for 21st Century Skills	X	X		X	X	X	X	
Secretary's Commission on Achieving Necessary Skills (SCANS), US Department of Labor	X	X	X	X	X	X	X	X
Workforce Skills Certification System; CASAS and Learning Resources	X	X						X

The College and Career Readiness Success Center provides the following guidelines for teaching employability skills:

- Employability skills, along with academic and technical skills, are a critical component of college and career readiness.
- Documenting employability skills that are embedded in classroom practice helps students realize the connection between education and employment.
- Opportunities exist for teachers to integrate employability skills in everyday lessons, at every age, and in every content area.
- Development of employability skills does not occur in one or two classes but grows during a student's educational career.
- Classroom activities can emphasize various employability skills, but not all skills can be addressed in every lesson.

A lesson planning checklist from the Employability Skills Framework is a tool to support the instruction and assessment of employability skills. Teachers can use it to document how employability skills are being reinforced in the classroom as a planning and reflection tool and as a vehicle for communicating with parents, students, employers, their peers, and other stakeholders. State and local administrators can use the tool to inform curriculum development, classroom observations, and professional development activities and as confirmation of classroom practice through teachers' self-reports (US Department of Education, n.d.). Figure 11.5 provides an example of the checklist for applied knowledge.

FUTURE WORK SKILLS: THE REWORKING OF WORK

The Institute for the Future (IFF) produced a report that examined six key drivers that will reshape the landscape of work and identified key work skills and competencies needed in the next 10 years (Davies, Fidler, & Gorbis, 2011). These changes are driven by global connectivity, smart machines, and new connectivity. The key drivers for change include (1) increasing lifespans globally and new perceptions of the aging workforce, (2) the rise of smart machines and systems that will displace human workers from rote and repetitive tasks, (3) massive increases in sensors and processing power that will result in enormous quantities of data, (4) new multimedia technologies that will reshape everyday communication and create new vernacular, (5) new technologies and social media platforms that are driving unprecedented reorganization that drives value creation outside of traditional organizational boundaries, and (6) increased global

Employability Skills Components	
APPLIED KNOWLEDGE	
Applied Academic Skills	**Reading skills** Student applies/demonstrates reading skills by interpreting written instructions/ project directions and constructing responses, using print and online materials as resources, completing worksheets, and seeking clarification about what they have read. **Writing skills** Student relies on writing skills to construct lab reports, posters, and presentation materials, take notes, and compose responses to essay questions. **Math strategies/procedures** Student uses computational skills appropriately and make logical choices when analyzing and differentiating among available procedures. Outside of math class, this includes creating/interpreting tables and graphs and organizing/displaying data. **Scientific principles/procedures** Student follows procedures, experiment, infer, hypothesize (even as simple as "what if we do it this way"), and construct processes to complete a task (can occur outside of math/science classes).
Critical Thinking Skills	**Thinks creatively** Student creates innovative and novel ideas/solutions and display divergent thinking. This can be seen in oral presentations and creative writing assignments, open-ended tasks, and project design. **Think critically** Student displays analytical and strategic thinking. This can be seen in debating an issue, converging on an understanding, assessing a problem, and questioning (playing devil's advocate). **Makes sound decisions** Student differentiates between multiple approaches and assess options (could be linked to thinking critically). **Solves problems** Student assesses problems involving the use of available resources (personnel and materials) and reviews multiple strategies for resolving problems (could be linked to thinking creatively). **Reasons** Student negotiates pros/cons of ideas, approaches, and solutions and analyzes options using "if-then" rationale. **Plans/organizes** Student plans steps, procedures, and/or approaches for addressing tasks. This occurs naturally in most assignments, ranging from solving one problem to completing a long-term project.

Figure 11.5 Lesson planning checklist for applied knowledge.

connectivity that drives organizational diversity and adaptability in order to remain competitive. Figure 11.6 provides an overview of the key drivers and skills needed in the future workforce.

Instead of considering what will be the jobs of the future by predicting specific job categories and labor requirements, the IFF focused on the future of

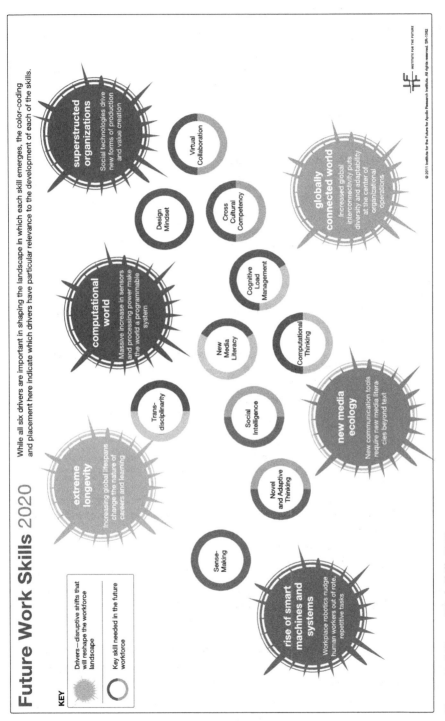

Figure 11.6 Future Work Skills 2020.

SOURCE: *Future Workskills 2020*, Institute for the Future, 2011.

work skills—proficiencies and abilities required across different jobs and work settings that will make humans relevant in the work world in which machines dominate. These future work skills include the following:

1. *Sense-making*: The ability to determine the deeper meaning or significance of what is being expressed. As smart machines take over routine manufacturing and rote services jobs, there will be an increasing demand for the kinds of skills machines are not good at performing, such as those that help us create unique insights critical to decision-making. For example, a computer may be able to beat a human in a game of chess, but if you ask if it wants to play a game of pool, it will not be able to tell you whether you are talking about swimming or billiards.

2. *Social intelligence*: The ability to connect to others in a deep and direct way, to sense and stimulate reactions and desired interactions. Socially intelligent employees are able to quickly assess the emotions of those around them and adapt their own words, tone, and gestures accordingly. This will become even more important to collaborate with larger groups in different settings and will be a comparative advantage over machines.

3. *Novel and adaptive thinking*: Proficiency at thinking of and coming up with solutions and responses beyond those that are rote or rule-based. Employment growth is polarizing into high-skill and low-skill jobs, both of which require the capacity for novel thinking and situational adaptability—the ability to respond to unique unexpected circumstances at the moment. Tasks as different as writing a convincing legal argument or creating a new dish out of a set of ingredients require novel thinking and adaptability.

4. *Cross-cultural competency*: The ability to operate in different cultural settings. In a truly globally connected world, workers' skill sets could enable them to be posted in any number of locations—they need to be able to operate in whatever environment they find themselves. Cross-cultural competency will become an important skill for all workers, not just those who have to operate in diverse geographical environments. Organizations increasingly view diversity as a driver for innovation by forming groups that have a combination of different ages, skills, disciplines, and working/thinking styles.

5. *Computational thinking*: The ability to translate vast amounts of data into abstract concepts and to understand data-based reasoning. As the amount of data increases exponentially, many more roles will require computational thinking skills in order to make sense of the

data. In addition to computational thinking skills, workers will need to also be aware of the limitations of models—even the best models are approximations of reality and not reality itself.

6. *New media literacy*: The ability to critically assess and develop content that uses new media forms and to leverage these media for persuasive communication. The explosion of user-generated media, including video, blogs, and podcasts that dominate social media, will also impact the workplace. Static slide show approaches such as PowerPoint will become obsolete, just as overhead transparencies became obsolete in the 1990s. The next generation of workers will need to become fluent in creating and presenting their own visual information using new interactive formats.

7. *Transdisciplinarity*: Literacy in and the ability to understand concepts across multiple disciplines. The ideal worker of the next decade will be "T-shaped" and will bring a deep understanding of at least one field but will also have the capacity to converse in the language of a broader range of disciplines. This requires a sense of curiosity and a willingness to continue learning far beyond formal education.

8. *Design mindset*: The ability to represent and develop tasks and work processes for desired outcomes. Sophisticated sensors, communication tools, and processing power will bring new opportunities to create optimal environments for design work. Workers of the future will need to become adept at recognizing the kind of thinking that different tasks require and making adjustments to work environments that enhance outcomes.

9. *Cognitive load management*: The ability to discriminate and filter information for importance and to understand how to maximize cognitive functioning using a variety of tools and techniques. A world rich in information streams in multiple formats from multiple devices raises the issue of cognitive overload. Organizations and workers will only be able to turn the massive influx of data into an advantage if they can learn to effectively filter and focus on what is important. This will require the use of social filtering tools such as ranking, tagging, or adding other metadata to higher quality or more relevant information so that it is more salient.

10. *Virtual collaboration*: The ability to work productively, drive engagement, and demonstrate presence as a member of a virtual team. Connective technologies make it easier than ever to work, share ideas, and be productive despite physical separation. However, virtual work environments require a new set of competencies, such as engaging and motivating a dispersed group.

RECOMMENDATIONS FOR LINKING EDUCATION AND EMPLOYMENT SUCCESS IN A CHANGING WORK WORLD

Foundational academic and workplace skills and competencies are important for college, career, and work success. States, employers, educators, and individuals can all play a role in emphasizing the importance of incorporating foundational competencies into both traditional and nontraditional education and training programs to better prepare students for a rapidly changing world of work. The following recommendations provide strategies for each of these groups:

1. *States* can play a leadership role in highlighting the necessity of foundational competencies in their labor forces and increasing skill acquisition by
   - working with business and education leaders to implement a framework that provides a common language for developing skills and competencies needed for workplace and career success;
   - directing education and workforce development resources to better address gaps in skills and competencies between employers' needs and the available workforce; and
   - attracting new business/industry into the state by focusing on the common, identifiable skills and competencies that can document the work readiness of the state and local workforce.
2. *Educators* at all levels can help guide the skilling up of the workforce by
   - engaging in efforts to align relevant educational standards and goals to local and state workforce development needs;
   - reinforcing the importance of a common set of employability skills and foundational competencies for work success with students by showing that foundational competencies learned in school are also useful in work;
   - identifying and employing effective interventions that help students and workers build these foundational competencies; and
   - establishing a system of periodic review that allows them to be responsive to the changing local, state, regional, and national workforce development needs.
3. Although the development of foundational academic competencies typically occurs within formal educational settings, the *business community* can take an active role in promoting foundational workplace competencies by

- using business resources to enhance formal education settings and provide an appropriate workforce development perspective by
  - aligning community college offerings with local workforce development needs,
  - providing job shadowing, internship, and other job-related opportunities, and
  - providing industry-related instructional tools and other resources to local education systems;
- using measures of foundational competencies to hire workers who have a better chance of success;
- using foundational competency measures to identify training needs for potential and current employees; and
- working with local and state entities to develop feedback systems for reporting on the importance of foundational workplace competencies at work and the levels needed by potential employees.

4. *Individuals* can also actively increase their chances for obtaining jobs and work success by
   - including their scores from measures of foundational competencies on job applications, on resumes, and in interviews to let potential employers know they have what it takes to learn and perform effectively on the job; and
   - using scores from measures of foundational competencies to identify areas in which improvement is needed and seeking out the training needed to develop additional knowledge and skills; and
   - comparing their own foundational competency levels to the levels needed for a wide range of jobs (e.g., using occupational profiles) in order to set career goals and obtain the training and development needed to achieve these goals.

CONCLUSION

This chapter presented an overview of various frameworks that attempt to link education to employment outcomes and to create a common language between educators and employers. Although the various frameworks reviewed in this chapter share commonalities, there are some inconsistencies and differences among them. For example, there is inconsistent use of the terms skills versus competencies. Often, these terms are used interchangeably when in fact they are distinct concepts. To add further to this complexity, skills and competencies can be broken down into cognitive and noncognitive factors that may or may not have a differential impact on academic versus workplace outcomes. This has implications for how we measure skills and competencies and further impacts how we validate them in education and workplace settings.

Another key difference is that some frameworks are aligned more with college and/or career readiness versus work readiness. Although there is obvious overlap between the various types of readiness, there is evidence of unique contributions of academic and workplace readiness to various education and employment outcomes. It could be hypothesized that there is significant interaction between college, career, and work readiness on the overall career success of an individual.

In conclusion, both academic and workplace skills and competencies are important for the future of work, and we must not attempt to place focus on one over the other. Focusing on whole-person assessment is necessary in order to understand the relationship between cognitive and behavioral competencies and future career success in a rapidly changing world of work.

ACKNOWLEDGMENTS

I acknowledge Mary LeFebvre, Principal Research Scientist at ACT, Inc., and Dr. Krista Mattern, Senior Director of Validity and Score Interpretation at ACT, Inc., for their significant contributions to defining the concepts of college, career, and work readiness in a way that is meaningful for education and workforce practitioners.

REFERENCES

ACT. (n.d.). *Occupational profiles*. Retrieved from http://www.act.org/workkeys/analysis/occup.html

ACT. (2006). *Reading between the lines: What the ACT reveals about college readiness in reading*. Retrieved from https://www.act.org/research/policymakers/pdf/reading_report.pdf

ACT. (2007). *Impact of cognitive, psychosocial, and career factors on educational and workplace success*. Retrieved from https://www.act.org/research/policymakers/pdf/CognitiveNoncognitive.pdf

ACT. (2008a). *College readiness standards for EXPLORE, PLAN, and the ACT*. Retrieved from http://files.eric.ed.gov/fulltext/ED510457.pdf

ACT. (2008b). *College readiness system: Meeting the challenge of a changing world*. Retrieved from https://www.act.org/research/policymakers/pdf/crs.pdf

Cascio, W., & Aguinis, H. (2005). *Applied psychology in human resource management* (6th ed.). Upper Saddle River, NJ: Pearson Prentice Hall.

Center on Great Teachers and Leaders. (2014). *Integrating employability skills: A framework for all educators.* Washington, DC: American Institutes for Research. Retrieved from http://www.gtlcenter.org/technical-assistance/professional-learning-modules/integrating-employability-skills-framework-all-educators

Clark, H. (2012). *Work readiness standards and benchmarks: The key to differentiating America's workforce and regaining global competitiveness.* Iowa City, IA: ACT. Retrieved from http://www.act.org/research/policymakers/pdf/Work-Readiness-Standards-and-Benchmarks.pdf

Davies, A., Fidler, D., & Gorbis, M. (2011). *Future work skills 2020.* Palo Alto, CA: Institute for the Future. Retrieved from http://www.iftf.org/futureworkskills

Duncan, A. (2011, February 2). *Pathways to prosperity: Meeting the challenge of preparing young Americans for the 21st century* [Prepared remarks at the release of the Pathways to Prosperity Project, by W. Symonds, R. Schwartz, and R. Ferguson]. Cambridge, MA: Pathways to Prosperity Project, Harvard University.

Harris, M. (1998, October). Practice Network: Competency modeling: Viagraized job analysis or impotent imposter? *TIP The Industrial Organizational Psychologist, 36*(2). Retrieved from http://www.siop.org/tip/backissues/tipoct98/7harris.aspx

HR Roundtable. (2011, October 18). *What's the difference between skills and competencies?* Retrieved from https://www.tlnt.com/2011/10/18/hr-roundtable-whats-the-difference-between-skills-and-competencies

HumRRO. (2014). *The content alignment between the NAEP and WorkKeys assessments. A report prepared for the National Assessment Governing Board.* Alexandria, VA: National Assessment Governing Board. Retrieved from https://www.nagb.org/content/nagb/assets/documents/what-we-do/preparedness-research/content-alignment/naep_workkeys_final.pdf

Manufacturing Institute. (n.d.). *NAM-endorsed certifications.* Retrieved from http://www.themanufacturinginstitute.org/Skills-Certification/Certifications/NAM-Endorsed-Certifications.aspx#AWC

Mattern, K., Burrus, J., Camera, W., O'Conner, R., Hanson, M., Gambrell, J., . . . Bobek, B. (2014). *Broadening the definition of college and career readiness: A holistic approach.* Iowa City, IA: ACT. Retrieved from http://www.act.org/research/researchers/reports/pdf/ACT_RR2014-5.pdf

National Network of Business and Industry Associations. (2014, July 22). *Common employability skills—A foundation for success in the workplace: The skills all employees need, no matter where they work.* Retrieved from http://businessroundtable.org/sites/default/files/Common%20Employability_asingle_fm.pdf

Neumann, G., Olitsky, N., & Robbins, S. (2009). Job congruence, academic achievement, and earnings. *Labour Economics, 16*(5), 503–509.

President's Jobs Council. (2011, October 11). *Recommendation to prepare the American workforce to compete in a global economy.* Retrieved from http://files.jobs-council.com/jobscouncil/files/2011/10/JobsCouncil_InterimReport_Oct11.pdf

Schneider, C. (2012). Is it finally time to kill the credit hour? *Liberal Education, 98*(4). Retrieved from https://www.aacu.org/publications-research/periodicals/it-finally-time-kill-credit-hour

Sparks, S. (2014, June 2). Student motivation: Age-old problem gets new attention. *Education Week.* Retrieved from http://www.edweek.org/ew/articles/2014/06/05/34overview.h33.html?intc=EW-DPCT14-TOC

US Department of Education. (n.d.). *Employability skills framework: Lesson planning checklist.* Retrieved from http://cte.ed.gov/employabilityskills/index.php/developing-skills/create_checklist

US Department of Labor. (n.d.). *Competency model clearinghouse.* Retrieved from http://www.careeronestop.org/CompetencyModel/models-in-action.aspx

US Department of Labor. (n.d.). *Occupational information network.* Retrieved from https://www.onetcenter.org

US Department of Labor. (2010, December 15). *Employment and training guidance letter No. 15-10.* Retrieved from https://wdr.doleta.gov/directives/attach/TEGL15-10.pdf

US Department of Labor. (2012, January). *Technical assistance guide for developing and using competency models—One solution for the workforce development system.* Retrieved from http://docplayer.net/84092-Technical-assistance-guide-for-developing-and-using-competency-models-one-solution-for-the-workforce-development-system.html

US Office of Personnel Management, Personnel Assessment and Selection Resource Center. (n.d.). *Assessment and selection.* Retrieved from https://www.opm.gov/policy-data-oversight/assessment-and-selection/job-analysis

US Office of Personnel Management, Personnel Assessment and Selection Resource Center. (n.d.). *What is a competency and competency-based assessment?* Retrieved from https://www.opm.gov/policy-data-oversight/assessment-and-selection

Combining Cognitive and Noncognitive Measures

Expanding the Domain of College and Workforce Performance and Its Prediction

NEAL SCHMITT ■

Organizations seek to hire employees who are the most likely to be excellent performers, and colleges and universities seek to admit and recruit the best students who will do well academically. Traditionally, college admissions personnel use high school grade point averages (HSGPAs), standardized tests of cognitive ability in the areas of verbal and mathematical skills (SAT/ACT), and sometimes records of achievement in specific subject matter areas to assess student potential. Each factor provides unique information about the applicant. Letters of recommendation, essays, or interviews are being used increasingly by universities to complement these HSGPA and SAT/ACT scores. Schools vary widely in their use of the information contained in these supplemental materials. For example, whereas a reviewer at one school might assign a subjective rating to each component of the application, a reviewer at another school might form ratings of personal qualities (e.g., leadership). Such holistic reviews of student potential are common although not often systematically used both across and within universities (Rigol, 2003). Clearly, any systematic and thorough processing of this information, especially when large numbers of applicants must be processed in a short period of time, places a heavy burden on admissions personnel. In addition, research on the incremental validity above standardized test scores and HSGPA of such material is largely missing.

This chapter first discusses the research on the prediction of college student success and the prediction of performance in the work context. Then, it describes the conceptual literature in both employment and academic worlds that suggests that organizations and universities expand the criterion domain to include more than task performance and academic grades when evaluating the outcomes produced by their personnel. In both domains, the consideration of these alternate criteria suggests that it should be important to consider social, motivational, and other personal characteristics when evaluating the potential of job or student applicants. The chapter then focuses on the assessment of noncognitive skills in the college domain, their validity, and their incremental validity beyond SAT/ACT scores and HSGPA. Finally, it considers the implications of including such measures for the diversity of the student body. Limitations of the use of these measures in high-stakes situations and the need for continued research in several areas are noted.

PREDICTION OF COLLEGE SUCCESS

Standardized cognitive ability tests or achievement tests (e.g., the SAT and the ACT) can be administered to large numbers of students efficiently, and they have demonstrated consistently high criterion-related validities (approximately $r = .45$) with cumulative college GPA, in addition to smaller but practically significant relationships with study habits, persistence, and degree attainment (Hezlett et al., 2001). Higher validities are often observed if the outcomes assessed are more proximal, such as first-year college GPA (Kuncel, Hezlett, & Ones, 2004). Sackett, Kuncel, Arneson, Cooper, and Waters (2009) examined various large data sets and found strong relationships between standardized tests and academic performance ($r = .44$). Even when controlling for socioeconomic status, these relationships were strong. Both HSGPA and standardized tests have been shown to have predictive validity in determining a variety of academic performance outcomes (Bridgeman, McCamley-Jenkins, & Ervin, 2000; Kuncel, Credé, & Thomas, 2007; Kuncel & Hezlett, 2007).

PREDICTION OF WORKFORCE PERFORMANCE

Prediction of workforce performance using both cognitive and noncognitive measures is well documented (for a review, see Schmitt, 2014). Sackett and

Lievens (2008) provide the last updating of this literature in the *Annual Review of Psychology*. Ones, Dilchert, and Viswesvaran (2012) provide a meta-analytic review of general cognitive ability and specific aspects of cognitive ability as predictors of training success and performance. A more general narrative review of the validity of cognitive ability tests is provided by Ones, Dilchert, Viswesvaran, and Salgado (2010). Schmitt and Fandre (2008) present a summary of various meta-analyses of general cognitive ability as well as specific mental abilities. Hulsheger, Maier, and Stumpp (2007) provide an analysis of the validity of cognitive ability tests in Germany, and Salgado and colleagues (Salgado, Anderson, Moscoso, Bertua, & De Fruyt, 2003; Salgado et al., 2003) report similar investigations in the European community.

Beginning with Barrick and Mount (1991), there have been numerous meta-analyses that establish that there is a relationship between some aspects of the Big Five personality constructs and job performance. Barrick, Mount, and Judge (2001) provide a meta-analysis of meta-analyses of what was at that time a burgeoning effort. Barrick and Mount (2012) provide a review of the relationship between personality and various work outcomes, and Hough and Dilchert (2010, p. 309) provide a summary of the relationships between various personality constructs and aspects of work performance.

The results of the previously mentioned reviews are summarized by Schmitt (2014) and are directly relevant to this chapter in that they address the degree to which job performance is predicted by both cognitive and noncognitive measures. Schmitt provides the following summary:

1. The validity of cognitive ability is generalizable across situations and the observed correlation between job performance and measured cognitive ability is usually in the .20s while validity corrected for range restriction and/or criterion unreliability is most often .40 or above.
2. The relationship between personality measures and performance varies with which of the Big Five constructs one considers and appears to be generalizable only in the case of conscientiousness. Observed correlations between performance and individual measures of personality are almost always less than .20 and corrected correlations rarely exceed .25.
3. Correlations between cognitive ability measures and personality measures are usually low. Judge, Jackson, Shaw, Scott, and Rich (2007) report meta-analytic correlations between four of the Big Five constructs and cognitive ability were less than .10; openness correlated .22 with cognitive ability. Similarly, Roth, Switzer, van Iddekinge, and Oh (2011) estimated the corrected correlation between conscientiousness and cognitive ability at .03.

4. Correlations between measures of the Big Five constructs are usually moderate (less than .40). Van der Linden, te Nijenhuis, and Bakker (2010) report meta-analytic correlations in absolute terms based on 212 separate correlation matrices and the responses of 144,117 individuals ranged between .12 and .32 (.17 and .43 corrected for unreliability).

5. These statements in combination suggest that both cognitive ability and personality are valuable predictors of job performance and given their relative lack of correlation with each other that combinations of the two will produce superior predictions of job performance. In addition, the low intercorrelations of Big Five measures suggest that personality combinations are also likely to produce validities that are larger in magnitude than are the validities of individual Big Five constructs. (p. 46)

EXPANSION OF THE DOMAIN OF WORKFORCE PERFORMANCE AND THE RESULT

Beginning perhaps with the work of Campbell, McCloy, Oppler, and Sager (1993), organizational psychologists have considered work outcomes in addition to those narrowly defined by one's job responsibilities. Their eight performance dimensions included non-job-specific task proficiency, facilitating peer and team performance, demonstrating effort, as well as job-specific task proficiency. On the negative side of performance, researchers have also focused on counterproductive work behavior such as theft, aggression, violence, destruction of property, and withdrawal. For a meta-analytic review, see Berry, Ones, and Sackett (2007). Research on employee turnover or withdrawal has a long history in organizational psychology (for a meta-analysis of turnover research, see Griffith, Hom, & Gaertner, 2000). Including these aspects of performance meant that the domain of predictor measures was also greatly expanded because many of these domains seem less likely to be a function of cognitive characteristics and more likely related to social and motivational attributes. Correlates of these dimensions as relevant outcomes meant that measures of personality, motivation, and social skills are relatively more important personal characteristics than would be the case if only task-specific performance were considered relevant.

Hoffman and Dilchert (2012) provide a review of the personality correlates of organizational citizenship behavior (for a meta-analysis, see Chiaburu, Oh, Berry, Li, & Gardner, 2011) and counterproductive work behavior. There has also been burgeoning research on adaptive performance (Pulakos, Mueller-Hanson,

& Nelson, 2012) and its predictability. To be useful considerations of individual performance, however, it is important that these performance constructs are indeed not highly redundant with measures of task performance or each other. This seems to be true for the distinction between organizational citizenship behavior (or contextual performance) and task performance; it may be less true for adaptive performance and task performance (Pulakos, Schmitt, Dorsey, Hedge, & Borman, 2002). Counterproductive work behavior and organizational citizenship behavior are not so highly correlated that they represent opposites on a single performance continuum (Dalal, 2005), and withdrawal measures are usually minimally correlated with task performance. This literature on the nature and dimensionality of performance points to the necessity of considering carefully what aspects of performance are relevant in a particular organizational context and that predictors be selected accordingly.

The academic prediction literature, however, does not often include a consideration of other dimensions of student outcome other than a focus on academic achievement. Even in that case, much of the prediction of college success employs first-year college GPA as the criterion of interest. There are some exceptions, and this literature is reviewed in the next section.

DOMAINS OF COLLEGE STUDENT PERFORMANCE AND STUDENT CAPABILITY

Willingham (1985) noted that conceptualizing and evaluating the successful development of college students depend on the multiple goals and outcomes desired by students, the school administration, legislators, and others. The concern in the educational literature for multiple dimensions of college performance parallels the development of multidimensional models of job performance in the industrial/organizational psychology literature. In an early attempt to understand multiple dimensions of college performance systematically, Taber and Hackman (1976) identified 17 academic and nonacademic dimensions to be important in classifying successful and unsuccessful college students, including intellectual perspective and curiosity, communication proficiency, and ethical behavior. It has also been demonstrated that college students who are actively engaged across numerous domains tend to achieve greater success in their overall college experience as reflected in their scholastic involvement, accumulated achievement record, or their graduation (Astin, 1984; Willingham, 1985). Student retention has also been the focus of some research (Braxton & Lee, 2005; Habley, Bloom, & Robbins, 2012).

Sternberg, Bonney, Gabora, and Merrifield (2012) have asserted that student potential for success be evaluated along four dimensions: analytical, creative, practical, and wisdom. In a more systematic study of what universities hope to develop in students, Stemler (2012) searched university websites. He found that universities stated the importance of a variety of dimensions usually considered cognitive (e.g., writing, interpretation, quantitative reasoning, and logical reasoning) but also several noncognitive dimensions, such as ethical reasoning; citizenship; designing, creating, and realizing; and intercultural literacy. Not easily classified as cognitive or noncognitive were informational literacy and speaking. Oswald, Schmitt, Kim, Gillespie, and Ramsay (2004) also content analyzed university web pages in an attempt to identify those dimensions universities claimed to develop in their students. Their 12 dimensions were knowledge, continuous learning, artistic appreciation, multicultural appreciation, adaptation, leadership, perseverance, social responsibility, ethics, interpersonal skills, health, and career orientation. Thus, there appears to be a recognition that the outcomes of a college education are noncognitive as well as the acquisition of a body of knowledge in one's area of interest. However, the measurement of student potential to develop these non-academic characteristics has not progressed as rapidly in the educational domain as has the measurement of potential in the organizational domain. There is also less consensus regarding the important noncognitive dimensions in the student realm.

ASSESSING NONCOGNITIVE SKILLS

Some previous studies have examined the role of noncognitive predictors of academic success, such as meta-cognitive skills (Zeegers, 2001), study attitudes (Zimmerman, Parks, Gray, & Michael, 1977), study motivation (Melancon, 2002), and even personality traits (Ridgell & Lounsbury, 2004). In a meta-analysis, Credé and Kuncel (2008) found that noncognitive factors such as study habits, skills, and study motivation accounted for variance in academic performance. Validities for the prediction of first-year college GPA were in the twenties across subscales for the Survey of Study Habits and Attitudes (Brown & Holtzman, 1967) and the Learning and Study Skills Inventory (Weinstein & Palmer, 2002). Corrected for unreliability in the criterion and range restriction, these correlations were approximately .30 across the various subscales in both measures. Even more encouraging, and relevant to a later section of this chapter, was the fact that these measures produced incremental validity over HSGPA and standardized test scores (change in R^2 ranged from .04 to .12 across the different subscales of the two tests).

Sternberg et al. (2012) have also reported success in developing measures that assess their hypothesized structure of student capabilities, as mentioned previously. Sternberg and the Rainbow Collaborators (2006) report that validities for the SAT Math and Verbal tests were .28 and .26, respectively, against first-year college GPA. By comparison, a battery of nine tests consisting of measures of creative, analytical, and practical abilities displayed validities of .35, .24, and .24, respectively. Other experimental tests of creativity and situational judgment had validities ranging from .15 to .29. In a subsequent effort labeled the Kaleidoscope project, measures of wisdom were added to the Rainbow tests. Sternberg et al. (2012) did not report the usual correlational statistics, but they reported that students admitted to a university using the expanded set of tests (beyond the SAT and HSGPA) performed as well as or better than students who had been selected using standard measures without the ethnic group differences usually observed on the SAT and HSGPA measures.

Schmitt and colleagues (Oswald et al., 2004; Schmitt et al., 2009) reported that biodata and situational judgment tests designed to measure the capability to perform well in the 12 areas listed previously were valid predictors of first- and fourth-year GPA. Correlations with first-year college GPA for four different samples of college students are presented in Table 12.1. As can be seen, ACT/SAT and HSGPA are consistently the best predictors of college GPA, but several alternative noncognitive measures (knowledge, ethics, and situational judgment inventory (SJI)) are consistent predictors of college GPA across all four samples. These measures were not developed to predict GPA but, rather, other student outcomes, such as dropout rates, class attendance, and organizational citizenship behavior. For these outcomes, the alternative measures were uniformly superior to ACT/SAT scores and HSGPA (Oswald et al., 2004; Schmitt et al., 2009; Table 12.2).

Habley et al. (2012) presented meta-analyses for retention and college GPA for a variety of noncognitive variables, HSGPA, and ACT/SAT scores. These data are summarized in Table 12.3. As can be seen in the table, several noncognitive predictors (academic goals, academic self-efficacy, and academic-related skills) were correlated above .20 with retention. Academic self-efficacy and achievement motivation were correlated above .20 with college GPA. Both HSGPA and ACT/SAT were highly correlated with college GPA and less so with retention. These data were used as the basis of the construction of the Engage instrument, or Student Readiness Inventory (http://www.act.org/engage/college_features.html), which has proven to be a valid predictor of GPA and retention (information on incremental validity is presented later).

More popular methods of obtaining the information these researchers attempted to collect with structured measures of noncognitive tests include achievement test scores, letters of recommendation, personal statements, lists of extracurricular activities, interviews, and peer references. In addition to the

Table 12.1 CORRELATIONS OF BIODATA, SITUATIONAL JUDGMENT, ACT/SAT, AND HIGH SCHOOL GPA WITH COLLEGE GPA[a]

	2001–2002 (N = 614)	2003–2004 (N = 568)	2004–2008 (N > 1,900)	2009–2010 (N > 550)
Knowledge	.22	.22	.26	.22
Learning	.05	−.02	.13	.10
Art. Appr.	.01	−.03	.18	.16
Mltcult. Appr.	.07	−.04	.11	.12
Leadership	.14	−.01	.09	.07
Interp. Skl.	.04			
Soc. Resp.	.08	.07	.13	.08
Health	.23	.14	.11	.04
Career. Ornt.	−.02	−.06	−.14	−.11
Adapt.	.21	.13	.05	.01
Perseverance	.15	.07	.07	.10
Ethics	.14	.22	.17	.13
SJI	.16	.11	.22	.09
HSGPA		.39	.53	.29
ACT/SAT	.33	.34	.53	.44

[a]All correlations were corrected for differential selectivity across schools when appropriate.

Adapt., adaptability; Art. Appr., artistic appreciation; Career Ornt., career orientation; HSGPA, high school grade point average; Interp. Skl., interpersonal skill; Mltcult. Appr., multicultural appreciation; SJI, situational judgment inventory; Soc. Resp., social responsibility.

work by Credé and Kuncel (2008), some support for the incremental validity and practical usefulness of such measures over the more common predictors mentioned previously has been reported (Cress, Astin, Zimmer-Oster, & Burkhart, 2001; Ra, 1989; Willingham, 1985). However, these authors and others have pointed to the fact that such supplementary measures are problematic insofar as (a) admissions personnel pay attention to, interpret, and weight this information in different ways; (b) admissions personnel rely on information about students' past experiences that is to some extent idiosyncratic and not in a standardized format; (c) collecting and evaluating this information requires extra cost in time and resources; and (d) the information is usually self-reported and/or may be difficult to verify (Willingham, 1998). Not implementing, scoring, or weighting such measures in a systematic manner across colleges and students precludes a conceptual understanding and a level of incremental validity above standardized test scores and HSGPA that would be of practical benefit in other academic settings even when such variables might be predictive.

Table 12.2 Validity of Biodata and the Situational Judgment Test (SJT) Measures Hierarchical Regression of Cumulative College GPA, Behaviorally Anchored Rating Scale (BARS), Organizational Citizenship Behavior (OCB), and Absenteeism on the Predictors[a]

	Cumulative GPA		BARS		OCB		Absenteeism	
	r	b	r	b	r	b	r	b
Step 1								
HSGPA	.531	.351*	.079	.070	−.007	.008	−.011	−.050
ACT/SAT	.539	.327*	.011	.002	−.098	−.107*	.149	.216*
ΔR^2		.398*		.008		.012*		.033*
Step 2								
Knowledge	.263	.046	.192	−.096	.056	−.045	−.161	−.063
Learning	.129	.064*	.226	−.011	.116	−.003	−.072	.041
Artistic	.174	.020	.200	.029	−.001	−.195*	−.082	−.037
Multicultural	.115	.022	.302	.199*	.184	.159*	−.115	−.084
Leadership	.092	−.014	.300	.043	.372	.286*	−.024	.112*
Responsibility	.136	.003	.274	.038	.298	.160*	−.107	−.004
Health	.101	.061*	.236	.157*	.093	−.036	−.121	−.131*
Career	−.144	−.132*	.220	.081	.174	.014	−.098	−.002
Adaptability	.054	−.043	.284	.087	.213	.110*	−.097	.004
Perseverance	.063	−.004	.363	.148*	.231	−.003	−.181	−.040
Ethics	.164	.004	.239	.098*	.102	.031	−.276	−.203*
SJT	.211	.070*	.223	.088	.087	−.021	−.194	−.102*
ΔR^2		.029*		.240*		.201*		.116*
Overall R^2		.426*		.247*		.214*		.149*
Adjusted R^2		.419		.227		.193		.127
N		1,155		547		558		556

[a]An asterisk indicates a significant beta, $p \le .05$. Correlations greater than .06 are statistically significant for the GPA relationships. Correlations greater than .09 are statistically significant for relationships with BARS, absenteeism, and OCB. *b* refers to standardized regression weights.

SOURCE: Adapted from Table 5 in Schmitt et al. (2009).

INCREMENTAL VALIDITY

In considering the use of noncognitive measures of student potential, very few, if any, researchers or admissions specialists would advocate the replacement of the traditional cognitive measures (e.g., the SAT/ACT and HSGPA). If so, they often replace these measures with similar ones (e.g., see the Sternberg et al. (2006, 2012) descriptions of the measures designed to assess the analytical

Table 12.3 META-ANALYSES OF COGNITIVE AND NONCOGNITIVE PREDICTORS
OF COLLEGE STUDENT RETENTION AND GPA

Predictor	No. of Students	No. of Studies	*r* with Retention	No. of Students	No. of Studies	*r* with GPA
Achievement motivation	3,208	7	.105	9,330	17	.257
Academic goals	20,010	33	.210	17,575	34	.155
Institutional commitment	20,741	28	.204	5,775	11	.108
Social support	11,624	26	.199	12,366	33	.096
Social involvement	26,263	36	.166	15,955	33	.124
Academic self-efficacy	6,930	6	.257	9,598	18	.378
General self-concept	4,240	6	.059	9,621	21	.037
Academic-related skills	1,627	8	.298	16,282	33	.129
Financial support	7,800	6	.181	6,849	5	.195
Socioeconomic status	7,704	6	.212	12,081	13	.155
High school GPA	5,551	12	.239	17,196	30	.413
ACT/SAT scores	3,053	11	.121	16,648	31	.368

SOURCE: This table was adapted from Tables 8.3 and 8.4 of Habley et al. (2012, pp. 145–146).

dimension of their model of student potential). Thus, in deciding how measures of noncognitive dimensions might be used in admissions decisions, it is important to know how predictive a combination of these two types of measures are in admissions contexts. The usual question, then, is whether the noncognitive measures (or novel measures of cognitive ability) produce a statistical and practically significant increment to the prediction of academic success. Sternberg et al. (2006) report that adding measures of creative, practical, and analytical abilities to SAT math and verbal tests as well as HSGPA produced a multiple R^2 of .244. This is compared to a value of .164 when only the SAT tests and HSGPA were used to predict college GPA. Most of the increment in validity was a function of the creative abilities; analytical and practical abilities did not produce an increment. The increment provided in this case (i.e., .08) was statistically significant, and most researchers would agree that it is also practically significant.

Schmitt and colleagues (Oswald et al., 2004; Schmitt et al., 2009) have also examined the incremental validity of their noncognitive measures (for a description of these measures, see Oswald et al., 2004) in the prediction of college GPA as well as alternative outcome measures. Unlike most studies of the validity of admissions procedures, the 2009 sample included the students' final college GPA. The results of hierarchical regression of final college GPA on the SAT/ACT scores, HSGPA, and biodata and situational judgment measures are presented in the second and third columns of Table 12.2. As was the case in the tests of incremental validity in the Sternberg et al. (2006) work described previously, the traditional measures were entered first in this regression. The traditional measures were highly related to college GPA (R^2 = .398). Even in this case, the noncognitive variables added significantly to R^2 (.029). Biodata measures of continuous learning, health, and career orientation and the situational judgment measure were significant predictors in this hierarchical regression.

Similar regressions were conducted for three alternative student outcomes. The first was a self-report behaviorally anchored rating scale (BARS) of student performance, the content of which represented the 12 dimensions listed previously. The second alternative outcome was an academic adaptation of organizational citizenship behavior (OCB; Organ, 1988). The last outcome measure presented in Table 12.2 was a self-report measure of class attendance (negative correlations indicate that high scores on a measure were associated with fewer missed classes). As can be seen when considering alternate student outcomes, the role of noncognitive and cognitive predictors is reversed. For self-ratings of performance along these 12 dimensions, almost all the predictability comes from the noncognitive predictors. It is the case that both measures are derived from the same source, but data for predictors were collected in the first semester of college and outcome data were collected more than 3 years later in the second semester of students' senior year. Data regarding the OCB measure were very similar; ACT/SAT scores were actually negatively related to this outcome, whereas leadership, multicultural appreciation, social responsibility, and adaptability were relatively important predictors of OCB. Absenteeism was not as well predicted as were the other outcomes, but particularly ethics, health, and the SJI were important predictors of class attendance. For graduation status (not shown in Table 12.2), the best predictors were HSGPA and SAT/ACT scores, with minimal predictability afforded by the noncognitive predictors.

Habley et al. (2012) also presented incremental validity data for several noncognitive predictors derived from the Student Readiness Inventory (e.g., academic discipline, social activity, and emotional control). In a hierarchical regression in which several demographic variables and HSGPA, socioeconomic status, and ACT/SAT scores were entered first, they found an incremental validity of .031 in predicting the college GPA at 4-year institutions. A similar logistic regression analysis using retention as an outcome also produced a significant incremental validity for noncognitive variables. The increment of .031 in the prediction of GPA is remarkably similar to that reported by Schmitt et al. (.029; see column 3 of Table 12.2).

The conclusions of this research on incremental validity are similar to those summarized previously for employment selection. Cognitive ability (as represented by standardized tests and HSGPA) is significantly related to student academic performance. Noncognitive measures are also related to student academic performance, but less so than cognitive measures. To the degree to which these two sets of measures are unrelated (for one set of data relevant to this issue, see Schmitt et al., 2009), the combination of cognitive and noncognitive predictors results in better prediction than either alone. If one considers student outcomes other than academic performance, the role of cognitive and noncognitive predictors is likely reversed in that noncognitive predictors are superior to the cognitive predictors.

IMPLICATIONS FOR STUDENT BODY COMPOSITION AND PERFORMANCE

Aside from the potential to add to the accuracy with which student performance is predicted, another major advantage is that noncognitive measures display markedly smaller score differences between minority and majority groups than do measures of cognitive ability. Cognitive score differences occur in both the employment and the academic context and are resistant to various attempts to minimize them (Sackett, Schmitt, Ellingson, & Kabin, 2001). For example, the African American–Caucasian differences for the sample described in this chapter (Schmitt et al., 2009) were –1.18 standard deviation units for ACT/SAT scores and –.88 for HSGPA. Hispanic American–Caucasian differences were –.83 for ACT/SAT scores and –.62 for HSGPA (in all cases, the negative numbers imply that Caucasians' scores were superior). Asian Americans scored better on ACT/SAT scores (.35) and HSGPA (.07) than did Caucasians. Differences of the magnitude reflected in the comparisons of Hispanic and African American students with Caucasian students will result in markedly different admissions rates when these measures are used to select students (Sackett & Ellingson, 1997). By contrast, minority–majority group differences on the noncognitive measures in that study averaged near zero; in 14 of 36 comparisons, the minority group scored better than the Caucasian group. Differences favoring minority groups were largest for the multicultural appreciation measure and career orientation for the African American group. Caucasians were most superior to minority groups on the health measure. A full summary of these differences is provided in Table 9 in Schmitt et al. (2009).

These subgroup differences suggest that using the noncognitive measures in combination with cognitive measures may serve to dampen the large differences observed between groups for the cognitive measures (note, however, that this is not always the case for predictor composites; Schmitt, Rogers, Chan, Sheppard, & Jennings, 1997). To demonstrate what might happen if some such combination were to take place, composites of the cognitive and noncognitive measures were formed. A sum of the noncognitive measures was formed and then standardized. It was combined with standardized versions of HSGPA and ACT/SAT scores to form a single summed composite, which results in each component being approximately equally weighted. This composite was then used to rank order the students in the sample and identify the top 15%, top 50%, and top 85% of the students. The latter was taken to represent what might occur in highly selective, moderately selective, and low selective institutions, respectively. Next, the proportion of students belonging to different racial groups that would have been admitted were this strategy used to admit students was identified. The result of this process is displayed in Table 12.4. As can be seen from the table, and is evident in previous analyses (Sackett & Ellingson, 1997), differences in scores across groups impact lower scoring groups the most when an institution is highly selective. For example, if only cognitive measures are used in the highly selective institutions, less than 1% of the student body would be African American. If these indices were combined with a noncognitive battery of tests, more than 4% of the student body would be African American. A similar but smaller impact would be observed on the proportion of Hispanic American students (i.e., 4.3% vs. 6.4%). Smaller proportions of students from higher scoring groups would be admitted using a composite that includes the noncognitive tests. These differences are most pronounced in the case of the highly selective institution; when 85% of the applicants are admitted, the differences in proportions of students of differing racial background admitted using the two different composites are minimal.

Table 12.4 is only an illustration. The samples of the different groups are small, and very few, if any, institutions would use the mechanical approach to combining and using test scores that was used to provide this illustration. However, the trend in these data would be observed in other instances, and differences would be smaller or larger depending on a number of factors, including the following: (1) the mean differences between subgroups on the various tests, (2) the weighting of the various test components, (3) the selectivity of the institution, and (4) the intercorrelations between the test components.

Because the use of the noncognitive measures might produce a less academically competent group of students due to the lower validity of these tests, an important question is whether the performance of students admitted using noncognitive measures is lower than that when only cognitive measures are used. The means and standard deviations of the college GPA of the groups

Table 12.4 PERCENTAGE OF MEMBERS OF EACH GROUP ADMITTED USING DIFFERENT ADMISSION RATES AND DIFFERENT TEST SCORE COMPOSITES

	Hispanic American		Asian American		African American		Caucasian	
	Cog	Cog+	Cog	Cog+	Cog	Cog+	Cog	Cog+
Top 15%	4.3	6.4	17.8	14.9	0.9	4.1	77.0	74.6
Top 50%	4.0	4.6	10.5	10.1	8.3	10.0	77.1	75.3
Top 85%	4.5	4.7	7.6	7.7	18.4	18.7	69.5	69.0
All		3.7		9.0		19.4		67.8

Cog, equally weighted composite of HSGPA and SAT/ACT. Cog+, equally weighted composite of HSGPA, SAT/ACT, and noncognitive measures.

SOURCE: Table is an adaptation and correction of Table 7A of Schmitt et al. (2009).

of students that were the subject of the analysis depicted in Table 12.4 were computed to illustrate what might happen for these students. The results of these computations for highly selective schools indicated that the GPA of the Hispanic American students selected using noncognitive tests as one aspect of the admissions procedure would be lower by .10; that of Asian American students would be .04 lower, and that of Caucasian students would be .01 lower. There was only one African American in this highly selective group, so comparisons were not possible. In cases in which the institution was minimally selective, there were no noticeable differences; in fact, use of a noncognitive test actually resulted in slightly better grades. Again, these results are based on small samples and a hypothetical approach to using the tests, but the general trend of the outcome should be expected in other situations; that is, the GPA of students admitted using the noncognitive tests as one criterion for admission would be slightly lower when the school is highly selective. The full set of these calculations is available in Table 7B of Schmitt et al. (2009).

Yet another outcome resulting from the use of an expanded set of admissions criteria is cited by Sternberg et al. (2012). After the measures used in their Kaleidoscope project at Tufts University were introduced, the number of applications from African American students increased by 30% and those from Hispanic American students by 15%. The number of African American students who were admitted increased by 25%. At the same time, the SAT scores and HSGPA of the applicant pool increased during the years in which Kaleidoscope measures were an optional part of the admissions process. Sternberg et al. also found that ratings on the Kaleidoscope measures were related to extracurricular participation, satisfaction in leadership, and active citizenship—variables similar to the alternate outcomes that were the subject of analyses summarized in Table 12.2.

ISSUES ARISING FROM THE USE OF NONCOGNITIVE ADMISSIONS CRITERIA

In talking with admissions personnel about the use of noncognitive assessments, a very common question is whether these assessments might be used in ways other than to make a simple accept/reject decision. Their notion is that these indices might inform the university as to how to intervene more successfully with students to make their college experience more successful. Schmitt et al. (2007) presented one feasible way in which such measures along with SAT/ACT scores and HSGPA might be used in this manner. They first computed a profile of the students' scores on 12 noncognitive measures, their SAT/ACT scores, and their HSGPA. Schmitt et al. then clustered these profiles and suggested, based on the configuration of scores, interventions that might be effective with each of the five groups identified in this manner. For example, one group was characterized by low scores on traditional measures of academic potential and relatively high scores on several biodata dimensions, including career orientation. Schmitt et al. suggested that members of this group would be particularly well motivated to work to improve their academic skills and that they would benefit from remedial courses and programs. Another group was characterized by relatively low scores on all measures. Members of this group would need to receive early and effective motivational and academic interventions or they would be likely to drop out or be placed on academic probation. Yet another group had high scores on all dimensions; individuals in this group might be recruited as mentors or tutors for low-performing students. No interventions were employed with these groups of students, but this represents one alternative potential use of these data. An examination of differences among these profile groups represented expected differences across groups in terms of majors selected, first-year college GPA, class absenteeism, self-performance ratings, organizational citizenship behavior, intent to quit school, and satisfaction. Habley et al. (2012, pp. 150–153) also present a similar idea in providing examples of four students with different profiles of scores on cognitive and noncognitive measures.

Certainly, the major concern regarding many noncognitive measures is the ease with which student applicants might provide desired responses. If these measures become widely used, coaching programs will certainly be available, and even relatively simple instructions as to the nature of the intended constructs targeted by the measures appear to be relatively effective in raising student scores (Ramsay, Schmitt, Oswald, Kim, & Gillespie, 2006). In most of the work done by the author and associates, the student respondents were first-semester college freshman who were research-only participants; scores were not used in any way to impact their admission or treatment at a university. In two situations, however, they were able to ask students who were still in the admissions process to respond to their measures. The standardized mean differences of these two sets of respondents are presented in Table 12.5. As can be seen, the scores are between .21 and .62 standard deviation units higher when the students were still in the admissions process compared to the situations in which they were completing the measures for research purposes only. Also note that members of the applicant groups were assured that their responses would not be used to make admissions decisions; it is hypothesized that the differences would be greater if no such assurance had been provided. These results are consistent with those of a meta-analysis by Ones and Viswesvaran (1998), in which the authors reported that the difference between the scores of examinees who were instructed to "fake good" and the scores of those who were given normal test instructions was .60. Respondents who were asked to respond to an instrument twice under "fake" instructions and normal instructions displayed scores .72 standard deviations higher when faking.

Detection of faking respondents and corrections for faking have a long history in personality research, beginning with the use of "lie" scales in the Minnesota Multiphasic Personality Inventory used for clinical diagnosis. There are at least two concerns about faking. One is the impact that widescale faking might have on the validity of the resulting test scores. The second is the impact of faking on the individuals who do (or do not) fake good or respond in a socially desirable way. Those who do not fake when others do so may not gain admission to a desired college or job. Those who do fake may be more likely to fail at school or work. The impact of corrections to faking on validity (and, by implication, the impact of faking on validity) is not likely to be consequential

Table 12.5 Mean Standardized Differences Between Applicants and Admitted Students in Two Comparisons

Measure	2004 Samples	2006 Samples
Knowledge	.55	.54
Continuous learning	.43	.49
Artistic appreciation	.35	.30
Multicultural appreciation	.48	.40
Leadership	.43	.35
Social responsibility	.46	.46
Health	.26	.30
Career orientation	.25	.21
Adaptability	.22	.25
Perseverance	.39	.32
Ethics	.62	.53
Situational judgment	.50	.52

given the usual level of validity and the intercorrelations among predictors and criteria and faking measures (Schmitt & Oswald, 2006).

Various methods other than statistical corrections have been used to minimize faking. Dwight and Donovan (2003) meta-analyzed results of studies in which respondents were warned not to fake by indicating that the instrument contained a scale that would identify fakers and that there would be consequences for those test takers who were so identified. Warning statements containing consequence elements reduced respondent scores by .30, whereas simply noting that fakers could be identified did not have an impact. Schmitt and Kunce (2002) showed that a requirement that respondents to a biodata measure "elaborate" claims that they had certain experiences lowered respondent scores, but subsequent research indicated that this effect was observed only for elaborated items. Because elaboration was often not possible for all items (e.g., those with qualitative options) and because elaboration of many items would turn objective measures into essay examinations, this alternative does not seem feasible in large-scale testing situations. Faking remains a significant concern for those interested in using noncognitive measures in high-stakes testing situations.

Another concern that must be taken into account in high-stakes situations in which noncognitive test use is proposed is the reaction of various consumer groups. In the case of college admissions tests, these groups include the students themselves, but also their parents, college admissions personnel, and perhaps high school counselors who are providing students with advice regarding colleges to which they might apply. In addition, the general public appears to have an active interest in the college admissions process.

The only systematic data collection on reactions to the use of noncognitive measures in college admissions of which I am aware was reported by Schmitt, Oswald, Kim, Gillespie, and Ramsay (2004). After responding to the authors' biodata and SJI items, approximately 654 respondents were asked to indicate the fairness, relevance, and perceived validity of each of the data collection methods. Responses in the case of each reaction measure were made on four Likert-type items with 5-point scales; hence, scores could range from 5 to 20. As can be seen in Table 12.6, these students were generally favorable in their reaction to all four methods. The largest difference in reactions across methods was on the fairness dimension, on which students perceived HSGPA and ACT/SAT scores to be a fairer measure of their potential than the biodata or SJI measures. Students' judgments of the relevance of various measures of potential were almost identical across the four measures, with HSGPA perceived to be the most relevant. Finally, perceptions of validity were almost the same for three methods of measurement, with a slight preference for HSGPA over the other three.

Table 12.6 Reactions of Students to Biodata, Situational Judgment Intervention (SJI), High School GPA (HSGPA), and ACT/SAT Measures in College Admissions[a]

Measure	Biodata	SJI	HSGPA	ACT/SAT
Fairness	14.78 (5.84)[b]	14.40 (6.08)	17.59 (5.51)	16.63 (5.38)
Relevance	13.27 (4.55)	13.30 (4.16)	14.02 (3.75)	13.11 (3.78)
Validity	14.39 (5.19)	14.52 (4.69)	15.96 (4.61)	14.84 (4.25)

[a]Numbers are means (standard deviations) based on a sum of responses to four Likert-type items with 5-point response scales; hence, possible scores ranged from 5 to 20.

SOURCE: Adapted from Schmitt et al. (2004).

On at least three issues (use of noncognitive measures for purposes other than admissions, the minimization of faking, and the role of reactions to these measures in determining their successful implementation), more research and practical solutions are required. If these measures are to be used continuously in high-stakes admissions, then we also need to know how to create additional equivalent forms. There also needs to be more research on the use of these measures and others like them with foreign student applicants. The freshman class at my home university is now 10% Chinese. I suspect that the biodata and SJI items developed with American students (some of whom were of Chinese heritage) simply reflect experiences and opportunities that are relatively meaningless to native Chinese. This may also be true for students of other backgrounds. One goal of this chapter was to draw a parallel between employment selection research and college admissions research insofar as there is an interest in using noncognitive measures to complement cognitive assessments. This suggests that researchers consider the long-term stability or development of these measures as individuals move from high school to college to employment. Mumford has long maintained that individuals' responses to questions about their background and experiences exhibit a pattern that is evident in college behavior and subsequent early career experiences (Mumford, Barrett, & Hester, 2012; Mumford, Wesley, & Shaffer, 1987). Finally, the labels attached to the noncognitive measures that have been used in the college admissions arena are diverse and likely address several different constructs, and some with different labels likely represent the same construct. From a scientific perspective, and likely from a practical generalizability standpoint, attention to the constructs measured within and across attempts to assess noncognitive attributes is desperately needed.

CONCLUSION

Based on both the employment selection and the academic admissions literature, it appears that measures of noncognitive constructs can contribute to the prediction of personal success beyond measures of cognitive ability; their use in combination is most likely to maximize students' and employees' performance. In the academic admissions domain, there is less research, and several important questions need more attention. In concluding this chapter, I highlight five issues that seem particularly important to me. First, perhaps most difficult, concerns about faking and coaching of noncognitive measures need to be addressed, and their effects need to be minimized or eliminated. Second, it is possible that these measures can be used in ways other than to enhance the accuracy of the admissions decision; the efficacy of these alternatives should be explored. If they were used in this manner, the motivation to fake would not exist. Third, attention to the constructs measured by the noncognitive measures used in the academic admissions literature is most apt to make generalizations possible across various institutions and to make the data collected most useful in guiding interventions. Fourth, the use of noncognitive measures among international students must be evaluated; it may be the case that different measures need to be developed to assess similar constructs for these populations. Finally, there must be attention to the reactions of various constituencies affected by academic admissions decisions if implementation of these measures is to be successful.

REFERENCES

Astin, A. W. (1984). Student involvement: A developmental theory for higher education. *Journal of College Student Personnel, 25*(4), 297–308.

Barrick, M. R., & Mount, M. K. (1991). The Big Five personality dimensions and job performance: A meta-analysis. *Personnel Psychology, 44*, 1–26.

Barrick, M. R., & Mount, M. K. (2012). Nature and use of personality in selection. In Schmitt (Ed.), *The Oxford handbook of personnel assessment and selection* (pp. 225–251). New York, NY: Oxford University Press.

Barrick, M. R., Mount, M. K., & Judge, T. A. (2001). Personality and performance at the beginning of the new millennium: What do we know and where do we go next? *International Journal of Selection and Assessment, 9*, 9–30.

Berry, C. M., Ones, D. S., & Sackett, P. R. (2007). Interpersonal deviance, organizational deviance, and their common correlates: A review and meta-analysis. *Journal of Applied Psychology, 92*, 410–424.

Braxton, J. M., & Lee, S. D. (2005). Toward reliable knowledge about college student departure. In A. Seidman (Ed.), *College student retention* (pp. 107–129). Westport, CT: Praeger.

Bridgeman, B., McCamley-Jenkins, L., & Ervin, N. (2000). *Predictions of freshman grade point average from the revised and recentered SAT I: Reasoning Test* (College Board Rep. No. 2000-1). New York, NY: College Entrance Examination Board.

Brown, W. F., & Holtzman, W. (1967). *Survey of study habits and attitudes, SSHA Manual* (pp. 4–30). New York, NY: Psychological Corporation.

Campbell, J. P., McCloy, R. A., Oppler, S. H., & Sager, C. E. (1993). A theory of performance. In N. Schmitt & W. C. Borman (Eds.), *Personnel selection in organizations* (pp. 35–70). San Francisco, CA: Jossey-Bass.

Chiaburu, D. S., Oh, I. S., Berry, C. M., Li, N., & Gardner, R. G. (2011). The five-factor model of personality: Traits and organizational citizenship behavior. *Journal of Applied Psychology, 96,* 1140–1166.

Credé, M., & Kuncel, N. R. (2008). Study habits, skills, and attitudes. *Perspectives in Psychological Science, 3,* 425–453.

Cress, C. M., Astin, H. S., Zimmer-Oster, K., & Burkhardt, J. (2001). Developmental outcomes of college students' involvement in leadership activities. *Journal of College Student Development, 42,* 15–27.

Dalal, R. S. (2005). A meta-analysis of the relationship between organizational citizen behavior and counter-productive work behavior. *Journal of Applied Psychology, 90,* 1241–1255.

Dwight, S. A., & Donovan, J. J. (2003). Do warnings not to fake reduce faking? *Human Performance, 16,* 1–23.

Griffith, R. W., Hom, P. S., & Gaertner, S. (2000). A meta-analysis of antecedents and correlates of employee turnover: Update, moderator tests, and research implications for the next millennium. *Journal of Management, 26,* 463–488.

Habley, W. R., Bloom, J. L., & Robbins, S. (2012). *Increasing persistence: Research based strategies for college student success.* San Francisco, CA: Jossey-Bass.

Hezlett, S. A., Kuncel, N. R., Vey, M. A., Ahart, A. M., Ones, D. S., Campbell, J. P., & Camara, W. (2001, April). The predictive validity of the SAT: A meta-analysis. Paper presented in D. Ones & S. Hezlett (Chairs), *Predicting performance: The interface of I-O psychology and educational research.* Symposium presented at the 16th Annual Convention of the Society for Industrial and Organizational Psychology, San Diego, CA.

Hoffman, B. J., & Dilchert, S. (2012). A review of citizenship and counterproductive behaviors in organizational decision-making. In N. Schmitt (Ed.), *The Oxford handbook of personnel assessment and selection* (pp. 543–569). New York, NY: Oxford University Press.

Hough, L., & Dilchert, S. (2010). Personality: Its measurement and validity. In J. L. Farr & N. T. Tippins (Eds.), *Handbook of employee selection* (pp. 299–320). New York, NY: Taylor & Francis.

Hulsheger, U. R., Maier, G. W., & Stumpp, T. (2007). Validity of general mental ability for the prediction of job performance and training success in Germany: A meta-analysis. *International Journal of Selection and Assessment, 15,* 3–18.

Judge, T. A., Jackson, C. L., Shaw, J. C., Scott, B. A., & Rich, B. L. (2007). Self-efficacy and work-related performance: The integral role of individual differences. *Journal of Applied Psychology, 2,* 107–127.

Kuncel, N. R., Credé, M., & Thomas, L. L. (2005). The validity of self-reported grade point averages, class ranks, and test scores: A meta-analysis and review of the literature. *Review of Educational Research, 75*, 63–82.

Kuncel, N. R., & Hezlett, S. A. (2007). Standardized tests predict graduate students' success. *Science, 315*, 1080–1081.

Kuncel, N. R., Hezlett, S. A., & Ones, D. S. (2004). Academic performance, career potential, creativity, and job performance: Can one construct predict them all? *Journal of Personality and Social Psychology, 86*, 148–161.

Melancon, J. G. (2002). Reliability, structure, and correlates of Learning and Study Strategies Inventory scores. *Educational and Psychological Measurement, 62*, 1020–1027.

Mumford, M. D., Barrett, J. D., & Hester, K. S. (2012). Background data: Use of experiential knowledge in personnel selection. In N. Schmitt (Ed.), *The Oxford handbook of personnel assessment and selection* (pp. 353–382). New York, NY: Oxford University Press.

Mumford, M. D., Wesley, S. S., & Shaffer, G. S. (1987). Individuality in a developmental context: II. The crystallization of development trajectories. *Human Development, 30*, 291–321.

Ones, D. S., Dilchert, S., & Viswesvaran, C. (2012). Cognitive abilities. In N. Schmitt (Ed.), *The Oxford handbook of personnel assessment and selection* (pp. 179–224). New York, NY: Oxford University Press.

Ones, D. S., Dilchert, S., Viswesvaran, C., & Salgado, J. F. (2010). Cognitive abilities. In J. L. Farr & N. T. Tippins (Eds.), *Handbook of employee selection* (pp. 255–275). New York, NY: Taylor & Francis.

Ones, D. S., & Viswesvaran, C. (1998). The effects of social desirability and faking on personality and integrity assessment for personnel selection. *Human Performance, 11*, 245–270.

Organ, D. W. (1988). *Organizational citizenship behavior: The good soldier syndrome.* Lexington, MA: Lexington Books.

Oswald, F. L., Schmitt, N., Kim, B. H., Gillespie, M. A., & Ramsay, L. J. (2004). Developing a biodata measure and situational judgment inventory as predictors of college student performance. *Journal of Applied Psychology, 89*, 187–207.

Pulakos, E. D., Mueller-Hanson, R. A., & Nelson, J. K. (2012). Adaptive performance and trainability as criteria in selection research. In N. Schmitt (Ed.), *The Oxford handbook of personnel assessment and selection* (pp. 595–613). New York, NY: Oxford University Press.

Pulakos, E. D., Schmitt, N., Dorsey, D. W., Hedge, J. W., & Borman, W. C. (2002). Predicting adaptive performance: Further tests of a model of adaptability. *Human Performance, 15*, 299–323.

Ra, J. B. (1989). Validity of a new evaluative scale to aid admissions decisions. *Evaluation and Program Planning, 12*, 195–204.

Ramsay, L., Schmitt, N., Oswald, F. L., Kim, B. H., & Gillespie, M. (2006). The impact of situational context variables on responses to biodata and situational judgment inventory items. *Psychology Science, 48*, 268–287.

Ridgell, S., & Lounsbury, J. W. (2004). Predicting collegiate academic success: General intelligence, "Big Five" personality traits, and work drive. *College Student Journal, 38*, 607–618.

Rigol, G. W. (2003). *Admissions decision-making models: How U.S. institutions of higher education select undergraduate students*. New York, NY: The College Board.

Roth, P. L., Switzer, F. S., III, van Iddekinge, C. H., & Oh, I.-S. (2011). Toward better meta-analytic matrices: How input values can affect research conclusions in human resource management simulations. *Personnel Psychology, 64*, 899–936.

Sackett, P. R., & Ellingson, J. E. (1997). The effects of forming multi-predictor composites on group differences and adverse impact. *Personnel Psychology, 50*, 707–721.

Sackett, P. R., Kuncel, N. R., Arneson, J. J., Cooper, S. R., & Waters, S. D. (2009). Does socioeconomic status explain the relationship between admissions tests and post-secondary academic performance? *Psychological Bulletin, 135*, 1–22.

Sackett, P. R., & Lievens, F. (2008). Personnel selection. *Annual Review of Psychology, 59*, 419–450.

Sackett, P. R., Schmitt, N., Ellingson, J. E., & Kabin, M. B. (2001). High-stakes testing in employment, credentialing, and higher education: Prospects in a post-affirmative action world. *American Psychologist, 56*, 302–318.

Salgado, J. F., Anderson, N., Moscoso, S., Bertua, C., & de Fruyt, F. (2003). International validity generalization of GMA and cognitive abilities: A European community meta-analysis. *Personnel Psychology, 56*, 571–605.

Salgado, J. F., Anderson, N., Moscoso, S., Bertua, C., De Fruyt, F., & Rolland, J. P. (2003). A meta-analytic study of general mental ability validity for different occupations in the European community. *Journal of Applied Psychology, 88*, 1068–1081.

Schmitt, N. (2014). Personality and cognitive ability predictors of effective performance at work. *Annual Review of Organizational Psychology and Organizational Behavior, 1*, 45–65.

Schmitt, N., & Fandre, J. (2008). The validity of current selection methods. In S. Cartwright & C. L. Cooper (Eds.), *Oxford handbook of personnel psychology* (pp. 163–193). New York, NY: Oxford University Press.

Schmitt, N., Keeney, J., Oswald, F. L., Pleskac, T., Billington, A. Q., Sinha, R., & Zorzie, M. (2009). Prediction of four-year college student performance using cognitive and noncognitive predictors and the impact on demographic status of admitted students. *Journal of Applied Psychology, 94*, 1479–1497.

Schmitt, N., & Kunce, C. (2002). The effects of required elaboration of answers to bio-data questions. *Personnel Psychology, 55*, 569–588.

Schmitt, N., & Oswald, F. L. (2006). The impact of corrections for faking on the validity of noncognitive measures in selection settings. *Journal of Applied Psychology, 91*, 613–621.

Schmitt, N., Oswald, F. L., Kim, B. H., Gillespie, M. A., & Ramsay, L. J. (2004). The impact of justice and self-serving bias explanations for the perceived fairness of different types of selection tests in college admissions. *International Journal of Selection and Assessment, 12*, 160–171.

Schmitt, N., Oswald, F. L., Kim, B. H., Imus, A., Drzakowski, S., Friede, A., & Shivpuri, S. (2007). The use of background and ability profiles to predict college student outcomes. *Journal of Applied Psychology, 92*, 165–179.

Schmitt, N., Rogers, W., Chan, D., Sheppard, L., & Jennings, D. (1997). Adverse impact and predictive efficiency using various predictor combinations. *Journal of Applied Psychology, 82*, 719–730.

Stemler, S. E. (2012). What should university admissions tests predict? *Educational Psychologist, 47*, 5–17.

Sternberg, R. J., Bonney, C. R., Gabora, L., & Merrifield, M. (2012). WICS: A model for college and university admissions. *Educational Psychologist, 47*, 30–41.

Sternberg, R. J., & the Rainbow Collaborators. (2006). Augmenting the SAT through assessments of analytical, practical, and creative skills. In: *Choosing students: Higher education admissions tools for the 21st century* (pp. 159–176). Mahwah, NJ: Erlbaum.

Taber, T. D., & Hackman, J. D. (1976). Dimensions of undergraduate college performance. *Journal of Applied Psychology, 61*, 546–558.

Van der Linden, D., te Nijenhuis, J. T., & Bakker, A. B. (2010). The general factor of personality: A meta-analysis of Big Five intercorrelations and a criterion-related validity study. *Journal of Research in Personality, 44*, 315–327.

Weinstein, C. E., & Palmer, D. R. (2002). *User's manual for those administering the Learning and Study Strategies Inventory.* Clearwater, FL: H & H Publishing.

Willingham, W. W. (1985). *Success in college: The role of personal qualities and academic ability.* New York, NY: College Entrance Examination Board.

Willingham, W. W. (1998). *Validity in college selection: Context and evidence.* Paper presented at the Workshop on the Role of Tests in Higher Education Admissions, Washington, DC.

Zeegers, P. (2001). Approaches to learning in science: A longitudinal study. *British Journal of Educational Psychology, 71*, 115–132.

Zimmerman, W. S., Parks, H., Gray, K., & Michael, W. B. (1977). The validity of traditional cognitive measures and of scales of the Study Attitudes and Methods Survey in the prediction of the academic success of Educational Opportunity Program students. *Educational and Psychological Measurement, 37*, 465–470.

Establishing an International Standards Framework and Action Research Agenda for Workplace Readiness and Success

JULIYA GOLUBOVICH, RONG SU,
AND STEVEN B. ROBBINS ■

The 21st century global economy has witnessed the evolution of traditional jobs and the emergence of new jobs that create a changing landscape in the skill sets required for individuals to be successful in the labor market (Pellegrino & Hilton, 2012). The success of students entering the workforce for the first time or workers seeking new employment largely depends on their possession of the right skills to respond to the needs of the ever-changing workplace. Likewise, the competitiveness of organizations or countries in the global economy relies heavily on their capability to develop and maintain a pool of workers who can meet such skill requirements (Organization for Economic Co-operation and Development (OECD), 2012). However, employers in the United States and throughout the world frequently report a skill gap between the current workforce and the 21st century job requirements. A disconnect exists between the skills that students develop in the formal education system and the skill requirements in the labor market (McKinsey Center for Government, 2013). One of the primary reasons for this skill gap and mismatch, we argue, is the lack of a standards framework of fundamental skills that defines workplace readiness and predicts workplace success. Establishing such a standards framework is critical for aligning the expectations and goals of formal education, organizational practices in selection and staffing, and workers' continuing training and development within an organization or in informal learning environments. It is essential for building a more prepared, competitive workforce in the 21st century global economy. In this chapter, we propose an international standards framework of foundational skills using a combination of theoretical and empirical approaches. We discuss an active research agenda to assess this set of skills and to determine the minimum levels of these skills individuals need to meet the demands of the workplace.

We begin the chapter by presenting the concept of talent supply chain management, explaining our choice to focus on middle-skill jobs (jobs that require a high school diploma, training in vocational schools, an associate's degree, or a 4-year bachelor's degree), highlighting the gap between the skills that workforce entrants have and those required by employers throughout the world, and discussing the need for a standards framework. We then provide an overview of various domains of predictors of work readiness and success (including knowledge, abilities, skills, personality traits, and career interests) to introduce the types of attributes that should be considered when trying to identify critical dimensions of attributes required for middle-skill jobs. Next, we detail our methodology for establishing these critical dimensions of attributes required within the international job space and present the results of our analyses. Thereafter, we outline a methodology for choosing assessments of known critical attributes, establishing minimum score levels needed for entry into various segments of jobs, and profiling jobs to understand their specific requirements. We conclude with a discussion of the extent to which we would expect particular types of assessments to be usable across jobs of different types and across different levels of complexity, as well as across different cultures.

TALENT SUPPLY CHAIN MANAGEMENT

Organizations have become very good at managing global supply chains. Supply chains are generally made up of different "tiers" of suppliers working to meet the requirements and schedules of subsequent contributors in the manufacturing process. Supply chains work well when the company that manufactures the final product (the "original equipment manufacturer" (OEM)) clearly communicates requirements and schedules to all parties in the supply chain so that they can respond appropriately with high-quality goods and services.

Applying this analogy to workers, preschools and primary, secondary, and postsecondary institutions comprise the "talent supply chain" for employers (the OEMs). To supply employers with workers who meet their standards, the consecutive suppliers in the supply chain need to align to a common set of standards for workplace readiness and success. We need to work with employers to articulate these standards.

The notion that there may be a common set of standards, or specifically a set of skills, that individuals need to be ready to meet the demands of the 21st century workplace (i.e., to be "workplace ready") is not inconsistent with the idea that occupations may differ in how much of a certain skill individuals need to be successful in that occupation or the minimum level of a skill employers would accept for a new hire. Furthermore, industries and occupations certainly have skill set requirements unique to them (i.e., job-specific skills). In light of occupational differences, talent supply chains need to develop systems akin to those used by manufacturers, who plan production and "pull" appropriate amounts of materials through the supply chain. Similarly, employers representing various occupations could pull needed workers through the supply chain by informing educational institutions and potential workers themselves about the skills (and skill levels) required and the forecasted demand for employees.

MIDDLE-SKILL JOBS

In trying to articulate a set of standards for workplace readiness and success, we focus on the "middle-skill" sector of jobs that may or may not require some education (e.g., associate's degree, 4-year college degree) or training (e.g., certifications) beyond high school. There are several reasons for this focus. First, workers in these occupations represent the majority of the workforce. Eighty-three percent of the occupations in the international work space are middle-skill jobs. Examples of these occupations include air traffic controllers, nuclear power reactor operators, dental hygienists, criminal investigators, nurses, flight attendants, telecom technicians, firefighters, police officers, mechanics, construction workers, electricians, and plumbers. Second, because many of these jobs require interaction with others, judgment, and complex problem solving, they are more difficult for technology to automate relative to transaction- or production-based jobs (McKinsey Global Institute, 2012). As such, middle-skill occupations are projected to evidence above average growth in the coming decade, in contrast to low-skills jobs, for which below average growth is expected (Lockard & Wolf, 2012). This means that skilled workers in these jobs will be in high demand. Third, because many of these jobs also pay fairly well— it is estimated that two out of five middle-skill jobs in the United States offer an annual salary of at least $50,000 (Georgetown Public Policy Institute, 2012)— they can provide livable wages for workforce entrants. However, reports detail an ongoing global "skills gap" or "skills shortage," in which emerging and industrialized countries are experiencing difficulty filling available middle-skill and other jobs with qualified workers (McKinsey Center for Government, 2014; McKinsey Global Institute, 2012; OECD, 2012).

SKILLS GAP

As technology and global competition drive workplace expectations to evolve and demand higher quality and efficiency, the future of work in advanced economies is being hampered by a growing mismatch between the skills employers want and the skills the workforce has (McKinsey Global Institute, 2012). Thirty-nine percent of employers surveyed in nine countries (Brazil, Germany, India, Mexico, Morocco, Saudi Arabia, Turkey, the United Kingdom, and the United States) reported that a skills shortage was a leading reason for entry-level vacancies (McKinsey Center for Government, 2013). Youth are one of the groups most impacted by the skills gap. In 2011, the unemployment rate for the 15- to 29-year-old age group was 15% across 148 countries and areas—three times the unemployment rate for the 30- to 49-year-old and 50- to 69-year-old age groups (Gallup, 2012). Although the possession of a diploma or degree signals that a job applicant met some threshold of training, employers are often uncertain about applicants' levels of skills (McKinsey Center for Government, 2013). Education providers do not always understand how to help their students get jobs commensurate with their education and interests or even recognize improving the education to employment system to be one of their responsibilities (McKinsey Center for Government, 2013). Relatedly, across nine countries, just half of recently surveyed youth believed that pursuing postsecondary education improved their employment opportunities (McKinsey Center for Government, 2013).

These issues pertaining to the skills shortage are of growing domestic and international concern and reinforce the need for a comprehensive system to identify, build, and certify critical workplace skills so as to better bridge the education and work systems (Council on Competitiveness, 2008; Deloitte & National Association of Manufacturers, 2005; National Commission on Adult Literacy, 2008; OECD, 2013). The OECD (2012) is calling for those with a stake in skills policies (e.g., governments, education providers, organizations, and industries) to work together to develop strategies of addressing the mismatch between worker skills and employer needs. Suggestions include improving the alignment of education and training with labor market requirements via (a) provision of more and better information regarding the skill demands of and opportunities in the labor market, which education and training providers can respond to with curriculum changes; and (b) development of transparent national and cross-national qualifications frameworks tied to skill assessments that allow educators and employers to communicate about the levels of job-relevant skills of individuals flowing through the education to employment system (OECD, 2012, 2013).

The increasing emphasis on development of competencies through formal education or informal training programs reflects this movement toward establishing necessary competencies or skills rather than assuming that formal degree programs are the only path to workplace access and success (Bartram, 2005; Shippmann et al., 2000). Use of valid and reliable assessments as the basis for recognizing and certifying individuals' proficiency in job-relevant skills is critical. Skill levels can be certified regardless of how they were acquired—via formal education or more recent work experiences—allowing individuals' continued learning past formal education to be recognized by future employers (OECD, 2012).

Although employers report that workforce entrants also lack occupation-specific skills (e.g., technical and engineering skills; McKinsey Global Institute, 2012), a shortage of general skills that transverse different occupations (e.g., work ethic, teamwork, and problem solving) is acknowledged as a key issue in the skills gap (McKinsey Center for Government, 2013, 2014). Our focus is on the skills gap in these general, 21st century workplace skills.

ESTABLISHING A STANDARDS FRAMEWORK

Although there are a multitude of calls for, and efforts to, identify critical 21st century skills (an overview of these frameworks is provided later; Burrus, Jackson, Xi, & Steinberg, 2013; Markle, Brenneman, Jackson, Burrus, & Robbins, 2013; Pellegrino & Hilton, 2012; US Department of Labor, 1991), there is no consensus on a framework that organizes the essential workplace skills and establishes standards and benchmarks for these skills for middle-skill jobs within the United States and globally. It is essential to establish such a framework with evidence-based standards and benchmarks tied to workplace performance requirements in order to (a) enable employers to communicate with educational institutions about skill requirements for workers in middle-skill jobs, (b) guide educational institutions in preparing students with the necessary skills for entry into such jobs, (c) assist organizations in selecting and training employees (to raise employees' levels of critical skills) to establish a strong workforce in a global economy, and (d) ensure a supply chain to meet the demands of traditional and emergent jobs within an international context.

We propose to (a) identify a set of critical workplace skills for middle-skill jobs that will form the basis of the framework and (b) subsequently describe a process for identifying and validating a set of assessments that may be used to measure and certify individuals' proficiency in these skills and establishing minimum levels of these skills that individuals require to be considered ready to meet the demands of the workplace. These critical skills will serve as a foundation on top of which job-specific competencies can be "stacked."

We begin by turning to the research literature (mainly in the field of industrial/organizational psychology) to identify domains of individual differences that are important predictors of work readiness and success. We conceptualize work readiness and success as including training performance, job performance, job satisfaction, job tenure, and earnings.

CRITICAL DOMAINS OF PREDICTORS FOR WORK READINESS AND SUCCESS

Economists and psychologists have studied a variety of personal resources or attributes (often called "human capital") that are developed through experience, schooling, and other forms of training and contribute to individuals' work readiness and success (Heckman, Hsee, & Rubinstein, 2000; Judge, Klinger, & Simon, 2010). Although levels of education, training, and work experience are often used as indicators of human capital, what human capital really reflects are the foundational and job-relevant competencies acquired or influenced through educational attainment and these other experiences, including knowledge, skills, abilities, personality traits (i.e., reflected in systematic behavioral tendencies), and interests. As we further explain next, individual differences in these factors help explain differences in individuals' levels of work readiness and success. Our goal is not to review the extensive literature on these individual difference domains but, rather, to highlight their importance for work readiness and success.

Knowledge

Individuals develop two types of knowledge: declarative and procedural (Campbell, McCloy, Oppler, & Sager, 1993). Declarative knowledge refers to a collection of interrelated facts ("book" knowledge) about a certain domain, such as chemistry, geography, history, or math. Procedural knowledge pertains to knowing how to apply one's declarative knowledge to perform a certain task. Individuals vary with respect to the domains in which they have deep knowledge (Ackerman, 1996). In Campbell et al.'s (1993) model of performance, declarative and procedural knowledge (and skills) are considered two major determinants of job performance. A specific type of knowledge should be a determinant of performance to the extent that it is relevant to an individual's occupation (i.e., job-related); job-related knowledge tests have been shown to be valid predictors of performance both on their own and incrementally above measures of cognitive ability (Hunter, 1986; Schmidt & Hunter, 1998).

Abilities

Abilities are relatively stable psychological characteristics that allow individuals to perform particular types of tasks (Tippins & Hilton, 2010). A commonly used framework of abilities organizes 52 specific abilities under 15 more general abilities, which are in turn organized into cognitive, physical, psychomotor, and sensory ability categories (Fleishman & Reilly, 1992; Peterson, Mumford, Borman, Jeanneret, & Fleishman, 1999). Cognitive ability is considered the best predictor of job performance and training success (Ree & Earles, 1991; Ree, Earles, & Teachout, 1994). Other abilities (e.g., physical ability) are also important for many jobs, but their importance across job types varies much more (Schmidt, 2002). In Campbell et al.'s (1993) model of performance, abilities are viewed as indirect determinants of performance. Whereas, as mentioned previously, declarative and procedural knowledge and skills are viewed as direct determinants of job performance, abilities, which are less malleable, tend to provide a foundation and ceiling for individuals' declarative and procedural knowledge and skills (Campbell et al., 1993).

Skills

A skill can be defined as a set of strategies and processes than enable individuals to acquire and work with information within a specific performance domain (Tippins & Hilton, 2010). Some examples of skills include listening, writing, reading comprehension, critical thinking, complex problem solving, time management, social skills, and technical skills (e.g., programming). Skills are developed over time through training or experience (Tippins & Hilton, 2010). Skills that involve performing physical tasks require cognitive abilities for initial performance during acquisition and psychomotor abilities (e.g., manual dexterity) for later performance following consistent practice (Ackerman, 1988). In Campbell et al.'s (1993) model of performance, skills are one of the direct determinants of job performance. Next, we highlight several types of skills that are important for work readiness and success.

Many jobs require individuals to effectively navigate social interactions to be successful. Not surprisingly, social skills have been found to be related to job performance (Ferris, Witt, & Hochwarter, 2001). Importantly, the effects of social skills on job performance may be moderated by conscientiousness and cognitive ability (Ferris et al., 2001; Witt & Ferris, 2003). Those who are socially skilled can better meet the social demands of work if they are likewise conscientious and/or intelligent. On the other hand, individuals who are not conscientious or intelligent will tend to not perform well regardless of their level of social skills. Social skills become especially important as individuals get promoted into managerial positions that require communicating with, understanding, and motivating individuals with diverse backgrounds and needs (Kilduff & Day, 1994). Socially skilled individuals are more likely to be viewed as promotable and get promoted in the first place (Kilduff & Day, 1994; Wayne, Liden, Graf, & Ferris, 1997).

Critical thinking and problem solving are other examples of skills employers deem highly important for workforce readiness and success and that are found to be associated with job performance (Ejiogu, Yang, Trent, & Rose, 2006; Kesselman, Lopez, & Lopez, 1982; Liu, Frankel, & Roohr, 2014; Watson & Glaser, 2009). As mentioned previously, as the world of work becomes more complex due to technology and increasing efficiency, workers will be expected to perform more complex, non-automated tasks. This means that critical thinking and problem solving skills will become even more important.

Personality Traits

Personality traits can be defined as relatively stable individual differences in people's tendency to behave, think, and feel in particular ways (Caspi, 1998). The five-factor model is the dominant framework used to measure personality. The five factors are Extraversion, Conscientiousness, Agreeableness, Neuroticism (or reversely, Emotional Stability), and Openness to Experience. Individual differences in personality predict a range of work-related outcomes (e.g., job search effort, training performance, job performance, and wages) (Almlund, Duckworth, Heckman, & Kautz, 2011; Barrick, Mount, & Judge, 2001). Notably, the importance of a given trait varies by job type and nature of the criterion examined (Barrick et al., 2001; Sackett & Walmsley, 2014). For example, Extraversion predicts leadership particularly well (Judge, Bono, Ilies, & Gerhardt, 2002), and Openness predicts decision-making performance better when adaptability is required and work performance better in jobs with strong innovation or creativity requirements (Judge & Zapata, 2015; LePine, Colquitt, & Erez, 2000). However, Conscientiousness, Emotional Stability, and Agreeableness are related to performance in different types of jobs more so than the other traits (Barrick et al., 2001; Sackett & Walmsley, 2014).

There can also be value in examining more narrow personality traits as predictors of certain workplace behavior and performance (Bergner, Neubauer, & Kreuzthaler, 2010; Griffin & Hesketh, 2004; Judge et al., 2002; Paunonen & Ashton, 2001). For example, results of Judge et al.'s study suggested that two of the facets of Extraversion (dominance and sociability) may predict leadership better than may overall measures of Extraversion. As another example, Griffin and Hesketh's study suggested that Openness *to internal experience* and Openness *to external experience* may have different associations with performance, and these associations may differ in direction (i.e., positive vs. negative correlations). Similarly, Hough's (1992) meta-analysis showed that facets of Conscientiousness (achievement and dependability) were differentially related to performance outcomes; achievement was a stronger positive predictor of overall performance and sales effectiveness. Furthermore, achievement showed a positive association with creativity, whereas dependability showed a negative association. Drasgow et al. (2012) reasoned that optimal prediction of criteria may be achieved by combining the narrow personality traits that comprise separate traits within the Big Five into composite predictors (e.g., integrity).

Career Interests

Individuals vary in their preferences for particular types of activities and situations (dispositional interests) and tend to prefer and seek out work environments that allow the expression of these interests (Holland, 1997; Rounds & Su, 2014; Su, Rounds, & Armstrong, 2009). Holland's (1959, 1997) interest model, the most widely used framework for interest measurement, specifies six types of career interests: Realistic, Investigative, Artistic, Social, Enterprising, and Conventional. Both interest levels and interest congruence, or the fit between individuals' interests and work environments, have been shown to be positively related to individuals' levels of task performance, willingness to assist colleagues, job satisfaction, job tenure, and earnings (Neumann, Olitsky, & Robbins, 2009; Nye, Su, Rounds, & Drasgow, 2012; Su, 2012; Tsabari, Tziner, & Meir, 2005, van Iddekinge, Putka, & Campbell, 2011; van Iddekinge, Roth, Putka, & Lanivich, 2011). Interests serve as a source of motivational force that drives engagement and persistence in pursued activities (Nye et al., 2012; Rounds & Su, 2014). In Campbell et al.'s (1993) model of performance, interests serve as indirect determinants of job performance via their influence on the acquisition of declarative knowledge and procedural knowledge and skills.

CRITICAL DIMENSIONS OF WORKFORCE KNOWLEDGE, SKILLS, ABILITIES, AND OTHER CHARACTERISTICS IN THE INTERNATIONAL JOB SPACE

Building on the critical domains of individual differences in predicting work readiness and success discussed previously, we continue to identify a standards framework of workforce knowledge, skills, abilities, and other characteristics (KSAOs, a term commonly used in industrial and organizational psychology; the "other" characteristics refer to personality traits and interests) in the international job space. By "standards framework," we suggest that the KSAOs in the critical domains of individual differences can be meaningfully organized into a number of factors or dimensions. These dimensions of KSAOs reflect the complex nature of worker requirements in the 21st century in that they cut across multiple individual difference domains and represent the core competencies needed for individuals to succeed in today's workplace.

As a first step to develop this standards framework of workplace readiness and success, we identified a pool of required KSAOs from the prevailing US occupational classification system. We obtained the KSAOs from the Occupational Information Network (O*NET) production database 18.1 (National Center for O*NET Development, 2014). Developed under the sponsorship of the US Department of Labor/Employment and Training Administration, the O*NET database provides comprehensive and regularly updated information on various aspects of worker attributes, including 52 abilities, 33 knowledge components, 35 skills, 16 work styles (which reflect personality traits), and 6 interest types for more than 900 US occupations (Peterson et al., 1999). The importance of the ability, knowledge, skill, and work style requirements for O*NET occupations is rated by job incumbents and occupation experts on a scale of 1 to 5, where 1 = not important, 2 = somewhat important, 3 = important, 4 = very important, and 5 = extremely important. The interest profiles for O*NET occupations are on a scale of 1 to 7, where higher scores indicate that an occupation is more representative of a certain type of work environment. The O*NET occupations are organized by the 2010 Standard Occupational Classification system (SOC; US Bureau of Labor Statistics (BLS), 2010) and stratified by their required levels of education, training, and experience—that is, job zones: job zone 1, some of these occupations may require a high school diploma or GED certificate; job zone 2, most of these occupations require a high school diploma; job zone 3, most of these occupations require training in vocational schools, related on-the-job experience, or an associate's degree; job zone 4, most of these occupations require a 4-year bachelor's degree; and job zone 5, most of these occupations require graduate school training (Oswald, Campbell, McCloy, Rivkin, & Lewis, 1999).

Next, to determine the required KSAOs in the international job space, we crosswalked the International Standard Classification of Occupations (ISCO; International Labour Organization (ILO), 2008) to occupations in the O*NET system (Peterson et al., 1999). First adopted in 1957 and most recently updated in 2008, ISCO was developed to serve as (a) a basis for the international reporting, comparison, and exchange of statistical and administrative data about occupations; (b) a model for the development of national and regional classifications of occupations; and (c) a system that can be used directly in countries that have not developed their own national classifications (ILO, 2008). The 2008 ISCO system organizes 619 occupational titles. By building a crosswalk between the prevailing US and international occupational systems, we were able to link the ISCO occupations with the rich occupational information from the O*NET database and determine the job zone and required KSAOs for each of the ISCO occupations.

Furthermore, we identified salient KSAOs across middle-skill ISCO occupations. As previously discussed, our current analysis focuses on occupations in the middle-skill job space (i.e., occupations that are in job zones 2, 3, and 4). We define salient KSAOs as those deemed moderately important and above (i.e., importance rating ≥ 3) for two-thirds (66.7%) or more of middle-skill ISCO occupations.

Finally, we conducted principal component analysis (PCA) on the previously discussed list of salient KSAOs to identify core dimensions of workplace readiness and success in middle-skill jobs. Five dimensions were identified: (a) Critical Thinking and Complex Problem Solving, (b) Oral and Written Communication, (c) Intrapersonal and Interpersonal Skills, (d) Achievement and Innovation, and (e) Detail Orientation. Next, we detail our procedures and findings.

Development of the ISCO-O*NET Crosswalk

We crosswalked the ISCO occupations to the O*NET database using the existing BLS crosswalk between the 2008 ISCO system to the 2010 SOC system (BLS, 2012) and the 2010 SOC–O*NET taxonomy (National Center for O*NET Development, 2010). As previously described, information on 52 abilities, 33 knowledge components, 35 skills, 16 work styles (personality traits), and 6 interests required by each occupation was obtained from O*NET database 18.1. This database was last updated in July 2013. Because some ISCO codes correspond to more than one O*NET occupation, we performed several additional procedures to ensure that the O*NET occupations within any ISCO code had sufficient agreement in their KSAOs before they were aggregated. First,

$r_{WG(J)}$ was computed for every ISCO code as an index of within-group interrater agreement (IRA; James, Demaree, & Wolf, 1993; LeBreton & Senter, 2008). The overwhelming majority (93.7%) of ISCO occupations had an $r_{WG(J)}$ above .90, indicating very strong agreement. Seventeen ISCO occupations had an $r_{WG(J)}$ between .85 and .90, and 1 ISCO occupation had an $r_{WG(J)}$ of .78, indicating strong agreement. These ISCO occupations were examined closely to identify and exclude any O*NET occupation that potentially lowered the interrater agreement and should not be classified within an ISCO code. Second, profile correlations of KSAO ratings for O*NET occupations within an ISCO code were computed as an index of within-group interrater reliability (IRR; LeBreton & Senter, 2008). Most profile correlations were above .80. Any O*NET occupations with a profile correlation below .80 were again inspected, and the ISCO–O*NET crosswalk was revised. In addition, a subject matter expert further reviewed the entire crosswalk to identify any ISCO–O*NET linkage that required revision. Twelve ISCO codes without meaningful corresponding O*NET occupations (e.g., 1439-Service managers not elsewhere classified, 4414-Scribes and related workers, and 6123-Apiarists and sericulturists) were excluded from the crosswalk. As a result, a total of 408 ISCO occupations were matched with O*NET occupations in the crosswalk. Among these ISCO occupations, the majority (91.42%) correspond to less than 5 O*NET occupations. One ISCO code (2310-University and higher education teachers) corresponds to 35 O*NET occupations (university professors in different subjects) with satisfactory IRA and IRR. A frequency table with the number of O*NET occupations within ISCO codes is presented in Table 13.1.

If an ISCO occupation had multiple corresponding O*NET occupations, the means were taken from the KSAOs of all corresponding O*NET occupations to represent the KSAOs of that ISCO occupation. Similarly, the average job zone of all corresponding O*NET occupations was used to represent the job zone for an ISCO occupation. For example, the ISCO occupation "Computer Network Professionals" has two corresponding occupations in the O*NET system: "Computer Network Architects (15-1143.00)" and "Telecommunications Engineering Specialists (15-1143.01)." "Computer Network Architects" is an occupation in job zone 4, for which considerable skills and experience are needed and a 4-year bachelor's degree is usually required, whereas "Telecommunications Engineering Specialists" is an occupation in job zone 3, for which medium levels of skills and experience are needed and training in vocational schools or associate's degrees are typically required. Therefore, the ISCO occupation "Computer Network Professionals" received a mean job zone of 3.5 in the ISCO–O*NET crosswalk. The ratings on 52 abilities, 33 knowledge components, 35 skills, 16 work styles (personality traits), and 6 interests for "Computer Network Architects" and "Telecommunications Engineering

Table 13.1 NUMBER OF O*NET OCCUPATIONS
WITHIN ISCO CODES—FREQUENCY

Count	No. of ISCO Codes	%
1	168	41.2
2	97	23.8
3	58	14.2
4	30	7.4
5	20	4.9
6	8	2.0
7	8	2.0
8	3	0.7
9	3	0.7
10	3	0.7
11	2	0.5
12	3	0.7
13	1	0.2
14	1	0.2
15	1	0.2
16	1	0.2
35	1	0.2

Specialists" were averaged to represent the KSAOs for "Computer Network Professionals."

Identifying Salient KSAOs Across Middle-Skill ISCO Occupations

Next, we examined salient KSAOs across all middle-skill ISCO occupations. Middle-skill occupations were classified as all occupations in job zones 2, 3, and 4. These job zones include occupations that range from requiring some previous work-related skill, knowledge, or experience and typically a high school diploma to occupations requiring considerable skills and experience and usually a 4-year bachelor's degree. This group of jobs constitutes the majority of the workforce (338 out of 408, or 83% of the ISCO jobs). Therefore, identifying the fundamental KSAOs required to be successful in these jobs is critical for building a qualified workforce and a strong economy.

Because the job zone value for each ISCO occupation was calculated from the average of one or more O*NET occupations, it may be a noninteger. Job zones for ISCO occupations were recoded using the following parameters: An occupation was assigned to job zone 1 if its job zone value was less than 1.5; an occupation was assigned to job zone 2 if its job zone value was greater than or equal to 1.5 and less than 2.5; an occupation was assigned to job zone 3 if its job zone value was greater than or equal to 2.5 and less than 3.5; an occupation was assigned to job zone 4 if its job zone value was greater than or equal to 3.5 and less than 4.5; and an occupation was assigned to job zone 5 if its job zone value was greater than or equal to 4.5. This procedure resulted in 138 occupations in job zone 2, 112 occupations in job zone 3, and 88 occupations in job zone 4—a total of 338 occupations in the international, middle-skill job space.

Each of the KSAOs across all of the occupations in job zones 2, 3, and 4 was examined. A salient ability, knowledge, skill, or personality (work style) requirement was defined as one that had an importance rating greater than or equal to 3 (i.e., important to extremely important) in two-thirds (66.7%) or more occupations within the targeted job zones. In total, 15 of the 52 abilities (primarily verbal abilities, idea generation and reasoning abilities, and sensory abilities), 2 of the 33 knowledge components (customer and personal service and English language), 12 of the 35 skills, and all 16 of the work styles were identified as integral to success across the majority of middle-skill jobs. A complete list of salient KSAOs across all middle-skill occupations and within each job zone is provided in Table 13.2. All six interest types were included because each describes the preference for a certain type of work environment.

Determining Core Dimensions of KSAOs Across Middle-Skill Occupations

To determine the key dimensions of KSAOs across middle-skill occupations and within each job zone from the previously presented list, we conducted PCA with oblique promax rotation because these core competencies required for workplace success are likely to be correlated. Parallel analysis was used to indicate the number of components that should be extracted in a PCA.

Thirty-seven KSAOs that are salient across all occupations in job zone 2 to job zone 4 from Table 13.2 were included in the analysis of all 338 middle-skill occupations. In addition, six interest types were included in the analysis because of their critical role in predicting job performance and career success. Five components were extracted and labeled as Critical Thinking and Problem Solving, Communication, Intrapersonal and Interpersonal Skills, Innovation and Achievement, and Detail Orientation. Item loadings on their corresponding components are listed in Table 13.3. As shown in this table, each dimension cuts across multiple individual difference domains. For example, the dimension of *Critical Thinking and Problem Solving* includes reasoning and information ordering abilities, critical thinking, decision-making, and coordination skills,

		Job Zone 2	Job Zone 3	Job Zone 4	Overall (2–4)
Abilities	Oral comprehension	**89.1**	**98.2**	**100.0**	**95.0**
	Written comprehension	50.7	**90.2**	**100.0**	**76.6**
	Oral expression	**84.8**	**99.1**	**100.0**	**93.5**
	Written expression	23.2	**75.9**	**97.7**	60.1
	Fluency of ideas	5.1	33.0	**79.5**	33.7
	Originality	6.5	25.9	**75.0**	30.8
	Problem sensitivity	**90.6**	**96.4**	**100.0**	**95.0**
	Deductive reasoning	**70.3**	**95.5**	**100.0**	**86.4**
	Inductive reasoning	53.6	**88.4**	**97.7**	**76.6**
	Information ordering	**80.4**	**96.4**	**100.0**	**90.8**
	Category flexibility	34.1	**84.8**	**97.7**	**67.5**
	Selective attention	63.0	**75.0**	**79.5**	**71.3**
	Arm–hand steadiness	**68.1**	47.3	9.1	45.9
	Manual dexterity	**67.4**	39.3	2.3	41.1
	Near vision	**96.4**	**100.0**	**100.0**	**98.5**
	Speech recognition	**76.1**	**96.4**	**98.9**	**88.8**
	Speech clarity	**71.7**	**95.5**	**98.9**	**86.7**
Knowledge	Administration and management	18.8	38.4	**69.3**	38.5
	Customer and personal service	56.5	**82.1**	**80.7**	**71.3**
	Computers and electronics	10.1	50.9	**73.9**	40.2
	English language	47.1	**85.7**	**98.9**	**73.4**
Skills	Reading comprehension	47.1	**88.4**	**100.0**	**74.6**
	Active listening	**79.0**	**99.1**	**98.9**	**90.8**
	Writing	18.1	65.2	**98.9**	54.7
	Speaking	**68.8**	**93.8**	**100.0**	**85.2**
	Critical thinking	**73.9**	**99.1**	**98.9**	**88.8**
	Active learning	8.7	62.5	**95.5**	49.1
	Monitoring	**71.0**	**85.7**	**98.9**	**83.1**
	Social perceptiveness	34.1	**67.0**	**86.4**	58.6
	Coordination	45.7	**76.8**	**93.2**	**68.3**
	Complex problem-solving	28.3	**72.3**	**96.6**	60.7
	Judgment and decision-making	37.7	**83.0**	**98.9**	**68.6**
	Time management	32.6	**75.9**	**95.5**	63.3
Work styles	Achievement/effort	**97.1**	**100.0**	**100.0**	**98.8**
	Persistence	**95.7**	**100.0**	**100.0**	**98.2**
	Initiative	**97.8**	**100.0**	**100.0**	**99.1**

(*continued*)

Table 13.2 CONTINUED

	Job Zone 2	Job Zone 3	Job Zone 4	Overall (2–4)
Leadership	79.7	**93.8**	**97.7**	89.1
Cooperation	**100.0**	**100.0**	**100.0**	100.0
Concern for others	**94.2**	**99.1**	**97.7**	96.7
Social orientation	**76.8**	**82.1**	**72.7**	77.5
Self-control	**98.6**	**100.0**	**100.0**	99.4
Stress tolerance	**97.1**	**99.1**	**98.9**	98.2
Adaptability/flexibility	**99.3**	**100.0**	**100.0**	99.7
Dependability	**100.0**	**100.0**	**100.0**	100.0
Attention to detail	**100.0**	**100.0**	**100.0**	100.0
Integrity	**99.3**	**100.0**	**100.0**	99.7
Independence	**100.0**	**100.0**	**98.9**	99.7
Innovation	**85.5**	**99.1**	**96.6**	92.9
Analytical thinking	**82.6**	**98.2**	**98.9**	92.0
Achievement	35.5	**94.6**	**100.0**	71.9
Working conditions	50.7	**92.0**	**98.9**	76.9
Recognition	18.1	74.1	**100.0**	58.0
Relationships	**90.6**	**94.6**	**96.6**	93.5
Support	**92.0**	**92.9**	**97.7**	93.8
Independence	**68.1**	**96.4**	**100.0**	85.8

[a]Bolded values denote that the job characteristic is important in two-thirds or more occupations within a specific job zone.

as well as the analytical thinking work style; the dimension of *Communication* encompasses oral and written expression and comprehension abilities, active listening and speaking skills, knowledge about the English language, and Enterprising interests; and the dimension of *Detail Orientation* comprises the attention to detail work style, near vision ability, and Investigative interests.

A notable finding from the current study is the importance of "noncognitive" skills for workplace success, as highlighted by two of the five critical dimensions: Intrapersonal and Interpersonal Skills and Innovation and Achievement. The *Intrapersonal and Interpersonal Skills* dimension is marked by intrapersonal attributes including self-control, stress tolerance, dependability, adaptability/flexibility, as well as interpersonal attributes including social orientation, concern for others, cooperation, and Social interests; the *Innovation and Achievement* dimension is composed of innovation, initiative, achievement/ effort, persistence work style, and Artistic interests. The previously mentioned

KSAO	Component 1	Component 2	Component 3	Component 4	Component 5
Deductive reasoning—ability	**0.91**	0.64	0.29	0.39	0.36
Problem sensitivity—ability	**0.91**	0.43	0.33	0.25	0.21
Critical thinking—skill	**0.91**	0.68	0.29	0.50	0.34
Inductive reasoning—ability	**0.90**	0.63	0.29	0.41	0.35
Judgment and decision-making—skill	**0.88**	0.63	0.30	0.51	0.21
Information ordering—ability	**0.82**	0.46	0.15	0.34	0.53
Monitoring—skill	**0.79**	0.43	0.40	0.31	0.08
Analytical thinking—work style	**0.74**	0.45	0.25	0.57	0.61
Category flexibility—ability	**0.73**	0.47	0.04	0.45	0.44
Coordination—skill	**0.70**	0.69	0.57	0.45	-0.07
Selective attention—ability	**0.57**	0.05	0.04	0.05	0.21
Speaking—skill	0.57	**0.95**	0.60	0.44	0.19
Oral expression—ability	0.58	**0.94**	0.59	0.45	0.23
Oral comprehension—ability	0.62	**0.92**	0.58	0.42	0.31
Active listening—skill	0.65	**0.92**	0.55	0.43	0.31
Speech clarity—ability	0.56	**0.92**	0.60	0.43	0.15
Speech recognition—ability	0.57	**0.90**	0.59	0.39	0.21
Realistic—interest	-0.18	**-0.85**	-0.51	-0.38	-0.28
Written comprehension—ability	0.68	**0.83**	0.35	0.40	0.59
Reading comprehension—skill	0.70	**0.81**	0.30	0.44	0.60
Enterprising—interest	0.35	**0.76**	0.44	0.28	-0.06
English language—knowledge	0.42	**0.75**	0.47	0.46	0.57
Integrity—work style	0.37	**0.73**	0.66	0.42	0.44
Customer and personal service—knowledge	0.13	**0.61**	0.60	0.24	0.13

(continued)

Table 13.3 CONTINUED

KSAO	Component 1	Component 2	Component 3	Component 4	Component 5
Self-control—work style	0.24	0.49	**0.91**	0.20	0.06
Concern for others—work style	0.09	0.42	**0.89**	0.21	-0.03
Social orientation—work style	0.17	0.51	**0.88**	0.23	-0.09
Stress tolerance—work style	0.43	0.58	**0.83**	0.37	0.29
Cooperation—work style	0.30	0.58	**0.82**	0.37	0.30
Dependability—work style	0.33	0.54	**0.80**	0.50	0.32
Adaptability/flexibility—work style	0.54	0.63	**0.76**	0.65	0.38
Social—interest	0.18	0.63	**0.74**	0.40	-0.02
Leadership—work style	0.63	0.52	**0.66**	0.55	0.03
Innovation—work style	0.40	0.32	0.31	**0.88**	0.24
Initiative—work style	0.59	0.63	0.54	**0.80**	0.41
Achievement/effort—work style	0.46	0.52	0.42	**0.77**	0.43
Persistence—work style	0.53	0.53	0.47	**0.77**	0.39
Artistic—interest	0.03	0.20	0.04	**0.72**	0.13
Independence—work style	0.02	0.43	0.36	**0.47**	0.16
Conventional—interest	-0.06	0.26	0.04	**-0.46**	0.39
Attention to detail—work style	0.30	0.28	0.27	0.42	**0.79**
Near vision—ability	0.49	0.14	-0.07	0.07	**0.63**
Investigative—interest	0.51	-0.02	-0.26	0.21	**0.52**

[a]Extraction method: principal component analysis; rotation method: promax with Kaiser normalization; components extracted: (1) Critical Thinking and Problem Solving; (2) Communication; (3) Intrapersonal and Interpersonal Skills; (4) Innovation and Achievement; and (5) Detail Orientation. Bolded values denote KSAOs loaded most highly on each component.

Table 13.4 REQUIRED LEVELS OF MATHEMATICS AND ENGLISH LANGUAGE SKILLS
BY JOB ZONE: JOB ZONE 2[a]

	Scale (Against Anchor Statements)						
	≥0	≥1	≥2	≥3	≥4	≥5	≥6
Importance							
Mathematics	100.0	100.0	79.0	2.9	0.0		
English Language	100.0	100.0	98.6	47.1	1.4		
Level							
Mathematics	100.0	97.8	83.3	36.2	2.9	0.0	0.0
English Language	100.0	100.0	94.2	31.2	1.4	0.0	0.0

[a]Scale anchors for Mathematics: level 1, add two numbers; level 4, analyze data to determine areas with the highest stakes; level 6, derive a complex mathematical equation. Scale anchors for English Language: level 2, write a thank-you note; level 4, edit a feature article in a local newspaper; level 6, teach a college English class.

five dimensions represent the core competencies required to be successful in today's workplace.

It may seem surprising that knowledge in Mathematics is not deemed critical across all middle-skill jobs (only 44.4% of these ISCO occupations have importance ratings on math knowledge of ≥ 3), primarily due to the lower complexity of the occupations in job zones 2 and 3 and the limited importance of math knowledge to these jobs. However, essentially all of the middle-skill jobs require basic levels of numeracy knowledge and skills, including comprehending and calculating fundamental mathematics such as addition, subtraction, multiplication, and division (Tables 13.4–13.6). Similarly, knowledge in

Table 13.5 REQUIRED LEVELS OF MATHEMATICS AND ENGLISH LANGUAGE SKILLS
BY JOB ZONE: JOB ZONE 3[a]

	Scale (Against Anchor Statements)						
	≥0	≥1	≥2	≥3	≥4	≥5	≥6
Importance							
Mathematics	100.0	100.0	92.0	10.7	0.0		
English Language	100.0	100.0	100.0	85.7	11.6		
Level							
Mathematics	100.0	100.0	97.3	67.0	17.0	0.9	0.0
English Language	100.0	100.0	99.1	83.0	19.6	0.0	0.0

[a]Scale anchors for Mathematics: level 1, add two numbers; level 4, analyze data to determine areas with the highest stakes; level 6, derive a complex mathematical equation. Scale anchors for English Language: level 2, write a thank-you note; level 4, edit a feature article in a local newspaper; level 6, teach a college English class.

Table 13.6 REQUIRED LEVELS OF MATHEMATICS AND ENGLISH LANGUAGE SKILLS
BY JOB ZONE: JOB ZONE 4[a]

	Scale (Against Anchor Statements)						
	≥0	≥1	≥2	≥3	≥4	≥5	≥6
Importance							
Mathematics	100.0	100.0	93.2	36.4	1.1		
English Language	100.0	100.0	100.0	98.9	46.6		
Level							
Mathematics	100.0	100.0	96.6	81.8	48.9	13.6	0.0
English Language	100.0	100.0	100.0	97.7	69.3	10.2	0.0

[a]Scale anchors for Mathematics: level 1, add two numbers; level 4, analyze data to determine areas with the highest stakes; level 6, derive a complex mathematical equation. Scale anchors for English Language: level 2, write a thank-you note; level 4, edit a feature article in a local newspaper; level 6, teach a college English class.

English Language is not deemed critically important for occupations in job zone 2. Nonetheless, it is reflected in the component of communication, and the basic ability to read and write (literacy) is required for almost all the middle-skill jobs (see Tables 13.4–13.6).

Comparing the Current Findings to Existing Frameworks

Table 13.7 presents a comparison of our list of core dimensions for workforce readiness and success with findings from four previous reports: "Education for Life and Work: Developing Transferable Knowledge and Skills in the 21st Century" from the National Research Council (Pellegrino & Hilton, 2012), "What Work Requires of Schools: A SCANS Report for America 2000" from the Secretary's Commission on Achieving Necessary Skills (US Department of Labor, 1991), and two Educational Testing Service (ETS) reports— "Synthesizing Frameworks of Higher Education Student Learning Outcomes" (Markle et al., 2013) and "Identifying the Most Important 21st Century Workforce Competencies: An Analysis of the Occupational Information Network (O*NET)" (Burrus et al., 2013). Among these reports, one was based on analysis of the O*NET database, with a somewhat different method from the current study (Burrus et al., 2013); the others are synthetic reviews of workforce readiness frameworks (Markle et al., 2013; Pellegrino & Hilton, 2012; US Department of Labor, 1991). Therefore, they provide meaningful comparisons for the current findings in understanding core dimensions of workforce readiness.

Table 13.7 Comparison of Workforce Readiness and Success Frameworks

Current Study	US Department of Labor (1991)	Pellegrino and Hilton (2012)	Markle et al. (2013)	Burrus et al. (2013)
Critical Thinking and Problem Solving	Thinking skills (creative thinking, decision-making, problem solving, seeing things in the mind's eye, knowing how to learn, reasoning)	Cognitive processes and strategies Knowledge (information literacy)	Critical thinking Digital information literacy	Problem solving Fluid intelligence
Communication	Basic skills (reading, writing, arithmetic/mathematics, listening, speaking)	Knowledge (communications technology literacy, oral and written communication, active listening) Leadership (assertive communication, self-presentation)	Effective communication	Communication skills
Intrapersonal and Interpersonal Skills	Personal qualities (responsibility, self-esteem, sociability, self-management, integrity/honesty)	Teamwork and collaboration Intellectual openness (flexibility, adaptability, personal and social responsibility) Positive core self-evaluation (self-regulation)	Teamwork Citizenship Life skills (time management, goal setting, adaptation, flexibility)	Teamwork
Innovation and Achievement	Not included in the framework	Creativity Work ethic/conscientiousness Intellectual openness (intellectual interest and curiosity)	Creativity	Achievement/innovation
Detail Orientation	Not included in the framework	Not included in the framework	Not included in the framework	Not included in the framework

As shown in Table 13.7, the five core dimensions of workforce readiness from the current study map onto respective components from previous frameworks. The current framework covers all the previously identified dimensions and includes a Detail Orientation dimension that is not reflected in any of the previous frameworks. In addition, the current framework includes interests as an important component of workforce readiness and success based on a review of supporting evidence in the literature, which were also omitted from the previous frameworks. Overall, the current study presents a comprehensive, logical, and effectively organized framework of predictors for workforce readiness and success.

Examining a Standards Framework Within the Context of Stackable Credentials

Our focus has been on identifying the KSAOs that emerge as central to work based on occupational classification systems (i.e., O*NET and ISCO). We have established a framework of five critical work readiness dimensions. However, it is also important to embed this framework within a larger context of work requirements. Figure 13.1 demonstrates how our five dimensions of work readiness can be considered within a broader model that also includes (a) education and training work requirements and (b) job-specific competencies. This model includes education and training requirements as a base on which other work requirements (including the work readiness dimensions and job-specific competencies) can be stacked. We have grouped the three dimensions of Intrapersonal and Interpersonal Skills, Innovation and Achievement, and Detail Orientation together in the model for simplicity. The extent to which individuals possess the education, training, and competencies represented in the model can be gauged using scores on relevant assessments and attained degrees, licenses, and certifications. The issue of how to choose and validate relevant assessments of identified work requirements is discussed next.

CREATING AN ACTION RESEARCH AGENDA: PROCESS FOR VALIDATING AN ASSESSMENT OF CRITICAL WORKPLACE SKILLS

Armed with the knowledge of the core competencies that are critical for middle-skill jobs, we can proceed to identify, validate, and establish minimum levels of these skills. We illustrate this process using an assessment that measures some of the critical work styles (or, technically, narrow personality traits) identified in

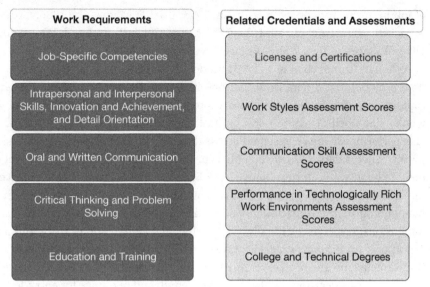

Figure 13.1 Preparation for the workforce and indicators of readiness.

the previous section (e.g., analytical thinking and leadership from the Critical Thinking and Problem Solving component, cooperation and dependability from the Intrapersonal and Interpersonal Skills component, innovation and achievement/effort from the Innovation and Achievement component, and attention to detail from the Detail Orientation component). In light of the fact that our plan was to examine the assessment's validity across different types of middle-skill jobs and across different countries, we developed a standard performance evaluation survey to use as a criterion measure, keeping in mind that the survey items would need to apply to most jobs and be amenable to translation into multiple languages.

Performance Evaluation Survey to Address Differential Workplace Outcomes

A 48-item performance evaluation survey was developed to capture behaviors representing six dimensions of employee performance—general task performance, safety and rule compliance, counterproductive work behavior (or, if reversed, work discipline), teamwork, customer service (with customers defined broadly as those who expect quality results, who are either internal or external, and whose role as customers is either explicit or implied), and commitment to quality—based on a review of a number of conceptualizations and measures of job performance (Borman & Brush, 1993; Brief & Motowidlo, 1986; Gruys & Sackett, 2003; Le et al., 2011; Liao & Chuang, 2004; Piedmont & Weinstein, 1994; Wallace & Chen, 2006; Wallace & Vodanovich, 2003).

Although Campbell et al.'s (1993) model of performance is widely used, we used a model that differs from that one in several respects in order to better capture, in a standardized way, the job requirements of entry-level jobs as a whole. Campbell et al.'s job-specific task performance and non-job-specific task performance are represented across three of our dimensions: general task performance, safety and rule compliance, and customer service. Our commitment to quality, counterproductive work behavior, and teamwork performance dimensions roughly correspond to Campbell et al.'s demonstrating effort, maintaining personal discipline, and facilitating peer and team performance dimensions, respectively. Finally, Campbell et al.'s written and oral communication task proficiency, supervision/leadership, and management/administration dimensions are not represented in our performance evaluation survey because of considerations related to survey length and relevance for entry-level jobs. As can be seen, our survey basically taps many of the same dimensions identified as important by Campbell et al.'s performance model, but our performance dimensions are more oriented toward discriminating between different entry-level jobs.

To pilot and refine this performance evaluation survey, a sample of supervisors evaluated 610 employees in a variety of jobs within ETS in the United States on their performance using a frequency rating scale (1 = never; 6 = always). The items were then subjected to exploratory and confirmatory factor analyses and reliability analyses, during which items with relatively weak loadings on their primary dimensions and high cross loadings, items with high error covariance with other items, and ambiguous items were dropped to improve the fit of the six-factor model and the internal consistency reliabilities of the six performance dimensions. Thirty-two items—27 based on survey refinement procedures plus 5 additional items as a buffer in case some of the retained 27 items would subsequently not hold up well during translation into other languages and data collections in different jobs/cultures—were retained for subsequent data collections. Based on the 27 items that remained after survey refinement, the six-factor solution fit the data well: $\chi^2 = 870.248$ (df = 309), $p < .01$, comparative fit index = .95, Tucker–Lewis index = .95, and root mean square error of approximation = .055. Performance dimension reliabilities ranged from .81 for counterproductive work behavior to .96 for customer service.

The six performance dimension scores can be used as criteria in analyses to examine the validity of the work styles assessment. The work styles assessment and performance evaluation survey have been translated into multiple languages (e.g., Spanish, Chinese, and Korean), and work is underway to collect data in various types of middle-skill jobs and in a number of different countries (e.g., the United States, South Korea, Costa Rica, Colombia, Brazil, Vietnam, and China). Job incumbents will complete the work styles assessment, and their supervisors will rate their job performance using the standard performance evaluation survey. Data will be examined to check for statistically significant relations between scores on the work styles assessment and those on the performance evaluation survey.

Establishing Minimum Levels of Competencies

Our belief is that to inform the education-to-work pipeline, it is important to set minimum competencies in the core dimensions we have highlighted. The challenge is to identify appropriate assessments of the competency domains of interest and conduct large-scale validation studies in jobs sampled from different job zones. Here, we describe the process we plan to use to establish minimum score levels on the skills assessed by ETS's work styles assessment, which we use for illustrative purposes. Note that the proposed methodology is novel, and if it does not prove feasible, we will explore other approaches (e.g., Angoff's method).

First, we will identify a sample of job types for which to validate the work styles assessment. We will aim for 20% of jobs from zone 2, 60% from zone 3, and 20% from zone 4, for a total of approximately 100 jobs. We will oversample jobs from zone 3 because, at least in the United States, occupations in zone 3 represent the largest proportion of the occupations (e.g., dental assistants and concierges) projected to grow most rapidly in the next few years (2012–2022) (National Center for O*NET Development, 2015) and employers most commonly post job openings for jobs in this zone (Woock, 2010). We will administer the work styles assessment to incumbents in these various job types and ask their supervisors to evaluate these individuals' performance using the standard performance evaluation survey.

Next, we will ask a sample of supervisors for each job type to complete an additional "survey of satisfactory work performance." The questions in the survey and the response scale correspond to those in the standard performance evaluation survey, but instead of rating the performance of a particular employee, supervisors will rate the performance of a "satisfactory" hypothetical employee performing at just an "acceptable" level (i.e., they will indicate how frequently an employee needs to perform the behaviors asked about in the survey to be considered just satisfactory/acceptable). Supervisors' aggregate ratings on the items comprising the six performance dimensions in the survey will represent minimally acceptable levels of performance on these performance dimensions.

Then, we will examine the level of agreement between supervisors within a job type and supervisors across the sampled middle-skill jobs on minimum levels on the various performance dimensions. Assuming that there is an adequate level of agreement (according to commonly used cutoffs for acceptable values on indices of rater agreement) among supervisors *within* a job type on what constitutes minimum performance on the rated job dimensions, we will try to establish the work styles assessment scores that correspond to the minimum levels of job performance indicated by supervisors. We will do so using the data (incumbents' work styles assessment test scores and performance ratings provided by supervisors) from that job type. Assuming that there is an adequate level of agreement among supervisors *across* job types on what constitutes minimum performance, we will try to establish the work styles assessment scores that correspond to those minimum levels of performance using the combined data (again, incumbents' test scores and supervisors' ratings) from individuals in those different job types. Before performing further analyses, we will verify that scores on the work styles assessment demonstrate statistically significant associations with job performance ratings within the data set to be analyzed. Otherwise, identifying work styles assessment scores associated with minimum levels of job performance will not be possible (i.e., the analysis assumes an association between test scores and job performance).

Next, regression analysis, where performance ratings assigned to job incumbents are regressed onto their work styles assessment scores, will be used to determine the score on a given behavioral skill that is associated with the modal or mean rating on a given job performance dimension. Alternatively, scores on the different job performance dimensions may be combined into an overall job performance score for these analyses.

Job Profiling

We believe that building a library of well-understood jobs tied to known assessment validities and minimum competencies on those assessments will help promote the adoption of a standards framework that transports across jobs and that can be applied across different countries. Continuing with our example of ETS's work styles assessment, we will be profiling jobs as part of the data collections to validate this assessment and establish minimum skill levels for entry into various types of jobs. Jobs will be profiled so that they may be described in terms of the work activities performed and the worker attributes required for job performance and added to a library of known jobs that have behavioral skill assessment validities and minimum behavioral skill level requirements associated with them. We will use a standard job profiling tool developed for this purpose (described in Golubovich, Chatterjee, & Robbins, 2015) and ask subject matter experts (incumbents, job supervisors, and hiring managers) to provide information about the profiled job using this tool. Incumbents will provide information about work activities performed on a target job, supervisors will provide information about worker attributes required for the job (including abilities, skills, and work styles), and a hiring manager will indicate educational, experience, and training requirements for the job.

GENERALIZABILITY OF ASSESSMENTS PREDICTING WORKPLACE READINESS AND SUCCESS

The ability to use an assessment to evaluate the work readiness of individuals in different countries and to establish score minimums for entry into various middle-skill jobs depends on the extent to which an assessment's validity generalizes across the types of jobs of interest, different levels of job complexity, and different cultures/languages. Here, we review the research literature regarding the generalizability of the validity of ability and personality assessments. We particularly focus on the findings pertaining to personality to anticipate the extent to which our work styles assessment may be used with job applicants on an international basis. The validity generalization of assessments of skills is not commonly examined in the research literature; researchers focus instead on validity generalization of cognitive ability and personality assessments. In fact, these attributes are predictors of skill acquisition (Ackerman, 1988; Oakes, Ferris, Martocchio, Buckley, & Broach, 2001), and tests are commonly used to assess individual differences on broader attributes underlying the development of various skills rather than to evaluate specific skills (Mumford, Baughman, Supinski, & Anderson, 1998).

Job Type

Research finds a strong association between cognitive ability (compare to Critical Thinking and Problem Solving component) and job performance (Schmidt & Hunter, 1998), and this finding generalizes across different types of jobs (Salgado et al., 2003b; Schmidt, 2002). The findings with regard to the generalizability of personality variables are more nuanced; relative to cognitive ability–performance relationships, associations between personality variables and performance are more likely to be moderated by other variables, such as how performance is measured and the type of criterion considered (Johnson & Schneider, 2013). Of the Big Five personality traits, assessments of

Conscientiousness have the best generalizability across different types of jobs and performance criteria (e.g., teamwork and training; Barrick & Mount, 1991; Barrick et al., 2001; Salgado, 1997). Emotional Stability has also been found to be related to performance in a number of different job types, but its validity for predicting overall performance generalizes better than its validity for specific performance criteria (Barrick et al., 2001; Salgado, 1997). Validity of other personality traits differs more across different job types or performance criteria. Openness tends to be a valid predictor of performance during training (Barrick et al., 2001) and when navigating unfamiliar or complex environments (Griffin & Hesketh, 2004). Agreeableness predicts performance in training and in jobs requiring interpersonal interactions, particularly when those interpersonal interactions are of the teamwork variety as opposed to of the direct customer service variety (Mount, Barrick, & Stewart, 1998; Salgado, 1997). Similar to Agreeableness, Extraversion may predict performance in training and in jobs requiring interpersonal interactions (e.g., managers and police officers; Barrick et al., 2001).

Job Complexity

Research findings indicate that the validity of cognitive ability for predicting job performance increases as job complexity increases (Gottfredson, 2002; Salgado et al., 2003b; Schmidt, 2002; Schmidt & Hunter, 2004). There is less evidence for the moderation of personality test validities by job complexity. Barrick and Mount (1991) examined validities of Conscientiousness for jobs that varied in complexity but did not find evidence of validity differences across jobs (however, they did not actually perform moderator analysis). Le and colleagues (2011), however, found some support for the idea that at a certain point, higher levels of a trait (e.g., Conscientiousness and Emotional Stability) become detrimental to, rather than facilitative of, task performance and that the level at which an otherwise positive trait may become detrimental to performance may be lower for less complex jobs.

Culture

There is some research examining the validities of cognitive ability and personality assessments in international contexts, and it suggests that validities generalize fairly well (Lievens, 2007). Cognitive ability predicts performance across different cultures (Ployhart, Sacco, Nishii, & Rogg, 2004, as cited in Lievens, 2007; Salgado & Anderson, 2002; Salgado, Anderson, Moscoso, Bertua, & De

Fruyt, 2003a; Schmidt & Hunter, 1998; Ziegler, Danay, Vogel, & Bühner, 2011), although some studies indicate differences in the sizes of validity coefficients for predicting job performance across cultures (e.g., United States vs. European countries; Salgado et al., 2003a).

Salgado's (1997) European meta-analysis of the validity of personality found results that were similar to research findings from North America (Barrick & Mount, 1991; Hough, Eaton, Dunnette, Kamp, & McCloy, 1990; Hurtz & Donovan, 2000; Tett, Jackson, & Rothstein, 1991). Ployhart et al. (2004, as cited in Lievens, 2007) examined validity of measures of team skills, work ethic, commitment, and customer focus across 10 countries and concluded that validities were mostly unaffected by culture. Research on the extent to which measures' validity generalizes across samples from Asia, Australia, Africa, the Middle East, and South/Central America is limited (or at least not written in English and less accessible) (Lievens, 2007).

To our knowledge, there is limited research examining the extent to which validities of narrow personality traits (like those measured by our work styles assessment) generalize across job types, job complexity, and cultures (e.g., in 1992, Hough examined the validity of achievement and dependability for predicting proficiency in two job types). Work that is underway to validate our work styles assessment in different types of middle-skill jobs and across different cultures will inform this area of research.

CONCLUSION

In this chapter, we discussed the notion that the education-to-work supply chain is broken, with many individuals completing their education without the basic skills they need to enter the workforce. We highlighted the need to bridge education and work systems by developing qualifications frameworks tied to skill assessments. We took an empirical approach to develop such a framework by identifying critical dimensions of knowledge, skills, abilities, work styles, and interests for middle-skill jobs. These are (a) Critical Thinking and Complex Problem Solving, (b) Oral and Written Communication, (c) Intrapersonal and Interpersonal Skills, (d) Achievement and Innovation, and (e) Detail Orientation. Valid assessments of critical "skills" (broadly defined) reflected in this framework are needed to test individuals and certify them ready for the workforce. Using an assessment of some of these skills as an example, we suggested a process for validating the assessment for international use and defining minimum skill levels individuals should meet for entry into middle-skill jobs. Research indicates that validities of cognitive assessments generalize very well across different contexts within a given level of job complexity, but validities of assessments of certain personality variables are somewhat more situationally specific. As such, we are conducting validity field trials for our work styles assessment in multiple countries and across multiple job types. We recommend similar steps be taken for validating other assessments of critical skills within the framework we have presented.

ACKNOWLEDGMENTS

We thank Travis Liebtag for his assistance in the preparation of this chapter and Dan Putka, Rod McCloy, and Cristina Anguiano Carrasco for their helpful feedback on an earlier version of this chapter.

REFERENCES

Ackerman, P. L. (1988). Determinants of individual differences during skill acquisition: Cognitive abilities and information processing. *Journal of Experimental Psychology: General, 117*(3), 288–318.

Ackerman, P. L. (1996). A theory of adult intellectual development: Process, personality, interests, and knowledge. *Intelligence, 22*(2), 227–257.

Almlund, M., Duckworth, A. L., Heckman, J. J., & Kautz, T. D. (2011). *Personality psychology and economics* (No. w16822). Cambridge, MA: National Bureau of Economic Research.

Barrick, M. R., & Mount, M. K. (1991). The Big Five personality dimensions and job performance: A meta-analysis. *Personnel Psychology, 44*, 1–26.

Barrick, M. R., Mount, M. K., & Judge, T. A. (2001). Personality and performance at the beginning of the new millennium: What do we know and where do we go next? *International Journal of Selection and Assessment, 9*(1-2), 9–30.

Bartram, D. (2005). The Great Eight competencies: A criterion-centric approach to validation. *Journal of Applied Psychology, 90*, 1185–1203.

Bergner, S., Neubauer, A. C., & Kreuzthaler, A. (2010). Broad and narrow personality traits for predicting managerial success. *European Journal of Work and Organizational Psychology, 19*(2), 177–199.

Borman, W. C., & Brush, D. H. (1993). More progress toward a taxonomy of managerial performance requirements. *Human Performance, 6*(1), 1–21.

Brief, A. P., & Motowidlo, S. J. (1986). Prosocial organizational behaviors. *Academy of Management Review, 11*(4), 710–725.

Burrus, J., Jackson, T., Xi, N., & Steinberg, J. (2013). *Identifying the most important 21st century workforce competencies: An analysis of the Occupational Information Network (O*NET)*. Princeton, NJ: Educational Testing Service.

Campbell, J. P., McCloy, R. A., Oppler, S. H., & Sager, C. E. (1993). A theory of performance. In N. Schmitt & W. C. Borman (Eds.), *Personnel selection in organizations* (pp. 35–70). San Francisco, CA: Jossey-Bass.

Caspi, A. (1998). Personality development across the life course. In W. Damon & N. Eisenberg (Eds.), *Handbook of child psychology: Social, emotional, and personality development* (pp. 311–388). New York, NY: Wiley.

Council on Competitiveness. (2008). *Thrive: The skills imperative*. Retrieved from http://all4ed.org/wp-content/uploads/2008/08/Thrive.-The-Skills-Imperative-FINAL-PDF.pdf

Deloitte & National Association of Manufacturers. (2005). *2005 Skills gap report: A survey of the American manufacturing workforce*. Retrieved from http://www.themanu-facturinginstitute.org/~/media/738F5D310119448DBB03DF30045084EF/2005_Skills_Gap_Report.pdf

Drasgow, F., Stark, S., Chernyshenko, O. S., Nye, C. D., Hulin, C. L., & White, L. A. (2012). *Development of the Tailored Adaptive Personality Assessment System (TAPAS) to support Army selection and classification decisions* (Technical Report 1311). Fort Belvoir, VA: US Army Research Institute for the Behavioral and Social Sciences.

Ejiogu, K. C., Yang, Z., Trent, J., & Rose, M. (2006, May). *Understanding the relationship between critical thinking and job performance*. Poster presented at the 21st annual conference of the Society for Industrial and Organizational Psychology, Dallas, TX.

Ferris, G. R., Witt, L. A., & Hochwarter, W. A. (2001). Interaction of social skill and general mental ability on job performance and salary. *Journal of Applied Psychology*, 86(6), 1075.

Fleishman, E. A., & Reilly, M. E. (1992). *Handbook of human abilities: Definitions, measurements, and job task requirements*. Potomac, MD: Management Research Institute.

Gallup. (2012). *Global unemployment at 8% in 2011*. Retrieved from http://www.gallup.com/poll/153884/global-unemployment-2011.aspx

Golubovich, J., Chatterjee, D., & Robbins, S. (2015). *Educational Testing Service (ETS) Job Profiler for Validity Studies: Overview and planned application* (Educational Testing Service Research Memorandum ETS RM-15-01). Princeton, NJ: Educational Testing Service.

Gottfredson, L. S. (2002). Where and why g matters: Not a mystery. *Human Performance*, 15, 79–132.

Griffin, B., & Hesketh, B. (2004). Why openness to experience is not a good predictor of job performance. *International Journal of Selection and Assessment, 12*, 243–251.

Gruys, M. L., & Sackett, P. R. (2003). Investigating the dimensionality of counterproductive work behavior. *International Journal of Selection and Assessment, 11*(1), 30–42.

Heckman, J. J., Hsee, J., & Rubinstein, Y. (2000). *The GED is a mixed signal: The effect of cognitive and non-cognitive skills on human capital and labor market outcomes*. Unpublished manuscript.

Holland, J. L. (1959). A theory of vocational choice. *Journal of Counseling Psychology*, 6(1), 35.

Holland, J. L. (1997). *Making vocational choices: A theory of vocational personalities and work environments*. Lutz, FL: Psychological Assessment Resources.

Hough, L. M. (1992). The Big Five personality variables—Construct confusion: Description versus prediction. *Human Performance, 5*, 139–155.

Hough, L. M., Eaton, N. K., Dunnette, M. D., Kamp, J. D., & McCloy, R. A. (1990). Criterion-related validities of personality constructs and the effect of response distortion on those validities. *Journal of Applied Psychology, 75*(5), 581.

Hunter, J. E. (1986). Cognitive ability, cognitive aptitudes, job knowledge, and job performance. *Journal of Vocational Behavior, 29*(3), 340–362.

Hurtz, G. M., & Donovan, J. J. (2000). Personality and job performance: The Big Five revisited. *Journal of Applied Psychology, 85*(6), 869.

International Labour Organization. (2008). *International standard classification of occupations.* Retrieved from http://www.ilo.org/public/english/bureau/stat/isco/isco08/index.htm

James, L. R., Demaree, R. G., & Wolf, G. (1993). r_{WG}: An assessment of within-group interrater agreement. *Journal of Applied Psychology, 78*, 306–309.

Johnson, J. W., & Schneider, R. J. (2013). Advancing our understanding of processes in personality–performance relationships. In N. Christiansen & R. Tett (Eds.), *Handbook of personality at work* (pp. 30–52). New York, NY: Routledge.

Judge, T. A., Bono, J. E., Ilies, R., & Gerhardt, M. W. (2002). Personality and leadership: A qualitative and quantitative review. *Journal of Applied Psychology, 87*(4), 765.

Judge, T. A., Klinger, R. L., & Simon, L. S. (2010). Time is on my side: Time, general mental ability, human capital, and extrinsic career success. *Journal of Applied Psychology, 95*(1), 92.

Judge, T. A., & Zapata, C. P. (2015). The person–situation debate revisited: Effect of situation strength and trait activation on the validity of the Big Five personality traits in predicting job performance. *Academy of Management Journal, 58*(4), 1149–1179.

Kesselman, G. A., Lopez, F. M., & Lopez, F. E. (1982). The development and validation of a self-report scored in-basket test in an assessment center setting. *Public Personnel Management, 11*(3), 228–238.

Kilduff, M., & Day, D. V. (1994). Do chameleons get ahead? The effects of self-monitoring on managerial careers. *Academy of Management Journal, 37*(4), 1047–1060.

Le, H., Oh, I., Robbins, S., Ilies, R., Holland, E., & Westrick, P. (2011). Too much of a good thing: Curvilinear relationships between personality traits and job performance. *Journal of Applied Psychology, 96*(1), 113–133.

LeBreton, J. M., & Senter, J. L. (2008). Answers to 20 questions about interrater reliability and interrater agreement. *Organizational Research Methods, 11*, 815–852.

LePine, J. A., Colquitt, J. A., & Erez, A. (2000). Adaptability to changing task contexts: Effects of general cognitive ability, conscientiousness, and openness to experience. *Personnel Psychology, 53*, 563–593.

Liao, H., & Chuang, A. (2004). A multilevel investigation of factors influencing employee service performance and customer outcomes. *Academy of Management Journal, 47*(1), 41–58.

Lievens, F. (2007). Research on selection in an international context: Current status and future directions. In M. M. Harris (Ed.), *Handbook of research in international human resource management* (pp. 107–123). Hillsdale, NJ: Erlbaum.

Liu, O. L., Frankel, L., & Roohr, K. C. (2014). *Assessing critical thinking in higher education: Current state and directions for next-generation assessment* (ETS Research Report Series). Princeton, NJ: Educational Testing Service.

Lockard, C. B., & Wolf, M. (2012). Occupational employment projections to 2020. *Monthly Labor Review, 135*, 84.

Markle, R., Brenneman, M., Jackson, T., Burrus, J., & Robbins, S. (2013). *Synthesizing frameworks of higher education student learning outcomes* (Research Report No. RR-13-22). Princeton, NJ: Educational Testing Service.

McKinsey Center for Government. (2013). *Education to employment: Designing a system that works.* Retrieved from http://www.mckinsey.com/industries/social-sector/our-insights/education-to-employment-designing-a-system-that-works

McKinsey Center for Government. (2014). *Education to employment: Getting Europe's youth into work.* Retrieved from http://www.mckinsey.com/insights/social_sector/converting_education_to_employment_in_europe

McKinsey Global Institute. (2012). *Help wanted: The future of work in advanced economies.* Retrieved from http://www.mckinsey.com/insights/employment_and_growth/future_of_work_in_advanced_economies

Mount, M. K., Barrick, M. R., & Stewart, G. L. (1998). Five-factor model of personality and performance in jobs involving interpersonal interactions. *Human Performance, 11*(2-3), 145–165.

Mumford, M. D., Baughman, W. A., Supinski, E. P., & Anderson, L. E. (1998). A construct approach to skill assessment: Procedures for assessing complex cognitive skills. In M. D. Hakel (Ed.), *Beyond multiple choice: Evaluating alternatives to traditional testing for selection* (pp. 75–112). Hillsdale, NJ: Erlbaum.

National Center for O*NET Development. (2010). *Updating the O*NET-SOC taxonomy: Incorporating the 2010 SOC structure: Summary and implementation.* Retrieved from http://www.onetcenter.org/reports/Taxonomy2010.html

National Center for O*NET Development. (2014). *Production database—O*NET 18.1.* Retrieved from http://www.onetcenter.org/database.html

National Center for O*NET Development. (2015). *Rapid growth bright outlook occupations.* Retrieved from http://www.onetonline.org/find/bright?b=1&g=Go

National Commission on Adult Literacy. (2008). *Reach higher, America: Overcoming crisis in the U.S. workforce.* Retrieved from http://www.caalusa.org/ReachHigherBUSINESSPullout/ReachHigherBUSINESSPullout.pdf

Neumann, G., Olitsky, N., & Robbins, S. (2009). Job congruence, academic achievement, and earnings. *Labour Economics, 16*(5), 503–509.

Nye, C. D., Su, R., Rounds, J., & Drasgow, F. (2012). Vocational interests and performance a quantitative summary of over 60 years of research. *Perspectives on Psychological Science, 7*(4), 384–403.

Oakes, D. W., Ferris, G. R., Martocchio, J. J., Buckley, M. R., & Broach, D. (2001). Cognitive ability and personality predictors of training program skill acquisition and job performance. *Journal of Business and Psychology, 15*(4), 523–548.

Organization for Economic Co-operation and Development. (2012). *Better skills, better jobs, better lives: A strategic approach to skills policies.* Paris, France: Author.

Organization for Economic Co-operation and Development. (2013). *OECD skills outlook 2013: First results from the survey of adult skills.* Retrieved from https://www.oecd.org/skills/piaac/Skills%20volume%201%20(eng)--full%20v12--eBook%20(04%2011%202013).pdf

Oswald, F., Campbell, J., McCloy, R., Rivkin, D., & Lewis, P. (1999). *Stratifying occupational units by specific vocational preparation.* Raleigh, NC: National Center for O*NET Development. Retrieved from http://www.onetcenter.org/dl_files/SVP.pdf

Paunonen, S. V., & Ashton, M. C. (2001). Big Five factors and facets and the prediction of behavior. *Journal of Personality and Social Psychology, 81*(3), 524–539.

Pellegrino, J. W., & Hilton, M. L. (2012). *Education for life and work: Developing transferable knowledge and skills in the 21st century*. Washington, DC: National Research Council of the National Academies.

Peterson, N. G., Mumford, M. D., Borman, W. C., Jeanneret, P., & Fleishman, E. A. (1999). *An occupational information system for the 21st century: The development of O*NET*. Washington, DC: American Psychological Association.

Piedmont, R. L., & Weinstein, H. P. (1994). Predicting supervisor ratings of job performance using the NEO Personality Inventory. *Journal of Psychology, 128*(3), 255–265.

Ployhart, R. E., Sacco, J. M., Nishii, L. H., & Rogg, K. L. (2004, April). *The influence of culture on criterion-related validity and job performance*. Poster presented at the annual conference of the Society for Industrial and Organizational Psychology, Chicago, IL.

Ree, M. J., & Earles, J. A. (1991). Predicting training success: Not much more than *g*. *Personnel Psychology, 44*, 321–332.

Ree, M. J., Earles, J. A., & Teachout, M. S. (1994). Predicting job performance: Not much more than *g*. *Journal of Applied Psychology, 79*, 518–524.

Rounds, J., & Su, R. (2014). The nature and power of interests. *Current Directions in Psychological Science, 23*(2), 98–103.

Sackett, P. R., & Walmsley, P. T. (2014). Which personality attributes are most important in the workplace? *Perspectives on Psychological Science, 9*, 538–551.

Salgado, J. F. (1997). The five-factor model of personality and job performance in the European Community. *Journal of Applied Psychology, 82*, 30–43.

Salgado, J. F., & Anderson, N. (2002). Cognitive and GMA testing in the European Community: Issues and evidence. *Human Performance, 15*, 75–96.

Salgado, J. F., Anderson, N., Moscoso, S., Bertua, C., & De Fruyt, F. (2003a). International validity generalization of GMA and cognitive abilities: A European Community meta-analysis. *Personnel Psychology, 56*, 573–605.

Salgado, J. F., Anderson, N., Moscoso, S., Bertua, C., De Fruyt, F., & Rolland, J. P. (2003b). A meta-analytic study of general mental ability validity for different occupations in the European Community. *Journal of Applied Psychology, 88*, 1068–1081.

Shippmann, J. S., Ash, R. A., Battista, M., Carr, L., Eyde, L. D., Hesketh, B., . . . Sanchez, J. I. (2000). The practice of competency modeling. *Personnel Psychology, 53*, 703–740.

Schmidt, F. L. (2002). The role of general cognitive ability and job performance: Why there cannot be a debate. *Human Performance, 15*, 187–210.

Schmidt, F. L., & Hunter, J. E. (1998). The validity and utility of selection methods in personnel psychology: Practical and theoretical implications of 85 years of research findings. *Psychological Bulletin, 124*, 262–274.

Schmidt, F. L., & Hunter, J. E. (2004). General mental ability in the world of work: Occupational attainment and job performance. *Journal of Personality and Social Psychology, 86*, 162–173.

Su, R. (2012). *The power of vocational interests and interest congruence in predicting career success*. Unpublished doctoral dissertation, University of Illinois at Urbana–Champaign.

Su, R., Rounds, J., & Armstrong, P. I. (2009). Men and things, women and people: A meta-analysis of sex differences in interests. *Psychological Bulletin, 135*(6), 859.

Tett, R. P., Jackson, D. N., & Rothstein, M. (1991). Personality measures as predictors of job performance: A meta-analytic review. *Personnel Psychology*, *44*(4), 703–742.

Tippins, N. T., & Hilton, M. L. (Eds.). (2010). *A database for a changing economy: Review of the Occupational Information Network (O*NET)*. Washington, DC: National Academies Press.

Tsabari, O., Tziner, A., & Meir, E. I. (2005). Updated meta-analysis on the relationship between congruence and satisfaction. *Journal of Career Assessment*, *13*(2), 216–232.

US Bureau of Labor Statistics. (2010). *Standard occupational classification*. Retrieved from https://www.bls.gov/soc/#classification

US Bureau of Labor Statistics. (2012). *Crosswalks between the International Standard Classification of Occupations (ISCO-08) and the 2010 Standard Occupational Classification (SOC)*. Retrieved from http://www.bls.gov/soc/soccrosswalks.htm

US Department of Labor. (1991, June). *What work requires of schools: A SCANS report for America 2000*. Retrieved from http://www.globalschoolnet.org/web/_shared/SCANS2000.pdf

van Iddekinge, C., Putka, D. J., & Campbell, J. P. (2011). Reconsidering vocational interests for personnel selection: The validity of an interest-based selection test in relation to job knowledge, job performance, and continuance intentions. *Journal of Applied Psychology*, *96*, 13–33.

van Iddekinge, C., Roth, P. R., Putka, D. J., & Lanivich, S. (2011). Are you interested? A meta-analysis of relations between vocational interests and employee performance and turnover. *Journal of Applied Psychology*, *96*, 1167–1194.

Wallace, C., & Chen, G. (2006). A multilevel integration of personality, climate, self-regulation, and performance. *Personnel Psychology*, *59*(3), 529–557.

Wallace, J. C., & Vodanovich, S. J. (2003). Workplace safety performance: Conscientiousness, cognitive failure, and their interaction. *Journal of Occupational Health Psychology*, *8*(4), 316–327.

Watson, G., & Glaser, E. M. (2009). *Watson–Glaser II critical thinking appraisal: Technical and user's manual*. San Antonio, TX: Pearson.

Wayne, S. J., Liden, R. C., Graf, I. K., & Ferris, G. R. (1997). The role of upward influence tactics in human resource decisions. *Personnel Psychology*, *50*(4), 979–1006.

Witt, L. A., & Ferris, G. R. (2003). Social skill as moderator of the conscientiousness–performance relationship: Convergent results across four studies. *Journal of Applied Psychology*, *88*(5), 809.

Woock, C. (2010). *The case for business to invest in post-secondary credentials* (Economics Program Working Paper Series no. EPWP 10-01). New York, NY: The Conference Board.

Ziegler, M., Dietl, E., Danay, E., Vogel, M., & Bühner, M. (2011). Predicting training success with general mental ability, specific ability tests, and (un)structured interviews: A meta-analysis with unique samples. *International Journal of Selection and Assessment*, *19*(2), 170–182.

Traversing the Gap Between College and Workforce Readiness: Anything But a "Bridge Too Far"!

Commentary

DANA M. MURANO AND RICHARD D. ROBERTS ■

Operation Market Garden was a notorious failure for the Allies during World War II. The operation was intended to allow joint militia from the United Kingdom, the United States, Canada, Poland, and the Netherlands to break through German lines and seize strategically important bridges in occupied territory to end the war by Christmas of 1944. Instead, overextending its resources, the Allies suffered a terrible defeat and the war lingered on for another year. These historical events led to an ensemble film, shunned by a patriotic America at the time—*A Bridge Too Far*—whose title derives from an unconfirmed comment attributed to British Lieutenant–General Frederick Browning who told Field Marshal Bernard Montgomery, the operation's architect, "I think we may be going a bridge too far."

We might ask ourselves whether the authors of the three chapter of this section (Clark; Schmitt; and Golubovich, Su, and Robbins) were buying (or rather being pressed by the four editors of this book, of whom the current senior author is one) into a similar situation. After all, as the chapters of the book attest, college readiness seems to sit uncomfortably within a chasm, neither quite the purview of kindergarten through grade 12 (K–12) education nor the colleges themselves, whereas workforce readiness adds a third player into the mix—the employer and the various components of the labor market, including policy, technology trends, and a range of economic factors. Ergo, we four editors may well have asked the authors of the three chapters in this section to go a bridge too far.

Although bridging the gap between college and workforce readiness is a feat that will take a great deal of advocacy, pioneers who believe in change, and steadfast implementation, it is far from impossible. A bridge initially perceived as "too far" becomes tangibly closer, more accessible, and more feasible once one considers a common denominator of both college and workforce readiness: noncognitive skills. Despite differences in domain-specific skill sets and competencies, both college and workforce readiness are rooted in a strikingly similar set of noncognitive skills. Through the development of noncognitive skills, which can be fostered through social–emotional learning programs, students could plausibly be prepared to face many of the challenges they meet, both in college and beyond into the workforce. Possessing qualities such as grit, resilience, cooperation, curiosity, and teamwork will help students succeed in multiple demanding environments, whether they are persisting in difficult university-level courses, maintaining positive attitudes when facing rejection in the job market, or assimilating to the demands of an entry-level job in their transition to the workforce. Juxtaposed, these three chapters suggest that by fostering noncognitive skills in students, we can effectively build a solid foundation of desirable noncognitive skills, which will enable individuals to succeed in college, in the workplace, and in life.

LINKING EDUCATION AND EMPLOYMENT: A FOUNDATIONAL COMPETENCY FRAMEWORK FOR CAREER SUCCESS

Arguably, Clark (Chapter 11) raises the largest concern regarding whether bridging college readiness and work readiness may be going a step too far. She presents three separate, rigid definitions of career, workforce, and college readiness, and an initial perception might have the reader assuming minimal, if any, room for overlap. There is a lack of cohesion between college and career and workplace readiness, the former of which emphasizes academic achievement, whereas the latter include both cognitive and noncognitive foundational skills, as well as increasingly domain-specific skill sets that qualify individuals to enter career clusters and specific jobs within them. However, Clark ultimately argues that the three readiness profiles are related and can be effectively developed via what she terms "foundational skills." These foundational skills are synonymous with "noncognitive skills," "21st century skills," and "soft skills" that have been discussed throughout this volume; she argues that focusing on these skills throughout K–12 education will better prepare students for college, careers, and specific job placements. After discussing the fallacies in labeling skills versus competencies in various models, she presents the Employability Skills Framework as an integrative readiness model, combining many common skills from 20 other competing frameworks and organizing them as subskills of three main skills: applied knowledge, effective relationships, and workplace skills. She concludes her chapter by presenting key skills that will be necessary in the next 10 years as a result of drivers in the workforce such as technology; local, national, and global market trends; and public policies that create constant, rapid change.

Whether intentional or not, Clark's chapter seems to suggest that the definition of college readiness be expanded to be more blatantly inclusive of noncognitive skills. She defines college readiness as "the level of achievement a student needs to be ready to enroll and succeed—without remediation—in credit-bearing first-year postsecondary courses" (Clark, Chapter 11). Although her definitions of career and workplace success both include explicit mention of "foundational skills," noncognitive skills are only inferred to be a part of her college readiness definition by the "and succeed" segment. Think about it: What exactly helped you succeed in college? Was it saying "no" to an invitation to a party so you could study for an upcoming exam? Working extra hard on a paper after receiving a failing grade on a prior assignment? Being able to delegate assignments and work cohesively with others on a group presentation? These actions exemplify conscientiousness, resilience, and cooperation, respectively, and are undoubtedly constituents of college success (Kyllonen, Lipnevich, Burrus, & Roberts, 2014). Research findings converge to suggest such noncognitive skills be included as constituents of college readiness, considering they are instrumental in predicting college success (McNeish, Radunzel, & Sanchez, 2015).

Although Clark admirably boils down 20 competing foundational skills models into the Employability Skills Framework, which can be appropriate for college, career, and work readiness, a question remains as to whether her ideas can be further integrated to fit within the Big Five factor model. During approximately the past 50 years, a consensus has been reached that in order for the field to advance, it is necessary to adopt a classification scheme through which to report, analyze, and compare empirical findings. In the industrial–organizational literature, the Big Five has become the predominant framework for understanding skills in the workforce and relating them to valued outcomes (Barrick & Mount, 1991; Sackett & Walmsley, 2014). The Big Five framework can also be validly applied to K–12 education (Lipnevich, Preckel, & Roberts, 2016; Poropat, 2009; Roberts, Martin, & Olaru, 2015) and to college readiness criteria (Credé & Niehorster, 2012; Kyllonen et al., 2014). If one accepts the meta-analytic findings on which these arguments rest, the Big Five framework appears appropriate for integrating all three readiness domains. The Employability Skills Framework includes components of the Big Five—for example, effective relationship skills, communication skills, and a range of personal qualities. In turn, we suggest the potential for further integration of even this comprehensive framework into the Big Five, which might be done for the sake of parsimony, integration, and ease of communicating to all constituents.

COMBINING COGNITIVE AND NONCOGNITIVE MEASURES: EXPANDING THE DOMAIN OF COLLEGE AND WORKFORCE PERFORMANCE AND ITS PREDICTION

Schmitt (Chapter 12) further highlights the significance of noncognitive constructs within discussions of both workforce and college readiness, and he advocates for the assessment of noncognitive constructs as constituents of not only college admissions but also subsequent outcomes of college success. It is as if Schmitt builds on the "and succeed" component of the college readiness definition provided by Clark and advances her argument by compiling evidence in support of the relevancy of noncognitive skills for college success. His advocacy for the inclusion of noncognitive constructs in college admissions is followed by a stimulating discussion of measurement, including current issues, potential solutions, and the demonstrated need for innovative approaches to assessment. Overall, Schmitt argues that noncognitive assessments should supplement traditional cognitive assessments in the college application process, especially considering that many of these constructs are already assessed in job applicants. The conclusion that can be extracted is that college and work require similar noncognitive skills, and we should be measuring them in college as well, considering that they are highly predictive of academic success (see also Kyllonen et al., 2014) and also colleges' value of noncognitive skills, as reflected through their mission statements (Stemler, 2012).

In terms of assessing noncognitive constructs, Schmitt calls for a move from the current subjective means of evaluating noncognitive skills, which include letters of recommendation, personal statements, and lists of extracurricular activities, to more objective, standardized, and innovative methodologies for measuring these constructs. He proposes that methodological advances will increase incremental validity, as well as objectivity. However, he points out concerns associated with noncognitive assessment: coaching to provide desirable responses; faking; and the reactions to these measures from students, parents, and admissions personnel. From his discussion of measurement, it becomes clear that this is an area in which more focused research is desperately needed but one in which psychometricians, educators, and policymakers need to become effectively co-joined. Assessments that are less susceptible to faking, generally well received by the public, and able to provide a baseline for formative assessment are needed if noncognitive constructs are to be assessed in tandem with traditional tests of cognitive ability. Measures that have the potential to fill this gap include situational judgment tests, forced-choice paradigms, and even big data as supplements to traditional self-report items (Lipnevich, MacCann, & Roberts, 2013). The future of the integration of noncognitive assessment with traditional cognitive assessment may depend on the emergence of such measures, which are capable of objectively measuring these constructs.

A particularly salient, and perhaps underemphasized, component of Schmitt's chapter is the finding of smaller score differences between minority and majority groups on noncognitive measures than on traditional measures of cognitive ability. Historically, minority students have tended to score lower on traditional measures of cognitive ability, including both IQ tests and college admissions entrance exams (Kobrin, Sathy, & Shaw, 2007; Nisbett et al., 2012). Potential reasons for this include cultural and psychometric bias (Kaufman, 2015). However, Schmitt's work showing an average of 0 in minority–majority differences on noncognitive measures, as opposed to differences between –.62 and –1.18 standard deviations on cognitive measures, suggests noncognitive measures may be much less biased, either culturally or psychometrically. Researchers also increasingly recognize that noncognitive skills are critical for college readiness, particularly in urban minority populations (Roderick, Nagaoka, & Coca, 2009), and possessing an unbiased way of measuring these skills, and moreover using them as an admissions criterion, appears to be a significant stride in the scheme of college admissions for minority students.

ESTABLISHING AN INTERNATIONAL STANDARDS FRAMEWORK AND ACTION RESEARCH AGENDA FOR WORKPLACE READINESS AND SUCCESS

Golubovich et al. (Chapter 13) also observe the lack of a framework for work readiness skills, which contributes to the disconnect between skills learned through formal education and those necessary for success in the 21st century workforce. These authors focus on establishing a framework specifically for middle-skills jobs, which are characterized by the need for training between a high school diploma and 4-year bachelor's degree, interpersonal interactions (insinuating these jobs cannot become automated), and the projected expansion of these types of jobs within upcoming years. Due to the relevancy of these jobs in the emergent job market, the framework presented targets these jobs specifically. A detailed research agenda and methodology is also presented for use in assessing critical attributes related to job success, establishing minimum scores for entry into job fields, and extracting specific requirements from various job profiles.

Commendable components of this chapter include the authors' detailed research agenda, inventive methodology, and effective use of principal component analysis (PCA) in establishing their standards framework. Their framework is both rooted in empirical data and derived from integrating data within O*NET and ISCO. Their goal was to identify the fundamental KSAOs required for success in each job in order to develop a comprehensive overview of KSAOs for middle-skills jobs. The five components that emerge are critical thinking and problem solving, communication, intrapersonal and interpersonal skills, innovation and achievement, and detail orientation, which were similar to those previously identified by a previous study cited by the authors. Moreover, Golubovich et al. have used these skills to develop a performance evaluation survey, which they intend to pilot and establish validity evidence using various workplace samples from multiple countries.

However, two areas of concern arise surrounding this particular chapter. First is the author-implemented limitation of the framework only applying to middle-skills jobs. It seems feasible that target skills identified as pertinent for middle-skills professions, such as detail orientation and critical thinking, could be both necessary and helpful in other levels of jobs, both higher and lower (indeed, this is entirely consistent with the arguments of another section of this book; see Sackett & Walmsley, Chapter 2). Burrus, Jackson, Xi, and Steinberg (2013) conducted an analysis of the O*NET database in order to identify a framework of crucial competencies for job zones 3–5, and they identified similar competencies to those identified by Golubovich et al. This further suggests the framework may be more broadly applicable and not necessarily limited to middle-skills jobs. Moreover, the standards framework includes both interpersonal and intrapersonal skills, as well as communication and detail orientation, which are noncognitive competencies that align closely with the Big Five (Roberts et al., 2015; Sackett & Walmseley, 2014). Such a narrow, specific framework limits the potential for a more inclusive, yet cohesive, framework that can identify critical skills for success across all postsecondary domains.

The second concern is the analogy of education as an almost factory-like process, through which individuals become trained and ready for workplace success following their education—a monotonous, drone-like phenomena that appears discrepant both with the arguably lofty goals of bridging education and workplace readiness and emerging technology trends that will likely one day see the re-imagination of the educational process. Instead, traits exemplified by a more holistic education, encapsulating noncognitive skills, will result in students who are better prepared for all aspects of postsecondary life. Instead of cogs in a factory assembly line, non-cog students (pun intended) will benefit from qualities such as critical thinking, interpersonal and intrapersonal communication competency, and the ability to think dynamically and critically in order to face any challenges that come their way.

ADVANCING THE OPERATION

Juxtaposed, these three chapters highlight the relevancy of noncognitive skills in discussions of both college and workplace readiness. However, this is not to say other factors do not play into the college and workplace readiness equation. Both high school grade point average (GPA) and SAT scores are powerful predictors of first-year college GPA (Kobrin, Patterson, Shaw, Mattern, & Barbuti, 2008), suggesting that cognitive ability plays a crucial role in college readiness. Golubovich et al. (Chapter 13) also cite cognitive ability as the best predictor of job performance. We are not advocating that noncognitive skills are the sole constituents of college and workforce readiness but, rather, that they instead supplement other predictors, such as cognitive ability. Just as Schmitt (Chapter 12) advocates for noncognitive assessments to supplement traditional assessments of cognitive ability, we are proposing that readiness at a noncognitive skills level can enhance students' readiness profiles as they enter college and the workforce. By considering multiple constituents of success, we can prepare students to succeed in both college and the workplace by cultivating a shared set of required noncognitive skills, in addition to the traditional cognitive skills in which students already receive instruction.

Through successfully cultivating and assessing noncognitive skills, we can bridge the gap between college and workplace readiness because these skills serve as a foundation for success in both domains. Some common themes discussed by the authors of Chapters 11–13 include the lack of a comprehensive framework, the need for a common language between educators and employers, and the need for innovative approaches to noncognitive assessment. Although currently treated as different skill sets, the authors make it clear that noncognitive skills underlie both college and workplace success, and cultivating such skills in K–12 education can prepare students for success in college and on through to the workforce. Based on the authors' contributions in support of noncognitive skills as foundational necessities to success in college and work, suggestions to advance the field are presented next.

Selection of an Integrative Framework Through Which to Study Noncognitive Skills in the Domains of College and Workforce Readiness

Multiple authors of the chapters in Section 3 comment on the lack of consensus for a theoretical framework for college and work readiness skills. As demonstrated by multiple meta-analyses, the Big Five framework is most suitable for studying the relationship between various skills and job success in the industrial–organizational psychology literature (Barrick & Mount, 1991; Barrick, Mount, & Judge, 2001). Furthermore, selection of one integrative framework enables us to match specific job characteristics with personality dimensions that will be most predictive of job performance within that work style (Burrus & Way, 2016). The Big Five is also a fitting framework through which to study academic achievement, both in K–12 and in college (Poropat, 2009; Roberts et al., 2015). Both frameworks presented by Clark as well as by Golubovich et al. could feasibly be considered within the larger realm of the Big Five. It seems appropriate that the Big Five receive consideration as an integrative framework, which could anchor all research and move the field forward.

Innovative Forms of Assessment for Noncognitive Readiness Skills

As demonstrated by Schmitt, work is needed in the domain of noncognitive skill assessment. The potential exists to measure noncognitive skills in a manner that removes cultural and psychometric bias and could provide an objective baseline of foundational readiness skills. Accurate assessments could be used in college admissions processes as a supplement to traditional measures of cognitive ability. Although the development of innovative approaches to noncognitive assessment is in its early stages, measures such as situational judgment tests, implicit association tests, and forced-choice approaches hold the potential as more unbiased, objective indicators (Lipnevich et al., 2013). Assuming the stance that all constructs we wish to assess can be encapsulated by the Big Five (John & De Fruyt, 2015; MacCann & Roberts, 2010; Roberts et al., 2015), innovative assessments (both summative and formative) could be built upon this framework in order to assess a multitude of noncognitive constructs.

Interventions to Improve Noncognitive Skills, Provided These Are Evaluated by Validated Assessments

During the past two decades, education has witnessed the emergence of a variety of programs designed to improve noncognitive skills in K–12 education, most often under the label of social and emotional learning (SEL) programs. The fact that personality is subject to change (Roberts, Walton, & Viechtbauer, 2006; Walton & Billera, 2016) implies that there may be systematic ways of influencing noncognitive skills, most likely at the facet level (MacCann, Duckworth, & Roberts, 2009). Meta-analytic evidence shows the value of SEL programs for a range of valued academic and behavioral outcomes (Durlak, Weissberg, Dymnicki, Taylor, & Schellinger, 2011; Durlak, Weissberg, & Pachan, 2010), and a recent study also demonstrates the economic advantages of SEL programs, with every $1 invested in SEL curricula yielding a mean return of $11 (Belfield et al., 2015). Innovative means of assessment will help with the advance of this field as well because it is still often the case that these programs rely excessively on self-reported assessments, which are subject to a variety of biases and validity threats (Duckworth & Yeager, 2015). Effective SEL programs, paired with equally effective program assessment, can bolster noncognitive skills in students from kindergarten to grade 16 (note we are arguing here that these might also be applied to college students as well), which can prepare them for success in both college and the workplace.

CONCLUSION

When the Allies faced the Germans in the infamous Operation Garden Market, an inus condition in their defeat was the lack and overextension of supplies and troops. On the horizon of bridging college and workplace readiness, our landscape differs vastly from that which the Allies faced in 1944. As exemplified by the contributors to this volume, we possess legions of qualified researchers, policymakers, and educators who are advocates for change. These individuals carry supplies such as methodologies of innovative assessment, social–emotional learning curricula, and the all-integrative Big Five framework. Most important, we are armed with the strategic knowledge on how to effectively bridge the gap—that is, through the identification, remediation, and perhaps even meaningful credentialing of noncognitive skills in students. Students who possess qualities such as grit, resilience, growth mindset, and the ability to cooperate will be able to succeed in all domains beyond secondary schooling, from college to the workplace. An operation to inculcate noncognitive skills in students could alter the status quo of deeming college and work readiness as disparate entities and effectively bridge the gap between college and workplace readiness.

ACKNOWLEDGMENTS

The views expressed in this chapter are the authors' and do not reflect the official opinions or policies of the authors' host affiliations. We thank the editors of this book for not only providing comments and feedback on the first draft of this chapter but also their professionalism throughout this long and arduous joint venture.

REFERENCES

Barrick, M. R., & Mount, M. K. (1991). The Big Five personality dimensions and job performance: A meta-analysis. *Personnel Psychology, 44*(1), 1–26.

Barrick, M. R., Mount, M. K., & Judge, T. A. (2001). Personality and performance at the beginning of the new millennium: What do we know and where do we go next? *International Journal of Selection and Assessment, 9*(1-2), 9–30.

Belfield, C., Bowden, B., Klapp, A., Levin, H., Shand, R., & Zander, S. (2015). *The economic value of social and emotional learning.* Center for Benefit–Cost Studies in Education, Teachers College, Columbia University. Retrieved from http://cbcse.org/wordpress/wp-content/uploads/2015/02/SEL-Revised.pdf

Burrus, J., Jackson, T., Xi, N., & Steinberg, J. (2013). *Identifying the most important 21st century workforce competencies: An analysis of the Occupational Information Network (O*NET).* Princeton, NJ: Educational Testing Service.

Burrus, J., & Way, J. (2016). *Using O*NET to develop a framework of job characteristics to potentially improve the predictive validity of personality measures* (ACT Research Report Series No. 9). Retrieved from http://www.act.org/content/dam/act/unsecured/documents/6168_RR_2016-9_Using_ONET_Develop_Framework_Job_Characteristics.pdf

Credé, M., & Niehorster, S. (2012). Adjustment to college as measured by the Student Adaptation to College Questionnaire: A quantitative review of its structure and relationships with correlates and consequences. *Educational Psychology Review, 24,* 133–165.

Duckworth, A. L., & Yeager, D. S. (2015). Measurement matters: Assessing personal qualities other than cognitive ability for educational purposes. *Educational Researcher, 44,* 237–251.

Durlak, J. A., Weissberg, R. P., Dymnicki, A. B., Taylor, R. D., & Schellinger, K. B. (2011). Enhancing students' social and emotional development promotes success in school: Results of a meta-analysis. *Child Development, 82,* 405–432.

Durlak, J. A., Weissberg, R. P., & Pachan, M. (2010). A meta-analysis of after-school programs that seek to promote personal and social skills in children and adolescents. *American Journal of Community Psychology, 45,* 294–309.

James, W. (1981). *The principles of psychology* (F. Burkhardt, Ed., 2 vols.). Cambridge, MA: Harvard University Press. (Original work published 1890)

John, O. P., & De Fruyt, F. D. (2015). *Framework for the longitudinal study of social and emotional skills in cities.* Retrieved from http://www.oecd.org/officialdocuments/publicdisplaydocumentpdf/?cote=EDU/CERI/CD(2015)13&docLanguage=En

Kaufman, J. C. (2015). Why creativity isn't in IQ tests, why it matters, and why it won't change anytime soon probably. *Journal of Intelligence, 3*(3), 59–72.

Kobrin, J. L., Patterson, B. F., Shaw, E. J., Mattern, K. D., & Barbuti, S. M. (2008). *Validity of the SAT for predicting first-year college grade point average* (College Board Research Report No. 2008-5). Retrieved from https://research.collegeboard.org/sites/default/files/publications/2012/7/researchreport-2008-5-validity-sat-predicting-first-year-college-grade-point-average.pdf

Kobrin, J. L., Sathy, V., & Shaw, E. J. (2007). *A historical view of subgroup performance differences on the SAT reasoning test* (College Board Research Report No. 2006-5). Retrieved from http://files.eric.ed.gov/fulltext/ED562569.pdf

Kyllonen, P. C., Lipnevich, A. A., Burrus, J., & Roberts, R. D. (2014). *Personality, motivation, and college readiness: A prospectus for assessment and development* (ETS Research Report Series). Retrieved from http://onlinelibrary.wiley.com/doi/10.1002/ets2.12004/full

Lipnevich, A. A., MacCann, C., & Roberts, R. D. (2013). Assessing noncognitive constructs in education: A review of traditional and innovative approaches. In D. H. Saklofske, C. B. Reynolds, & V. L. Schwean (Eds.), *The Oxford handbook of child psychological assessment* (pp. 750–772). New York, NY: Oxford University Press.

Lipnevich, A. A., Preckel, F., & Roberts, R. D. (2016). Psychosocial constructs: Knowns, unknowns, and future directions. In A. A. Lipnevich, F. Preckel, & R. D. Roberts (Eds.), *Psychosocial skills and school systems in the 21st century: Theory, research, and practice.* New York, NY: Springer.

MacCann, C., Duckworth, A. L., & Roberts, R. D. (2009). Empirical identification of the major facets of conscientiousness. *Learning and Individual Differences, 19*, 451–458.

MacCann, C., & Roberts, R. D. (2010). Prediction of academic outcomes from time management, grit, and self-control: The pervasive influence of conscientiousness. In R. E. Hicks (Eds.), *Personality and individual differences: Current directions* (pp. 79–90). Brisbane, Queensland, Australia: Australian Academic Press.

McNeish, D. M., Radunzel, J., & Sanchez, E. (2015). A multidimensional perspective of college readiness: Relating student and school characteristics to performance on the ACT (ACT Research Report Series). Retrieved from http://files.eric.ed.gov/fulltext/ED563774.pdf

Nisbett, R. E., Aronson, J., Blair, C., Dickens, W., Flynn, J., Halpern, D. F., & Turkheimer, E. (2012). Intelligence: New findings and theoretical developments. *American Psychologist, 67*(2), 130–159.

Poropat, A. E. (2009). A meta-analysis of the five-factor model of personality and academic performance. *Psychological Bulletin, 135*, 322–338.

Roberts, B. W., & DelVecchio, W. F. (2000). The rank-order consistency of personality traits from childhood to old age: A quantitative review of longitudinal studies. *Psychological Bulletin, 126*, 3–25.

Roberts, B. W., Walton, K. E., & Viechtbauer, W. (2006). Patterns of mean-level change in personality traits across the life course: A meta-analysis of longitudinal studies. *Psychological Bulletin, 132*, 1–25.

Roberts, R. D., Martin, J., & Olaru, G. (2015). *A Rosetta Stone for noncognitive skills: Understanding, assessing, and enhancing noncognitive skills in primary and secondary education.* New York, NY: Asia Society and ProExam.

Roderick, M., Nagaoka, J., & Coca, V. (2009). College readiness for all: The challenge for urban high schools. *Project Muse: The Future of Children, 19*(1), 185–210.

Sackett, P. R., & Walmsley, P. T. (2014). Which personality attributes are most important in the workplace? *Perspectives on Psychological Science, 9*, 538–551.

Stemler, S. E. (2012). What should university admissions tests predict? *Educational Psychologist, 47*, 5–17.

Walton, K. E., & Billera, K. A. (2016). Personality development during the school-aged years: Implications for theory, research and practice. In A. A. Lipnevich, F. Preckel, & R. D. Roberts (Eds.), *Psychosocial skills and school systems in the 21st century: Theory, research, and practice.* New York, NY: Springer.

The Future of Workforce Readiness

Research, Policy, and Practice[1]

BOBBY D. NAEMI, KRISTA D. MATTERN, JEREMY BURRUS,
AND RICHARD D. ROBERTS ■

The Building Better Student Conference was held in Washington, DC, on December 8–10, 2010, with the following explicit aim (Educational Testing Service, 2010): "A focused dialogue among the nation's college and workforce readiness researchers, policymakers and educators with the specific goal of finding ways to create an educational system that 'builds better students.'" As the conference and its various follow-up activities (including securing a book contract) unfolded, we began to realize this aim needed sharper focus. Too often, this lofty ambition had drawn past researchers and policymakers to consider mainly the preparation of high school students for college. Two logic-based factors drove our focus toward preparation for the workforce rather than higher education. First, there is a meager amount of books (or scientific articles, for that matter) distilling research, theory, and practice on workforce readiness relative to college readiness. This book could thus serve as a catalyst for greater focus in this domain. Second, given backgrounds in education and teaching and current industry experience, each of the editorial team members was attuned to how a focus on academic readiness could influence any given professor, who all too often is enamored with the small minority of undergraduate students who might go on to evangelize his or her chosen topic of academic interest. For even in college, the end goal should be workforce readiness (in addition to cultivating intellectual curiosity).

The journey to disseminate the results of all of these activities has been lengthy and circuitous, but as the organizers of this conference and the editors of the book, each of us has worked to sustain this conversation across many channels of communication. Whether through scientific conferences, policy summits, or business gatherings, we have cultivated and maintained the relationships forged in that conference in service of one overarching goal: a cross-disciplinary dialogue, based on a strong research foundation, to define a model of workforce readiness that builds better workers. By drawing from the expertise of the speakers and contributors to that conference, and over the course of 15 chapters and commentaries, this book has assembled a diverse array of experts in the fields of education, psychology, and economics to answer the burning question emanating from the conference and its aftermath: What builds workforce readiness?

In this concluding chapter, we synthesize the emerging themes across chapters to arrive at an operational framework for understanding, measuring, and impacting workforce readiness. Next, we look to the future of workforce readiness research by examining the global trends that will influence readiness over time—examining the impact on workforce *research* across academic disciplines, workforce *practice* in the field, and ways that both labor and educational *policy* might variously address these concerns. Finally, we integrate the themes and models presented throughout and propose a path forward by identifying areas in which more research is needed or more public policy might be warranted.

OPERATIONAL FRAMEWORK OF WORKFORCE READINESS

Before reviewing the various definitions of workforce readiness proposed throughout this volume, it is useful to engage in an exercise to demonstrate the effect that specific terms—meanings, uses, and adoption rates—have across fields. Given that many of the authors and editors of this book come from the discipline of industrial and organizational (I/O) psychology, a field that is nominally dedicated to the study of the workforce, it might be useful to examine how "workforce readiness" as a term appears within this literature.

If you browse the *APA Handbook of Industrial and Organizational Psychology* (Zedeck, 2011), the premier reference source of the field, you will see in Volume 2 ("Selecting and Developing Members for the Organization," which is most closely related to the focus of the current book) chapters with titles such as "Individual Differences: Their Measurement and Validity," "Personality and

Its Assessment in Organizations: Theoretical and Empirical Developments," "Training and Employee Development for Improved Performance," and "Organizational Socialization: The Effective Onboarding of New Employees." (Box 15.1 provides a complete listing of chapter titles from Volume 2.) What

---

Box 15.1

CHAPTER TITLES OF THE *APA HANDBOOK OF INDUSTRIAL AND ORGANIZATIONAL PSYCHOLOGY*, **VOLUME 2: SELECTING AND DEVELOPING MEMBERS FOR THE ORGANIZATION**

1. Work Analysis: From Technique to Theory
   Frederick P. Morgeson and Erich C. Dierdorff
2. Recruitment: A Review of Research and Emerging Directions
   Brian R. Dineen and Scott M. Soltis
3. Career Issues
   Yehuda Baruch and Nikos Bozionelos
4. Individual Differences: Their Measurement and Validity
   Oleksandr S. Chernyshenko, Stephen Stark, and Fritz Drasgow
5. Personality and Its Assessment in Organizations: Theoretical and Empirical Developments
   Frederick L. Oswald and Leaetta M. Hough
6. Interviews
   Allen I. Huffcutt and Satoris S. Culbertson
7. Assessment Centers
   Winfred Arthur Jr. and Eric Anthony Day
8. Situational Judgment Tests: A Critical Review and Agenda for the Future
   Robert E. Ployhart and William I. MacKenzie Jr.
9. The Appraisal and Management of Performance at Work
   Angelo S. DeNisi and Shirley Sonesh
10. Expanding the Criterion Domain to Include Organizational Citizenship Behavior: Implications for Employee Selection
    Dennis W. Organ, Philip M. Podsakoff, and Nathan P. Podsakoff
11. Organizational Exit
    Peter W. Hom
12. Applicant Reactions to Organizations and Selection Systems
    Donald M. Truxillo and Talya N. Bauer
13. Validation Support for Selection Procedures
    Neal Schmitt and Ruchi Sinha

(continued)

SOURCE: Zedeck (2011).

you will not see is a chapter or chapter heading referring to "workforce readiness," a term that is frequently referenced in the fields of education and policy and that is the central topic of the current book.

Is bemoaning the lack of "workforce readiness" in the I/O handbook just pedantic quibbling? Or is there something to the idea that the lack of common language and terminology between fields contributes to a gap, a lack of clarity in cross-disciplinary goals, and a loss of collaboration that draws from work that may have already been accomplished? Kyllonen (Chapter 5) identifies this "Tower of Babel" effect, where terminology shifts are said to inhibit the goals of progress. What can be done to get the disciplines of education, educational psychology, organizational psychology, public policy, and business to talk to one another? Our book is an attempt to bridge at least some of these gaps, where I/O psychologists can begin to think about how students learn, and educational researchers can begin to think about employee selection and high performers.

Each of the chapters in this book has grappled with the question of how to define workforce readiness in one way or another, whether through proposing specific models, focusing on specific aspects of a particular contributor, or summarizing existing definitions. The terms that are used vary: 21st century skills, workforce readiness KSAs (knowledge, skills, and abilities), noncognitive skills, interpersonal and intrapersonal skills, foundational workplace competencies, and even non-academic skills as suggested by the recent Every Student Succeeds Act of the US Congress. However, the themes that emerge point to a clear organizing framework and model.

Clark (Chapter 11) in particular reviews differing frameworks for organizing foundational academic and workplace competencies and defines work readiness narrowly as "the level of foundational skills an individual needs to be minimally qualified for a specific occupation/job as determined through an occupational profile or job analysis." Her proposed model differentiates between competencies and skills, as well as college, career, and work readiness. Murano and Roberts (Chapter 14) question this complex model, with its plethora of constructs, and yet for the sheer breadth of its reach, the point does need mentioning again.

Sackett and Walmsley (Chapter 2) are the most explicit in their attempt to review and synthesize definitions of workforce readiness into an arguably more manageable cluster. The authors review several prominent definitions of workforce readiness, including the ACT model described by Clark (Chapter 11) and numerous others. Sackett and Walmsley note the following differences across workforce readiness models: the degree of emphasis on cognitive and noncognitive attributes, occupation specificity, individual- versus aggregate-level distinctions, and the target outcome of preparedness. The conclusion from these findings is simple and obvious, almost to the point of tautology: Differing approaches of examining workforce readiness will yield differing definitions of workforce readiness and, thus, differing ways to evaluate success in building workforce readiness models and interventions. In this way, Sackett and Walmsley and Clark agree: The level of analysis (i.e., the individual worker or student vs. the aggregate school or workplace) can lead to differing conclusions about workforce readiness and the best way to improve it. The authors conclude their review by discussing a broad taxonomy first developed by an expert panel commissioned by the National Research Council (Pellegrino & Hilton, 2010) that categorizes the workforce readiness models into three overarching domains: interpersonal skills (e.g., communication, teamwork, and cross-cultural competence), intrapersonal skills (e.g., time management, adaptability, and conscientiousness), and cognitive skills (e.g., critical thinking, creativity, and problem solving). The five dimensions associated with readiness and success for middle-skills jobs identified by Golubovich, Su, and Robbins (Chapter 13) largely align with this model: (1) Critical Thinking and Complex Problem Solving, (2) Oral and Written Communication, (3) Intrapersonal and Interpersonal Skills, (4) Achievement and Innovation, and (5) Detail Orientation. Su and Nye (Chapter 8) introduce interests to the conversation as an important individual difference associated with good job performance, and Roberts and Hill (Chapter 9) drill down into conscientiousness as a "spectrum of constructs" that are key to workforce success. Clarke, Double, and MacCann (Chapter 10), in the course of reviewing this series of key indicators of workforce readiness, home in on the need to develop tools and training programs to foster both interests and skills. The conclusion across all chapters aligns with the insights provided by Schmitt (Chapter 12) on the need to expand the domain of workforce success to accommodate noncognitive measures.

Given the thrust of the research presented and the commonality of the terms that appear throughout this book, we can conclude that the broad taxonomy presented by Sackett and Walmsley (Chapter 2) is clear and of use for the following reasons. As the authors note, it is a model derived from multiple methods, multiple disciplines, and multiple sources. In addition, it extends the attributes of workforce readiness beyond the knowledge and skills typically identified by schools while also meeting the needs of employers who repeatedly state they seek a broader set of competencies. It is also a model that is flexible in addressing needs at both the individual and the aggregate level. In this way, this taxonomy can serve as a unified model that can be of use to stakeholders in schools, the workplace, and the government—each of which may be tasked with solving discrete problems around issues of workforce readiness. The suggested taxonomy in this chapter of interpersonal skills, intrapersonal skills, and cognitive skills should speak to these multiple audiences in a way that clarifies our thinking in the field and results in practical applications to address the issues involved. We believe, however, that a slight modification of the model would make it even more useful. We propose that cognitive skills be split into (a) cognitive skills, which include the "traditional" cognitive skills of general mental ability and job-specific/subject-specific knowledge, and (b) cross-cutting cognitive skills, which consist of what might be considered general "thinking skills" such as creativity and critical thinking that are useful across multiple domains ("cut across" multiple domains), although we concede the fact that general mental ability is clearly also "cross-cutting" (in a theoretical rather than a substantively meaningful manner). This framework is not without precedent, sharing a number of similarities with a holistic framework of student success recently developed by ACT (Camara, O'Connor, Mattern, & Hanson, 2015).

Table 15.1 fits most of the skills discussed in this book into the resulting four-part framework. Clark's chapter (Chapter 11) is not included in the table because that thesis introduces several frameworks that do not fit so easily. There are a few points to note from a closer examination of this table:

- It is clear that some skills received more attention than others in this book. This may indicate that these skills may be worthy of emphasized research attention in the future. Cross-cultural competence and ethics appeared to be the two most mentioned skills.

Table 15.1 WORKING FRAMEWORK OF WORKFORCE READINESS

General Mental Ability		Personality	
Cognitive	Cross-Cutting Cognitive	Interpersonal	Intrapersonal
Job knowledge/general knowledge (Ch. 2, 12)	Creativity/innovation (Ch. 3, 11)	Cross-cultural competence/multicultural appreciation (Ch. 3, 4, 6, 12)	*General motivation*
General mental ability (Ch. 2)	Critical thinking/problem solving (Ch. 3, 11)		Conscientiousness (Ch. 2, 9)
			Interests (Ch. 2, 8)
			Achievement (Ch. 11)
		Ethics/integrity	Detail orientation (Ch. 11)
	Judgment	Ethics/integrity (Ch. 2, 3, 12)	Perseverance (Ch. 12)
	Metacognition (Ch. 3)	Social responsibility (Ch. 12)	Openness (Ch. 2)
	Situational judgment (Ch. 12)		Continuous learning (Ch. 12)
		Working with others	
		Leadership (Ch. 3, 12)	*Context-specific motivation*
		Agreeableness (Ch. 2)	Career aspirations (Ch. 7)
		Communication (Ch. 11)	Career orientation (Ch. 12)
		Customer service (Ch. 3)	Leadership motivation (Ch. 7)
		Extraversion (Ch. 2)	Person–environment fit (Ch. 8)
		Interpersonal skills (Ch. 11)	Professional motivation (Ch. 7)
		Safety (Ch. 3)	Entrepreneurial motivation (Ch. 7)
		Teamwork (Ch. 3)	Artistic appreciation (Ch. 12)
			Stress management/adaptability
			Adaptability (Ch. 12)
			Boundaryless mindset (Ch. 7)
			Career adaptability (Ch. 7)
			Emotional stability (Ch. 2)
			Health (Ch. 12)
			Intrapersonal skills (Ch. 11)

- Many skills could be placed into multiple parts of our four-part framework. For example, cross-cultural competence has both interpersonal (e.g., perspective taking) and intrapersonal (e.g., stress management) aspects. For skills such as these, we placed the skill into the category we believed most appropriate.
- Many skills overlap. One of the most obvious examples of this has to do with the Big Five personality traits. For instance, agreeableness is listed as an interpersonal skill in the framework. However, teamwork is also listed as an interpersonal skill in the framework. Clearly, agreeableness is an important determining factor in how well one works in teams. This issue also applies to general mental ability and skills such as critical thinking/problem solving. We thus created subcategories to account for this overlap. This left us with a final framework that includes four higher-order skills with 11 lower-order skills in total:
  - *Cognitive*: Job knowledge/general knowledge; general mental ability, higher level reading comprehension, writing, mathematics
  - *Cross-cutting cognitive*: Creativity/innovation; critical thinking/problem solving; judgment
  - *Interpersonal*: Cross-cultural competence/multicultural appreciation; ethics/integrity; working with others
  - *Intrapersonal*: General motivation; context-specific motivation; stress management/adaptability
- Alternate models can be created by taking into account these lower-order skills. We present one such model in Figure 15.1, which represents workforce readiness as a function of general mental ability and personality. General mental ability is presented as the higher-order factor feeding into the cognitive and cross-cutting cognitive skills, and personality is presented as the higher-order factor feeding into the interpersonal and intrapersonal skills. Furthermore, we acknowledge that motivation is an important factor in creativity and the formation of knowledge, in that those who are more motivated will spend more time thinking of creative ideas and studying to create knowledge. This model is necessarily an oversimplification of reality, but it does represent one parsimonious, and possibly testable, way to model workforce readiness.

Figure 15.2 presents a theoretical model of the interplay between technological forces and globalization and how they impact the relative importance of cognitive, cross-cutting cognitive, interpersonal, and intrapersonal skills on workplace outcomes. Contributing to this model are the major forces outlined by Burrus, Mattern, Naemi, and Roberts (Chapter 1) and Whorton,

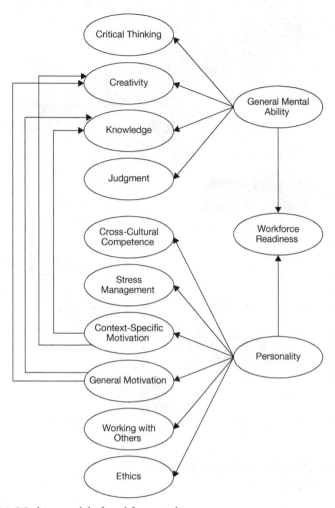

Figure 15.1 Working model of workforce readiness.

Casillas, Oswald, and Shaw (Chapter 3), particularly forces of technology and international (globalization) issues. On the bottom half of Figure 15.2, technology is shown to act as a lever that elevates the importance of the different skills, whereas globalization similarly influences the salience of all three factors. In short, a four-factor model of interpersonal, intrapersonal, cognitive, and cross-cutting skills is broad and inclusive enough to incorporate the individual concepts and models of workforce readiness proposed in each of the chapters in this book. Having synthesized a scientific model of workforce readiness, given this model, as researchers, where do we go from here? What does the future hold for workforce research? And how does this research in turn feed into issues of public policy? We aim to answer these questions in the next section.

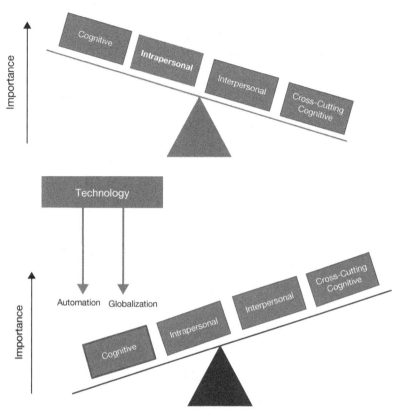

Figure 15.2 Technology as a lever of workforce readiness models.

POLICY IMPLICATION OF FUTURE GLOBAL MEGATRENDS

The organizational firm PWC, formerly known as PricewaterhouseCoopers, identified five global megatrends of paramount influence for the future of the global workforce: (a) demographic and social change, (b) shifts to emerging economies, (c) urbanization, (d) climate change and resource scarcity, and (e) technological breakthroughs. Similarly, Whorton et al. (Chapter 3) describe technology, customer service, and globalization as overarching economic forces that disrupt the 21st century workplace. Burrus et al. (Chapter 1) present a simple model outlining the factors leading to shifting skills of workforce readiness, describing how innovations in technology have led to shifts in work activities, the job market, and the skills required to survive this shifting job market. Other chapters in this book underscore the challenges and opportunities of diversity (Lester, Kravitz, & Klein, Chapter 6), cross-cultural competence (Klafehn, Chapter 4), and the "boundaryless" 21st century workplace

(Chernyshenko, Chan, Hoon-Ho, Uy, & Loo, Chapter 7) as factors that will influence the future.

How these commonly identified megatrends play out in the world of policy arguably depends on whether one views the glass as half full or half empty. The pessimistic take on the need to improve workforce readiness is a prominent one. The reader can look back to 1983 to see one of the more seminal examples: *A Nation at Risk: The Imperative for Educational Reform* from the Gardner Commission appointed by the administration of President Ronald Reagan (National Commission on Excellence in Education, 1983). The thesis of the report was that earning a high school diploma did not translate to a certain level of proficiency because many high school graduates lacked the knowledge and skills necessary to perform college-level work. The same themes reoccur in the more recent *America's Perfect Storm: Three Forces Changing Our Nation's Future*, a report produced in 2007 from the Educational Testing Service's Policy Information Center (Kirsch, Braun, Yamamoto, & Sum, 2007). The report stated that the lack of literacy and numeracy skills in the US adult population, changes in the structure of the US economy, and demographic shifts in the United States were three "forces" putting America's economic future at risk. The commonality in both these cases is the use of alarmism, but is this kind of heightened tension, produced for decade after decade, really the best way to lead to change? Politicians and social psychologists might have much to say on the topic of pessimistic alarmism as a clarion call to action, but we propose that there is an opportunity to define a program of research and action around workforce readiness framed in a positive way. Technological breakthroughs and the "boundaryless" global workplace need not be viewed as job-killing agents of economic destruction; rather, the possibility exists to frame workforce readiness as an opportunity for change, improvement, and adaptability. The proposed integrative model of workforce readiness can lead to such change by identifying the areas that can be targeted for improvement, whether cognitive, cross-cutting cognitive, interpersonal, or intrapersonal, across individuals or at the aggregate level. The future of workforce research will revolve around implementing programs of change around these areas, and it is along these lines that we can now examine the challenges associated with this kind of implementation in a particular illustrative use case.

THE FUTURE OF WORKFORCE READINESS IN POLICY AND PRACTICE

One particular implementation of workforce research in practice involves the recent popularity of an intrapersonal skill called "grit," which refers to a "perseverance or passion for long-term goals" (Duckworth, Peterson, Matthews, & Kelly, 2007). In an editorial for *The New York Times*, Angela Duckworth (2016), the psychologist most famous for popularizing this concept, argues against the assessment of this skill at schools despite the ability of this intrapersonal skill to predict success after school and in the workplace. The catalyst for this argument derives from the decision of nine California school districts to make use of assessments of grit as part of school accountability metrics. Duckworth argues that even though intrapersonal skills such as grit matter for workforce readiness and are able to be developed, these skills should nevertheless not be considered a part of student or school performance metrics. Duckworth cites issues with measurement of these skills such as reference bias as well as a punitive focus that may lead to cheating rather than true skill development and improvement.

If punitive accountability measures are an albatross preventing the full adoption of workforce readiness skills into school curricula, Duckworth's (2016) reticence is a key example of the challenges faced in applying workforce readiness research into practice. In this way, concerns regarding the accuracy of measurement are often woven into general institutional fears regarding the use of workforce readiness assessments. In a rejoinder to Duckworth's editorial, Martin and Burrus (2016) argue that although the specific methods of measuring grit discussed by the California districts have limitations, there are other methods of capturing intrapersonal skills, including multimethod measures with acceptable reliability and compelling validity evidence, that can address these limitations. The exchange illustrates the difficulties of translating the undeniable value of workforce readiness research into practice, gaining buy-in from schools, and ultimately the workforce. Questions in this area remain. Is the reluctance for implementation simply an issue with schools as opposed to employers? Is there a way to make use of measures in a nonpunitive manner that still meets the goal of preparing graduating students for the workforce? Can the conversation be reframed toward this kind of development? The future of workforce readiness research in the field lies in grappling with these issues. And although difficult issues, these seem not to have stopped cognitive assessment from playing a prominent role in global educational policy and practice.

Another research stream that must undoubtedly receive attention in the future is the effectiveness and development of interventions. Given that the title of this book refers to "building" better students, research presented throughout the volume has sought to extend the conversation on how to best develop workforce readiness skills. Klafehn (Chapter 4) notes the ineffectiveness of many current cross-cultural training interventions in the workplace (however, see Morris, Savani, & Roberts, 2014), whereas Whorton et al. (Chapter 3) note the ineffectiveness of current interventions for critical thinking. Lester et al.

(Chapter 6) note principles for interventions that effectively reduce prejudice and prepare students for diverse workplaces. Elsewhere, Kyllonen, Lipnevich, Burrus, and Roberts (2014) review a disparate body of literature that has focused on training interventions to change or improve the five factors of personality, from openness (whether critical thinking or cross-cultural competence) to conscientiousness (see Roberts and Hill, Chapter 9), to extraversion or leadership, to agreeableness or teamwork, to emotional stability or anxiety. The four-part model of workforce readiness we present can serve as an organizational framework for future intervention research that targets the key skills that will prepare students and, ultimately, workers for the 21st century workplace.

THE FUTURE OF WORKFORCE READINESS IN RESEARCH

A key challenge that all workforce readiness researchers inevitably face concerns issues regarding the measurement of workforce readiness skills and competencies. Interpersonal and intrapersonal skills are most frequently measured through simple self-reports that often make use of Likert-type scales. Although relatively inexpensive and easy to implement, this type of skill measurement is unfortunately the most susceptible to faking. There are numerous strategies to deal with faking (Ziegler, MacCann, & Roberts, 2011), but workforce readiness researchers will nevertheless need to be prepared to propose reliable assessment solutions that demonstrate face validity for any given audience at reasonable cost.

Table 15.2 (Naemi, 2012) presents several options for both self- and other-reported assessments (i.e., from peers, parents, teachers, and supervisors) that

Table 15.2 SOURCES AND TYPES OF NONCOGNITIVE INTERPERSONAL OR INTRAPERSONAL SKILL ASSESSMENT

Self		Others	
Ratings	Performance	Ratings	Performance
Self-assessments (Likert type)	Situational judgment tests	Others' ratings (Likert type)	Transcripts
Self-assessments (forced-choice)		Letters of recommendation	Observations
Biodata			
Day reconstruction method			

SOURCE: Naemi (2012).

can be used for varying types of interpersonal and intrapersonal skill assessment (either as a rating measure or as a performance measure). Although there are bodies of literature associated with each of these categories of assessment, future workforce readiness researchers will need to contend with each of these forms as the demand for cross-cutting cognitive, interpersonal, and intrapersonal skill assessment grows. Of particular interest is the intersection of each of these forms of assessment with new technologies. Perhaps a revolution in video delivery will lead to inexpensive and immersive forms of assessment that more accurately capture interpersonal skills of interest to employers. Disruptive technology that streamlines Internet or mobile communication methods may influence the ways in which noncognitive assessments are structured, shifting our understanding of the length or chunks of time that are necessary for valid and reliable assessment. From the impact of big data and deep learning artificial intelligence processes to gather and structure information, the possibilities are exciting and varied, and engaged researchers should be poised to take advantage of opportunities for innovation in workforce readiness assessment.

Finally, researchers must continue to advance the measurement models that underpin workforce readiness research. The model we present in this chapter integrates key concepts and dimensions that reoccur across research streams in chapters throughout this book, but work remains to be done to examine the compensatory or noncompensatory nature of these dimensions and factors. Sackett and Walmsley (Chapter 2) and Clark (Chapter 11) agree that pinning down the level of analysis is also a crucial issue, whether across all occupations or only in certain categories of interest (e.g., middle-skills workers). Should we as researchers focus on the individual worker or aggregate across schools and workplaces? Are there places where differing disciplines and fields can best attack the issues in differing ways, or can we unify and collaborate in a way that captures information that can meaningfully be relayed to both students and employers?

CONCLUSIONS AND THE PATH FORWARD

The goal of this chapter was straightforward yet complex: to arrive at a taxonomy of workforce readiness that integrates the many models presented in this book and streamlines the definition of workforce readiness for researchers, educators, and employers alike. In addition, we examined trends in workforce readiness research and practice that will influence the work being done in the near future and beyond. So, where do we go from here?

One path is to use the four-part integrated model of cognitive, cross-cutting cognitive, interpersonal, and intrapersonal skills of workforce readiness as a basis to streamline future research, policy, and practice across the many fields represented throughout this book. If funding agencies are explicit about making use of this model of workforce readiness in a cross-disciplinary fashion, researchers can hopefully work together to address problems in a way that is grounded in science, applied practice, and public policy.

How else can the work accomplished in forming this book be best used to serve the public need for workforce readiness research and practice? One thing that is clear is that older models of dissemination are outdated; academic jargon in cloistered segregated outposts is not going to lead to advances in workforce readiness for all. As thoughtful 21st century thought leaders, it is important for us to search for new avenues of dissemination with wider access that will activate the imaginations of the constituencies in the workforce we purport to serve. Conferences such as Building Better Students that formed the foundation of this book should be a starting point that leads to a greater effort to bring scientists, educators, government officials, and business leaders together, drawing from the resources each field has to offer in order to tackle the seemingly intractable problem of building and improving readiness in all students. It is likely that major international entities such as the Organization for Economic Co-operation and Development will play a role in such endeavors, especially as they continue to give greater credibility to noncognitive factors in large-scale group score assessments such as the Programme for International Student Assessment and the Programme for the International Assessment of Adult Competencies (Naemi et al., 2013).

With international meetings a mere Skype call away, improving Internet service, and even the prevalence of English as a lingua franca, the barriers to global collaboration have never been lower. Our book has made the case that technology has revolutionized the workforce and issues around the workforce, and how academics engage with and disseminate scientific research should be no exception. Researchers must find ways to embrace technology—not only to promote global collaboration but also to accelerate the advancement of scientific knowledge. Technology, in this case, refers not only to computer processing speed or advances in device tech but also to academic movements that embrace open global communication. We have seen the beginnings of this kind of work through efforts to promote free source software, publicly available data sets, and open access journals and repositories such as the Department of Open Access Journals. Our hope is that by demonstrating a cross-disciplinary framework for workforce readiness, we have informed not only future theory and research in this area but also future collaborative practice, policy, and application.

NOTES

1. All statements expressed in this chapter are the authors' and do not reflect the official opinions or policies of the any of the authors' host affiliations. Correspondence concerning this chapter should be addressed to bnaemi@ets.org.

REFERENCES

Camara, W., O'Connor, R., Mattern, K., & Hanson, M. A. (2015). *Beyond academics: A holistic framework for enhancing education and workplace success.* Iowa City, IA: ACT. Retrieved from http://www.act.org/research/researchers/reports/pdf/ACT_RR2015-4.pdf

Duckworth A. L. (2016, March 26). Don't grade schools on grit. *New York Times.* Retrieved from http://www.nytimes.com/2016/03/27/opinion/sunday/dont-grade-schools-on-grit.html?_r=0

Duckworth, A. L., Peterson, C., Matthews, M. D., & Kelly, D. R. (2007). Grit: Perseverance and passion for long-term goals. *Journal of Personality and Social Psychology, 92,* 1087–1101.

Educational Testing Service. (2010). *Building better students: Preparing for life after high school: Research conference.* Retrieved from https://www.ets.org/c/15481/index.html

Kirsch, I., Braun, H., Yamamoto, K., & Sum, A. (2007). *America's perfect storm: Three forces changing our nation's future.* Retrieved from https://www.ets.org/Media/Education_Topics/pdf/AmericasPerfectStorm.pdf

Kyllonen, P. C., Lipnevich, A. A., Burrus, J., & Roberts, R. D. (2014). *Personality, motivation, and college readiness: A prospectus for assessment and development* (ETS Research Report Series). Retrieved from http://onlinelibrary.wiley.com/doi/10.1002/ets2.12004/full

Martin, J., & Burrus, J. (2016). *Schools really can (and should) measure noncognitive skills.* Retrieved from http://gettingsmart.com/2016/04/schools-really-can-and-should-measure-noncognitive-skills

Morris, M. W., Savani, K., & Roberts, R. D. (2014). Intercultural training and assessment: Implications for organizational and public policies. *Policy Insights from Behavioral and Brain Sciences, 1,* 63–71.

Naemi, B. (2012). *Assessment methods.* Retrieved from https://www.ets.org/s/workforce_readiness/pdf/21333_big_5.pdf

Naemi, B., Gonzalez, E., Bertling, J., Betancourt, A., Burrus, J., Kyllonen, P. C., … Roberts, R. D. (2013). Large-scale group score assessments: Past, present, and future. In D. H. Saklofske, C. B. Reynolds, & V. L. Schwean (Eds.), *The Oxford handbook of child psychological assessment* (pp. 129–149). New York, NY: Oxford University Press.

National Commission on Excellence in Education. (1983). A nation at risk: The imperative for educational reform. *Elementary School Journal,* 113–130. https://books.google.com/books?hl=en&lr=&id=bFZpAgAAQBAJ&oi=fnd&pg=PA129&#v=onepage&q&f=false

Pellegrino, J. W., & Hilton, M. L. (Eds.). (2010). Education for life and work: Developing transferable knowledge and skills in the 21st century. Washington, D.C.: National Academies Press.

Zedeck, S. E. (2011). *APA handbook of industrial and organizational psychology*. Washington, DC: American Psychological Association.

Ziegler, M., MacCann, C., & Roberts, R. D. (Eds.). (2011). *New perspectives on faking in personality assessment*. New York, NY: Oxford University Press.

Page numbers followed by b, *f,* or *t* indicate a box, figure, or table, on the designated page